D1595980

SALMAN'S LEGACY

MADAWI AL-RASHEED

(*Editor*)

Salman's Legacy

The Dilemmas of a New Era in Saudi Arabia

OXFORD

UNIVERSITY PRESS

Oxford University Press is a department of the
University of Oxford. It furthers the University's objective
of excellence in research, scholarship, and education
by publishing worldwide.

Oxford   New York
Auckland   Cape Town   Dar es Salaam   Hong Kong   Karachi
Kuala Lumpur   Madrid   Melbourne   Mexico City   Nairobi
New Delhi   Shanghai   Taipei   Toronto

With offices in
Argentina   Austria   Brazil   Chile   Czech Republic   France   Greece
Guatemala   Hungary   Italy   Japan   Poland   Portugal   Singapore
South Korea   Switzerland   Thailand   Turkey   Ukraine   Vietnam

Oxford is a registered trade mark of Oxford University Press
in the UK and certain other countries.

Published in the United States of America by
Oxford University Press
198 Madison Avenue, New York, NY 10016

Library of Congress Cataloging-in-Publication Data is available
Madawi Al-Rasheed.
Salman's Legacy: The Dilemmas of a New Era in Saudi Arabia.
ISBN: 9780190901745

Printed in the USA on acid-free paper

In memory of Professor Peter Sluglett,
our great colleague and friend

CONTENTS

CONTENTS

PART III
FOREIGN RELATIONS

ACKNOWLEDGEMENTS

This book resulted from an international conference held at the Middle East Institute at the National University of Singapore in December 2016. Both individuals and institutions made this conference a success. Special appreciation goes to the late Professor Peter Sluglett, acting director of the institute at the time, Michelle Teo, deputy director, and Professor Engseng Ho, who joined the institute during preparations for the conference. They were all encouraging and supportive. The conference took place at a time when many observers anticipated King Salman's historic visit to South East Asia that took place early in 2017. They supported the timely idea of the conference and provided all necessary help. The Middle East Institute at NUS provided generous financial support without which the conference could not have taken place.

My colleagues Mohamed Ali Adraoui and Shuang Wen were appreciated for their chairing of panels and comments on presentations during the conference.

The organizational support of Sharifah Noor Huda Al-Junied, Zubaidah Abdul Jalil, Retna Devi, and Rommel Hernando is well appreciated. Finally two energetic, punctual, and enthusiastic National University of Singapore graduates added invaluable and much-appreciated insight into academic and social life at NUS. They also helped with preparing bibliographies for the introduction to this edited volume. Both Ismail Shogo and Anderson Yep were exemplary and dedicated interns who participated in the preparation for the conference.

Final preparation of this manuscript took place at the Middle East Centre at the London School of Economics, where I am currently a

ACKNOWLEDGEMENTS

visiting professor. Special gratitude is expressed to Professor Toby Dodge, the director of MEC. Both Sandra Sfeir and Ribale Sleiman Haidar are so supportive and deserve special thanks. Deputy director of MEC Robert Lowe has always been a great listener and adviser.

Finally, my greatest gratitude is for the contributors to this book who travelled to Singapore in the middle of very busy academic calendars, presented interesting papers, and produced the chapters in this volume on time. I thank them profusely for responding to my invitation and making the conference a great success.

As always, copy-editor Mary Starkey was meticulous in preparing the manuscript for publication. Her insight and familiarity with the topics discussed is unique. The support of Michael Dwyer at Hurst & Co. publishers is much appreciated.

LIST OF CONTRIBUTORS

Sultan Alamer is a Political Science doctoral student at George Washington University. His focus is on the Middle East region, and his research interests include identity-based politics, the political economy of resource-rich countries, and political violence. Alamer has co-authored three Arabic books on subjects that relate to political theory and nationalism. He also serves as a researcher for the Kuwaiti think tank the Gulf Center for Development Policies.

Cole Bunzel is a Ph.D. candidate at the Department of Near Eastern Studies at Princeton University, where his work focuses on the history of Wahhabism in Saudi Arabia and the Jihadi Salafi movement in modern Islam. He is the author of *From Paper State to Caliphate: The Ideology of the Islamic State* (Brookings Institution, 2015) and *The Kingdom and the Caliphate: Duel of the Islamic States* (Carnegie Endowment, 2016).

Nora Doaiji is a researcher and recent Master's graduate in Middle East Studies from the George Washington University, and holds two Bachelor's degrees in Political Science and Philosophy from the University of California, Irvine. She is currently a teaching assistant at the Elliott School of International Affairs. She has previously authored chapters in two Arabic books focusing on Arab nationalism.

Michael Farquhar is lecturer in Middle East Politics at the Department of Middle East Studies, King's College London. He recently published *Circuits of Faith* (Stanford University Press, 2016), a study of Saudi state-funded efforts to extend Wahhabi influence abroad

xi

from the mid-twentieth century. He is currently undertaking research on policing and social order in Egypt.

F. Gregory Gause III is Professor and holder of the John H. Lindsey '44 Chair in International Affairs at the Bush School of Government and Public Service, Texas A&M University, as well as serving as head of the school's International Affairs Department. His research focuses on the international politics of the Middle East, particularly the Arabian Peninsula and the Persian Gulf. He has published three books, most recently *The International Relations of the Persian Gulf* (Cambridge University Press, 2010).

Andrew Hammond is a doctoral candidate at St Antony's College, Oxford, researching interactions between Turkish and Arabic-language *'ulama'* and intellectuals in the early twentieth century, including their role in the development of the notion of Salafiyya. He worked for BBC Arabic radio and Reuters news agency in Egypt, Saudi Arabia, and the United Arab Emirates and as a policy fellow with the European Council on Foreign Relations. He has published extensively on pan-Arab media and contemporary Islamist movements in Egypt, Qatar, Turkey, and Saudi Arabia. He is the author of several books including *The Islamic Utopia: The Illusion of Reform in Saudi Arabia* (Pluto Press, 2012).

Steffen Hertog is Associate Professor of Comparative Politics at the London School of Economics and Political Science. His research interests include Gulf politics, Middle East political economy, political violence, and radicalization. His book *Princes, Brokers, and Bureaucrats: Oil and State in Saudi Arabia* was published by Cornell University Press in 2011. He is the co-author, with Diego Gambetta, of *Engineers of Jihad: the Curious Connection between Violent Extremism and Education* (Princeton University Press, 2016).

Toby Matthiesen is Senior Research Fellow in the International Relations of the Middle East at St Antony's College, Oxford. Matthiesen was previously a Research Fellow at Pembroke College, Cambridge, and at the London School of Economics and Political Science. He is the author of *Sectarian Gulf: Bahrain, Saudi Arabia, and the Arab Spring That Wasn't* (Stanford University Press, 2013), and *The Other Saudis: Shiism, Dissent and Sectarianism* (Cambridge University Press, 2015).

LIST OF CONTRIBUTORS

Madawi Al-Rasheed is Visiting Professor at the Middle East Centre, London School of Economics. In 2016 she was Visiting Professor at the Middle East Institute, National University of Singapore. Al-Rasheed specializes in the history, politics, and society of Saudi Arabia. Her latest book, *Muted Modernists: The Struggle over Divine Politics in Saudi Arabia*, was published by Hurst & Co. and Oxford University Press in 2015.

Nadav Samin is Lecturer in Anthropology and Government at Dartmouth College. His book *Of Sand or Soil: Genealogy and Tribal Belonging in Saudi Arabia* was published in 2015 by Princeton University Press, and is forthcoming in Arabic translation with Jadawel. Samin received his Ph.D. in Near Eastern Studies from Princeton University.

Naser al-Tamimi is an independent UK-based Middle East researcher and political analyst with particular research interests in energy politics, strategic studies of the Middle East, and Gulf–Asia relations. Al-Tamimi is the author of the book *China–Saudi Arabia Relations, 1990–2012: Marriage of Convenience or Strategic Alliance?* (Routledge, 2013). He has carried out extensive research on various aspects of Arab–China relations, Saudi Arabia in particular. In addition to his core research interests, Al-Tamimi has worked for numerous Arab newspapers, in the United Kingdom and a number of Arab countries. He holds a Ph.D. in Government and International Relations from Durham University.

INTRODUCTION

THE DILEMMAS OF A NEW ERA

Madawi Al-Rasheed

King Salman began his rule in 2015 with a series of unprecedented challenges. From leadership shuffles and falling oil prices to regional and international upheaval, he faced new dilemmas. This book focuses on this era and provides analysis of previous troublesome historical episodes and contemporary challenges. Although King Salman is old and looks frail, he has brought in several measures to deal with succession issues, the oil crisis, the Arab uprisings, regional rivalries with Iran and other troublesome Arab and Gulf neighbours, reached out to Asia to seek new opportunities, and finally mended relations with the USA under President Donald Trump. Whether his policies, viewed over a very short period—just over two years at the time of writing this introduction—have saved the kingdom from serious upheaval is yet to be seen, but no doubt that a new kingdom is emerging, rightly referred to in the title of this volume, *Salman's Legacy*, as a result of his actions. However, Salman's kingdom—or that of his son—may not be so drastically different from previous incarnations, as there are continuities and historical precedents to some but not all the decisions that Salman and

1

his young son Muhammad have made since 2015. This book is an attempt to provide historical depth and insights into the contemporary challenges that Salman's kingdom has faced, and is likely to continue to face, in the near future.

Since its creation in 1932, the Saudi regime continues to divide opinions. Among analysts and scholars, speculations about its resilience or imminent collapse remain abundant. But so far it is managing to hold on to power amidst two contradictory narratives. At one end of the spectrum there is a narrative that highlights its resilience and ability to contain shock and challenges at different historical moments.[1] In contrast, at the opposite end there is the story of the imminent collapse of the house of Saud, and even the fragmentation of the kingdom into smaller entities along sectarian and regional lines.[2] But the truth about Saudi Arabia may actually lie between these two scenarios. The triumphalist tone of the first narrative needs to be assessed against the wishful thinking that underlies the second one. In between, observers map the consequences of the collapse, described as potentially cataclysmic.[3]

Based on new research that moves beyond the two diametrically opposed narratives, contributors in this volume engage with Saudi history, contemporary social, political, and economic challenges, and foreign relations. The rich and nuanced studies offer a balanced understanding of the country and sophisticated interpretations of its domestic, regional, and international choices that may appear to outsiders as shrouded in secrecy and speculation. Several contributors engage in diachronic analysis that uncovers the recent past but also identify continuities and discontinuities emerging from both leadership and societal changes. While the contributors may not agree with each other on all matters related to Saudi Arabia—in fact, a few are critical of each other's work—they nevertheless engage in conversations that generate a better and balanced understanding of the country, its political dynamics, religious tradition, and new directions in its foreign policy. The value of an edited volume is enriched by the potential inherent both in the contrasting views of the contributors and in their criticisms of each other's work in ways that enhance understanding of the subject.

Observers who draw attention to the challenges facing the kingdom rightly list numerous problems that may undermine future stability. In the aftermath of the Arab uprisings in 2011 the kingdom is often believed to face several domestic concerns that need to be immediately addressed. The rivalry between disgruntled princes, the demographic youth bulge, the new class of educated women, the terrorists, the radical Wahhabi preachers, the aspiring middle classes, the marginalized poor, the unemployment crisis, the repressed minorities, and more recently the dramatic fall in oil prices are often among the list of potential structural problems that the kingdom will have to deal with sooner or later.

In addition, the advent of the internet and new communication technology from Twitter to Facebook are believed to open new avenues of dissent and resistance. Monitoring Saudi users of the new social media allows commentators to map and assess opinions that circulate widely and reach all citizens inside and outside the country. The new voices that are now heard in the virtual sphere are unusual in a country with no experience of an open and free press. Tapping into the voices of dissent among both men and women, even though the most critical remain virtual, points to a changing public sphere where Saudis assess the performance of their leadership and dare to launch criticism of their shortcomings online. They request more rights and entitlements, from women's driving campaigns to demands for better infrastructure in cities.

Since the Arab uprisings most virtual Saudi campaigns have focused on local demands for higher government salaries, and better welfare services such as health facilities, education, and housing.[4] Other campaigns have had overtly regional political objectives—for example, criticizing Saudi intervention against the elected Muslim Brotherhood government in Egypt in 2013, or the increase in subsidies to other monarchies such as Morocco and Jordan, or in 2017 the rift between Saudi Arabia and Qatar. But the corruption of government officials and the confiscation of land by senior princes remain topics hotly debated in the virtual world among active Saudi citizens with YouTube clips spreading news about local demonstrations, sit-ins, and resistance. Since the Arab uprisings women's rights issues, especially lifting the ban on women driving and abolishing the male guardian requirement, have attracted a lot of attention among local women, as well as in the international community.[5] Those who predict trouble in the kingdom often point out that the combination of economic, political, and social problems on the one hand and more active citizenry on the other is likely to produce serious internal upheaval in the future.

New Research on Saudi Arabia

Fortunately, recent scholarship on the kingdom is much richer and more nuanced than in the past. A plethora of new research in history, the humanities, and social sciences offers a complex prism through which Saudi Arabia can be understood. For instance, historians began to reflect on the Saudi past in novel ways that move beyond the cherished wisdom about the original eighteenth-century pact between the Al Saud and the Wahhabi tradition. Their analysis informs us about how the past is reproduced, shunned, or simply reconfigured in the present.[6] From historical studies we learn about Arabian society, the formation of the three Saudi states, Wahhabiyya, and the transformations that took place with the discovery of oil. But there is more to Saudi history than the state, religion, and oil. Recently, several studies have explored local and regional historiography before and after the formation of the state, thus enriching our knowledge of the Arabian Peninsula in general.[7] The ancient forgotten diversity of the country began to attract the attention of scholars fascinated by the religious and economic networks that tied Arabia in general to both the Red Sea and the Indian Ocean.[8]

For obvious reasons the so-called Saudi Islam, i.e. the Wahhabi tradition, has attracted the attention of many social scientists and Islamic studies specialists.[9] Understanding the state pact with Wahhabiyya continues to generate controversial debates and polemics among academics.[10] In the aftermath of 9/11 this attention led to serious academic scrutiny. The Wahhabi movement and its adherents suddenly became 'suspect' after decades of being considered a mere nuisance that allegedly set Saudi Arabia apart from the rest of the Muslim world. As Osama Bin Laden and fifteen of the hijackers who attacked the Twin Towers in New York were Saudis, Wahhabiyya, together with other Islamist trends in Saudi Arabia and beyond, became the focus of several valuable studies. In 2014 the Islamic State in Iraq and Syria (ISIS) put the books of the founder of Wahhabiyya, Muhamamd ibn 'Abd al-Wahhab, on its school curriculum, thus confirming a dominant narrative about how Wahhabiyya inspires radical jihadi groups. With the consolidation of the global jihadi movement, Wahhabiyya moved from being described as simply a literal, conservative, reformist, and puritanical interpretation of Islam to being a tradition that many observers accused of inspiring radicalization, sectarianism, and even terrorism. In the minds of many observers Wahhabiyya remains accused of galvanizing Muslims, precipitating a global terrorism crisis, and inciting generations of Muslim youth to commit atrocities across many continents.[11] Today many see the tradition as the ideological incubator of 'global jihad' and sectarian violence across the Middle East and beyond. This familiar accusation has been countered by other narratives about Wahhabiyya that try to absolve it from any wrongdoing.[12] The ideological affinity between Wahhabiyya and global jihad is complex, and can be elusive, but there is a persistent academic attempt to explore the underlying Saudi logic of spreading it across the globe. While much work has already been done on why the Saudi state was eager to export Wahhabiyya, i.e. focusing on the supply end, more research needs to be done on the demand for this tradition in local contexts spreading from Jakarta to Bosnia.

While many scholars continue to focus on the historical development of Wahhabiyya under the auspices of the Saudi state, others investigate Wahhabi transnational connections, educational outreach, charitable foundations, and religious institutions that propagate it around the world.[13] Many scholars examine the rationale of the Wahhabi mission, its theology, and the clerics who spread it. Above all, the controversy surrounding the name Wahhabiyya and its recent association with Salafiyya is now the focus of nuanced academic research. If we imagine Wahhabiyya as a coherent tradition, we have to revise our perceptions as we learn about the fragmentation that sets its spokesmen against each other in fierce theological debates.

Political scientists focus on regime strategies and policies to maintain power. From repression to co-optation, new research maps the spectrum of Saudi regime strategies over several decades. With the rise of the Islamist opposition since the 1990s, scholars explore the diverse Islamist groups that at one point challenged the Saudi regime through petitions, demonstrations, and deadly violence.[14] Since the 1920s the Saudi state has faced several challenges by armed groups, both to its domestic policies and its alliance with the West. The waves of contestation have led to serious confrontations with the leadership. From the Wahhabi tribal Ikhwan rebellion of 1927 to the current wave of ISIS terrorism, the regime has been confronted by home-grown groups committed to armed rebellion, or, more recently, terrorist attacks as ways to undermine and even overthrow it. Many of those groups question the regime's Islamic credentials and believe that it has betrayed the eighteenth-century Wahhabi movement and its pact with the Al Saud. While an Islamist opposition in a state that claims to rule according to the law of God may appear contradictory, many studies have demonstrated the contentious relationship between the Saudi state and both the Wahhabis and the Islamists. Recent research focuses on regime strategies to maintain its power, pacify the population, and counter the threat of violent jihadis. Others analyse successive Saudi calls for political reform and capture the core demands and aspirations of many peaceful intellectuals, professionals, and activists. We now have a rich literature explaining factors contributing to regime stability, including, among other things, repression, oil revenues, dynastic rule, tribal tradition, loyal Wahhabi clerics, the redistributive economy, and foreign support. At the same time, we know more about how Saudis mobilize and contest regime strategies.

However, the spectacular violence of Islamist groups, for example the 1979 Mecca Mosque siege and al-Qaeda terrorism in 2003–8, meant that the Islamist opposition is over-studied at the expense of other dissident groups with no overt Islamist agenda. In the 1950s and 1960s, long before the Islamist challenge of the 1990s, Saudi Arabia, like other Arab countries, witnessed the mobilization of both leftists and nationalists. It is only recently that this phenomenon became the focus of serious and nuanced research.[15] Both leftists and nationalists were part of the anti-imperial wave that swept the Arab world under the influence of Egyptian president Gamal 'Abd al-Nasser. It is no surprise that the Saudi oil fields with their international workers became the platform where activists and dissidents gathered and mobilized others. This era in Saudi history had almost been forgotten, but recently historians have begun to explore this episode of non-Islamist mobilization, thus adding great insight into how we interpret state–society relations over time. Others have explained the shift towards more Islamist agendas as a function of the intersection between local domestic state strategies, international pressure, and Cold War agendas.[16]

INTRODUCTION

Another contentious aspect of Saudi politics, Shi'a dissent, is now well documented and understood. Since the 1980s there have been several research papers and monographs explaining how the Shi'a of the Eastern Province continue to challenge the state and demand recognition of their religious, civil, political, and human rights.[17] Given the strategic and economic significance of the Eastern Province, where the majority of the Shi'a live, it is not surprising that scholarship focused on this group. Moreover, the Wahhabi denunciation of the Shi'a as heretics made it easier for them to be constructed as a minority that continues to experience marginalization and discrimination. Saudi–Shi'a relations continue to be analysed within the sectarian prism. However, as we shall see in this volume, young Saudi scholars are beginning to challenge this sectarian narrative.[18]

International-relations analysts map the contours and shifts, if any, in Saudi foreign policy with special attention paid to how they reflect domestic concerns or changing regional contexts and global power struggles. What is the future of the Saudi–US so-called special relationship? Why has Saudi Arabia intensified its outreach to Asia, both Muslim-majority countries and non-Muslim countries such as China and Japan? Can it succeed in opening new venues for greater economic and security integration with China? Can this evolve into greater military cooperation?

At the regional level, a plethora of studies explain the aggressive interventionist policies of the regime in places such as Yemen, Egypt, Bahrain, Syria, and beyond.[19] More recently the crisis with Qatar in 2014 and 2017 became the focus of recent speculations. The rivalry between Iran and Saudi Arabia since 1979, which intensified after the Arab uprisings, has also been hotly discussed in academic work, policy think tanks, and international media.[20] These are among the questions that dominate the recent interest in Saudi foreign policy. Such questions get even more complicated as they become entangled with oil, the country's main source of revenue.

With the sharp collapse of oil prices since 2014, political economists reflect on the future of the so-called social contract between rulers and ruled, the consequences of newly introduced cuts in subsidies, the gradual erosion of welfare services, and the imposition of new overt and hidden taxes on a society that has little experience of direct taxation.[21] Their attention is focused on whether, after the restructuring of the Saudi economy, embedded in the new Vision 2030 and the National Transformation Programme,[22] Saudis would eventually demand political representation, shaking the foundation of the absolute monarchy and the rentier state model, used to account for the Saudi redistributive economy and the perpetual loyalty of citizen to leadership. Speculation about the 2017 reversal of cuts in subsidies and welfare provision point to societal pressure and the desire of Muhammad ibn Salman to distance himself from an era of austerity. But when it comes to Saudi Arabia, there is more at stake than simply testing how far the rentier state model can be upheld to explain the resilience of the monarchy or the alleged acquiescence of the citizens. The country remains important not only for its oil but also for its role in the wider world. Many scholars have demonstrated that its stability may not only be a function of the regime's redistributive powers.

There are those who dismiss any suggestion that the kingdom is currently facing life-threatening challenges that would eventually lead to destabilizing the monarchy, or even the disintegration of the kingdom. Many writers assure markets, foreign governments, and global audiences that it is business as usual in the kingdom. To substantiate the narrative about the resilience of the monarchy, observers highlight the dynamic nature of the Saudi political decision-making process, attributing the stability of the kingdom to the good vision and charisma of both the old and new leadership or to the stabilizing dynamics of dynastic rule.[23] Recently, with the appointment of Muhammad ibn Salman as crown prince, analysis highlights the merits of the leadership's credentials as it remains eager to maintain stability, prosperity, and survival in a tormented and volatile Arab region. The step was applauded in the Saudi press as the right leadership move. Veteran Western diplomats, retired ambassadors, and others remind their audiences of the banality of the narrative about the imminent collapse of the house of Saud. 'We have heard it before' is a common response among many Western diplomats when the fate of the house of Saud is discussed. As the ruling house did not fall under pressure from the Arab nationalists and leftists in the 1960s, or after the terrorism crisis in the aftermath of 9/11, it is unlikely that the regime is on the verge of collapse now, according to some commentators. While this may be the public discourse, however, many observers privately express concern about the future of Muhammad ibn Salman and his policies.

In the wake of the smooth royal succession in 2015, the initial leadership shuffles a couple of months later, and the dramatic sacking of Muhammad ibn Nayif as crown prince and the promotion of Muhammad ibn Salman to the post, Saudi observers describe the regime as a careful, shrewd, and evolutionary force, always on a steady path to incremental reform. Some argue that those who forecast that Saudi Arabia is on the verge of a revolutionary upheaval are usually ignorant of the internal dynamics of state–society relations and the nature of a 'traditional' and 'conservative' Saudi society. In this Orientalist narrative, the alleged 'traditionalism', 'conservatism', and 'tribalism' of Saudi society are held responsible for delaying urgent social and political reform and inhibiting revolutionary action at the national level. In this discourse, the repressive measures taken by the regime since the 1950s to stifle civil society, prohibit demonstrations, and curb political and civil rights are not considered fundamental in containing and repressing reformist impulses among a plethora of Saudi leftists, nationalists, and Islamists—not to mention the large amount of space given in this resilience narrative to the Wahhabi tradition, believed to maintain obedience and loyalty to rulers. Added to this is the sectarian outlook that deepens the divide between the Sunni majority and the small but active Shi'a minority, thus delaying and obstructing the emergence of national solidarities across regional and sectarian divides.

It is ironic that the most threatening challenges to the regime did in fact originate from the so-called loyal Wahhabi tradition and its clerics. From the Sahwa shaykhs of the 1990s to the al-Qaeda operatives in the post-9/11 era, and the Islamic State since 2014, the challenge to the regime erupted from within the rank and file of the Wahhabi tradition among people who had been indoctrinated in its tenets. A possible explanation may point to the fragmentation of Wahhabiyya under state control or the radical trend that had always been part of its theology and doctrines that the Saudi state had not successfully suppressed or totally eliminated, even after institutionalizing the tradition in the 1970s.

The Saudi regime itself insists that the dangers facing the kingdom are mainly external. While the rivalry between Iran and Saudi Arabia dates back to 1979, the regime has certainly amplified the Iranian threat recently. The ongoing Saudi–Iranian rivalry has prompted scholars to consider it as the new Middle East Cold War.[24] The rivalry gathered momentum during the 2011 Arab uprisings, especially in Iraq, Bahrain, Yemen, Lebanon, and Syria. The so-called Middle East Cold War became extremely heated, threatening even the annual Pilgrimage to Mecca and deepening the decline in oil prices. Iranians boycotted the Pilgrimage in 2016 and continued to accuse the Saudis of resisting lowering their oil production, thus contributing further to low oil prices, which proved to hurt not only all oil-producing countries but also Saudi Arabia itself.

After unsuccessful attempts to draw the USA into a military conflict with Iran since 2008, the Saudi regime shifted its own policy towards more military interventionism. The Saudi regime regards its 2011 military intervention in Bahrain and later in Yemen in 2015 as necessary measures to protect itself from Iranian expansion. In Yemen it went further than it had in Bahrain, when it acted in alliance with the Gulf Cooperation Council (GCC) countries. In Yemen, in addition to GCC support, the Saudis assembled an Arab and Muslim coalition of several countries, declared the beginning of Operation Decisive Storm, and began to launch regular military strikes against the Iranian-backed Houthis, immediately after the latter stormed Sana'a and forced the Yemeni president, Abdrabbuh Mansour Hadi, into exile in Riyadh. Many observers may forget that Saudi military intervention in Yemen has a long history, for example in 1962 and 2009. The 2015 war is an escalation of a previous historical pattern, although the rationale and objective of the current Saudi war may be different from previous military engagement.

Moreover, after the Arab uprisings, the kingdom intensified its own outreach to Muslim countries, from Morocco to Malaysia. Saudi Arabia invited Muslim countries to joint military exercises.[25] These events became opportunities to demonstrate the solidarity of other Muslim nations and their support for the Saudis. These initiatives are also intended to isolate Iran in the Muslim world. It is in this context that Saudi Arabia projected itself as the defender of Sunni Muslims after decades of carrying the banner as defender of all Muslims. The pan-Islamic narrative of the regime, promoted since the reign of King

Faysal in the 1960s, gradually degenerated into a narrow sectarian agenda. While direct military engagement between Iran and Saudi Arabia remains unlikely in the near future, both countries rely on proxies who currently fight this new Middle East Cold War.

The Saudi amplification of the Iranian threat is used as a pretext to justify a shift in foreign policy from diplomacy to direct military interventions in the Arab region. Saudi Arabia claims to be defending its own borders against Iranian expansion in both Bahrain and Yemen. This new military interventionism immediately became popular among many Saudi constituencies, from Islamists to liberals. In particular, the war on Yemen fused Wahhabiyya, a sectarian religious tradition, with the nascent Saudi nationalism to strengthen the regime and bind it with a Saudi population indoctrinated in the belief that its leadership is destined to play a leading role not only in the region but also globally. By amplifying the undoubtedly genuine Iranian threat, the Saudi regime invoked both nationalism and sectarianism.

During the early years of the Arab uprisings, Saudi Islamists in particular began to show signs of dissent. This intensified after the regime overtly supported the 2013 coup in Egypt where the elected Muslim Brotherhood president, Muhammad Morsi, was ousted by the Egyptian army under General Abdel Fattah al-Sisi. Saudi foreign interventions in Bahrain and Yemen promised to silence a broad range of dissenting voices calling for political reform. It also designated the Muslim Brotherhood a terrorist organization. Intervention in Yemen in particular appeased many Islamists who were either driven by sectarian agendas or disappointed with the regime for its support for the Egyptian coup. Moreover, since the Syrian uprising in 2011, with a few exceptions Saudi Islamists have continued to frame events in Syria in sectarian terms, seeing them through the prism of Sunni–Shi'a divides.[26] This Saudi perspective also applies to the ongoing conflict in Iraq, where Sunnis lost their power in 2003, following the American occupation. Saudis viewed both Iraq and Syria through a sectarian prism, which only became more entrenched after several Iranian-backed Shi'a militias came to the rescue of both Bashar al-Assad in Damascus and the central government in Baghdad. Saudi Islamists lamented their own government's unsuccessful bid to reverse the situation in both countries despite diplomatic efforts and the sponsorship of multiple local rebel groups, especially in Syria. Many of them contrasted the role Iran plays among the Shi'a and its continuous support for their militia in places such as Lebanon, Syria, Iraq, and more recently in Yemen with their own government's reluctance to overtly support their Sunni counterparts in the same countries. From the Islamists' perspective the Saudi regime contributed to the downfall of the elected Islamist government in Egypt immediately after the Arab uprisings. Given that Saudi Arabia is still struggling to dissociate itself from extremism, its sponsorship of rebels in Syria is projected as an attempt to strengthen moderate forces fighting Bashar al-Assad. But as Saudi Arabia joined the international coalition against the Islamic State in Iraq in 2014, many hardline Islamists in Saudi Arabia questioned the logic of their own leadership. From the perspective of hardline Saudi Islamists, their regime has not done enough to counter Iran's penetration of the Arab world.

Therefore, the direct Saudi military intervention in Yemen in March 2015 sent a clear message to local constituencies that the regime is determined to act on the Iranian threat to its security and sphere of influence in the whole Arab world. Saudi Islamists wanted their regime to show more commitment to defending Sunni Islam against the onslaught of the Shi'a and the so-called Safavid expansion across the region.

Given the importance of Saudi Arabia for the stability of the global economy, it is no surprise that speculations about the regime and its ability to contain and absorb political, economic, regional, and international shocks remain abundant and persistent. Such speculations are central to understanding, explaining, and predicting the future of Saudi Arabia. Consequently, narrating Saudi Arabia especially to foreign audiences is always fraught with forecasts either about insurmountable domestic challenges or the leadership's ability to contain them. While many observers concur that there are serious challenges facing the kingdom even in the short term, they rarely agree on the nature of the potential threats.

This edited volume is a collection of chapters that explores Saudi Arabia's historical and contemporary trajectories, with each chapter focusing on important aspects of Saudi history, state–society relations, contestations, the politics of wealth distribution, local and transnational religious outlook, in addition to its international relations and choices. None of the chapters easily fall within either the narrative of resilience or that of collapse. These narratives have dominated other research agendas, and there is no urgent reason to make them central to the analysis in this book. Moving away from such narrow focus is a welcome attribute of the various studies in this book. Predicting the future of Saudi Arabia is left to the readers, who can make their own judgement on the basis of the material presented here.

Webs of Interrelated Challenges

The kingdom surprised observers in the wake of the Arab uprisings in 2011 by remaining relatively stable. Domestically, the regime appeared intact and ready to confront multiple challenges from restless groups, including Islamists, women, and religious minorities. Small-scale sporadic protests erupted immediately after demonstrations in Arab capitals. Saudis watched crowds in Tunis, Cairo, and Tripoli occupy public squares and chant 'The people want the downfall of the regime'. When demonstrators occupied central Manama in February 2011, Saudis on the other side of the causeway connecting the two countries began to stage demonstrations in support of their own detained prisoners, demanding their release. The Shi'a of Saudi Arabia were the first to stage demonstrations in the oil-rich Eastern Province.[27] However, Shi'a demonstrations failed to trigger a national solidarity campaign as other areas of Saudi Arabia refrained from joining the Shi'a's public display of frustration over their various grievances.

In the central province of Qasim, and in particular Buraydah, small-scale demonstrations by relatives of political prisoners took place in 2012–13.[28] Men and women marched to government buildings carrying signs that denounced Muhammad ibn Nayif, the minister of interior at the time, and other agencies of government for prolonged detentions without trial and torture in prisons. Surprisingly, women relatives of detained activists were most active in this wave of demonstrations (see Nora Doaiji's chapter in this volume). Demonstrators used the slogan *Fuku al-ani* (free the detained/captured), invoking a prophetic hadith reminding believers of the obligation to free captured Muslim prisoners. The government response took multiple forms on the carrot-and-stick spectrum. Severe repression, outlawing demonstrations, introducing new welfare benefits, and promises to provide employ-

ment gathered momentum in an attempt to contain dissent and miti-
gate its spread to other major cities. King 'Abdullah found it easy to
promise to augment the distribution of benefits, especially at times
when oil prices were high.

The most effective mechanisms for countering the Shi'a demonstrations in the Eastern Province and the sporadic protests in Qasim and to
a lesser extent Riyadh from coalescing into a national movement were
entrenched regionalism, the invocation of sectarian discourse, and the
continuous amplification of the Iranian threat. Religious opinion and
political rhetoric framed demonstrations among both Sunnis and Shi'a
as Iranian conspiracies featuring the Saudi Shi'a as a fifth column.
Passing very long prison sentences on several human rights and civil
society activists, who truly believed in peaceful dissent, also helped
silence voices calling for political reform.[29] The government described
these detainees, several among them prisoners of conscience, as terrorists threatening the security of the kingdom. New anti-terrorism laws
were introduced, with several peaceful activists and lawyers put on
trial in courts specializing in terrorism cases.

At the leadership level, a smooth succession in January 2015 brought
the ageing crown prince, Salman ibn 'Abd al-'Aziz, to the throne. The
transfer of power from King 'Abdullah to Salman was unchallenged,
and went ahead without noticeable dissent among the princes. The new
king's leadership shuffles, which brought his nephew Muhammad ibn
Nayif and his own son Muhammad ibn Salman so close to the throne,
went ahead amidst speculations and rumours about dissent within the
Al Saud family. The king simply changed the succession arrangement
that King 'Abdullah had put in place before he died in 2015. The new
king removed Prince Muqrin from his post as deputy crown prince and
elevated his nephew, thus moving the succession to the second generation of Al Saud for the first time. Yet the persistent narrative about
palace intrigues and silent coups continued to flourish in international
media. Royal solidarity was maintained in public in the face of rumours
about internal royal rivalries. The smooth succession assured observers
that the king was still in charge, with his two aides successfully running
government affairs. However, immediately after this succession reshuffle, new speculations emerged, this time about the rivalry between the
so-called two Muhammads, the crown prince and the deputy crown

prince. Succession issues in the kingdom remain important, and as such they attract analysis and speculation. In the absence of a flourishing civil society and representative institutions, any internal royal rivalries may pose a serious threat to the survival of the kingdom. The regime ensured that no alternative government to the Al Saud is imagined or allowed to emerge. Hence, should the regime show signs of weakness at the top level, a power vacuum is more likely to emerge and threaten its survival.

Saudi Arabia witnessed a new wave of terrorism with the Islamic State group's declaration of a caliphate in Mosul in July 2014. But sporadic IS terrorist attacks in 2015–16 did not seem to threaten the regime itself. While several minor attacks targeted the Saudi security forces, the American consulate in Jeddah, and the Medina Mosque, there were other, more deadly, attacks against the Shi'a in the Eastern Province. This new wave of terrorism differed from the previous terrorist era between 2003 and 2008, when al-Qaeda in the Arabian Peninsula targeted foreign compounds and killed hundreds of people.[30] However, in general IS terrorism empowered rather than undermined the regime. It confirmed its own general narrative about how Saudi Arabia is a target of terrorism rather than an incubator or supporter of radical groups such as ISIS and others. Since the beginning of the Syrian war and the Saudi support for radical rebel groups, which Saudi Arabia always denied, the country had become increasingly on the defensive against a plethora of accusations about its role in the Syrian conflict, and its religious tradition, especially Wahhabi interpretations of Islam that many continue to believe are at the heart of inspiring contemporary jihadis around the globe. The increasing ideological Wahhabization of jihad in both Iraq and Syria did little to counter the narrative about Saudi Arabia's responsibility for contemporary terrorism and the affinities between Salafi jihadis and the Saudi Wahhabi religious tradition. By the end of 2016 terrorist attacks were less frequent, while the regime tightened the security measures that had been consolidated and enforced immediately after the first terrorist episode in 2003.

One major domestic challenge that continues to cast its shadow on the reign of King Salman was the dramatic fall in oil prices since 2014. While King 'Abdullah enjoyed a period of *tufra* (affluence), with barrels of crude oil trading at a high of $147, the reign of the current king has coincided with a dramatic sharp decrease in oil prices. In 2016 it reached $40 per barrel. The fluctuation in oil prices is not new: Saudi Arabia has witnessed successive cycles of affluence and austerity since the 1970s. However, there seems to be a new dimension in the current oil crisis. Saudi Arabia is yet to adjust its economy to a changing oil market, mainly the new emerging sources of energy such as shale oil that threatens its own market share. Since 2014 it has refused during OPEC meetings to reduce production. Saudi Arabia hoped that the decline in oil prices would weaken its rivals, Iran and Russia, in this volatile market. However, as a result of declining oil prices it has suffered serious budget deficits since 2015, and was compelled to borrow money from international markets, and issue government bonds.

In 2016 the regime introduced a new economic plan, dubbed Vision 2030, to deal with the budget deficit and curb spending.[31] The plan promised economic diversification, Saudization, privatization, and other social and educational initiatives. The backbone of the Saudi economy, Saudi Aramco, became central to the new vision as Crown Prince Muhammad ibn Salman, the plan's creator, promised to float 5 per cent of the company. In 2016 economic austerity measures after the dramatic fall in oil prices were introduced as part of the new economic plan. Subsidies on essential goods and energy were lifted, and public-sector employees such as ministers and members of the Shura Council were told to expect 20 per cent salary cuts. Taxing citizens to raise money remains controversial among people who have become used to receiving rather than contributing to central government funds. Electronic-based dissent against these measures flourish online, but real resistance to the austerity measures is yet to emerge. Saudis are very active on social media, where they air their grievances. Since the introduction of Vision 2030, several informal discussion groups have invited experts to discuss the new measures and posted the discussion on YouTube.[32] So far this virtual resistance has not materialized in the form of real confrontation with the regime over its new austerity plans and economic cuts. In 2017 Muhammad ibn Salman perhaps sensed the dissent and declared that the cuts would be reversed. However, criticism of corruption and nepotism intensified on social media after cuts were announced. Many activists asked whether restructuring the Saudi economy is possible without serious political reform that involves the people in policy and government.

If the domestic front appeared relatively calm and unthreatening to the regime, regionally Saudis faced mounting challenges around their borders. The Syrian uprising turned into a quagmire that sucked in not only the Syrian people and other international actors but also the Saudi regime. Nowhere in the Arab world did the Saudi regime show so much enthusiasm for revolution as in Syria, where it immediately took the side of the rebels against Bashar al-Assad. This is contrasted with its denunciation of the overthrow of Mubarak of Egypt and Zayn al-Abidin Bin Ali of Tunisia, and the demonstrators in Bahrain. So when Saudi Arabia is described as a counter-revolutionary force, this needs to be qualified by explaining its multiple approaches to the individual uprisings that swept the Arab world. [33] From the beginning the Saudis demanded that al-Assad step down, but, more than five years later, the conflict continues and metamorphoses into sinister outcomes that neither the Saudi regime nor the international community seem to be able to contain. While many regional powers and non-state actors took sides in this conflict, the Saudi regime became increasingly involved in the prolonged civil war, arming Syrian rebels and leading international conferences in support of the Syrian opposition.

With the Arab uprisings, the regime seems to combine its old behind-the-scenes diplomacy with an aggressive regional foreign policy. Its main urgent objective in the Arabian Peninsula was to preserve the monarchy as a form of government. The regime also extended its support for the monarchies in Morocco and Jordan; both received substantial subsidies from the Saudis. The regime feared that the monarchies would start collapsing alongside the republics in Tunisia and Egypt. King 'Abdullah invited both Jordan and Morocco to join the GCC, proposed greater GCC unification to replace cooperation, and augmented Saudi aid to friendly regimes in the Arab world.

Moreover, Saudi Arabia became more determined to contain the expansion of Iran in the region. From the perspective of the Saudis, the Arab uprisings could potentially become a window of opportunity for Iran to increase its penetration of the Arab world. From Damascus to Sana'a, the Saudi regime began to apply a new foreign policy, dubbed Salman's doctrine, directed mainly against its Iranian arch-enemy in the region. While 'Salman's doctrine' was a public relations exercise, it translated into more aggressive rhetoric against Iran, a justification for the war in Yemen, and more recently in 2017 the crisis with Qatar. As

Saudi Arabia failed to enlist the USA in this regional goal, it actively sought to involve the Muslim world in its struggle against Iran, perceived to be encroaching on Saudi influence in Beirut, Damascus, Baghdad, and Yemen, to mention a few of the hot spots. In Bahrain, a combination of a military presence and subsidies stabilized the al-Khalifa regime and ensured that the Gulf monarchy remains secure against any political and economic upheaval. In Egypt, Saudi Arabia continued to support the new military regime against the threat of Islamists. In Syria the Saudis supported rebel groups against the Iranian-backed regime. However, in Yemen the Saudis directly bombed the Houthis to ensure that an Iranian-backed militia was destroyed before it could represent a serious threat to Saudi Arabia's southern borders. Aggressive intervention in Yemen is not new as the Saudis had previously participated in bombing the Houthis in 2009. The only difference is that in 2009 Ali Abdallah Salih, the president of Yemen at the time, was a Saudi ally. In 2015, after being deposed, he returned to Yemeni politics as an ally of the Houthis and an enemy of the Saudis. While this aggressive policy is still ongoing, it remains to be seen whether it actually stabilizes Yemen and allows the regime to emerge victorious in this proxy war with Iran. So far Saudi Arabia's performance in Yemen attests to an emerging reality that it may have started a war impossible to win. As in Syria and Iraq, the Saudi regime has yet to succeed in its plan to weaken Iran's penetration of the Arab world.

With Salman on the throne, his son Crown Prince Muhammad ibn Salman is currently struggling to make Saudi Arabia a serious regional power on a par with Turkey, Iran, and Israel. All these regional powers are currently flexing their muscles in a bid to emerge as the dominant force dictating the outcome of various conflicts in the Arab world. In this heated regional struggle, new alliances are formed, and old ones are reversed.

The young Saudi prince has continued the long-standing anti-Iranian rhetoric, and has even tried to encroach on Iran's traditional sphere of influence in the region. The American occupation of Iraq from 2003 helped Iran to increase its sway in neighbouring Arab countries. The Saudi leadership has come to appreciate that its previous policy of ostracizing Iraq in the post-2003 period has exacerbated the country's estrangement from its Arab neighbours, pushing it towards Iran. The current situation in Iraq, however, has made the government of Haidar al-Abadi more responsive to recent Saudi advances than former prime minister Nouri al-Maliki had been, and Saudi Arabia's advances to the controversial Shi'i cleric Muqtada al-Sadr have also been welcomed by the Iraqi government, which is hoping, especially after the defeat of ISIS in Mosul, to gain broader Arab support and dismiss accusations of being entrenched in Shi'i sectarian politics; al-Abadi is working to be seen as a leader for all Iraq rather than just the Shi'a. Good relations with the Saudis could help improve his image.

But without Iran's approval, Saudi Arabia will find it difficult to 'reconcile' with Iraq, and the presence of Iranian militia on Iraqi soil and the pro-Iranian position of its leading political party, Hizb al-Da'wa, along with Muhammad ibn Salman's erratic foreign policy, threaten any potential rapprochement between the two countries. It is unlikely that Saudi–Iraqi relations will improve in the short term without positive input from Iran.

Turkey, despite cooperating with Saudi Arabia over the Syrian civil war, sided with Qatar in the 2017 Saudi–Qatari crisis, when Saudi Arabia accused Qatar of sponsoring terrorism (including Hamas) and destablizing the region via its al-Jazeera media empire. Saudi Arabia even tried to interfere in Qatari domestic politics, precipitating a rift difficult to heal in the Gulf. More importantly, like other regional conflicts in the Arab world, this one has turned into an opportunity for regional powers—Turkey, Iran, and Israel—to become involved, with Israel demonstrating solidarity with the Saudi coalition by closing al-Jazeera's offices in Jerusalem.

Indeed, Muhammad ibn Salman has courted Israel, now jokingly dubbed the newest Sunni state, in a bid to form a pan-Islamic international alliance against both Iran and Qatar. There have been a number of contacts aimed at strengthening Saudi Arabia's military capabilities and enlisting the support of Israel in the event of a military confrontation with Iran. The Saudi media has also been less critical of Israel and its treatment of Palestinians. Muhammad ibn Salman must have pleased the Israelis by both this and his condemnation of Qatar's support for Hamas, and this should improve relations in the longer term, although it will take time to bear fruit. Under Salman, however, one can conclude that a serious reshuffle of foreign policy has taken place.

The regional concerns of Saudi Arabia were also entangled with a changing international scene. It seems that the rift with the USA after

9/11 has not been successfully healed. In fact, it appears to have wors-
ened in 2016 as the US Senate passed the Justice Against Sponsors of
Terrorism Act (JASTA) allowing the families of the 9/11 victims to sue
Saudi Arabia in American courts. This came as the final blow to the
troubled Saudi–US relations during the presidency of Barack Obama.
Despite several visits to Saudi Arabia, Obama remained aloof from the
country's leadership while continuing to sell them weaponry and provide logistical support for their war in Yemen. In the meantime, Russia
is becoming increasingly involved in Syria, and possibly in Yemen in the
future, while Saudi Arabia still clings to its old partnership with
America despite the latter's new hands-off approach to the troubles of
the region. However, it is uncertain that the US–Saudi relationship
reached breaking point during Obama's presidency. The relationship,
however, improved after the election of Donald Trump as president in
2016. The Saudi regime continues to enjoy close ties with America,
cemented by regular weapons purchases, cooperation against terrorism, and trade. The USA did little to restrain Saudi Arabia in its war on
Yemen. In fact, it approved the war and provided logistical support.
While the Saudis seem to rightly continue to worry about the JASTA,
and the American administration tries to contain the damage, the relationship is better described as aloof. Some will argue that a breaking
point may never be reached, as it will be costly to both parties, so there
is an understanding that the core of this relationship remains intact.
While most US presidents had supported Saudi Arabia, even Barak
Obama in his own way (for example, turning a blind eye to Saudi interventions in Bahrain, Yemen, and Syria), Saudi Arabia may not have successfully pacified the US Congress or the Senate, and both houses are
capable of creating some noise when it comes to the USA offering
unequivocal support to the Saudis.

This book is an attempt to look closely at the above-mentioned
interrelated webs of domestic, regional, and foreign challenges to
arrive at a better understanding of Saudi Arabia.

The Organization of the Book

In Part I, State and Society, several chapters examine regime stability,
the dynamics of statehood, the Saudi succession, the economic dis-

tributive power of the state, protest, and the emergence of a new feminism. Gregory Gause III highlights the intersection of three domestic factors behind regime survival: the oil-funded patronage networks, the religious establishment, and internal cohesion within the royal family. Added to this, he draws attention to the importance of the external support the regime receives from the international community, mainly the USA. While at times this relationship can be problematic and contentious, it nevertheless remains crucial for regime stability. He also points out that these factors are not constant but follow a certain trajectory that may change in the future.

In an absolute monarchy with barely any political institutions beyond the control of the royal family, succession at the highest level of government becomes crucial. Madawi Al-Rasheed examines how the current ambiguity of the succession in Saudi Arabia adds to the mystique of the monarchy and contributes to the flourishing of rumours about internal rivalry and strife. While most studies of the persistence of authoritarian rule focus on the authoritarian leader as a rational person and strategist, constantly preoccupied with his own survival, the shift from primogeniture to horizontal succession among the sons of the founder of Saudi Arabia, 'Abd al-'Aziz ibn Saud, generated an indeterminate succession with vague notions about eligibility and seniority. Al-Rasheed argues that the indeterminacy and ambiguity of Saudi succession contribute to a sense of irrationality, which in turn leads to the circulation of rumours about potential rifts between senior members of the royal family. She highlights how public speculation about royal rivalries is taboo inside the country, leading to the circulation of rumours as alternative ways in which citizens make their voices heard in the narrative about the succession. The advent of social media has added to the speed by which such rumours travel, granting its source celebrity status.

While succession has always been ambiguous in Saudi Arabia, whoever became the head of the royal household and the nation fully endorsed a redistributive economy in which oil profit was redistributed among the population, thus creating networks of patronage and clientelism. Such rent distribution, argues Steffen Hertog, was important to depoliticize the citizens and to stabilize the regime. He postulates that Arab monarchies that did not distribute oil rents were overthrown in the 1950s and 1960s. But Saudi Arabia, together with the rest of the

GCC countries, introduced pervasive welfare services and benefits that shielded their regimes from further demands for political reform. Hertog revisits the Saudi redistributive economy, especially in 2014 when oil prices started their dramatic decline. This prompted the Saudi government to rethink its old economic policies and introduce new initiatives to counter the shock. There is a lot at stake here. The public sector remains the greatest employment destination for Saudis, but is no longer capable of expanding at times of austerity. Hertog argues that the old rent system is under stress at the moment as it had been linked to oil and failed to diversify early on.

The importance of succession and the redistributive economy cannot be overstated. However, succession is not simply a domestic affair. Given the historical alliance between Saudi Arabia and the USA, it is also a matter of concern for the latter. In the process of deposing King Saud in the 1960s, the USA became entangled in the dispute between Saud and his brother Faysal. As leftist and nationalist opposition gathered momentum in the oil-rich province where the American oil company Aramco was based, the USA made sure that whoever becomes king must pledge to protect US interests against agitators.

Sultan Alamer examines the recent contestations witnessed after the Arab uprisings among both the Shi'a minority in Qatif and the Sunnis in Buraydah. He deconstructs the narrative about 'sectarian grievances' and 'Islamist dissent' as causes behind the mobilization that Saudi Arabia witnessed even before 2011. According to Alamer, protest is framed in those terms as a reflection of authors writing for specific, often Western, audiences, concerned with both real and imagined discrimination among the Shi'a and violence among Islamist dissidents. By considering the persistent regional identities among both the Sunnis and the Shi'a, albeit in two different cities, he offers a new revisionist perspective, grounded in understanding regional identities and regionalism. This regionalism should not be interpreted as a function of the failure of the state to create national identity; it is a product of a deliberate state strategy to control and map the population in administrative units. While some regions failed to produce regional elites who can mobilize their people, others such as Qatif and Buraydah succeeded, and so the enigma of these two 'protesting cities' persists.

In more recent years, state–society relations have become increasingly entangled with gender issues. Nora Doaiji points our attention to

INTRODUCTION

an emerging Saudi feminism that uses the internet to create new feminist spaces, away from the historical state-centric domains where gender issues have been debated and manipulated. Through a thorough analysis of the new debates, Doaiji links women's struggles to wider political campaigns such as that started by the Saudi nascent civil and political rights association Hasm. She therefore challenges the prevalent understanding of Arab women as trapped by religion and society, on the one hand, or as tools of legitimization for authoritarian states, on the other.

Part II, Saudi Arabia and Transnational Salafiyya, is an exploration of important dimensions in the Saudi religious tradition, its global expansion, and ideological affinities with radical groups such as ISIS.

Although a number of studies have delved into Wahhabiyya, its genesis, theology, and clerics, few scholars have explored its relation to Salafiyya. Andrew Hammond navigates the genealogy of Salafiyya, a complex historical phenomenon associated with the work of many Muslim scholars across several centuries and countries. He traces how Islam began to play a role in Saudi foreign policy in the 1960s. The 'Islamization of foreign policy' was a response to the Saudi government wanting to keep local *'ulama'* out of politics, by redirecting their energies abroad. Wahhabiyya was intrinsic to new understandings of normative Sunni Islam that came to be labelled Salafiyya. Several global Muslim institutions were created, for example the World Assembly of Muslim Youth, the Organization of the Islamic Conference, and the Islamic University of Medina, among others. Hammond explores how a Salafiyya strongly associated with Saudi Arabia has made its journey to an unlikely destination, known for its Sufi tradition. Hammond describes Salafiyya in Turkey as a project in translation. In the 1980s several Saudi-trained Turkish scholars introduced Salafiyya and translated the main Saudi texts into Turkish. Hammond's contribution points to an important aspect of transnational Salafiyya, which flourishes at the intersection between local political conditions and global trends. Without understanding the local Turkish context, first with its national military outlook and later its Islamic inclinations, it is difficult to imagine why a Saudi version of Salafiyya found a niche, however limited, in a country like Turkey.

Michael Farquhar considers the forms of border-spanning religious identity and community at stake in networks of migrant students that have grown up around the Islamic University of Medina (IUM). Focusing on the discourse of non-Saudi students who have passed through the IUM's system of Salafi-oriented religious instruction, he challenges the claim that Salafis spurn engagement with local and national issues in favour of an attachment to an idealized global Muslim community. At the same time, he resists a view of Salafis as constituting a transnational 'movement', engaging with local and national issues in diverse ways whilst being bound together by shared moral concerns. Instead, he suggests that the unpredictable ways in which the influence of Saudi state-funded missionary projects such as the IUM have played out beyond the kingdom's borders are best appreciated by thinking of Salafis as constituting a 'community of discourse', members of which are bound together as much by conflict and disputation as they are by shared commitments.

Since the Islamic State in Iraq and Syria (ISIS) announced the establishment of the caliphate in Mosul in 2014, speculation about the ideological affinity between this jihadi movement and Salafiyya/Wahhabiyya has been abundant. This prompted Saudi Arabia to ban the publication of any article or research that explores the connections at the theological levels. However, in this volume Cole Bunzel shows how the prominent ISIS ideologue Bahraini Turki al-Bin'ali adopted the theology of a Saudi scholar, 'Abdullah ibn Jibrin, known for his role in the Islamic awakening movement (Sahwa) since the 1990s. A defector from loyalist Wahhabis, Ibn Jibrin is associated with a defiant brand of Wahhabiyya. Bunzel traces the shift of the global jihadi project towards becoming more entrenched in Wahhabiyya, thus representing a departure from early association with Muslim Brotherhood thinkers. He warns that as 'ISIS adopts a decidedly Wahhabi posture, and as the kingdom moves further away from Wahhabism, the potential for jihadi unrest in Saudi Arabia continues to loom large'.

In fact, this warning has already materialized as Saudi Arabia witnessed more than fifteen ISIS attacks in 2015–16. More chilling is the novel wave of parricide that has accompanied suicide bombings. Nadav Samin explores ISIS's Saudi campaign by highlighting how it reflected local Saudi genealogical politics and a repudiation of this politics. Killing one's kin in the pursuit of political goals is not specifically Islamic or Saudi, but it was used to drive a wedge through the Saudi family unit. Furthermore, Samin explores the meaning of jihadi poetry in the Saudi tribal context where tension and accommodation already exist between tribal identities, Islam, and nationalism. The Syrian conflict prompted many Saudis to seek jihad there, but it also became an opportunity to denounce the Saudi regime for failing to rescue Sunnis. In this volatile and increasingly sectarian context, narratives of kin and faith emerge, combine, and clash, according to Samin.

In Part III, Foreign Relations, Saudi foreign relations are assessed in the light of both historical and new directions. This section is not meant to be comprehensive, as there are other studies that map Saudi foreign relations in more detail, but it is meant to offer a glimpse of its role in the Cold War, followed by a general assessment of its broad relations in the region and outside it. Toby Matthiesen argues that Saudi relations with the USA were shaped by the Cold War, in which Saudis increasingly came under American influence. The Saudis eventually turned into key funders of anti-communism in different parts of the world. The promotion of Islam as an alternative to communism was eventually entangled with jihad in Afghanistan, where Saudis 'matched US funding' to the Mujahidin. Islam was a crucial ideological weapon throughout the Cold War under the auspices of the Safari Club, an anti-communist alliance of countries under the umbrella of the American intelligence services. In retrospect, and given the pervasiveness of jihadi ideology and terrorism since the 1980s, no doubt many people would question the logic of this Cold War policy and the pivotal role that Saudi Arabia has played since then.

More recent Saudi regional policies are mapped in Madawi Al-Rasheed's chapter on Saudi relations with the West. As the Arab world was shaken by the uprisings in 2011, Saudi Arabia began to confront several challenges, all close to its borders. While Saudi frustration with the USA continued during the Obama administration, Saudis worked with Arab proxies to promote their own national interests. In Yemen, Saudis opted for 'flexing their muscles'. In several Arab hot spots, Saudi regional policy stumbled, leading to a sense of impotence, especially in Iraq, Yemen, Syria, and more recently Qatar. However, the greatest achievement was to court the American president, Donald Trump. The chapter focuses on why Saudi Arabia struggled to remain the main US partner and how it reversed its previous ambiguous status under Obama to become President Trump's first foreign destination in 2017 after his election. The new crown prince has not shown great interest in Europe. Suspicion is mutual, as many European countries are still unsure about his policies and may wonder whether Saudi Arabia is a reliable and good partner. The chapter concludes by asserting that Muhammad ibn Salman may have won the USA but lost the rest.

Considering its frustration with its US partner during the Obama administration, will Saudi Arabia succeed in turning its existing economic cooperation with China into a durable political and military alliance? Naser al-Tamimi explores the potential of the relatively new Saudi–Chinese relationship to develop beyond shared economic interest. Given that Saudi Arabia established diplomatic relations with China as late as the 1990s, economic ties moved quickly to become important for both countries. The chapter on Saudi–Chinese relations emphasizes economic and financial cooperation, but casts doubt on whether such a relationship would eventually lead to serious military cooperation at the expense of Saudi–US relations. Al-Tamimi questions that in the future Saudi Arabia would seek to use China as a military replacement for the USA.

Conclusion

Despite a plethora of new research on Saudi Arabia, a British author described it as 'one of the planet's enduring—and, for some, quite offensive—enigmas'.[34] But there is nothing exceptional about Saudi Arabia. More nuanced research has explored the 'enigma' and reinserted the country into the regional history of the Arab world and beyond.[35]

Perhaps Saudi Arabia will always remain an enigma in the minds of those who refuse to acknowledge that geographically and structurally it belongs to an Arab region suffering from serious prolonged repression and upheaval, with people expressing their frustration in multiple but similar ways. There is no Saudi exceptionalism that can be understood by invoking the concept of an enigma. While Saudi Arabia has not experienced the same level of contentious mass politics after the Arab uprisings, its people have not remained quiescent, passive, or unmoved by the waves of protest. Those who do not have an interest in investigating the various forms of protest in Saudi Arabia since 2011 and the wave of repression that followed may simply conclude that the regime is resilient and strong. However, deconstructing this narrative was not the main reason for producing a book on the challenges facing the kingdom after the Arab uprisings.

This book is an attempt to unravel the real dilemmas that Saudi Arabia faced and continues to face after the Arab uprisings. The research presented here paints a complex and nuanced picture of Saudi Arabia as it adopts new social and economic initiatives and projects. From succession issues to economic visions and national transformation programmes, the country is not the island of tranquillity and prosperity it used to be. Nor is it exceptional, a unique model of benevolent monarchical rule. I hope that this edited volume demonstrates the real dilemmas that the country is expected to deal with, in addition to its total immersion in the Arab world and its many problems. However, the book does not claim to be comprehensive. There are many unanswered questions related to Saudi Arabia.

As most research on Saudi Arabia continues to be shaped by concerns over regime stability, religious extremism, terrorism, and oil, certain aspects of Saudi politics and society have remained marginal and have received minimal attention. For example, the study of migration after the discovery of oil has not moved beyond statistical analysis. Unfortunately, this area needs to be more deeply studied, with research focusing on issues related to for example the contribution of Arab immigrant functionaries to state consolidation, the segregated development model associated with American oil and military interests and personnel, the liberal impulses among Saudi intellectuals and activists, and the hybrid Saudis who are a product of their parents' or their own prolonged presence outside the country for study or work. Young Saudi hybrids have articulated their integration and alienation from their own society in literature[36] and art, but we are far from understanding this rather large cohort and its impact on the future of society and politics in the kingdom. With this new hybridity, a counter-current is beginning to assert itself, namely the new tribalism.[37]

While the study of Saudi Shi'a is well established now, we are yet to have full ethnographies of other religious minorities and groups, for example Isma'ilis and Sufis. Moreover, rural and urban poverty in Saudi Arabia remains understudied, with only scattered reports on its prevalence among sections of society. I hope that these important sociological questions will be the focus of interest among a new generation of academics. They are important if a full and nuanced picture of Saudi Arabia is to emerge in the future. A new generation of scholars may take this task seriously, and enrich knowledge about Saudi Arabia in the future.

PART I

STATE AND SOCIETY

1

SAUDI REGIME STABILITY AND CHALLENGES

F. Gregory Gause III

The success of the Saudi regime in weathering the storms of the Middle East over the past six decades and remaining in power is based on three important domestic political factors:

(1) an oil-funded, patronage-based system that links important constituencies to the ruling elite while keeping them divided from each other;
(2) a strong relationship with the religious establishment that provides both legitimization ideologically and support from an important social constituency; and
(3) cohesion within the ruling family itself.

At the international level the Saudi regime's relationship with the United States is a problematic but important element of regime stability, at times creating problems at home but providing a security umbrella in a fractious region. It is possible that each of these pillars of regime stability could be undergoing change and that the Saudi leadership is recalculating its regime-security strategy. This chapter will

31

examine the forces of change in these areas and assess the prospects for regime stability in Saudi Arabia in the coming years. It concludes that the Al Saud are likely to survive the current round of domestic and regional crises, as they have the past rounds, but identifies scenarios that could lead to regime instability.

Regime Stability in Saudi Arabia

The longevity of the Al Saud regime continues to be a mystery to Western observers. Its demise has been foretold by generations of students of the region. Each regional crisis was seen as the last straw that would sweep away what was widely perceived as a political anachronism in the modern world. Nasserist pan-Arabism, the Islamic revolution in Iran, the heightened global scrutiny following the 11 September 2001 attacks by al-Qaeda on the United States, the Arab uprisings of 2011, and, most recently, the dramatic fall of oil prices in late 2014 have all been identified as the death knell of the regime. One needs only consider the titles of recent books and articles about political stability in the country to get a flavour of this kind of thinking: *Saudi Arabia: A Kingdom in Peril*; 'The Specter of Saudi Instability'; 'It is Time for the United States to Start Worrying about a Saudi Collapse'.[1] Christopher Davidson, in his book *After the Sheikhs: The Coming Collapse of the Gulf Monarchies*, had the courage to make a point prediction that the Al Saud and the other monarchical families on the Arab side of the Persian Gulf would fall by the end of 2017.[2] The jury remains out, but the clock is ticking. Davidson's work recalls a much earlier and celebrated account of politics on the Arabian Peninsula that, while eschewing a specific date for regime change, thought that the rulers were not long for this world. Fred Halliday's *Arabia without Sultans* foresaw leftist revolts bringing the regimes down.[3] The current crop of analytical pessimists sees the threat as coming from Islamist groups (both Sunni Salafi and Shi'i) or from the kind of broad popular mobilization witnessed in so many Arab states in 2010–11. The point here is not to denigrate this work. Much can be learned from it. Halliday's book remains a classic in the study of Arabian Peninsula politics, despite the fact that the sultans (and kings and amirs) remain. It is only to call into question the assumptions—stated and unstated—that the authors make about the underpinnings of the Saudi regime.

Those who seek to explain the underpinnings of that stability can be as wrong as those who forecast the regime's demise. In the wake of the Arab uprisings a number of analysts sought to explain the stability of the monarchical regimes (not a single monarch fell from power, while four leaders of republics did, and one, in Syria, held on by his fingernails) by the nature, or the 'legitimacy', of the regime type itself.[4] But monarchs have no special mandate to rule in the Arab world. As many have fallen in Arab countries since the Second World War (Tunisia, Libya, Egypt, Iraq, North Yemen, South Yemen) as have survived. If one extends the analysis to the greater Middle East, the fallen monarchs of Iran and Afghanistan can be added. There is no particular cultural affinity between Arabian society and monarchy either. The imams of North Yemen were no less Arabian and 'legitimate' than the rulers of the rest of Arabia and could claim a much longer historical pedigree, yet the imamate fell to a military coup in 1962 and has disappeared from history. The shaykhs and sultans who ruled the small states making up the South Arabian Federation, British protectorates that, along with the crown colony of Aden, became South Yemen, resembled the shaykhs of the United Arab Emirates (UAE) in everything but the possession of oil. They were swept aside by leftists who established the first (and only) Marxist regime in the Arab world in 1967. In short, those who seek to explain regime stability in Saudi Arabia and the other Gulf monarchies through some kind of imagined cultural 'legitimacy' have failed to make their case.[5]

An analysis of regime stability cannot be done in the abstract. Each regime has built a particular strategy for survival, based on specific institutions, partnerships with its society, and international alliances. Those strategies change over time, as regimes acquire new resources and deal with changes in their societies. In Saudi Arabia, since the 1970s, that survival strategy is based first and foremost upon oil wealth. Oil does not automatically guarantee regime security. If it did, the son of the late Shah of Iran would today be consulting with his royal courtiers in Tehran about how to deal with Saddam Hussein in Baghdad. But oil wealth gives rulers the ability to build institutions and to form social alliances aimed at maintaining their rule. Every regime does this, of course. But the enormous resources that the oil boom provided to the Al Saud in the 1970s allowed them to build extensive networks and develop a myriad of new institutions. They did not have to make the hard choices about where to invest their resources that other states do.

One element of the oil-based political economy built by the Al Saud is the broad distribution of economic benefits across the citizen population of the country. Those benefits include government jobs, free health care and education, and heavily subsidized public utilities, all without taxes. These benefits have been provided directly by the state to its citizens (or subjects), bypassing historically mediating social actors such as tribal shaykhs and other local elites, thus reducing the independent power of those elites (who receive their own financial and other benefits from the Saudi state) and subordinating them to the Al Saud.[6] The Saudi regime has maintained this generalized system of benefits even during periods of oil-revenue declines, most notably from the early 1980s through the late 1990s, by drawing down the state's financial reserves and by borrowing. By the late 1990s the government debt to GDP ratio was over 100 per cent.[7] The regime was saved from a fiscal crisis by the upturn in oil prices in the 2000s.

The importance of these generalized benefits to the citizenry as a whole in the regime-security strategy of the Saudis was apparent in Riyadh's reaction to the Arab uprisings of 2011. King 'Abdullah, in two royal decrees in February and March 2011, committed to spending over $100 billion on his subjects, much of it immediately. That included a two-month salary bonus for state workers and retirees, an increase in the minimum wage in the state and parastatal sectors, a continuation of a 5 per cent 'inflation allowance' in state salaries, and the creation of more than 60,000 public-sector jobs. The king also committed to build 500,000 homes over the subsequent five years and to vastly increase the availability of state loans for home purchase.[8]

Oil wealth also allowed the Saudi regime to build patron–client relations with specific social groups, vesting their interests in the continuation of the status quo. The Saudi business community became highly dependent upon the state for contracts, licences, credit, investment opportunities, subsidies, favourable labour regulations (including very liberal policies on the importation of labour), and the creation of a national market. Given the enormous increase in wealth in the country, the regime was able to create new business actors among its core constituency in Najd while also patronizing existing merchant families in the Hijaz and the Eastern Province.[9] The business community, including in Shi'i areas, have been supportive of the regime through the various crises it has faced since the oil revolution of the 1970s.

Another important social group patronized by the Saudis has been the religious establishment. That relationship long pre-dates the oil revolution, but the coming of great oil wealth changed the dynamic. When the Saudi state was living hand to mouth the Wahhabi men of religion served as the regime's bureaucrats, collecting its taxes and enforcing its law. With oil money in the post-Second World War era the regime began to build a modern bureaucracy, staffed with a broader range of Saudis. The men of religion themselves became bureaucratized, becoming just another set of state employees. The power relationship, more equal in the past, became one of subordination of the religious establishment. But in exchange the men of religion were given a significant cut of the vastly expanded state budget and allowed to build their own bureaucracies in various ministries and institutions. They used this status to exercise control over aspects of Saudi social life, manage the Pilgrimage, play a large role in education and the administration of justice, and proselytize their version of Islam throughout the Muslim world.[10] In exchange, they gave the Al Saud their loyalty, legitimizing every controversial decision the regime made and supporting it against its critics, both domestically and internationally.[11]

This change in the status of the religious establishment, from more independent and powerful to subordinate to the state, did not sit well with all of the men of religion or those who believed that the Al Saud were straying from the straight path. Osama Bin Laden rejected Saudi rule by forming al-Qaeda, propagandizing against the Al Saud globally, and conducting a campaign inside the country against regime targets in the mid-2000s.[12] The Saudis joining al-Qaeda and the Islamic State group in Iraq and Syria (ISIS) are 'voting with their feet' against the regime. More interesting than these extremists, however, are the domestic critics of the regime from within the Salafi–Wahhabi orbit. The Sahwa ('awakening') movement of religious critique against the regime developed in the 1980s, emerged with public criticism of Saudi policy in the Gulf War in the early 1990s, and felt the wrath of the state in that decade.[13] But after the 11 September 2001 attacks and the global criticism they brought to Saudi Arabia and its version of Islam, the leaders of this movement publicly supported the regime. They could not imagine an Arabia without Al Saud rule, because Al Saud rule and Wahhabism were inextricably linked for them.[14] While critics of regime policies, they too, when the chips were down, acted as clients and supporters of the regime.

Oil wealth provided the Al Saud with plenty of carrots, but also plenty of sticks. The strategy of regime survival was not all benefits. The Saudi regime built an extensive set of security services aimed at maintaining domestic order, vastly expanding the Interior Ministry and its various policing services, both public and secret. The National Guard developed into a sophisticated force aimed at balancing the regular armed forces in a 'coup-proofing' strategy and at providing for domestic security when the regular police were not enough.[15] These domestic security services allowed the Saudis to put down the al-Qaeda challenge in the mid-2000s, contain unrest in Shi'a communities in the Eastern Province, both in the aftermath of the Iranian revolution of 1979 and during the Arab upheavals of 2011, and crack down on a range of dissent at various times since the 1970s. This is not to argue that the Saudi internal security forces are more efficient, brutal, or frightening than those of other Arab states. It is hard to imagine that Saudis fear their police more than Tunisians, Egyptians, Libyans, or Syrians feared theirs, yet protesters filled the streets of all those countries in 2011 while Saudi Arabia remained quiet. But it would be equally mistaken to overlook the agencies of coercion and surveillance that oil money has allowed the Saudi regime to build.

Institutions of distribution and of coercion are essential elements of the Saudi regime-security strategy, but so is a unique institution of governance, the ruling family itself. Oil money allowed the remaking of the family into an institution of rule. In more penurious circumstances a monarch would need to cut his extended family out of politics because he could not afford to employ them all, and would see them as potential threats to his control of the resources of the state. With the oil boom, the Al Saud were able to cut most if not all of the large number of sons of the founding king in on the spoils.[16] The extended Al Saud family, or at least the senior members, formed a corporate group that ruled the country, particularly after the accession of King Faysal after the deposition of his half-brother, King Saud, in

1964. Saud tried to groom his son to succeed him; Faysal rallied almost all of the other sons of 'Abd al-'Aziz to oppose Saud. When Faysal emerged victorious he staffed his government with his half-brothers and established a succession mechanism that transferred kingship among them.[17] King Salman is, in all probability, the last of that generation to assume the top spot. The Al Saud formed themselves into a ruling elite and, since the Saud–Faysal struggle, have basically maintained their internal unity. That unity has allowed them to fend off domestic challenges and confront regional crises in a coherent fashion and has prevented outside powers and local actors from being able to play factions of the family against each other. Regime security requires that the ruling elite remain united, and the Al Saud have.

Generalized benefits to the citizenry, targeted patron–client relations with the business community, the religious establishment, and the tribes, institutions of coercion and surveillance, and the conversion of the ruling family into a corporate ruling elite have all been parts of the survival strategy of the Al Saud regime at the domestic level. In terms of foreign policy, the major element in the regime's survival strategy has been an alliance with the United States. That alliance has been problematic at times.[18] Riyadh confronted the United States directly with the oil embargo of 1973–4. The 11 September 2001 attacks by al-Qaeda, in which fifteen of the nineteen hijackers were Saudi citizens, led to intense American public scrutiny of the relationship and pressure on the Saudis. Saudi public opinion, though not a major factor in the making of Saudi foreign policy, has generally seen the United States as an untrustworthy ally, because of its strong support for Israel. Osama Bin Laden's breach with the regime was largely over its dependence on the United States and the presence of American troops in the country after the 1990–1 Gulf war. Despite all of these issues, the alliance has endured. It proved its worth to the Saudis most directly during the Gulf war, when the United States led an international coalition that ejected Saddam Hussein's Iraq from Kuwait and restored the monarchical regime. The American security umbrella provides the Saudis with protection against militarily stronger regional states and allows them to pursue more forward regional policies without having to worry about direct military retaliation by their foes.

The Reign of King Salman: A New Regime-Security Strategy?

Since the accession of King Salman in early 2015 every element of the regime's security strategy has come under pressure. The collapse of oil prices in late 2014 has called into question the ability of the state to sustain the government spending that underpins so much of the strategy. The changes in Saudi political economy promoted by the king's young son, defence minister and now the crown prince, Muhammad ibn Salman, through the Vision 2030 plan call into question some of the pillars of the strategy. The concentration of power in the hands of Prince Muhammad ibn Salman suggests a new dispensation within the ruling family itself that raises questions about future family unity. Belief in Riyadh that the United States is withdrawing from its military role in the Middle East has cast into doubt the core foreign alliance of the regime's survival strategy.

An examination of each of these issues in more detail will demonstrate that the Al Saud are not facing immediate challenges to regime stability. Taken together, however, they do suggest that Riyadh might be contemplating a rewriting of the regime-survival strategy that has served it so well over the past decades.

The key challenge facing the Saudi regime is fiscal. Oil prices have fallen from their historic highs in the early 2010s, losing over two-thirds of their value. In August 2013 oil reached $111.44 per barrel (West Texas Intermediate). In January 2016 it dipped below $30 per barrel. Toward the end of 2016 oil settled into a band between $40 and $50 per barrel, and stayed there in the early months of 2017.[19] Even with spending cuts in 2015 and 2016, the Saudi budget deficit in 2016 was 11.5 percent of gross domestic product (GDP), with a projected deficit in the 2017 budget of approximately 7.7 percent of GDP.[20] The Saudi reaction to the Arab uprisings of 2011 emphasized the importance of state spending and patronage to the Saudi regime-security strategy. As oil seems to be settling into a moderate price range for the foreseeable future, Riyadh faces hard choices about how to cope.

The past model was to maintain spending, run down reserves, and borrow. There has certainly been some of that so far. The 2015 government budget set expenditures at 860 billion Saudi riyals (SR), but actual spending was 975 billion SR, with a deficit that amounted to 15 per cent of GDP.[21] Saudi government financial reserves totalled over $725 billion in 2014. They are estimated to have fallen, by the end of 2016, to somewhere around $500 billion, a reduction of almost one-third in the space of two years. Government debt to domestic entities rose from below 2 per cent of GDP in 2014 to an estimate of 11.6 per cent by the end of 2016.[22] In October 2016 the government went for the first time to international markets for a $17.5 billion bond sale, the largest ever by an 'emerging-market' country.[23] The government also used tactics similar to those of the oil-price downturn of the late 1980s and 1990s to preserve cash, delaying payments to contractors.[24]

However, there are also strong indications that King Salman and Prince Muhammad ibn Salman are rethinking the distributional basis of the regime's survival strategy. In the prince's plan for economic restructuring, expressed in the Vision 2030 and National Transformation Programme (NTP) documents, subsidies on electricity and water are to be cut, a value-added tax is to be implemented, and the number of public-sector jobs is to be cut. The private sector is expected to take on the bulk of the responsibility for employing Saudis entering the work force.[25] Saudi electricity and water bills are already increasing, and in September 2016 salaries and perks for government employees were cut.[26] It is not clear how the government intends to push the Saudi private sector, whose business model is largely based on less-expensive foreign labour, to absorb so much greater a percentage of local job-seekers. But it is clear that the implementation of Prince Muhammad's plans will require sacrifices not only from the mass of the Saudi public, but also from the Saudi business community. Moreover, the Vision 2030 document envisages an increase in public entertainments in the country of a type opposed in the past by the religious establishment: concerts, movies, a more active social life in general. The state has already taken steps under King Salman to restrict the powers of the religious police.[27]

The ambitious plans laid out in the Vision 2030 and NTP documents call into question the patron–client relationships that the Saudi regime has built over time with the general population, the Saudi business community, and, to a lesser extent, the religious establishment. Planning documents are one thing; implementation is another. Almost every policy found in the Vision 2030 document can be found in previous planning documents that did nothing but gather dust on shelves in bureaucrats' offices. It is possible that, seeing the dangers of profound changes in the country's political economy, the regime will back away and trust fate (and the oil market) to allow them to sustain themselves. But this round of economic changes seems more serious than previous announcements, both because initial steps have been taken and because they have behind them the political will of the leading decision makers.

King Salman has also made an important change in another institution that is an element of the Saudi regime-security strategy: the ruling family. Since the time of King Faysal the senior princes of the Al Saud have ruled the country as a corporate body, parcelling out the major ministries among themselves and constituting a de facto veto group on important decisions. This arrangement had all the deficiencies of committees: it was slow to react, resistant to innovation, and unable to undertake major policy departures except in the most extreme circumstances. But it also had the virtues of committees: it was cautious, prudent, and unlikely to take dangerous risks. This 'dynastic monarchy' model kept the regime in power through numerous regional crises and internal challenges.[28] King Salman, most likely the last of those senior princes who sided with Faysal in the struggle for power in the late 1950s and early 1960s, has up-ended that system of shared governance in his transfer of power to the next generation. Rather than recreate a system of senior princes in the next generation, he has concentrated power in the hands of his son, defence minister and crown prince Muhammad ibn Salman. There are fewer members of the Al Saud in the current Saudi cabinet than at any time since Faysal became king. This concentration of power has permitted more decisive and risky decision making, exemplified both by Vision 2030 and by the Yemen war, both policies directed by and strongly identified with Prince Muhammad ibn Salman.

The risk in this shift of the structure of power within the Al Saud is that it will be rejected by other members of the family, creating rifts within the ruling elite and opening up the possibility of conflicts over power. There have been indications of disquiet. One prince went public with his complaints about the new order in an interview with a Western reporter.[29] Some princes have circulated a petition within the family calling for the deposition of King Salman and the two favoured princes of the third generation and the elevation of Prince Ahmad, one of the remaining sons of the founding king, to rulership (see chapter by Madawi Al-Rasheed in this volume).[30] These faint public signals of discontent have been few and far between. There are no indications of an overt split within the family that could lead to a real struggle for power. But the possibility remains.

It would be hard to argue that King Salman has changed the major foreign policy pillar of the Al Saud regime security strategy, the relationship with the United States. Washington and Riyadh continue to cooperate on a range of issues, including intelligence sharing and counter-terrorism. The United States continues to sell substantial amounts of weaponry to Saudi Arabia and has provided vital logistical support to the Saudi military operation in Yemen. Saudi Arabia publicly supported American policy initiatives, such as the Iran Nuclear Deal of 2015, about which it had qualms. But it is undoubtedly true that the Saudi leadership has less confidence in the American security guarantee than has been the case in the past. While agreeing in principle that Bashar al-Assad must go, the two allies differed substantially on how important that goal was. While the Saudis saw the spread of Iranian power through the region as the major threat, the United States focused on ISIS and Salafi jihadism as its primary target, while seeking to draw Iran into a new relationship.

This uncertainty about America's willingness to play a major military role in the region has led Saudi foreign policy under King Salman to take greater risks, most notably in Yemen. Saudi Arabia and the UAE used their own military forces in Yemen, beginning in April 2015, to halt the drive by the Houthi forces to capture Aden and consolidate their control over the country. While the Saudi-led coalition was successful in turning back the Houthi advance, it has not been able to dislodge the Houthis and their allies, forces loyal to former president Ali Abdallah Salih, from Sana'a. While the Saudis have committed few of their own ground troops to the fighting (the bulk of the ground forces come from the UAE with token contributions from other states joining the coalition), they have taken the lead in air attacks and in naval patrols aimed at preventing Iranian resupply of the Houthis.

The departure that the Yemen campaign represents in Saudi foreign policy can be exaggerated. The Saudis are not deploying significant ground forces into Yemen. They seem to be looking for a political set-tlement to the fighting, supporting various mediation efforts in 2016, though all have failed. Their involvement in the Syrian civil war is through the means that Saudi Arabia has used for decades to try to affect regional politics: money and guns to local clients, media and propaganda support for its side, diplomatic pressure regionally and internationally to achieve its aims. Yet there is a general sense that Saudi Arabia is taking a more activist role in regional politics, confronting Iran and using military force directly in Yemen to secure its interests.

The Saudi sense of uncertainty about the American security com-mitment is not simply a factor of their distaste for the Obama admin-istration's reticence to confront Iran and involve itself in Syria. While the atmospherics in Saudi–American relations improved with the advent of the Trump administration in January 2017, buoyed by the two leaderships' shared suspicions of Iran, important questions about the bilateral relationship remain. The substantial increase in American domestic oil production has raised doubts about the importance of Persian Gulf oil in overall American strategy, both in the USA and in Saudi Arabia. These doubts might well be misplaced. The Saudi–American relationship was forged when the USA did not import a drop of oil. It was the importance of the Gulf region for world energy sup-plies that led American defence planners to identify it as a strategic prize. That global importance has not lessened, even with the ups and downs of the world oil market over the decades. However, perceptions are central to policy, and many on both sides of the relationship won-der if the most recent changes in the oil market have decreased that importance. The adoption by the US Congress of the Justice Against Sponsors of Terrorism Act (JASTA), which permits American citizens to sue the government of Saudi Arabia for its alleged (though never proved) involvement in the 11 September 2001 attacks is a fresh dem-onstration that the kingdom has few if any friends in American public opinion. Congress overrode President Obama's veto of the bill by large bipartisan majorities in the midst of the 2016 election campaign.[31] That action reflected the continued belief by many in the American political elite that the Saudi promotion of its own interpretation of Islam—'Wahhabism' to those who oppose it—is a central element in the rise of the Salafi jihadist movement represented by al-Qaeda and ISIS.

Conclusion

Is the regime-security strategy of the Al Saud changing? It is too early to give a definitive answer to that question. None of these trends discussed above is irreversible. The regime could back away from the more serious changes set out in Vision 2030 and return to a policy of borrowing and hoping for a change in the oil market. There could be changes in the ruling family, particularly if King Salman's rule ends shortly; that could clip the wings of the young crown prince and return the more cautious structure of committee rule by a number of princes. The Saudi–American relationship has weathered plenty of crises in the past and not changed substantially. But, for the first time since King Faysal consolidated power in the early 1960s, one can entertain the question in a serious way. For the first time since the oil revolution of the early 1970s, there are serious plans being implemented in Riyadh to change the political economy of the distributive, rentier oil state. The structure of power within the ruling family is undergoing an important change. The relationship with the United States is being called into question, on both sides, in a serious way. It would be risky to hazard a guess as to the ultimate destination of these changes. But, if they are carried forward, the Al Saud will need to develop new strategies and mechanisms to sustain support within their society and in the international community.

2

MYSTIQUE OF MONARCHY

THE MAGIC OF ROYAL SUCCESSION IN SAUDI ARABIA

Madawi Al-Rasheed

On 23 January 2015 old King 'Abdullah ibn 'Abd al-'Aziz Al Saud (b. 1924) passed away. Within hours his half-brother Crown Prince Salman (b. 1935) became king and Deputy Crown Prince Muqrin (b. 1945) was promoted to crown prince. Interior Minister Muhammad ibn Nayif (b. 1959) became deputy crown prince. Such arrangements confirmed King Salman as respecting his deceased brother's succession plan. Before his death, King 'Abdullah had made it clear to other senior princes that the sequence of succession should remain as he had stipulated and confirmed in his royal orders. Saudis and outside observers breathed a sigh of relief over the swift and smooth succession. Many Saudis considered the succession to reflect the unity of the royal family. The smooth transfer of power was believed to silence those outside observers and dissidents who had always speculated about rivalries among senior royals.

However, King Salman felt free to alter this succession plan within two months of becoming king. In April 2015 he sacked his younger brother Crown Prince Muqrin and promoted his nephew, Deputy Crown Prince Muhammad ibn Nayif, to crown prince. He went further when he appointed his youngest son Muhammad (b. 1985) to the position of deputy crown prince. Young Prince Muhammad became second deputy prime minister, minister of defence, chief of the royal court, and chair of the Council of Economic Development Affairs, which excluded the crown prince, Muhamamd ibn Nayif. No other prince has ever held as many key positions at such a young age as Muhammad ibn Salman.[1] Even at the height of creating a centralized state, King Faysal (d. 1975) did not hold so many responsibilities. Deputy Crown Prince Muhammad was believed to be the key person and the power behind the throne. King Salman is 'possibly the last member of the Al-Saud who will be able to enjoy the unquestioned authority and prestige to impose his will irrespective of family consensus'.[2]

But on 21 June 2017 King Salman issued an expected royal decree. He sacked Crown Prince Muhammad ibn Nayif and promoted his young son Muhammad to crown prince. During the lifespan of the third Saudi state (which started in 1932), such a move had been made only once, in 1933, when 'Abd al-'Aziz ibn Saud appointed his own son Saud as crown prince. King Salman's bold decision may not be the last episode of royal reshuffles. It remains to be seen whether Salman will abdicate and allow himself to see his beloved son settle into his new role as king. Given the frequency of royal decrees that relate to succession, it will not be a surprise, as the king is over eighty years old at the time of writing this chapter.

These bold succession decisions, dubbed by foreign observers a 'palace coup' and a 'quiet revolution', ignited new rumours and speculations about royal intrigues.[3] Furthermore, reports about Muhammad ibn Nayif's ill-health had already been in circulation, especially among foreign intelligence observers in Washington. A royal decree in June 2017 places young Prince Muhammad ibn Salman immediately in line to inherit the throne, provided that no further succession changes take place during the king's lifetime. But in Saudi Arabia nothing can be taken for granted or expected to happen according to a rational plan. The survival and mystique of the monarchy are closely linked to its unpredictability even at the very top level.

King Salman's new appointments in June 2017 are destined to generate more ambiguity and speculation after he dies. The appointment
of Muhammad ibn Nayif initially created a bridge to move the throne
into vertical succession after it had followed a horizontal line. But after
June 2017, a new era was ushered following the appointment of the
king's son as crown prince.

But will Salman change the succession again before he dies? Will
Muhammad ibn Nayif ever challenge the royal decree that sidelined
him and brought his rival Muhammad ibn Salman so close to the
throne? Will Muhammad ibn Salman remain crown prince and wait for
his father to die to become king? Will King Salman abdicate in favour
of his son soon? These were the questions asked during the first two
years of Salman's rule. But by June 2017 it had become clear that
Salman wanted his son Muhammad to become the future king as he
sacked Muhammad ibn Nayif and deprived him of all his responsibilities in government. The king also changed the article relating to succession in the Basic Law of Government as will be discussed in this
chapter to ensure that Saudi Arabia truly becomes Salman's Kingdom,
with his own descendants occupying the highest post as future kings.

This chapter examines why it was difficult to answer these questions
during the first two years of Salman's rule. I explore the impulse
towards primogeniture as one of the principles for succession, and the
challenges its implementation has faced since the eighteenth century.
The principle was used several times before the succession moved to
the horizontal line from brother to brother. In the twentieth century,
this was done by the founder of the kingdom 'Abd al-'Aziz ibn Saud in
1933 when he appointed his son Saud as crown prince. Since then,
kingship moved horizontally from brother to brother, until the latest
royal decree in June 2017 when King Salman appointed his own son as
crown prince, thus excluding his nephew Muhammad ibn Nayif, other
nephews, his brothers, and the rest of his sons, some of whom are
older than Muhammad ibn Salman.

I argue that the unpredictability of succession among brothers and
now even sons of the king constantly rejuvenated the mystique of monarchy. I explore why King Salman completely ignored the Committee
of Allegiance, established by the late King 'Abdullah, and the latter's
wish that Salman respect the succession plan that he had put in place

before he died.[4] With the advent of social media, and given the ambiguity of succession, rumours became rife and further added to monarchical mystique. I explore how dissidents, royals, and commoners circulate rumours to puncture official narratives, and connect community and individual agency. Finally, the conclusion points out that endless rumours about the throne are a function of indeterminate succession, opacity, and secrecy. These qualities contribute to the mystique of absolute monarchy in Saudi Arabia. Ambiguity and inconsistency seem to serve the traditional emotional foundation of the politics of the royal family better than super-rationality, transparency, and openness. The regime survives because it mediates contradictory attributes, above all ambiguity versus clarity, and certainty versus uncertainty. The chapter confirms that the need for monarchy is neither innate nor universal, but a learned appetite. Its survival in Saudi Arabia can be attributed to the 'anaesthesia of un-reason', irrational impulses often ignored in the analysis of monarchy.[5]

By highlighting the mystical and magical aspects of uncertainty and unpredictability as contributing factors to regime survival, I do not dismiss structural domestic conditions and international and regional factors that have sustained the monarchy during the pressure of the Arab uprisings. In previous publications[6] I have argued that both US support and regional turmoil partially militated against the domino impact of the uprisings in the kingdom. So far the more civil wars raged around the kingdom, the less likely the monarch was to be challenged by mass contentious politics or his own kin. Furthermore, I shifted the analysis from regime strategies to societal conditions such as domestic fragmentation, sectarian divides, ideological polarization, and religious dogma in support of the status quo to explain why the Saudi regime survived the turmoil of the region. Neither a deterministic political economy approach (rentier state model and subsidies under the pressure of the Arab uprisings in return for loyalty) nor excessive repression fully explain the enigma of the kingdom. This chapter is a further development of themes that I have not tackled before.

Unlike presidential republics and other Arab quasi-constitutional monarchies (Jordan and Morocco), the Saudi monarchy generates both hope and illusion, thus creating a semi-magical mystique that contributes to an irrational expectation about affluence and prosperity even at times of falling oil prices, budget deficits, and shrinking welfare services. Instead of the image dominant in the literature on authoritarian survival of the calculating monarch who is constantly preoccupied with his own survival by deploying rational strategies, I shift the analysis to more emotional dispositions, attachments, and rumours all related to the power of uncertainty and hope, both often ignored in the analysis of authoritarian and autocratic rule.

The image of the rational autocrat dominates the political science literature on the 'resilience of authoritarianism', 'upgrading authoritarianism', 'robustness of authoritarianism', and 'modernisation of authoritarian rule'. This literature explains monarchical resilience by highlighting the rational strategies of the monarch from integrating the largest number of princes into state institutions (dynastic monarchies) to adopting certain trappings of democracy.[7] But a bundle of emotions such as fear, hope, uncertainty, apprehension, and illusion can equally be powerful forces in royal politics, sustaining monarchs. The image of the authoritarian ruler is often that of a highly rational autocrat, a shrewd player in the game of autocratic survival, always plotting how to remain unchallenged. He constantly deploys a combination of political control and repression in addition to deviant soft power, propaganda, coalitions, co-optation, and bribes. As autocrats try to minimize coercion and violence as much as possible, they build consensus that leads to voluntary servitude.[8] In other words, political science theorizing monarchical survival invokes the carrot and the stick; hence most analysis provides contextualization of the two strategies. In this literature, the shrewd and calculating prince eventually emerges as a savvy wolf.[9]

Recent scholarly work on the survival of monarchies, especially in GCC countries, is beginning to challenge previous rationalist perspectives. It is often the case that politics in certain contexts such as that practised in GCC countries, including above all Saudi Arabia, may elude 'calculating rationality'.[10] If irrational, unpredictable, and even counterproductive measures and forces are attributes of the person who occupies the highest post, namely the king/father of the nation and the benevolent autocratic monarch, such characteristics have so far no doubt added to the mystique and magic of the monarch rather than contributing to his overthrow.

The more the Saudi monarch seeks to project himself as endorsing a Weberian political rationality,[11] for example establishing the Committee of Allegiance to deal with succession to the throne, or adopting economic rational transformation models such as that of Deputy Crown Prince Muhammad ibn Salman's Vision 2030, the more salient irrational and unpredictable features become. If rationalization is tantamount to the increasing pervasiveness of the means–end (*zweckrational*)—purposive and instrumental social action—disenchantment, and de-magnification, the Saudi monarch relies heavily on non-rational elements for survival, a continuous state of 'the anaesthesia of un-reason'.[12]

Historical Perspective on Succession

The Al Saud adopted multiple modes of succession at different historical moments. In the eighteenth century the founder of the first Saudi–Wahhabi emirate (1744–1818), Muhammad ibn Saud (d. 1765), struck an alliance with the founder of the Wahhabi movement, Muhammad ibn 'Abd al-Wahhab (1703–92) to expand his authority beyond Deriyyah, the Al Saud's first capital. In order to ensure continuity, he adopted primogeniture to regulate the succession and guarantee that only his son would inherit the position of imam, as the first Al Saud chiefs were known.[13] When Muhammad ibn Saud died, his son 'Abd al-'Aziz (1765–1803) became the second imam. He in turn was succeeded by his son, Saud (r. 1803–14) who later appointed his own son 'Abdullah (r. 1814–18) to be his successor and fourth imam.[14]

'Abdullah was defeated by the Egyptian troops who invaded Arabia at the request of the Ottoman sultan in 1818. The Egyptians took 'Abdullah to Istanbul, where he was beheaded. The demise of the Deriyyah emirate came at the hands of an external power, endowed with much more advanced military capabilities than those that the Saudi imams had mastered in eighteenth-century Arabia. The stable primogeniture principle worked against the centrifugal forces that surrounded the emirate's rise. From shifting tribal loyalties and religious resistance to Wahhabi domination, the emirate was able to expand and control swathes of the Arabian Peninsula. This control was shaky, but many regions occasionally paid *zakat* (Islamic tax) to the Saudi imam, a token of their submission and recognition of his authority.[15]

In the nineteenth century the unstable and weak Saudi–Wahhabi revival in Riyadh, known as the emirate of Riyadh (1818–91), proved to be precarious, and eventually it collapsed under the pressure of rising rivals. The Rashidis, together with the Ottoman–Egyptian forces still stationed in Arabia, exploited the internal power struggles that had already erupted within the house of Saud.[16] Turki ibn 'Abdullah (r. 1824–34), the son of the beheaded Saudi ruler, became imam in the new capital, Riyadh. Turki was assassinated by his cousin Mishari. Turki's son Faysal (r. 1834–8) immediately killed Mishari and appointed himself imam, following the primogeniture path of succession that his Deriyyah ancestors had put in place in the previous century.

Faysal was deposed in a fresh Egyptian expedition and sent to Cairo. He later escaped and returned to Riyadh to rule for the second time after killing the Egyptian-appointed Al Saud ruler, 'Abdullah ibn Thunayan. Faysal reverted to the primogeniture mode of succession and appointed his son 'Abdullah (r. 1865–71) as the next imam. At this point 'Abdullah's three half-brothers—Saud, Muhammad, and 'Abd al-Rahman, the father of 'Abd al-'Aziz ibn Saud (Ibn Saud, the founder of the current kingdom)—were competing with each other. Their sons also entered the fray. The brother-versus-brother and uncle-versus-nephew axis became the focus of serious internal Saudi rivalries that were fuelled and exploited by many Arabian tribes aspiring to free themselves from Saudi rule. This rivalry is typical of pre-state attempts to centralize power, routinize succession, and ensure stability against centrifugal tribal traditions in which succession was not an automatic right from father to son. In such a diffused authority system, all male members of a chiefly household had in theory equal claim to become central chiefs, who remained *primus inter pares*. The rhetoric of such succession masked serious inequality between brothers. The stated values and norms of political succession collided with the reality of personal ambition, rivalry, and power struggles between men of chiefly households.

The Saudi rivalries resulted in the total demise of the Riyadh emirate in 1891, after which 'Abd al-Rahman, the father of the founder of the kingdom, Ibn Saud, fled to Kuwait with his children. Internal strife among brothers and between rulers and nephews was one of the reasons behind the fall of the house of Saud in the last decade of the nineteenth century.

Primogeniture Only Once

With the establishment of the kingdom in 1932, Ibn Saud was aware of the detrimental consequences of the rivalry that had undermined his ancestors' second weak revival in Arabia in the previous century. So he reverted back to primogeniture immediately when he appointed his son Saud (r. 1953–64) as crown prince. He first sidelined his own brothers and other collateral Al Saud branches, for example his Araif paternal cousins. The latter staged a rebellion against him in 1908 after they struck an alliance with the Ajman tribe. He subdued them militarily and later married his sister Nura to Saud al-Kabir, the head of the Araif.[17]

The king did not expect his son Saud to follow primogeniture and appoint one of his own sons as crown prince. But the monarch's expectation was unrealistic as, from 1953 onward, once he became king, Saud began to place his own sons in key positions in preparation for a new primogeniture arrangement. This move led to the rebellion King Saud faced in the early 1960s, orchestrated by his half-bother Crown Prince Faysal, who eventually organized a coup against Saud and systematically relegated all his sons to marginal positions within the royal household. Saud's fifty or so sons never recovered from this sidelining, despite several attempts to revive their father's heritage and seek important positions in government. One of these sons, Sayf al-Islam, resorted to literature to highlight this marginality, even amounting to defamation of King Saud and his descendants.[18] King Ibn Saud made it clear that agnatic seniority should be the principle determining succession after his death as he limited it in his own sons, numbering thirty-four princes at the time. But rivalry between brothers manifested itself during the turbulent relationship between King Saud and Faysal, then between Faysal and the Free Princes, led by Talal in the early 1960s.

The principle of agnatic seniority introduced by Ibn Saud was a royal order to be respected by his sons. Nevertheless, it was contentious as it assumes *a priori* that the founder's sons are theoretically equal and respect the seniority that comes with age. While young princes are expected to respect older ones, it was common for the young to challenge their elders (Faysal challenged Saud, and Talal challenged Faysal). Also, the principle rules out succession within a king's line of descent, which Ibn Saud himself had implemented in 1932 and his son Saud aspired to do in 1953. Furthermore, the ambiguous agnatic seniority magnified opportunities for the sons of the founder to compete and enter a potentially divisive power struggle.

Given that the mothers of Ibn Saud's sons were unequal, inequality between his sons was unavoidable, as they inherited their mothers' status. Ibn Saud included among his wives women from religious families (Al Shaykh, maternal kin of King Faysal), tribal Bedouin chiefs (Bani Khalid, maternal kin of King Khalid, and the Shammar, maternal kin of King 'Abdullah), sedentary families (Sudayris, maternal kin of Fahd, Salman, Nayif, Sultan, 'Abd al-Rahman, Turki, and Ahmad), Levantine concubines (Armenian and Alawite slave mothers of Princes Talal and Mansur, the so-called Free Princes of the 1960s) and Yemeni concubines (the mother of Prince Muqrin). Added to this is the vast age gap between the older sons and those whom Ibn Saud fathered later in his life.

A previous generation of anthropologists saw in tribal segmentary systems equality and solidarity across a large group of male agnates, but this was a misconception sustained by nostalgia for an imagined bygone era of tribal equality rather than a historically accurate conclusion.[19] In Ibn Saud's case, serial marriages, polygamy, and concubinage contributed to creating a vast clan where inequality rather than the principle of *primus inter pares* reigned. The multiple-marriage strategies led to subclans/segments united by maternal links within the Al Saud clan. Hence observers of royal politics talked about the Sudayris as a sub-clan consisting of seven sons born to Husa al-Sudayri. The so-called Sudayri Seven were constructed as enjoying a special kind of 'womb solidarity' against all the other sons, who were in turn further divided by their matrilineal descent.[20] However, their assumed solidarity was shaken by King Salman in 2015 when he sidelined Princes Ahmad, Turki, and 'Abd al-Rahman, all members of this sub-clan, and appointed Muhammad ibn Nayif as crown prince. This may have possibly happened because of the age of the remaining Sudayris and the urgent need to shift the succession to the second generation. King Salman favoured both Muhammad ibn Nayif and his own young son Muhammad over his full brothers and also his own other sons, some of whom had more experience and acumen than the young Muhammad.[21] He then swiftly promoted his son to crown prince after sacking Muhammad ibn Nayif in June 2017.

The principle of seniority associated with the Saudi succession is an ambiguous requirement. It is not about age or the credentials that supposedly come with seniority. Throughout the twentieth century, royalty understood seniority to mean the fittest and ablest (*al-aslah*), but this was not necessarily the case, as senior princes had been excluded despite demonstrating leadership initiatives. Moreover, both Kings Saud and Khalid may not have fulfilled these criteria. The appointment or exclusion of princes must have been related to internal rivalry, animosity, dissidence, and other factors that divided the sons of Ibn Saud, most of whom were half-brothers. Since 1932 the king has been able to skip a brother regardless of seniority and appoint a crown prince of his own choice. He can also dismiss a crown prince appointed by his predecessor. The ambiguity of seniority, coupled with the age of all Ibn Saud's sons, especially from the 1980s onward, made this horizontal succession pattern susceptible to speculation and rumours.

Primogeniture Again

While King Saud failed to appoint any of his sons to the post of crown prince, King Salman succeeded in 2017 simply because most of his remaining brothers were old or incapacitated. There were no longer groups within the Al Saud clan and Salman's contemporaries that could have challenged his swift decision to appoint his own son as crown prince. By 2017, Salman appeared likely to be the last ageing prince to ascend to the throne. After his death, there would not be a legitimate senior brother to succeed him. His initial appointment of Muhammad ibn Nayif as crown prince may have been a tactic to delay the shock of promoting his own son to the post, thus changing the Saudi succession from horizontal to vertical.

Towards Rationality: The Basic Law of Government

In 1992 King Fahd (r. 1982–2005) was considered to have injected some rationality into Saudi politics, starting with 'institutionalizing' the succession. The 1990 Gulf war and the crisis that followed the invitation of foreign troops to defend the kingdom prompted the king to act against dissenting Islamist voices who began to question the policies and even the right of the Al Saud to rule.[22] In 1992 the king introduced *al-Nitham al asasi lil-hukm*, the Basic Law of Government. The law was meant to formalize the succession and fix the right of the house of Saud to rule. Article 5 of the Basic Law states that:

> The system of government in Saudi Arabia shall be monarchical. The dynasty right shall be confined to the sons of the Founder, King Abdul Aziz bin Abdul Rahman Al Saud (Ibn Saud), and the sons of sons. The most eligible among them shall be invited, through the process of 'bay'a', to rule in accordance with the Book of God and the Prophet's Sunnah. The King names the Crown Prince and may relieve him of his duties by Royal Order.[23]

There is nothing in the Basic Law that specifies the criteria for the 'most eligible', an ambiguous requirement allowing multiple interpretations and speculations. But the introduction of a text called the Basic Law ushered in what was then dubbed a new era of 'systemization of Saudi politics' or 'ornamental constitutionalism'.[24]

The new Basic Law, mistakenly seen by outsiders as the constitution of Saudi Arabia, simply failed to systematize the succession. It also failed to institutionalize a transparent unambiguous pattern that would end speculation about who the next king would be, especially when the Al Saud ran out of brothers to occupy the throne. It proved the limits of textuality and reaffirmed the king as the supreme commander who can appoint and dismiss princes, and exclude his own full and half-brothers from important positions.

The introduction of this law must be seen in the context of a turbulent moment in the short history of the kingdom. Although Fahd secured the support of his full brothers, Nayif and Sultan, both of whom occupied very senior positions, he was suspicious of half-brother Crown Prince 'Abdullah, who lived long enough to become both de facto and de jure king after Fahd suffered a debilitating stroke in 1995.

In June 2017 King Salman modified article B of the Basic Law to ensure that vertical succession from father to son is now the rule for succession, rather than the vague stipulation that it should be in the family as a whole. As his young son Muhammad became crown prince, the text pertaining to succession became clearer, stating that succession vests in the sons and the sons of the sons of the king. This was interpreted as a way of ensuring that the children of his beloved son, the crown prince, inherit the throne. The exclusion of the descendants of other sons of Ibn Saud as potential candidates is now confirmed.

The Committee of Allegiance

In 2005 Crown Prince 'Abdullah became king. Other senior princes respected the line of succession that had been in place during King Fahd's life, and swore allegiance to 'Abdullah. However, it was clear that 'Abdullah had to coexist with the most powerful princes that a Saudi king had had to deal with, namely Crown Prince Sultan, Interior Minister Nayif, and Salman, who was the governor of Riyadh. The internal politics of the kingdom at the time appeared to be dominated by powerful concentric circles akin to multiple fiefdoms within the state.[25] 'Abdullah felt helpless, and introduced a new initiative. He did not simply want to reassert the right of the Al Saud to rule, but to contain the potentially volatile struggles within the clan itself and the imminent power vacuum that was on the horizon with the ill health of both the crown prince and interior minister. He wanted to ensure that he did not face a rebellion by his powerful senior brothers.

In 2007 'Abdullah introduced the Committee of Allegiance, reportedly to regulate, rationalize, and routinize the succession to the highest office. The thirty-three-member Committee was meant to reassure the many princes in this secretive body that they still matter, and to enlist their support for 'Abdullah. However, in addition to reassurances, the king's main objective was to prevent a takeover of the state by the powerful princes Nayif, Sultan, and Salman. 'Abdullah wanted to widen the circle of princes who are theoretically consulted by including them in the Committee. His objective was to enlist allies within the Al Saud clan against the three most powerful princes. 'Abdullah relied on a wide circle of marginal princes to counter the rising influence of the three princes and their extended clans. He perhaps naively thought that the future king should be voted into office, thus entertaining the idea of an elected king.

It was perhaps fortunate for 'Abdullah that both Sultan and Nayif fell seriously ill and eventually died during his lifetime, in 2011 and 2012 respectively. This was unprecedented, as no previous king had had to deal with a vacuum at the top two levels of government. However, the senior princes' deaths complicated the succession and fuelled fresh speculation. 'Abdullah had hoped that the Committee of Allegiance would provide the solution, but it remained dysfunctional.

After the deaths of Sultan and Nayif 'Abdullah invented the new position of deputy crown prince and nominated Prince Muqrin, an outsider to the circle of more powerful princes, as the first deputy crown prince. He also ordered the princes to respect this arrangement after his death. As mentioned earlier, King Salman did not respect his deceased brother's wish. Muqrin held his position during 'Abdullah's life but it was certain that he would lose it immediately after his death, which he did. As mentioned earlier in this chapter, all these supposedly 'rational' decisions to routinize politics at the top level were annulled by King Salman. Choosing an heir to the throne is never about eligibility or seniority; it is mainly about mediating struggles within the royal family.

Regardless of the drive towards a Weberian rational authority that followed the establishment of the Committee of Allegiance and the propaganda associated with it, succession remains the prerogative of the king, who nominates his successor(s) with or without consultation. He is not obliged to respect seniority, regardless of how this is interpreted.

Both the Basic Law and the Committee of Allegiance failed to end speculation and create the conditions for rationalization and routinization of the royal succession. Hence, Salman's appointment of a grandson of Ibn Saud (Muhammad ibn Nayif) rather than a son of Ibn Saud to be crown prince, although it had been predicted by some, was largely unexpected, and fuelled unprecedented rumours and speculations. Moreover, Salman's promotion of his own son to crown prince was also predicted but was seen as a bold move in June 2017, only two years after this young prince became the rising star in Saudi Arabia. Princes openly expressed dissatisfaction and criticism, as will be discussed later. Salman's reshuffle proved the limits of Weberian rationality in the traditional context of the Saudi state. He simply ignored the Committee of Allegiance, although the Saudi press reported that thirty-one out of thirty-four members of the Allegiance Committee voted for young Prince Muhammad ibn Salman as crown prince and offered their allegiance, including the deposed Muhammad ibn Nayif. The king exercised his personal prerogative without any concern for the views and opinions of other senior princes, among whom are his full brother Prince Ahmad and his own sons, most of them older and more experienced than the prince he favoured. In the Saudi absolute monarchy it is almost impossible to invoke rationality and inject predictability. Not being able to anticipate the actions and decisions of the monarch perhaps enhances his mystique and magic.

Royal Rumours

Political rumours about the Saudi succession—which often coincide with ambiguity such as the ill health of kings and senior princes, the imminent death of the king, or abrupt royal reshuffles, such as those of King Salman—have recently been abundant. Rumours are ways of communicating special messages, creating meaning, and making sense of situations of ambiguity and secrecy. Unlike gossip, rumours circulate 'on a national or international scale and often relate to collective hopes and fears that reach beyond the moral behaviour of individuals'.[26] When rumours circulate to convey political messages in the context of heavy censorship, they become dangerous and threatening to the political order, and Saudi law criminalizes those who spread them when they are related to power struggles within the ruling house or the ill health of senior princes. However, studying these rumours is a window of opportunity to observe both Saudi subalterns and the elite. According to Scott, rumours are 'hidden transcripts that allow subordinate people to express views that differed markedly from those of their superiors'.[27] However, Scott does not seem to contemplate how marginalized elites such as some in the Saudi royal family may contribute to spreading rumours to overcome their marginality and undermine the dominance of other princes.

The official narrative about the smooth royal succession generates rumours about disgruntled and sidelined princes, either removed from office 'according to their own wish', as often announced in official media, preferring the comfort and luxury of self-exile abroad, or silently sitting in their palaces waiting for the next royal reshuffle to bring them back into the spotlight. Given the large number of princes, estimated to be around seven or eight thousand, there is no shortage of minor royalty who will never be asked to perform any public role. Government bureaucracy cannot absorb such a large number, not all of whom are fit to occupy even minor government positions or wish to work. Rumours function to make sense of the vast royal family and mediate anxiety and marginalization. Above all, both ordinary Saudis and sidelined royalty articulate their isolation by spreading rumours.

Since Salman became king rumours about palace coups have been abundant; but, like all rumours, they either vanish without any evidence or persist against all evidence to the contrary. However, rumour should not be dismissed in a country where people cannot express themselves freely. Rumours become an important mechanism for resistance. With the advent of social media, anonymous commentators spread rumours about internal royal intrigues online, and there is no clear indication as to who can be behind them. However, they can be read as transcripts that express distress and alarm, but also hope, aspiration, and wishful thinking.[28]

One rumour focused on the rivalry between Muhammad ibn Nayif and his deputy, Muhammad ibn Salman. The rumour stated that Muhammad ibn Salman was about to oust Muhammad ibn Nayif in a bid to ensure that he inherits the throne immediately after his father's death. This rumour, which became reality when Salman appointed his son as crown prince, sacking Muhammad ibn Nayif, drew on the sudden rise of Muhammad ibn Salman, who had been consolidating more power and achieving global visibility, through a series of media interviews in respectable international sources and regular visits to the USA and Europe. The rumour capitalized on some facts and amplified them, thus adding a political dimension to the power struggle among senior royalty.

A second rumour is woven around the disgruntled brothers of King Salman, amongst them Princes Ahmad and Talal. Their complete marginalization is often interpreted as a sign that they are plotting a sinister comeback, defying the king's wish to secure the throne in the hands of his son. Talal was critical of Nayif when he became crown prince in 2005 and declared that he was not obliged to offer the oath of allegiance to him should he become king. Talal's age and current ill health removed him from the spotlight, but the rumour persists.

A third rumour revolves around the second-generation princes. This includes above all the half-brothers of Muhammad ibn Salman, Mit'ib, the son of King 'Abdullah, and 'Abd al-'Aziz, the son of King Fahd, in addition to lesser-known junior and marginalized princes, some of them the sons of King Saud. With the advent of social media, Saudis either applaud the new succession measures or undermine the decision by circulating rumours about angry and marginalized second-generation princes. The princes tend to use their real names when they applaud the king, but those who circulate rumours about palace intrigues remain anonymous.

Rumours provide an important window of opportunity to observe the Saudi royal succession and Saudis' reaction to their status as marginalized citizens. By June 2017, one rumour about the king preparing his son for kingship had turned out to be true, while the other rumours are still circulating. A fourth rumour may emerge soon, as Muhammad ibn Nayif is apparently departing from the scene, but is widely anticipated to be planning a comeback.

An Urgent Warning to the Al Saud

Added to these rumours was the circulation of anonymous online letters between 2015 and 2017. One such letter, entitled *Nathir ajil li kul Al Saoud* (Warning to all the Al Saud), suddenly appeared online in September 2015. The warning letter invoked the wisdom of several previous kings, but denounced King 'Abdullah and Prince Sultan, and King Salman. The anonymous author reminded the Al Saud of two important traditions that are attributed to the founder of the kingdom. The letter invoked the succession principle that stipulates seniority and the best (*al-aslah*) for the highest office. It reminded readers of the requirement to consult the rest of the family members and remain faithful to the Islamic character of the state. Ibn Saud was mentioned to remind his sons that he had advised them not to mix trade and politics. The letter claimed that welfare services had deteriorated. Excessive spending, corruption, and the exclusion of senior princes had become common, to the detriment of stability and consensus. Finally, there was a call to the remaining thirteen sons of Ibn Saud to hold a general meeting to discuss the future and propose policies. Princes Talal, Ahmad, and Turki, all sidelined by Salman, were identified as capable senior princes. They should depose 'the incapacitated king, the arrogant Muhammad ibn Nayif, and the thief and destroyer of the country Muhammad ibn Salman'.[29] The letter called not only for the abolition of the post of deputy crown prince, but for a new king to be chosen.

The letter was meant to highlight serious rifts within the royal house and to resist the official narrative about the smooth succession. A second letter entitled *Idhahat* (clarifications) followed, with five clarifications. The anonymous authors stated that,

1. They are the grandsons of Ibn Saud who think that King Saud, who was deposed, had committed only a fraction of the mistakes that are currently being made by King Salman.
2. King Salman is mentally incapable of running the affairs of the state because of his health, and hence he has left his son to mismanage the affairs of the country.
3. They are worried about the continuous depletion of state resources and sovereign reserves, and the appropriation of state funds by Muhammad ibn Salman.
4. They demand the appointment of an honest person to be the head of the royal court; this should be the equivalent of the head of administration in the White House. The appointment should help prevent the rise of people such as 'Abd al-'Aziz ibn Fahd, the son of King Fahd, and Khalid al-Tuwaijri, as heads of the royal court; both used their position to promote themselves.
5. They called for a wise foreign policy that reverses the loss of four Arab capitals to Iran.[30]

The two letters called for a palace coup, and supported the rumour that there is a royal rift. By the end of September 2015 the two letters had been read by 2 million people. While it is difficult to assess the true identity of the author(s),[31] I was told in a private conversation that the three princes Sultan ibn Turki, Saud ibn Sayf al-Nasr ibn Saud, and Turki ibn Bandar, all of whom had recently vanished, had composed the letters.[32] Saud ibn Sayf al-Nasr endorsed the letters on Twitter. His last statement was recorded on 10 September 2015.[33] Their disappearance seriously intimidated other princes, who are unable to challenge King Salman and his son.[34] The letters were simply used to prove rumours about palace intrigues.

The Mujtahid Phenomenon

Secret royal circles and the quest for more information about royal intrigues gave rise to a novel and unique Saudi Twitter phenomenon: an anonymous tweeter known as Mujtahid ibn Harith ibn Hamam, dubbed a 'Saudi Julian Assange', a mysterious 'whistle-blower', and 'rebel tweeter'.[35] He has captured the imagination of international and regional media since he started his Twitter account in 2011. Mujtahid is also a reflection of the global phenomenon that came to haunt established democracies in the last decade when Edward Snowden, Julian Assange, and others employed in businesses turned into whistle-blowers. The phenomenon is not a reflection of authoritarian rule per se, but is prevalent as a result of citizens' demand for greater transparency in an age when even well-established democracies have proved susceptible to secret intrigues. However, Mujtahid does not often offer documents to support his whistle-blowing; rather, he claims to be informed by anonymous sources close to the king and senior princes. Many observers suspect that he is a member of the royal family, but this is yet to be confirmed. It is astonishing that he suddenly became so important, followed on Twitter by many people not only in Saudi Arabia but outside it even without providing hard evidence in support of his commentaries and rumours.

With over 1.5 million followers and 10 million tweets at the time of writing this chapter, Mujtahid has forced even domestic media to comment on his regular stories, if only to dismiss them as fabrications and lies. His regular tweets prompted the mufti 'Abd al-'Aziz Al Shaykh to issue several opinions condemning those who 'undermine the unity of the country, create rifts between society and the rulers and cause dissent on Twitter'.[36] His rumours are closely monitored for their subversive nature. International media such as the *Financial Times*, BBC, CNN, Arabian Business, and many others were also compelled to comment on the Mujtahid phenomenon and conduct interviews with him by email. The *Financial Times* Middle East editor, Roula Khalaf, wrote: 'Although there is no way to separate truth from fiction in his claims, many observers are convinced that he is an estranged member of the royal family and are engaged in a guessing game over his possible identity.'[37]

Mujtahid became particularly famous when he volunteered opinions and predictions on succession and royal reshuffles after Salman became king. While it is important but difficult to ascertain Mujtahid's identity, his success and popularity need to be situated at the intersection of Saudi domestic politics and global interest in the country.

Mujtahid explains that his popularity is attributed, first, to the obsession of Saudi society with royal secrets that he fully exposed and, second, to the accuracy of his rumours, which subsequent events have confirmed. His credibility rests, in his opinion, on disseminating information in respectable language, guided by strict moral and religious codes. In addition to his linguistic skills, he avoids sensational and unwarranted stories that delve into the private lives of princes. In this respect, Mujtahid distinguishes himself from previous opposition figures whose discourse often degenerated into personal attacks on royalty.[38]

Mujtahid explains his objectives in circulating information about royal succession intrigues. His main purpose is to help other more vocal opposition figures to use the information with a view to undermining the legitimacy of the regime. He insists that he wants to contribute to the big project of political change. His contribution consists of exposing lies and intrigues in order to undermine the mystique of monarchy. In the context of controlled media and propaganda, the regime appears intact, powerful, and frightening. Delving into behind-the-scenes information and exposing cracks within the royal household contribute to this project, according to Mujtahid. The regime has 'a false and fabricated *hayba* [mystique]', that he tries to expose.

The issue of the succession occupied Mujtahid for several months after Salman became king in 2015. According to Mujtahid, Muhammad ibn Salman was determined to become king before Muhammad ibn Nayif. This requires consolidating his powers before his father dies. Muhammad ibn Salman wants to be in charge of foreign affairs, religion, the economy, and the media, and has already accomplished these objectives, according to Mujtahid. In the first three months of 2016 Muhammad ibn Salman's interviews with the *Economist*, Bloomberg, and al-Arabiyya television in advance of announcing Vision 2030, a blueprint for economic reform, had already confirmed him as the economic decision maker. He also curbed the powers of the Committee for the Promotion of Virtue and Prohibition of Vice, thus expanding his control over religion. Moreover, he moved swiftly to dominate Saudi foreign policy regarding the war in Yemen, the Syrian file, and above all rivalry with Iran, in which oil and politics are now closely and increasingly interlinked. More recently and since 2017, he became the main figure to lead Saudi Arabia's embargo on Qatar. He toured the USA and Europe twice within a year of becoming deputy crown prince. These successive initiatives simply confirmed Mujtahid's early rumours about Muhammad ibn Salman's ambitions.

According to Mujtahid, the expansion of the young prince's powers would eventually leave Muhamad ibn Nayif with no powers, thus further isolating the crown prince and paving the way for his dismissal. Muhammad ibn Salman's speedy encroachment on the various functions of the state reflects his fear that his plan may not be fully accomplished before his father dies. The king is currently providing cover for his son's political ambitions. Mujtahid predicts that he plans to control further military and policing agencies, for example the Special Forces, the Emergency Units, Border Control Forces, and the Intelligence Directorate, in addition to his current job as minister of defence.

Mujtahid was of the opinion that the king was unlikely to dismiss Muhammad ibn Nayif, saying that senior royals would seriously object to this unwise move. It had taken almost two years to sack the minister of interior. Mujtahid insisted that several military units in the kingdom would refuse to be engaged in a struggle in support of one prince against another should the latent rivalry between the two princes become public. He felt that the dismissal of Muhammad ibn Nayif would be detrimental to the credibility of the royal family. But the current brewing rivalry seems to have been contained so far with the silent departure of Muhammad ibn Nayif.

The popularity of Mujtahid among domestic and global audiences stems from his ability to spread rumours to anticipate certain royal reshuffles and expose corruption at all government levels. However, although Mujtahid does not openly call for the implementation of a specific political system, he is critical of Saudi liberals and Islamists, especially those loyal to the government. He is also critical of official 'ulama', for example those who unquestioningly accept and defend all government decisions. In his view, true Islam 'requires one to reject injustice, repression, and corruption. I circulate information that exposes those hypocrites among state intellectuals, 'ulama', and also

Islamists.'[39] He sees his role as a whistle-blower who 'exposes secret scandals' to weaken the regime's mystique. He believes that reform and justice can only be achieved after real regime change.

In conversation with Mujtahid, he explains why Saudis do not rebel given that they are aware of all the corruption and mismanagement. According to him,

> the forces that can cause change are still loyal to the regime, for example the religious elite, tribal groups, businessmen, and notables. Moreover, repression is conducted by security forces who are well paid and remain loyal to the regime. Also, Saudis are not the type who will practise peaceful protest like the one that swept the rest of the Arab world. They believe in armed struggle but the way this had been practised by for example jihadis is used by the government to intimidate people.[40]

Furthermore, Mujtahid's focus on people's everyday problems relating to corruption in local authorities, confiscation of land by princes, and the incompetence of municipalities during flooding made him close to people's issues without being overtly ideological. His short Twitter statements oscillate between predictions, facts, and rumour, thus pointing out a continuum between fact and fiction in the context of Saudi politics.

Those Who Know and Those Who Don't

A previous generation of dissidents with leftist and nationalist inclinations, such as Nasir al-Said, had extensively highlighted the moral and personal bankruptcy of royalty in the 1960s.[41] Although poorly documented, and harshly critical of the house of Saud, al-Said's famous book, *Tarikh Al Saud* (History of the Al Saud),[42] represented an emerging genre of sensational subjective and personalized Saudi opposition texts. It transformed oral opposition embedded in everyday gossip, narratives, and, more importantly, damning oral poetry into text. Unlike previous oral historical opposition genres, al-Said's text is accompanied by pictures of drunk and gambling kings and princes. Saudi Arabia banned the book. Al-Said was kidnapped in Beirut in 1979 by Palestinian armed factions allegedly working for the Saudi regime at the time.[43] Since then, he has disappeared without a trace. His book is available across many Arab capitals and in Europe.

Since the late 1970s Islamists, like al-Said, have opposed royalty on the basis of their immorality and personal corruption. Character assassination of royalty continued to be endorsed by many Islamists, the heirs of dissidence in the kingdom after the fleeting moment of leftist and nationalist politics in the 1960s. In 1979 Juhayman al-'Utaybi, who led the Mecca Mosque siege, was equally determined to expose the moral corruption of royalty, which in his view had also corrupted society.[44] More recently, a Salafi critic of the decision to partially lift the restriction on mixing between men and women, Shaykh Nasir al-Omar, felt free to criticize King 'Abdullah's son-in-law, who was in charge of the Ministry of Education at the time and was believed to be behind violating the segregation tradition. In a sermon he highlighted the fact that while the prince may accept exposing his own honour (his female relatives) to non-*muhram* men (men with whom women should not mix), Saudi society rejects this unlawful policy. The criticism focused on the prince's personal morality and integrity. In the context of Saudi society, accusing someone of not worrying too much about the honour of his own women is a serious insult.

This personalized opposition is a reflection of the gap between the controlled and glorified official reporting on the princes' public personae and the reality of their private lives. Their publicly celebrated religious charitable activities tend to be highlighted in official media, while some citizens seem to be occupied with finding opportunities to debunk the official narrative. Hence, the contradiction between the staged public piety and the private lives of most princes undermines the grand meta-narrative. Rumours about extravagant spending on 'immoral pursuits' tend to create social solidarity among those who spread them. They also assert their own morality against the background of corrupt princes.

Dissidents, princes, and citizens often delve into the binary opposites of the public lives of princes: their kindness, generosity, meanness, debauchery, and corruption. Those who oppose the royal family often descend into outright character assassination and personal onslaughts on kings and princes, their arrogance, corruption, and private wealth. They substantiate their position by citing rumours that support their assessment. Whether Islamist, liberal, nationalist, or leftist, the *ad hominem* criticism reflects the personalized character of both

Saudi royal politics and opposition. From princely intrigues to lavish spending, corruption, and criminality, rumours are fuelled by new sources of information, emanating from individual citizens or sidelined princes who spread statements and images of other princes that official media prefers to remain buried.

While royalty is always engaged in secret speculation and anticipation of the king's wishes, ordinary Saudis are equally active in contributing to the speculations and rumours. However, those loyalists who would like to see an end to rumours often reiterate the saying that 'those who don't know talk and those who know prefer to remain silent', thus dismissing any truth in rumours about royal succession, especially at the top level. The saying anchors discussion of royal succession in *ghaybiyyat*, those issues related to the unknown or afterlife. Whether royalty or commoners, not to mention outsiders with limited access to Saudi Arabia, those who indulge in such speculation are better understood as fortune tellers/soothsayers, according to a defensive Saudi. The prohibition on having a meaningful and open discussion on the succession contributes to its mystique. New anti-terrorism laws criminalize a whole range of acts, including tarnishing *al-that al-malakiyya* (the royal persona). So, for example, the rumour about King Salman having Alzheimer's disease will definitely lead to imprisonment for anyone found to be spreading it. In an attempt to identify the source of this rumour, a Saudi claims that the king's marginalized sons, who resent the rise to power of their half-brother Muhammad, are behind it.

Any rumour about royal power struggles is subversive. As such it becomes a criminal act. In 2013 Muhammad al-'Abd al-Karim, an Islamist intellectual who posted a short article on Facebook discussing possible royal struggles, was arrested in his office at the university and interrogated. Since then he has stopped making any meaningful statements about royalty.[45] He had violated the taboo of discussing royal power struggles and intrigues, with serious implications for the future of the kingdom. Rumours about the health of senior princes is also taboo, with one Reuters journalist asked to leave the country within forty-eight hours of reporting that Prince Sultan had cancer.[46] Even when accurate and true, such news is considered rumour in Saudi Arabia until officially announced.

The saying 'those who don't know talk and those who know prefer to remain silent' is also meant to render speculation about the future of royal succession not only taboo but also an unrealistic and futile exercise, a venture into the realm of rumours. The prohibition on speculation and the harsh punishment for transgressors depoliticizes citizens, whose role is simply to applaud any swift royal decree or reshuffle that removes a prince from power and replaces him with another. Such sudden changes are always described in official media as 'putting the right person in the right place'. Consequently, the appointments of both Muhammad ibn Nayif and Muhammad ibn Salman were dubbed overdue decisions to ensure a great transition to the young second-generation princes, thus securing the future stability of the monarchy in a turbulent Arab world in which three presidents were unexpectedly toppled with unprecedented speed. One Saudi commentator applauded the new appointments as a necessary step to 'slim royalty' and move succession towards primogeniture.[47] Other disgruntled princes consider it a step towards their own isolation.

While the congratulatory discourse of official media is taken for granted in the Saudi domestic public sphere, especially in state-owned print and visual media, in the privacy of homes and among trusted friends Saudis feel free to discuss and circulate rumours. Such discussion always starts with *yaqulun* (an anonymous saying). The sayings are rumours about royal affairs, dissecting the intrigues of both their private lives and public roles. Like others, Saudis are fascinated by the scandals, intrigues, and conspicuous consumption of their royalty. However, there is something peculiar about this fascination, as rumours about royal intrigues are integral to Saudi dissent and opposition to the regime.

Discussing politics with a spectrum of Saudi activists of all ages and persuasions is bound to descend at some point into rumours about the future of this or that prince and whether he is likely to remain in his position in the near future. The personalized attacks and rumours about the immorality of royals constitute a great concern for opposition politics. Today, information and images circulate on social media and reach far beyond the limited confines of *shila*, a gossip and entertainment network of trusted kin and friends. Mimicking the voices of princes, composing video clips to ridicule the king's speeches, and circulating critical poetry to tarnish the princes' reputations and humiliate them have all become an established dissident strategy. These scattered outpourings of resistance find a virtual niche. Saudi officials endorse comedy undermining terrorism, radicalization, and social and religious tradition on Saudi-owned television, but royalty remains above humour, satire, and caricature. Citizens have moved their resistance from the private realm of orality to the public sphere of online textuality, imagery, unlicensed comedy, and rumour. Today there are no fixed boundaries between orality and textuality; rather, a continuum dominates this age-old illusory division.

With the proliferation of online visual media, images of the king returning from trips abroad, the royal court in session, funerals of senior princes, and news about long absences from the country for medical reasons or holidays all become subject to intense rumours. Rumours in the social context remain oral, but, with the interactive internet venues, such discussions enter the public sphere with force. Saudis speculate about the presence or absence of princes at televised royal councils (*majlis*). An absent senior prince is immediately thought to be boycotting a royal public event, a sign of dissatisfaction or ill health.

News about princes spending a long time abroad in opulent holiday palaces (for example, Prince 'Abd al-'Aziz ibn Fahd in New York), or permanently residing in luxury hotel suites abroad (for example Turki ibn 'Abd al-'Aziz, who moved to a Cairo hotel for several years after he was removed from office following a scandal involving his extravagant al-Fasi wife in California), forms the basis of many rumours. Rumours claim that these are signs of deteriorating health or 'self-exile', believed to reflect rifts and conflict with more established senior princes.

In contrast, to counter rumours that Muhammad ibn Nayif and Muhammad ibn Salman were on a collision path, royalists circulated images of young Deputy Crown Prince Muhammad passionately kissing the hand of his senior cousin, Crown Prince Muhammad ibn Nayif. Audiences were expected to draw the conclusion that the seniority principle was being respected and that the alleged rift between the two most influential princes was simply rumour. When Muhammad ibn Nayif was sacked in June 2017, an official video circulated on the internet showing Muhammad ibn Salman kissing Muhammad in Nayif's hand.

Those Saudis loyal to princes, or pretending to be loyal, are likely to defend every royal succession decision. But they too may also engage in rumours about the future of the succession, without feeling that they have undermined or compromised their position as loyal subjects. While they may applaud a new prince in a senior position, they might privately express a preference for another one, believed to be more suitable for the job. While most Saudis do not actually know what kind of relations—warm, affectionate, or hostile—exist between the king and the princes or between princes, they resort to rumours on the basis of very limited evidence. Princes are rumoured to communicate through messengers who go between palaces to relay messages or orders. There are always a few 'commoner' confidants in the inner circle of each senior prince, who may spread such rumours. In this universe of rumours, women play an important role, especially the wives and ex-wives of princes and their courtiers. These marginalized circles where royal intrigues are exposed remain so far untapped as a source of rumour.[48]

Conclusion

According to common wisdom, the remaining authoritarian monarchs are calculating rational strategists who carefully introduce policies that ensure their survival. From increasing subsidies and welfare to stepping up repression, they are often described as constantly engaged in planning how to remain unchallenged. But the Saudi case demonstrates the limits of monarchical rationality. Foreign support, regional upheavals, and economic benefits are important but not sufficient conditions underlying the survival of monarchy. The impulse to inject rationality into the royal succession in order to 'routinize' it and minimize internal power struggles has been limited. Two initiatives, the Basic Law and the Committee of Allegiance, were already in place. But King Salman shook up these measures, and demonstrated that the king is the only arbiter.

Saudis engage in rumours about succession, constantly interpret fragmented information, and follow anonymous sources online. The mystical monarch pushes citizens to turn to rumours to anticipate the future and decode the quasi-magical awe of royalty. All this adds to the mystique and power of the Saudi monarch and enhances conspicuous submission.

Multiple rumours about succession are a great distraction from real long-term structural problems such as social upheaval, unemployment, housing shortages, budget deficits, corruption, detentions, and gender discrimination. Rumours have become central to the mystique of the Saudi monarchy, in which people transcend their powerlessness, marginalization, and, above all, fragmentation by region, class, tribe, race, and sect. Engaging in rumours is not a descent into *ghaybiyyat* (the unknown), irrational impulses, or wishful thinking, but an assertion of agency against forces that continue to marginalize citizens. Those who start and spread rumours insert themselves into the public narrative about stability and politics in a monarchy that allows its citizens almost no modern participation in decision making. The recent surge in Saudi cyber-resistance through the circulation of letters and rumours are modern forms of challenging official narratives and inserting one's voice into a mystical political realm.

The survival of the monarchy may be partially related to the 'anaesthesia of un-reason', irrational impulses that are often ignored in the analysis of the durability of monarchy. The previous analysis demonstrates that monarchs may rely on a certain degree of quasi-magic to maintain their mystique and, eventually, survival. Citizens find refuge in rumours about royal intrigues, where they can participate in the politics of their country.

While rumours continue to spread, no one in Saudi Arabia and abroad anticipated the bold move when Muhammad ibn Salman detained eleven senior princes and an unknown number of ministers and wealthy businessmen on 4 November 2017. They were arrested under an anti-corruption crackdown, with more rumours spreading that Muhammad asked them to hand over a substantial amount of money in return for their release from the Ritz Carlton hotel where they are held. At the time of writing this chapter, the purge is still going on and there are no clear signs that a resolution is close to being reached.

3

CHALLENGES TO THE SAUDI DISTRIBUTIONAL STATE IN THE AGE OF AUSTERITY

Steffen Hertog

With oil prices dropping to below half their 2014 levels, Saudi Arabia faces an unprecedented challenge of economic adjustment. In 2015 the government's reported salary and allowance spending alone exceeded its total oil income. Its current distributional obligations in terms of state employment, provision of free public services, and energy subsidies are unsustainable. The Saudi wealth-distribution regime has contributed to the kingdom's political stability for more than half a century. It does now, however, pose unique challenges to the economic modernization of Saudi Arabia. These challenges, and the state's attempts to overcome them, are the main focus of this chapter.

The chapter will start with a brief exploration of the historical origins of the Saudi rent-distribution regime, which goes back to the era of Arab nationalism in the 1950s and 1960s and was, as I will argue, to an important extent a reaction to political challenges emerging from nationalist movements. It will outline how Saudi elites quickly built a distributive state that, while itself fragmented into different fiefdoms, rapidly expanded its intervention in society and created many layers of material dependency. The chapter will illustrate how distribution of state resources has been the key factor in shaping (and distorting) economy and labour markets. After a quick overview of the government's post-2014 adjustment policies, I will analyse the unique economic and institutional constraints that the distributive state has created for economic diversification and fiscal sustainability—which in some cases seem to be underappreciated by decision makers. Just like the building of the distributive state, economic adjustment in Saudi Arabia will constitute a unique historical experiment. But it is not clear that the ruling elite will enjoy the same degree of autonomy and eventual success in the process, even if the first steps of adjustment have come faster and met less resistance than many observers expected.

The chapter's main conclusions are forward-looking, but will also discuss key aspects of change and continuity since the publication of *Princes, Brokers, and Bureaucrats*, my 2010 account of the Saudi political economy and its historical roots.[1] While it is clear that we are in a new era of policy making and that elite-level politics have changed drastically, I will argue that many of the structural factors characterizing and constraining the Saudi state have remained exactly the same.

Wealth Sharing in Saudi Arabia

Like most of its peers in the Gulf Cooperation Council (GCC), the state of Saudi Arabia is deeply authoritarian but—by the standards of a middle-income country—exceptionally generous towards its population. Two-thirds of all Saudi workers are employed by government, energy and fuel for households as well as inter-city transport remain subsidized, while healthcare and education are free. While the quality of education and health services is generally considered as not on a par with those in most advanced countries, the improvement in the provision of basic public goods in Saudi Arabia since the 1960s has been remarkable. Figures 3.1 and 3.2 show that Saudi Arabia has been much faster than its Middle East and North Africa (MENA) peers in increasing literacy levels and reducing child mortality—although the MENA region, perhaps surprisingly, is already among the fastest-improving regions in the developing world on these two indicators.

Figure 3.1: Literacy ratio of population (per cent)

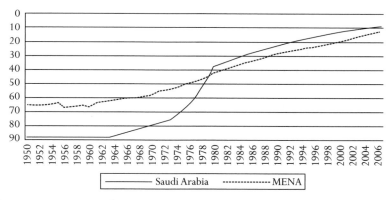

Source: Barro & Lee dataset.

It seems obvious that an oil-rich state would share some of its wealth with the population, but Saudi Arabia—and the Gulf monarchies more broadly—stand out even among oil-rich countries in their material generosity. Other oil-rich states in the developing world do no better on the provision of basic welfare than their neighbours, and some, notably in sub-Saharan Africa, do markedly worse.[2]

Figure 3.2: Infant mortality (per 1,000 births)

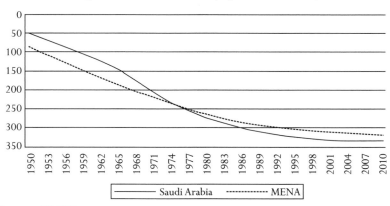

Source: UNDP.

Historical Background

The reasons for the Saudi state's broad-based welfare regime are historical and, as I will argue, have to do with largely forgotten ideological challenges that the Al Saud family faced in the 1950s and 1960s—challenges that I underestimated in *Princes, Brokers, and Bureaucrats*, which focused on elite competition as the primary cause of state expansion. The following section will outline how this elite competition in fact interacted with what key princes perceived as substantial subversive threats, leading them to prioritize mass welfare policies in the process of Saudi state building. I draw on both secondary historical literature and primary sources from diplomatic archives; the latter in particular illustrate key motivations of the ruling elite in building a distributive state.

The modern Saudi state had little modern administration before the onset of oil exports in 1947.[3] The Al Saud ruling elite faced an institutional *tabula rasa* when they started to build the country's modern bureaucracy. They were also unconstrained by constitutional processes or modern interest-group politics in their decision making. Elite whims and conflicts hence played a particularly large role in shaping the institutional landscape.[4]

Early Ideological Challenges and Patronage

At the same time, however, at important junctures of state building in the 1950s and 1960s, Saudi rulers felt threatened by the nationalist and leftist ideologies coursing through the Arab world. These never gave birth to a mass movement in the kingdom.[5] Yet repeat threats of assassinations and military coups, combined with a febrile regional environment in which several Arab monarchies had already fallen, pushed key Al Saud players to start sharing wealth with the population—a process that also allowed them to build their own institutional fiefdoms.

After the takeover of the republican Free Officers in Egypt in 1952 and the death of Saudi founder King 'Abd al-'Aziz in 1953, Arab nationalism found adherents among Saudi army officers, the nation's small intelligentsia, and its student population. The spread of socialist-tinged nationalist ideology across the Arab world happened at a time when rapidly rising oil income made the creation of modern welfare state institutions possible at least in principle. In this context, a nationalist

'Front of National Reforms' formed in 1953; it called for a constitution and an elected parliament as well as the abolition of illiteracy, schools for girls, and the expansion of higher and technical education[6]—all demands that would have been unthinkable without the new oil income. Nasser's republican Egypt started an active campaign of subversion in Saudi Arabia in the mid-1950s. As a result, the largely illiterate bulk of the population was increasingly exposed to radio propaganda from Cairo.[7]

In 1955 there was an aborted military coup by nationalist officers,[8] and in July 1956 'Abd al-'Aziz's successor King Saud was met by mass anti-Western demonstrations on a visit to the oil-rich Eastern Province.[9] The same year, tens of thousands of Saudis cheered Nasser during a visit to Riyadh in the hitherto largest non-religious public display in the kingdom.[10] In May 1957 evidence emerged that the Egyptian military attaché in Jeddah had been working on a plot to assassinate Saud.[11]

Saud's personal profligacy was well known. He brought the kingdom to the brink of fiscal crisis in 1958, while Egyptian attacks and nationalist subversion were continuing. Fearing the end of the dynasty, the Al Saud family installed King Saud's brother Faysal as head of government.[12] Faysal was unable to publicly distance himself from Nasser, instead professing his nationalist and reformist convictions to placate republican tendencies.[13] In practice, Faysal stalled on political reforms, but increased the kingdom's education and communication budgets in 1958–9 while decreasing the king's privy purse.[14]

King Saud managed to wrest government power back from Faysal in 1960 and styled himself even more of a Nasserist, recruiting nationalist technocrats and a number of radical princes as ministers and making even more extensive promises of development, especially in education.[15] Saud's policies were seen as a direct reaction to nationalist threats. According to a 1962 UK diplomatic report, Saudis outside the royal circle reportedly liked Nasser's Voice of the Arabs radio attacks on Saud, as they heard that these made the king contemplate the economic development of the country more.[16]

In 1962 the country once again reached a crisis as the Egyptian military supported a nationalist revolution in neighbouring Yemen, a small number of Saudi troops defected, and Egyptian subversion in Saudi Arabia picked up. Faysal again took over from Saud with the support of a number of powerful half-brothers.[17] At the time both the *Financial Times* and *The Guardian* expected the Saudi monarchy to follow the fate of its peers in Egypt and Iraq and be overthrown.[18] Other Gulf rulers were similarly concerned about a Nasserist revolution in the kingdom.[19]

Faysal once more reacted to the subversive threats with material welfare. The 'ten-point programme' he announced in 1962 promised education, health, and social welfare improvements; the programme's political components included a constitution, a consultative assembly, local government, and the creation of an independent judiciary. While Faysal implemented the welfare promises,[20] and once again cut royal allowances,[21] he largely did not deliver political reforms.[22]

The political motivation behind the regime's generosity was obvious to contemporary observers. A 1963 British assessment was that 'Faisal knows that he must bring about reforms quickly if the regime is to survive'.[23] Faysal had personally told his fellow ruler Rashid of Dubai that revolution came from poverty and that development was needed to forestall it.[24]

As in the rest of the region, subversion did not disappear overnight. Revolutionary networks remained in the armed forces.[25] A coup attempt was reported in 1965,[26] followed by a more serious plot among nationalist army officers in 1969.[27] The 1969 crisis seems to have pushed Faysal, who had become king in 1964, to pursue further social reforms and initiate the kingdom's first five-year development plan in 1970.[28]

Gradually, material welfare seemed to de-fang the militant opposition: a member of the Saudi Communist Party complained of sagging revolutionary spirits after the 1960s as a broad-based consumer society emerged in the kingdom.[29] In the 1970s the Saudi regime proved particularly adept at co-opting dissidents, often into lucrative bureaucratic positions.[30] At the same time, the distributive state managed to gradually envelop all of Saudi society through provision of infrastructure, public services, and employment. The dependence of both Saudi households and businesses on state resources reached unprecedented levels.[31] As local business expanded rapidly, it did so almost exclusively on the back of state-provided privileges and demand, and largely based on low-cost expatriate labour that substituted for a local working class.[32]

Organized opposition virtually disappeared during the 1970s, and only returned in Islamist garb in the early 1990s when it again was undercut by a mixture of repression and co-optation.[33] The deep patronage of the Saudi state seems to have bought 'peace' for a very long time, both among the ruling elite and the population. Politics has not stopped, of course, but it tends to happen within the state. To the extent that there is ideological contestation, this is usually with Islamist forces, and often over social issues and the control of state resources in education and the judiciary rather than control of the political system per se.[34]

In contrast to what rentier state theory leads us to expect, oil wealth did not automatically create political quiescence in the kingdom. Instead, if anything, it initially augmented political challenges from society as the potential material rewards from political contestation suddenly increased drastically. The regime's reaction to these challenges—large-scale patronage—did then however produce the political quiescence and fragmentation that rentier theories predict. The fact that very similar patterns of contestation and co-optation unfolded in other GCC countries from the 1950s to the 1970s suggests that there is a shared causal pattern.[35]

State Fragmentation and Fiefdoms

Broad-based distribution was a key motivation driving the expansion of the Saudi state apparatus. Yet the sudden availability of huge fiscal resources and the absence of formal political constraints also left much space for elite agency in shaping individual institutions. As a result of the princely rivalries and bargains of the 1960s, a number of parallel fiefdoms emerged that continue to dominate the Saudi state today. The Al Saud-controlled Ministry of Defence, National Guard, and Ministry of Interior developed into full-fledged states-within-a-state, each with hundreds of thousands of employees (the Interior Ministry recently seems to have reached a million), their own health and education systems, residential cities, and large land banks. As oil income grew and senior princes competed for patronage and generosity, their institutions sprawled. At the same time, oil surpluses allowed Al Saud elites to build a number of smaller, insulated elite institutions headed by commoner technocrats and to co-opt traditional social forces such as the religious establishment into new educational and judicial bureaucracies.[36]

This fragmented process of state growth has made it hard to coordinate policy making, while the use of state employment as distributive tool has made it difficult to hold bureaucrats accountable on a day-to-day level. As the state has become weighed down by its various distributional obligations, its autonomy to create or change institutions or economic policies has declined, as shown by its paralysis during the more austere 1980s and 1990s.[37]

When oil prices picked up again in the 2000s, the kingdom in many ways went back to the 1970s: new institutions and fiefdoms were built, state employment growth accelerated, and subsidy and social-transfer regimes were expanded. At no point in history has the Saudi state penetrated people's lives as deeply as it did at the peak of the boom in the early 2010s—a factor that has probably contributed to the muted local reaction to the Arab uprisings in 2011. At the same time, the dependence of Saudi business on state protection and support arguably increased again during the recent boom, after it had gained a modicum of autonomy in the 1980s and 1990s.

Long-Term Consequences of Wealth Sharing

The Saudi brand of wealth sharing is not egalitarian: state salary scales are less equal than in most Arab republics; women are excluded from large parts of state employment, and even young men often have to wait for many years until a government job becomes available. Energy subsidies are regressive, as they disproportionately benefit larger and richer households. Saudi business remains dominated by a limited number of families with close government connections. Yet the breadth of wealth sharing is impressive and unlike anything seen in wealthy oil states outside the Middle East (with the one exception of Brunei, which has a population of only 400,000).

The extent of wealth distribution also means that its distortionary effects on the Saudi economy are particularly wide and deep. These effects make the Saudi system costly and unsustainable in the long run. They are increasingly well known yet difficult to tackle without a wholesale re-engineering of the Saudi political economy, key features of which have become deeply ensconced since at least the 1970s oil boom.

The IMF estimates Saudi Arabia to have the highest energy subsidies in the GCC, reaching almost 10 per cent of GDP in 2011.[38] This has led to significant distortions in the Saudi economy which, unlike most other countries in the world, has witnessed declining energy efficiency over the last decades (see figure 3.3). This falling efficiency has increasing economic opportunity costs, as growing domestic energy consumption has started to eat into the kingdom's energy export capacity. Very low energy prices have also spawned state-dependent industries and consumption habits that might not be economically sustainable when energy prices are brought closer to opportunity costs.

The Saudi patronage system gives even more problematic incentives in the local labour market, where two-thirds of the national labour force remains employed in government (see figure 3.4).

This open-handed provision of government jobs has created labour-market attitudes that in turn reinforce dependency on and expectation of state employment. Figure 3.5, based on a 2014 survey, shows that most Saudi job seekers rank the majority of jobs available in the local private sector as unattractive. Figure 3.6 shows that even Saudis currently employed in the private sector would largely prefer government employment.

Figure 3.3: Energy use (kg of oil equivalent) per $1,000 GDP (constant 2005 PPP)

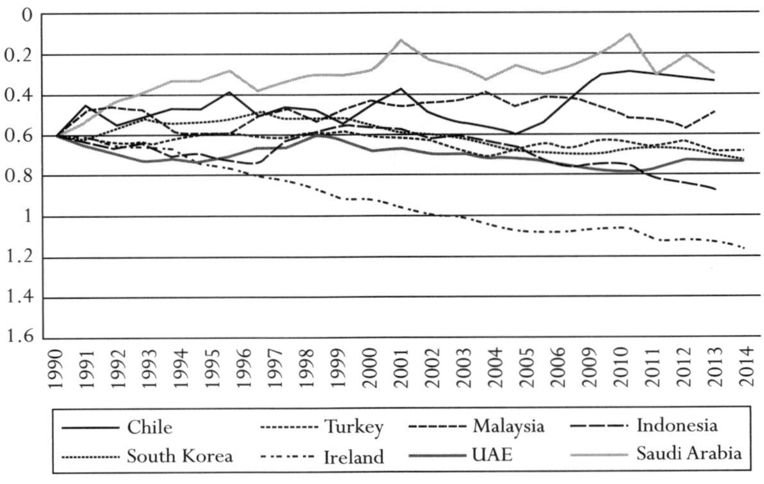

Source: World Bank.

Figure 3.4: Share of government employees in the economically active citizenry of select countries[39]

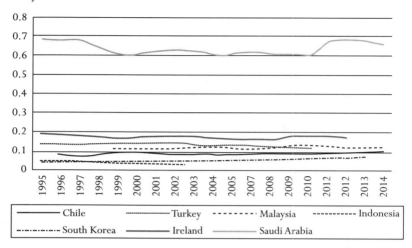

Source: World Bank, ILO, Saudi Labour Force Survey, and SAMA.

Figure 3.5: Saudi job seekers' ranking of occupations by attractiveness

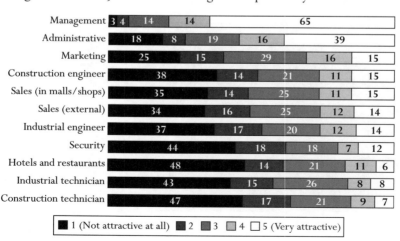

Source: 2014 Accenture/Yougov Saudization survey.

Figure 3.6: Would you accept a government job with similar salary, higher job security, and working hours from 7.30 to 2.30 over your current job?

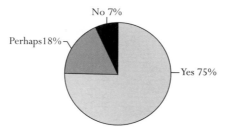

Source: 2014 Accenture/Yougov Saudization survey.

Saudi expectations have been further raised by a higher education system that by now enrols almost three-quarters of recent secondary-school graduates, creating widespread expectations of white-collar employment despite the often questionable quality of tertiary degrees. Saudis are disproportionately enrolled for humanities degrees, which are not in demand in the private sector but have historically provided the formal credentials needed to apply for government positions. Again, patronage has been self-reinforcing, creating dependencies and expectations that lead to demands for further patronage. The very welfare demanded by the nationalist opposition in the 1950s and 1960s has made Saudi society deeply dependent on the paternal, authoritarian state controlled by the Al Saud.

While the Saudi private sector has matured since the 1970s,[40] it also remains directly or indirectly dependent on the state for most of its activities. Both subsidies and state-generated demand have created easy opportunities for profit that have undercut incentives to seek independent markets and sources of demand.

Figure 3.7 shows that the ratio of government spending to non-oil GDP in the kingdom is uniquely high, while figure 3.8 documents a very high ratio of public to private consumption. Both measures have, if anything, trended up during the last decade. They suggest that (a) much domestic demand is directly government created and (b) the fiscal multiplier through which government spending stimulates private economic activities is quite low. One reason for this is that much of the government-created demand 'leaks' abroad as the private economic

Figure 3.7: Share of government spending in non-oil GDP

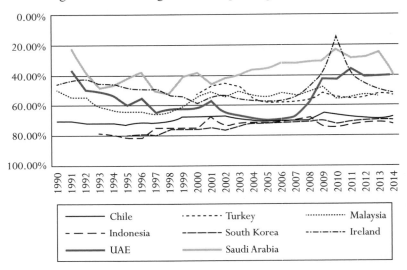

Source: Calculated from UNSTATS and IMF data.

Figure 3.8: Ratio of government to private consumption in Saudi Arabia and select comparative cases, 1971 to 2014

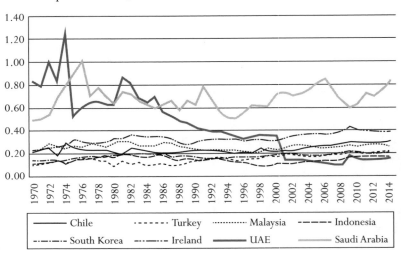

Source: Calculated from UNSTATS data.

activity it stimulates leads to subsequent imports of foreign goods and services that are not part of local GDP, rather than creating knock-on demand for local goods and services.

Much of the demand that is technically private is in fact also government created: government salaries and allowances constituted more than 18 per cent of GDP in 2015, while private salaries to Saudis accounted for only about 4 per cent of GDP (a further 5 per cent is accounted for by salaries to expats, which are largely remitted abroad and hence do not create much local demand).[41]

Unsurprisingly, the size of total private-sector GDP in the kingdom remains closely linked to the total volume of state expenditure (see figure 3.9). As there are few domestic taxes to finance government spending, it is clear that causality runs from (oil-financed) spending to private economic activity rather than the other way around.[42]

Private employment remains dominated by foreign workers, who outnumber Saudis in private jobs by about five to one. This is part of the distributive bargain for both businesses and households: businesses obviously profit from cheap and easily controlled foreign labour, especially at times of rent-financed economic expansion. Saudi households too benefit from cheap services provided by foreigners. As important, the presence of a large foreign workforce has historically obviated the

Figure 3.9: Private-sector contribution to Saudi GDP vs. total government expenditure (million SR)

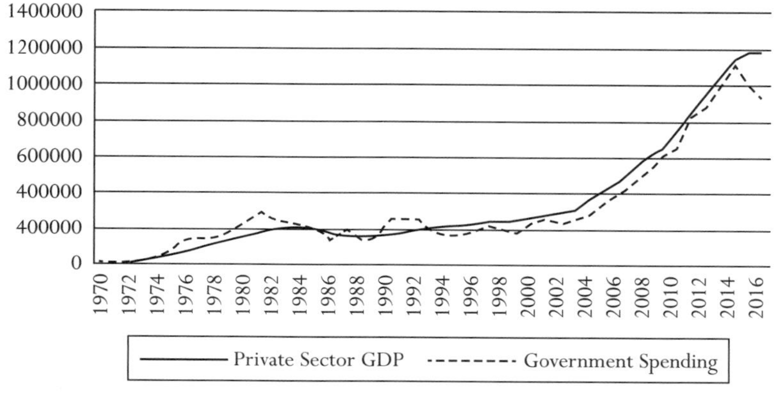

Source: Based on SAMA data.

structural need for citizens to participate in the more demanding private labour market; a majority of national households can instead draw on more convenient government salaries and transfers.

Reliance on low-cost foreign workers does not only limit privately financed household demand in the Saudi economy. The predominant focus on low-skilled workers also has led to low and stagnant productivity levels (see figure 3.10). As private Saudi employers effectively face a flat international labour-supply curve, they can always expand production by just adding more cheap foreign labour instead of investing in skills or upgrading their production structures. The labour scarcity that has pushed Western or other Asian countries into industrial deepening does not apply in the Saudi distributive state.

While Saudi business can pay low wages to its expatriate labour, non-wage costs of migrant labour recruitment are substantial and foreign workers' reservation wages for work in Saudi Arabia significantly higher than what they expect to be paid in their home countries. This means that labour cost in Saudi Arabia, while lower than in advanced countries, is still high compared to low-wage developing countries—and this is even more so where Saudis are privately employed. This means that the labour-intensive strategy of industrialization with which most successful emerging economies have started their industrial upgrading process is not feasible.

Figure 3.10: Relative labour productivity growth in comparison
(1980 = 100)

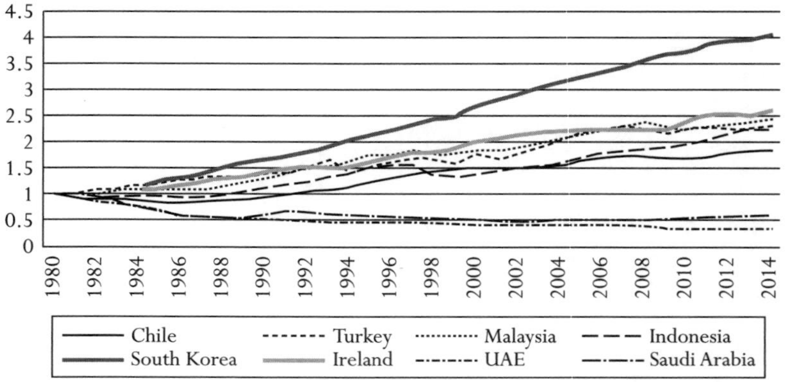

Source: Conference Board.

The Saudi combination of low and stagnating productivity with relatively high operating costs creates a unique development trap that is hard to escape. Saudi businesses—incentivized to cater to a captive local market—have found it difficult to break into the production of exportable goods outside energy-intensive industries that rely on state-provided cheap energy. The kingdom's exports outside oil and heavy industry are minuscule and mostly low tech; according to the World Bank, less than 1 per cent of Saudi manufacturing exports are classified as high tech.

The Saudi wealth-sharing regime has bolstered political stability since the 1970s, but has created deep dependencies and distortions that have become a threat to the kingdom's economic sustainability. Even incomes and activities that are formally private—and which are supposed to drive the kingdom's future non-oil diversification—are often predicated on continued state patronage. While there would be ways to re-engineer rent distribution to make it less distortionary and to incentivize more genuinely private activities, creative thinking about such alternatives remains in short supply.[43]

New Fiscal Challenges

Three years after the 2014 collapse of the oil price, public employment and cheap energy remain the main channels of broad-based rent distribution and economic stimulus in the kingdom. That being said, a sense of crisis has set in much faster in Riyadh than was the case during the austere years of the 1980s and 1990s under King Fahd. The policy reactions to growing deficits, while partial, have been much quicker—and they have been accompanied by changes to the ruling elite that are comparable in depth only to the royal reshuffle the kingdom saw in the troubled 1950s and 1960s.

Adjustment Steps

Key components of the kingdom's post-2014 economic policies are the Vision 2030 and the 2016–20 National Transformation Programme (NTP) that were published in the first half of 2016 and hold out the promise of a private-driven, post-oil economy. At the same time, and more concretely, the government undertook several significant steps of fiscal adjustment in 2016.

The accelerated decision making is the result of a fundamental shift in the kingdom's elite politics. The key economic policy maker behind recent measures has been Crown Prince Muhammad ibn Salman. His father King Salman succeeded King 'Abdullah in January 2015, and has since given his favourite son wide latitude to shape the kingdom's economic and military strategy.

Salman is the last surviving player of a core group of brothers and half-brothers who ruled Saudi Arabia collectively since they wrested power from King Saud in 1962, resulting in the above-mentioned institutional fragmentation and elite-level checks and balances.[44] Now that all of the old veto players are gone, Salman has enjoyed unprecedented autonomy in reordering the ruling family. Two of his brothers have been able to bequeath core state institutions to their sons, but this proved temporary: Muhammad ibn Nayif remained in charge of his father's Interior Ministry until June 2017, while Mit'ib ibn 'Abdullah controlled the National Guard until November 2007, which his father had previously controlled for more than fifty years (for a variety of reasons, sons of Salman's senior brothers Fahd and Sultan were less lucky).

Both institutions remain large and important, providing employment and patronage for hundreds of thousands of Saudi households. Yet they did not convey as much power on the top level as they did under the previous generation. Personality and relationship to the current king matter much more: Mit'ib was of far lesser stature than his father, for example, and Muhammad ibn Nayif, although an experienced policy maker, was sidelined during much of 2015 and 2016, even while still crown prince, in favour of Muhammad ibn Salman in all policy areas bar internal security. He was later sacked in 2017. Similarly, the Riyadh governorate, once Salman's key fiefdom, now is of much less importance under his successor as governor, Khalid ibn Bandar.

All this indicates that power structures at the top level are determined by informal family politics at least as much as princes' formal positions or the sheer weight of the institutions they control—as important as the latter remain in structuring quotidian wealth distribution and bureaucracy in the kingdom. As the transition to the next generation of Al Saud was delayed until almost all members of the old ruling generation had died, no one in the new generation, with the partial exception of Muhammad ibn Nayif, has been able to establish anything like the autonomous political stature that members of the old guard enjoyed. However, even Muhammad ibn Nayif was deposed.

The more centralized new generation leadership has fewer political sensitivities about established family hierarchies and a much larger appetite for risk than the consensus-oriented previous leadership had. That said, the top-level reshuffle has also produced some familiar patterns of bureaucratic politics: similar to the growth of new institutions around the new leadership in the 1960s and 1970s, new institutions have come into being or been empowered as personal tools of the deputy crown prince, notably the new Council of Economic Development Affairs (which, unlike its predecessor, the Supreme Economic Council, excludes the minister of interior), the Public Investment Fund, various new economic commissions, and a re-engineered and expanded royal court—all while most of the existing institutions remained untouched. As in the transition to the de facto rule of Muhammad ibn Zayed in Abu Dhabi after his father Zayed's death in 2004, international consultants have also suddenly started to play a key role in policy making at the very top level of government, adding another layer of complexity and parallel structures to government.

The main sign of the new centralization of power and risk appetite on the domestic front has been the unexpectedly strong fiscal adjustment the kingdom has gone through since late 2015, involving energy-price increases, hikes in various administrative fees, the announcement of (still to be implemented) land taxes and a VAT, a freeze in public-sector hiring, and, most notably, substantial cuts to the allowances of public-sector employees in September 2016, which according to some estimates amount to close to $20 billion. In December 2016 the government announced a four-year 'Fiscal Balance Program' that will lead to further taxes on soft drinks and cigarettes as well as, more substantially, gradually increasing fees on foreign workers and further hikes in energy prices—albeit partially cushioned through a new, means-tested household cash grant.

This fairly rapid adjustment differs drastically from King Fahd's days of cautious austerity in the 1980s and 1990s, when the regime went to great lengths to spare the population from any broad-based cuts, and when government employment continued to grow every year.[45] The only salient commonality between Fahd's austerity and the current fiscal policies are freezes in government payments to private contractors and drastic cuts in capital expenditure—generally seen as politically less sensitive as they do not directly affect most of the citizen population.

The NTP, published in early June 2016, aims to increase the government's non-oil revenue from SR165 billion in 2015 to SR530 billion by 2020 with a view to re-balancing the Saudi budget by then. SR530 billion is equivalent to 44 per cent of the Saudi private sector's contribution to GDP in 2015 which—assuming that most non-oil revenue has to be generated locally—would potentially entail going from practically no local taxes to OECD-style taxation levels within four years. While this objective is unlikely to be accomplished in such a short timeframe, it gives a sense of the new leadership's ambitions.

Reactions to Fiscal Adjustment

The most immediate impact of the austerity has been a sizeable dent in the growth and confidence of the local private sector, which expanded by only 0.1 per cent in real terms in 2016, which, given the kingdom's continued population growth, implies significant shrinkage per capita. This contrasts sharply with real annual growth levels between 5 and 10 per cent during the boom years from 2009 to 2014. The construction sector has been hit particularly hard by non-payment of government contracts and reduction of capital expenditure. But consumer-focused sectors that were relatively protected during the 1980s and 1990s austerity such as retail also contracted between mid-2015 and mid-2016. Manufacturing has similarly shrunk due to partial increases in energy prices.

Total private-sector growth during the third quarter of 2016 was negative. The overall mood among both population and businesspeople in Riyadh shifted discernibly from the first half of 2016, when Vision 2030 and the NTP were announced, to the second half, when deeper austerity kicked in. Available statistics on foreign-exchange transactions indicate significant private-capital flight from the kingdom, unlike the 1990s when Saudi banks and large families repatriated capital to purchase government bonds.

The negative impact of austerity seems to have been stronger than the government expected, yet should have been predictable given the private sector's deep dependence on state spending outlined above. The allowance cuts alone, if fully implemented, would have cut average incomes of Saudi state employees by up to 20 per cent. To get a sense of the magnitude of these cuts relative to private-sector activities, consider that their aggregate volume is equivalent to two-thirds of the aggregate of all private-sector salaries paid to Saudis—creating a potentially substantial gap in consumer demand. Based on 2016 IMF estimates of fiscal multipliers,[46] the allowance cuts alone could have shaved about 2 percentage points off non-oil GDP over a period of two years, had they been fully implemented. The belated realization of this impact led to the reversal of the allowance cuts in April 2017. Further cuts through the Fiscal Balance Programme would further eat into domestic demand generation.

While the generation of non-oil revenue is a worthwhile target, the centrality of state spending in the economy means that the kingdom's domestic tax base itself is dependent on state spending. High levels of taxation would reduce the state's effective demand stimulus, depress business activity, and potentially lead to further capital flight at a time when local business is already sceptical of investing in the Saudi economy because of plateauing or declining state spending. The higher domestic price levels resulting from taxation would also exert upward pressure on government expenditure that relies on local suppliers—the financing of which in turn could require even higher taxation levels. Tax-induced inflation would also lead to real appreciation of the (pegged) Saudi riyal, reducing the competitiveness of future non-oil exports and potentially diverting more domestic spending towards imports.

In tax-based economies, fiscal stimulus can potentially enlarge the tax base, allowing governments to recoup some or all of the extra spending through taxes. But Saudi Arabia is still far away from such a 'Keynesian multiplier' mechanism: for the foreseeable future, leakage of state-generated demand towards imported goods and services will remain large, blunting the growth spill-overs of fiscal policy, while taxes as a share of the private economy will remain too low for the state to be able to recoup much of whatever local stimulus it generates.

Generating non-oil revenue is important and the government's efforts appear serious, but there are strict short-term structural limits to increasing such revenue without shrinking the local economy. Available estimates of the revenue potential of most new fees and taxes are modest: a recent discussion of Saudi VAT plans by JP Morgan indicates that the kingdom will raise SR22 billion in revenue through this tax, which is a mere 0.8 per cent of GDP (the IMF estimates a more optimistic 1.5 per cent). The new foreign-worker levy alone is likely to raise more substantial revenue, reaching an estimated SR65 billion per year by 2020—but probably with significant knock-on effects for inflation and business profits.

Most private business activities in the kingdom are predicated on direct or indirect state support. For the same reason, the diversification promised by Vision 2030 and the NTP remains a long-term ambition. While the Saudi private sector has built real capacities since the 1970s, it mostly caters to a domestic market that relies on state-generated demand, and has developed production models that rely on state protection and state-provided subsidies. Some private-sector leaders confidentially admit their confusion over which concrete policy measures the Vision 2030 entails and ask why the government has not systematically consulted them in the process of drafting it. The contrast between the concrete fiscal cuts that have hit the profits of Saudi business and the lofty but long-term ambitions of Vision 2030 has created some frustration among Saudi merchants.

As discussed above, the Saudi distributive state has also created deep institutional legacies, which include an overstaffed, slow-moving, and fragmented bureaucracy as well as the historical co-optation into the judiciary of religious forces with little understanding of modern commercial law. These create a difficult regulatory and bureaucratic environ-

Figure 3.11: Estimated revenue from a 5 per cent VAT as share of GDP (IMF)

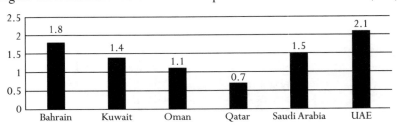

Source: IMF.

ment that has changed little since 2014 according to local lawyers and businessmen as well as international rankings of institutional performance. While civil service reforms are an important component of the NTP, changing the behaviours and incentives of about 3.5 million state employees after decades of patronage employment is a secular and politically difficult task—as was reflected in the public backlash after the then civil service minister stated on TV in October 2016 that Saudi bureaucrats only work an average of one hour per day. The kingdom's challenging institutional environment is a further factor that disincentivizes the taking of entrepreneurial risks and investment in new sectors.

While the Saudi regime enjoys an increased level of political autonomy at the top level, the structural legacy of the distributive state below the top is deep: low productivity and dependence on cheap but low-productivity foreign labour which substitutes for a local working class, dependence of both business and Saudi households on state support, a relatively high domestic cost base, and a sprawling bureaucracy that serves as an employment machine for citizens are deep-seated and in many ways interdependent. They will all make competitive, export-oriented economic development difficult.

Saudi Arabia would be the first high-rent oil country to achieve genuine private-driven diversification. While the task is not impossible, it is not clear that the NTP and Vision 2030 address the key structural constraints, price distortions, and institutional bottlenecks resulting from the distributive legacy of the Saudi state. Specifically, without a move from state employment and subsidies towards more incentive-neutral ways of sharing the kingdom's wealth with business and citizenry, incentives will remain stacked against autonomous private growth.

Households in the Era of Austerity

Real incomes and employment for Saudi households have been affected surprisingly quickly by the new austerity policies. As the private economy remains strongly state dependent, private job creation has stalled at exactly the time when the Saudi government has stopped hiring, leading to flat employment growth in 2016 despite a rapidly growing working-age population.

Austerity has led to fairly open expressions of discontent on Saudi social media, and even some local newspapers. That being said, to the surprise of many observers (including local ones), the scaling down of decades-old distributional commitments has not given rise to any open unrest or oppositional mobilization. There are diffuse complaints about the fact that royal family allowances seem to be almost the only budget item untouched by austerity, and the deep involvement of many royals in local land markets at a time when the national housing shortage has become acute. Some intellectuals also mention the link between taxation and political representation. Yet none of this amounts to an organized political reaction to the regime's partial reneging on its patronage commitments. Instead, there seems to be a widespread sense of fatalism among Saudis, who compare the stability in the kingdom to the chaos in many neighbouring countries and see no realistic alternative to the present regime.

The ability of the leadership to impose austerity suggests that much of the previous elite commitment to stable mass patronage in the 1980s and 1990s might have been self-imposed: the result of elite bargaining and princely risk aversion—potentially rooted in royal memories of the tumultuous 1960s—rather than genuine pressures from below. It is clear that recent austerity steps violate established clientelist expectations. Yet decades of patronage have also made Saudi society so state dependent, and have undermined the formation of independent social groups to such an extent,[47] that society has been unable to mobilize against austerity. Should fiscal cuts be slowed down or reversed in the future, this is likely to be the outcome of elite whims or conflict rather than anything else.

The swift, unchallenged imposition of austerity after the oil-price collapse presents a striking contrast to the politics of patronage in the 1950s and 1960s, the last time the royal leadership was fundamentally reshaped and the future of rent distribution was at stake: back then, the Al Saud faced and feared open ideological challenges, and reacted with increased generosity. Nowadays, decades of patronage seem to have removed ideological alternatives to the Al Saud, whose rule over the kingdom is not even challenged by most political dissidents. The rentier state, whose growth was once triggered by subversive challenges, seems to have done its work of undercutting independent opposition most thoroughly. ISIS alone poses an ideological challenge of sorts to the Al Saud, but it has so far directed most of its energies towards the Syrian and Iraqi theatres—and it certainly does not make any concrete programmatic demands on public goods provision the way the nationalists and leftists did two generations ago.

None of this is to say that more contentious politics might not return, possibly if harsher steps such as a reduction in the number of civil service workers are taken or if continued current account deficits and capital flight lead to a devaluation of the riyal and hence an imported inflationary shock. For the time being, however, it seems that the depoliticizing effects of patronage that set in from the 1960s on are long lasting, even at a time when patronage is reduced. The Al Saud family sits at the centre of the omnipresent Saudi distributional state, and thereby has become an indelible fact of Saudi life.

The most likely future scenario right now seems to be survival of the Saudi system, but with diminished patronage powers. A less distorted labour market might gradually emerge as new public jobs remain scarce and Saudis reorient themselves towards less lucrative private employment—although a truly integrated labour market would require substantial reforms to the migrant-labour regime that both businesses and households might resist. The least optimistic economic scenario would be a gradual 'Egyptianization' of Saudi Arabia, under which real incomes decline and public-service provision is stretched thin but households and businesses continue to be oriented towards government patronage, while a bloated bureaucracy makes life difficult for citizens and businesses alike.

Conclusion

Saudi Arabia has entered another era of fundamental political, social, and economic change, similar to the one it witnessed in the late 1950s and early 1960s. The full consequences are not yet clear—arguably not even to the kingdom's current leaders. What is clear is that the legacies of the distributive state that was created half a century ago will continue to strongly constrain the policy options of even the most ambitious leadership. The level of patronage entitlements in the Saudi economy is unique for a middle-income country. The experiment to try to move this system from a state-driven onto a private growth path is similarly unprecedented.

The two years of elite change and reform since early 2015 do allow us a few comparative remarks against the background of earlier periods of state building. First, while the large institutional fiefdoms of the Saudi state have not disappeared, they now convey less power at the top level, indicating that the influence of senior regime players has at least as much to do with their history and position in the family as with the institutional resources they control. Politics at the top remains informal. Second, it is now clear that some of the past patronage obligations of the regime have been voluntary and potentially reversible, possibly created and maintained through a contingent power balance among ruling elites. Again, personality and elite politics continue to matter more in the mature Saudi state than I anticipated in *Princes, Brokers, and Bureaucrats*. Third, and in line with past patterns, political change is once more accompanied by the creation of new, often parallel, institutions, potentially deepening institutional fragmentation below the top leadership—despite the centralization of the latter. Oil rents and political autonomy of the leadership still allow institutional experiments. Fourth, structural change below the top level of the state apparatus remains very slow, often disconnecting the bulk of the state apparatus from the current leadership's ambitious top-down reform projects.

The Saudi oil state provides much better infrastructure and public goods than its more kleptocratic peers in other world regions. Yet, in pursuing economic adjustment, it now is probably more hampered by its distributive legacies than klepto-states such as Angola, Gabon, or Equatorial Guinea. While these legacies will continue to guarantee comparatively high (if potentially declining) levels of citizen welfare, they will also reproduce structures of state dependence for households and businesses. These would appear to be good ingredients for political survival, but also for gradual economic decline.

4

BEYOND SECTARIANISM AND IDEOLOGY

REGIONALISM AND COLLECTIVE POLITICAL ACTION IN SAUDI ARABIA

Sultan Alamer

While much ink has been spilled in addressing the question of why some Arab states witnessed protests and revolutions during the Arab Spring and others did not, there has been less interest in explaining why some regions within each state protested whereas others did not. In Saudi Arabia the wave of protest between 2011 and 2013 was concentrated in two regions: Qatif and Buraydah. From 17 February 2011 there were recurring protests in Qatif. While the demands of the early protests focused on releasing Qatifi prisoners, from 16 March the demonstrations were directed against the Saudi military intervention in Bahrain. In response, the state adopted a strategy that included targeted arrests, a heavy security presence in the form of checkpoints, and the use of the community's elite as a broker to contain the situation. By April 2011 the protests in Qatif became much smaller and less frequent. In Buraydah the month-long protest wave, which took place between 25 February and 27 March 2013, came after two years of small, sporadic demonstrations. The main demand of this month of protest was the release of prisoners who had been held without charge or trial for many years. The state used the same strategy it had employed in Qatif, which led the protests to fade out by 27 March. The question of why some regions protest but others do not is puzzling, and becomes even more so if we consider that Qatif and Buraydah are distinguished from other Saudi regions by long histories of protest. Before the Arab Spring, Qatifis engaged in recurring protest action from the major intifada in 1979 until 2009, when they took to the streets following the attack on Shi'a women in the city of Medina. On the other hand, Buraydah had its own intifada in 1994 where the protests were directed against, among other things, the state's decision to allow American troops onto Saudi soil. The protests kept recurring until 2009, when relatives of Buraydah's prisoners gathered in front of the *mabahith* (secret police) building demanding their release.[1] Given the history of protest in these two cities, it is important to provide not only an explanation of why protests concentrated there in the context of the Arab Spring, but also why they had occurred there constantly over the previous four decades. In other words, why do some Saudi cities become sites of protest while others remain quiet?

In this chapter I will move beyond the dominant sectarian and ideological explanations of protests in Saudi Arabia that have treated the two cities as if they belong to two different countries. I will argue that in an authoritarian regime such as the Saudi state, where freedom of speech is not totally monopolized by the state, but controlled situationally, people in cities with strong regional identities are more likely than those in other places to act collectively against the state. I will show that the Saudi state-making process played an important role in allowing some cities to invent strong regional identities. Moreover, the regionally imbalanced socio-economic distribution of oil rents caused a rapid domestic migration between Saudi regions which affected the ability of big cities to mobilize their inhabitants on the basis of a unifying regional identity. This left few cities with the potential to mobilize against the state. When a protest occurred, for any reason, it was more likely to be repeated if the state's response included policies that were regionally indiscriminate.

The chapter will be divided into three sections. In the first I provide a critical assessment of how protests and opposition activities have been dealt with in the literature on Saudi Arabia. Then, in the second section I build my argument for why the existence of strong regional identities is essential in explaining why some cities periodically protest and others do not. The third section shows how regional identities were constructed in the Saudi context, and why some, with an emphasis on Buraydah and Qatif, are stronger and more able to mobilize people than others.

Why Regional Variations Went Unnoticed in Saudi Literature

Studies of opposition activity in Saudi Arabia tend to provide an image of a country that is divided into two separate sectarian worlds: Shiʻi and Sunni. The political dynamics and history of one world are perceived to have no relation to those of the other. In the Shiʻi world, studies tend to emphasize the role of 'sectarian grievances' in motivating Saudi Shiʻa to challenge the government.[2] Although some of these studies recognize the role of economic and geopolitical factors in influencing the political behaviour of Saudi Shiʻa, they consider sectarian grievances as the root of any opposition. According to this line of reasoning, it is appropriate to treat the history of the Shiʻa in Saudi Arabia separately, and to understand it as a series of attempts by the Shiʻi minority to challenge the religious discrimination of the Wahhabi state.

To illustrate the problems with this kind of scholarship, I will use the example of Toby Matthiesen's book *The Other Saudis: Shiism, Dissent and Sectarianism*, which he considers 'the first book that tells the political history of the Shia in Qatif and al-Ahsa since the late nineteenth century'.[3] The first problem in this work is his approach to sectarian identity. Although he promises that the book will be useful 'to gain insights into how and why people identify with a particular group … in competition with other possible markers of identity', his account of the 'Shiʻi' identity is ahistorical. In other words, it is a history of the Shiʻa in Saudi Arabia, not a history of the Shi'i identity there and how it developed. This is evident throughout the book, where we find Qatifi actors described as 'Shi'a notables', 'educated Shi'a elite', 'Shi'a workers' etc. For Matthiesen they are politically Shi'a even if they do not identify politically with their sectarian identity. To show how problematic this approach is, I will focus on the term 'Shi'a notables'. It is understandable to call someone a 'Shi'i judge' because Islamic judges belong to different schools of religious jurisprudence. However, calling a notable from Qatif a 'Shi'a notable' is not analytically justifiable unless notables who happen to be Shi'a behave differently from notables of other religious beliefs. From the account that Matthiesen provides about the politics of notables in Qatif, we do not see any significant difference between their political behaviour and any other situation that involves politics of notables. Therefore, replacing the qualifier 'Shi'a' with 'Qatifi' would be more meaningful and useful in Matthiesen's argument because those notables were representatives of Qatif as a town and preoccupied in securing its interests. Notwithstanding this criticism, Matthiessen's work is meticulous in documenting the history of protest in the region and its relations with the Saudi state. But had he compared Qatifi protest with that taking place in Buraydah, a different picture would have certainly emerged, which would have diluted the strong focus on sectarianism.

The heavy focus on sectarianism undermines a theoretical explanation of the regional variations in political behaviour between the people of Qatif and al-Ahsa (both of them considered Shi'a regions). Indeed, the crucial focus of his story, most of its key actors, and most of its major events (such as the intifada), is about Qatif and its people. Although al-Ahsa and its people appear here and there in his book, their existence and role in these major events is mostly marginal. Although the author hints in different places about this difference between the two regions,[4] he does not provide a theoretical justification for why some Shi'a protest more than others. His inability to recognize and theorize this regional variation is because it would undermine his own argument. In other words, if, for Matthiesen, Shi'a engage in protest because they are discriminated against as Shi'a, then it is reasonable not to assume any regional variation.

If sectarian analysis prevented studies on the Saudi Shi'i world from taking regional variation in protests in the Eastern Province into account, it is their preoccupation with Islamist ideology that has prevented other scholars from recognizing regional variation in protests in the Sunni world. For example, Buraydah is an important region in Lacroix's *Awakening Islam* and Heghammer's *Jihad in Saudi Arabia*. The first shows that an intifada occurred in Buraydah in 1993, but that a comparable attempt failed in Riyadh. However, the author does not provide any explanation for this variation. Heghammer's book emphasizes the role of what he calls the Shuʻaybi school in the transformation of the jihadi movements in Saudi Arabia. Although he acknowledges that most of the school's members are from Buraydah, he does not provide an explanation for this. The reason for this lack of interest in explaining such a variation has to do with the nature of the audience to which these studies were addressed. After 9/11 the growing Western interest in understanding how al-Qaeda was founded led some scholars to investigate the Islamist context in Saudi Arabia. This means that these studies are governed by the following major question: what are the domestic context and factors that helped in creating al-Qaeda or global jihadism? Needless to say, understanding regional variations and the recurrence of protest action was not directly relevant to providing an answer to such a question and similar post-9/11 preoccupations.

Regional Identity and Protest

In order to provide a theoretical approach that goes beyond the aforementioned two-worlds paradigm, I will rely on a modified version of Timur Kuran's theoretical framework on revolutions and protests.[5] Kuran accepts the conclusion that mass discontent does not necessarily lead to protest, and then provides a rationalist account for why individuals join mass protests and revolutions. In authoritarian settings, Kuran argues, each individual has two political preferences. The first is the public preference, where the individual has to choose whether to publicly support the authoritarian regime or not. The second preference is the private one, the one that he keeps to himself and which might be different from his public preference. When the latter is different from the former, then the individual is engaged in what Kuran calls self-falsification. Each individual with self-falsification has a revolutionary threshold. By this, he means a moment when the individual adopts a public preference against the government that corresponds to her private preference. The revolutionary threshold varies from one person to another, and two factors influence this variation. The first is the individual's evaluation of her chances of being prosecuted if she reveals her true preferences. One way for the individual to calculate this is by the number of people who join a protest. If it is high, then the risks of her being singled out for prosecution is low. The second factor is the individual's ability to sustain the discomfort of a life in which her true preference is hidden. If the individual's animosity towards the government is high, then his tolerance for such a psychologically stressed life will be low, and he will thus be more likely to join a protest before others who need more people to join before they can resolve their self-falsification and take action in accordance with their true preference.

In order to make use of this framework in the context of Saudi Arabia, I will add two important modifications. First, Kuran's framework is designed to apply to full authoritarian settings where any form of expression against the status quo is not tolerated and is repressed. However, not all authoritarian regimes monopolize the public sphere. Some of them, such as Saudi Arabia, differ in their approach to freedom of speech in two ways. First, they dominate, but do not monopolize, the media. Their domination serves an important function: to prevent any popular counter-narrative. In this kind of regime, counter-narratives exist but are weak nationally. For instance, if an incident of political significance occurs, the ability of the regime to spread its narrative about what happened to a much wider audience is greater than any opposition group. Although the narrative might be strong within the group, its ability to disseminate it nationally is relatively weak. Besides dominating the national narrative, the Saudi method of limiting expression can be described as 'situational repression'. By this I mean that it is not the content of what is said that results in repression, but who articulates it, when, and through what media, etc. In this murky situation, what makes individuals act politically is not their knowledge of the real preferences of others, it is their trust in others' willingness to join them.

The second modification to Kuran's framework has to do with his understanding of preference. As Nathan Brown correctly notes, Kuran 'gives us few tools other than the coincidences of individual preferences for understanding how consensual agendas can quickly emerge and be enthusiastically embraced in situations in which individuals are just beginning to feel free to act on their private views'.[6] Thus, if individual preferences are not exclusively individual and fixed, then the role of social context and groups in shaping and reshaping individual identities and preferences are important and ought to be taken into account. If a group manages to create some marginal or local public sphere, which is relatively independent of the state's control and where unifying identities and narratives can be produced, then the ability of this group to resist the state's dominant narratives and shape the preferences of its members is higher than that of other groups.

These two modifications imply that in some authoritarian regimes, where the territory is large and where freedom of speech is not fully monopolized by the regime, but rather controlled situationally, the likelihood of regional collective political action against the regime is higher than nationwide political collective action. Moreover, even where sub-national (such as tribal or sectarian) identities are present, regional identity has more potential to be manipulated by political actors to homogenize preferences and build trust within groups. The reason why regional identity is more powerful than other sub-national identities has to do with its geographical concentration. The territorial aspect is important given the regime's method of controlling communication. Since the regime is interested in preventing a nationwide counter-narrative, it is possible for a territorially concentrated counter-narrative to develop. This is because local sites of communication, such as mosques, social gatherings, intellectual meetings, etc., are not as subject to state control as are nationwide radio stations, newspapers, TV channels, etc.

However, since they cannot compete with the regime at the national level, the state is ultimately always able to win by its ability to frame any protest within its own chosen parameters. This serves two purposes: it isolates the regional protest from any national solidarity; and it legitimizes the state's repressive measures against such regional protest. However, the regime's representation of the situation remains weak in the region in question. This is especially the case if the state uses indiscriminate repressive measures there. These include regionally concentrated checkpoints, a regional ban on public religious sermons and other activities, mass arrests, etc. The local counter-narrative framing of such policies is available to the region's inhabitants. This creates a distinct local memory of what happened, and consequently helps to solidify the regional identity. This, in turn, makes the likelihood of another cycle of protest higher than other regions.

The Infrastructure of Regional Identities and Protest

The previous section concludes that the likelihood for a Saudi region to protest can be explained by the existence of a strong regional identity that is shared by most of its inhabitants. In this section I will show how this is applied to Qatif and Buraydah. First, I will show why some regions were able to construct a strong regional identity, while others were not. Second, I will propose two factors to explain why among the areas that developed strong regional identities, some were able to influence protests while others were not. The first factor is domestic migration, and the other is the reproduction of a regional elite.

Inventing Regional Identities

Regional identities in Saudi Arabia are similar to tribal and sectarian ones in that they are modern constructs. Although their existence is often understood as signifying a crisis in the state's project to build a national identity, I would argue that their invention is closely linked to, or even a product of, the very process of state making. As Scott et al. have put it, 'there is no state-making without state-naming'.[7] By this they mean that an important part of state-making measures is to name and classify people, places, roads, and property. These measures help the state to accurately identify individuals and locations without requiring local brokers. The modern state-making project is to a large extent a project against illegibility. The more individuals, places, and properties are legible to the state, the less local brokers are needed for the state to rule. Legibility is a key for facilitating the state's reach and direct rule. However, this form of standardized, rational knowledge that the modern state needs to rule directly is sometimes in conflict with the prevalent local customary practices of knowledge and identification. The emergence of regional identity in Saudi Arabia is closely linked to the interaction between these two forms of knowledge. Paradoxically, the Saudi state, in its process of naming and classification, also lays the groundwork for some local forms of identification to be reconstructed as modern regional identities. In the following, I will show how this was done by focusing on two of these naming processes.

The first is the state's administrative division of the country. This process divides the country into different administrative units, each with a distinct name. Generally speaking, these units can be classified into three categories. The first category is drawn up and named to serve the state's needs without any regard to the identities of the region's inhabitants. For the people living in these regions, the name and boundaries of their region have no historical or local significance. For example, although the meaning of the Northern Borders region is relevant in defining the relation between the region and the state's centre, its boundaries and name have no local meaning or significance for its inhabitants. The naming process of this category prevented local forms of identification from being reconstructed and imagined through the administrative categories, which resulted in weak regional identities.

The second regional category includes modern cities that were founded after the formation of the Saudi state. Their names were invented by either the state or the oil company Aramco, and mostly borrowed from the names of surrounding mountains, valleys, and the like. For example, the biggest city in the aforementioned Northern Borders is called Arar. This city was founded in 1950 along the Tapline, which was a pipeline built by Aramco to transfer oil from the Saudi east coast to the Lebanese Mediterranean port of Sidon. Aramco called it Arar after the nearby Arar Valley. The same applies for Dhahran in the Eastern Region, as the city was founded by Aramco, which named it after the Dhahran Mountain. The fact that the state and Aramco were able to impose names on these regions shows how weak the ties were between them and their inhabitants. This is because these new cities are populated by people who migrated from other regions with strong identities. These people tend to not give up these identities, since they have social and economic value, through which they can secure jobs, celebrate holidays, marry, etc. The durability and appeal of these original identities undermine the creation of alternative strong collective regional identities for the new cities and regions, which could then shape the preferences of their inhabitants.

The third category of administrative units uses words borrowed from the names of towns or regions that existed before the formation of the Saudi state and are locally identifiable by the inhabitants. Although the boundaries of the administrative units in this category do not correspond exactly to the historical boundaries of the towns that held those names, the adoption of these labels nonetheless contributes to a sense of historical continuity. For example, the administrative unit that is labelled Riyadh is much larger than the historical city of Riyadh, which comprises two out of the fifteen municipal units that make up contemporary Riyadh. Nonetheless, the sense of historical continuity that the name provides for its inhabitants is not challenged. This variation in naming places made it easier for the inhabitants of this category to imagine a historical continuity for their regions, and paved the groundwork for regional identity to be constructed.

The other factor that influences the creation of regional identity is the Saudi identification card or *tab'ia*. Although these cards are extremely helpful for the state to prevent people from concealing their identities, they also constitute a medium through which individuals can relate to each other. Among the information in these cards, two items are important in serving this function. The first is, obviously, the individual's name. According to Al-Fahad, the state pursued different naming procedures for Bedouin and Hadar (the sedentary population). This is because the former were not territorially confined. Therefore, it asked each Bedouin individual to provide five names: his name, his father's name, his grandfather's name, his lineage name, and his tribal name.[8] This gives the state the ability to locate the individual through his tribal affiliation. However, as Al-Fahad notes, 'this naming system originally designed to ensure state control would eventually bring about unintended consequences'. By 'unintended consequences' he means the construction of a tribal identity. For the Hadar, this means that if the last name in the card is not a tribal name, then the individual is a Hadari. While the last name in the cards differentiates between Hadar and Bedouin, another piece of information in the ID cards, the individual's place of birth, helped Hadari people to recognize those from their home towns without knowing them personally. If an individual's card indicates that their place of birth is X and their name does not end with a tribal name, then it is fair to assume that the individual belongs to X, and allows others from the same town to relate to him or her without knowing him or her personally. These ways of imagined regional relations would become important for public officials inclined to channel the state's resources (jobs, services, funds, etc.) to their regional brethren to be able to easily identify them.

I do not mean to say that these two naming systems (administrative division and identification cards) directly created regional identities, but they did make it structurally easier for some local forms of identification to be reconstructed. From the 1960s different intellectual projects, some led by the state and others not, helped in the construction of regional identities. The main example of such projects is the series of sixty-seven local histories that the General Presidency of Youth Welfare supervised between 1982 and 2004. The series title was *This is our Country*, and it covered many cities and towns from all around the country.[9] A similar project was led by the famous Saudi historian and intellectual Hamad al-Jasir and called the *Geographic Dictionary of the Kingdom of Saudi Arabia*. This project divided the kingdom into small geographical units, and a local researcher was tasked to conduct fieldwork in each unit. The purpose of the project was to survey the names of all the places and document them and their history.[10] Beside these collective projects, different local historians published local histories of their own regions. The surge in such local histories made them accessible to a wider audience, and helped to draw the boundaries of regions' identities. Moreover, they substantiated the sense of historical continuity, with narratives, events, and local heroes. This played an important role in the creation of regional identities for different groups.

To show how this intellectual activity played a part in creating regional identities I will focus on Qatif and Buraydah. Scholars have paid more attention to the role of local historians in constructing identity in Qatif.[11] This is understandable given the two sectarian worlds paradigm discussed above. However, this paradigm does lead these scholars to confuse the construction of regional with sectarian identity. Here, I will use the work of Muhammad al-Muslim, *Sahil al-dhahab al-aswad* (The coast of black gold), to show how the author was driven by more regional than sectarian concerns. The book is important since it is the first comprehensive history of Qatif. Al-Muslim is a well-known Qatifi poet, intellectual, Arab nationalist, and banker. He was born in 1922 to a wealthy notable family in Qatif. He spent most of the 1950s in Iraq, where there was a small neighbourhood which was inhabited by a Qatifi migrant community. The author became friendly with a poet from this community who convinced him to write the history of their own region. Indeed, the motivation for writing the book was the author's discomfort with the neglect of the history of Qatif in Arab historiography. 'I do not know any Arab city', says al-Muslim,

> that has been neglected to the point of oblivion, as has Qatif ... I was deeply concerned when I found that many people do not know anything—even its geographical location—about Qatif. It was painful to me to see that those who wrote about the Arab Gulf, such as Jean-Jacques Berreby, do not even mention Qatif despite the fact that it was one of the most prosperous towns on the Gulf.[12]

As this quotation indicates, the author was concerned about the marginalization of his home town's history—not in the national historiography, but in the broader Arab and Western historiographies. To give his town its proper place in history, he started collecting information and sources during his stay in Iraq. In 1959 he returned to Dammam, where he worked in the local branch of Riyadh Bank, and began work on his book. He finished it in August 1960. In 1964 he was jailed on suspicion of involvement in the Arab nationalist and communist movements that were active at the time.[13] In 1989 he was commissioned by General Presidency of Youth Welfare to write about Qatif in *This is our Country*. Before his death in 1994 he published a revised edition of his book on Qatif.

His book is important for two reasons. First, it was written before Shi'i Islamist movements monopolized the public sphere in Qatif. It gives the perspective of a non-sectarian author about the history of his home town. Second, it is the first systematic historical account that is devoted completely to the history of Qatif. The narrative that he provides is straightforward. He starts by discussing the geographical and geological characteristics of Qatif, and goes on to deal with its political history. Three types of conflict drive his narrative. The first is the imperial conflict over control of the city. Throughout its history Qatif was a place of contestation between different imperial powers, from the Persian to Muslim, Ottoman, Portuguese, and British. The second conflict is its location on the periphery of empires, which makes it a natural base for anti-imperial movements. The prime example is the Qarmatians, who rebelled against the Abbasid caliphate in the ninth century. The third conflict is local tension between the sedentary residents and nomads. For al-Muslim, the fact that the Ottomans were not able to protect Qatif's sedentary population from nomad attacks was the reason for the latter's support of Ibn Saud's capture of the city. In his view, the fact that the people of Qatif were Shi'a plays virtually no role in these conflicts. Generally speaking, al-Muslim's account provides its readers with a local history from the pre-Islamic era to modern times. This way of writing history brings the locality to the centre of events, and highlights the roles played by its inhabitants. It produces heroes, 'ulama', fighters, politicians, and poets.

While Qatif received a certain amount of attention from historians, their interest in Buraydah was marginal. The first important work on Buraydah is the long section written by Muhammad Nasir al-Obodi in his *Dictionary of Qasim Towns*. Qasim is the northern region of Najd, which includes cities such as Buraydah, Unayzah, and Rass. Al-Obodi's work is part of Hamad al-Jasir's project *The Geographic Dictionary of the Kingdom of Saudi Arabia*. Al-Jasir tasked al-Obodi to write the part on the Qasim region. Al-Obodi is a well-known intellectual, historian, traveller, and genealogist. He was born in Buraydah in 1930. In the 1960s Saudi Arabia formed the Muslim World League, and al-Obodi was appointed as its assistant secretary. His job involved travelling to many countries. This created an opportunity for him to write a book on each country he visited, and he wrote more than a hundred travel books. Besides his interest in travel, he published many books on local culture, poetry, genealogy, and history. His *Dictionary of Qasim Towns*, which was written in 1978, is one of the earliest books about the Qasim region and its towns. Many later authors have relied on his work when writing about the region. He aimed to craft a unique character for Qasim's people that distinguishes them from other people from Najd. For him, Qasim's people are 'the most active among Najdis in trade, industry, and communication with external world. When the word "Najdi" was uttered in surrounding regions such as Iraq and Syria, people would mean the people from Qassim.'[14] When he speaks about Qasim's towns, such as Unayzah and Buraydah, he says that 'before the recent economic prosperity, Qasim's towns were the most developed

Najdi towns'. In the section on Buraydah, al-Obodi describes it as 'the base of Qasim, its administrative capital, its largest city ... and its beating heart'.

Building on al-Obodi's work, another author from Buraydah, Muhammad al-Rebdi, wrote a more systematic and comprehensive book on the city in 1986, *Buraydah: Its Urban Development and Regional Relations*.[15] Al-Rebdi belongs to one of the wealthiest families in central Arabia in the nineteenth and early twentieth centuries. Since his graduation from University of Southampton in 1990 he has been a professor in the geography department at Imam Muhammad ibn Saud University. His book is divided into two volumes. The first is about Buraydah's natural and demographic characteristics, while the other deals with its political and urban history. I will emphasize three elements in the account he provides. The first is his division of Buraydah's history into three main periods: from the formation of the city in 1577 until 1818; from 1819 until 1908; and from 1909 until 1980. The author used the town's walls as markers of its history: each period starts with the building of a new wall. This way of writing the history of the town privileges the local context over the main regional and international context. While the national history is divided into periods based on the attempts of the Al Saud family to establish a state, al-Rebdi disregards these events and only mentions them when their effects are relevant on the urban and political development of Buraydah. This strategy liberates the history of Buraydah from the dominant national history of the country, and provides the reader with an independent account of its people. The second is his emphasis on the political role of Buraydah in the nineteenth-century conflict between different local powers for control over the whole of Najd. While dominant history focuses on either the internal war among the Al Saud family, or the war between the Al Saud and Al Rashid, al-Rebdi presents Buraydah as an important and significant third party in these conflicts. This strategy provides readers with local heroes, who are not necessarily Saudi national heroes, to be proud of.

These two cases show how regional identities were developed by local intellectuals. They also show how they manipulated structural conditions that the state-making naming processes produced and allowed certain regions to claim some sort of historical continuity and means of imagination. Moreover, they show how this intellectual activity is important in crafting an independent history and imagined community that treat the Saudi state as marginal, or only a phase in the region's history. This creates a space for local actors to construct anti-regime claims and narratives. It also increases the sense of belonging, which allows the region's members to trust each other more and enhances local channels of communication that can serve as a medium for a counter-narrative.

Domestic Migration, Regional Elites, and Mobilization

It is important to note that these constructed regional identities differ in their ability to mobilize inhabitants and shape their preferences. This variation is due to two factors. The first has to do with whether a city or a region has witnessed high domestic migration. If it did, then those who identify with the region would become a numerical minority, and the ability of the regional identity to shape the preferences of the region's inhabitants is limited. Although Jeddah and Riyadh were constituted before the state and had strong regional identities, the fact that they witnessed a rapid increase in their populations due to in-state migration led to a weakening of their regional identities. In 1950 Riyadh's population was 83,000. Now it is around 4,000,000. Within one or two generations the city's population increased by 4,719 per cent. This rapid change made these cities resemble Khobar and Dammam in that the majority of their inhabitants maintain their distinctive original identities. The fact that each local migrant group tends to live in a specific neighbourhood in these big cities makes it difficult for them either to maintain their previous identity or construct a new one as city dwellers. However, some might argue that the Hijaz still possesses a strong regional identity in spite of in-state migration. For example, Mai Yamani's book *The Cradle of Islam: The Hijaz and the Quest for an Arabian Identity* makes a case for the existence of such a strong regional identity.[16] The core of her argument is that Hijazi elite families developed cultural rituals to preserve their identity as a response to Najdi rule. She then provides a detailed analysis of these private rituals. Although it is true that such an identity exists, it applies to a small group of people in different cities of the western regions. The

111

author is very explicit that the group's identity is not shared by other inhabitants of their towns. This means that their identity, which was once that of the majority, has been reduced, due to in-state migration, to a minority identity.

The second element is the ability of a region to reproduce its own local elite. By local elite I mean the group that acts as brokers, directly or indirectly, between the state and the local population. These elites play a significant role in shaping, framing, and channelling the region's grievances and issues. They can be local public officials, religious scholars, merchants, intellectuals, professors, etc. Some regions are able to keep reproducing their own elites, while others are not. Different factors influence this outcome. For example, the local elites of the small towns around Riyadh tend to migrate to Riyadh. This is because the city has better education, job opportunities, higher government positions, and so on. This migration prevents these small towns from having stable local elites that can manipulate their own identity and reshape it in ways that make it able to mobilize their inhabitants. The same situation applies to the towns in the southern regions. The population there needed to migrate to big cities in order to secure jobs and have better education. Beside these socio-economic reasons, the fact that religious institutions are dominated by religious scholars from the central regions means that the judicial and religious positions in these towns are filled by people who do not share the same regional identity.

There are two factors that helped Buraydah to reproduce its regional elite. The first is its distance from Riyadh, which meant that several universities opened branches there. In the late 1970s and early 1980s the two universities in Riyadh, King Saud University (KSU) and Imam Muhammad Ibn Saud University, opened branches in Buraydah. The KSU branch taught agriculture, veterinary science, economics, and administration. Later, in 1998, a new science college was added, and in 2001 a medical school was included. The Imam branch taught Islamic studies, social sciences, and literature. In 2004 the two branches were amalgamated to form a new university called Qassim University. The existence of higher education in a variety of disciplines ensures that a significant segment of the youth will remain in the region to complete their studies. Moreover, it has helped to supply the local administrative units with manpower from the region.

The other factor that has facilitated this phenomenon is the fact that Buraydah was an important religious centre. This means that, unlike most of the other regions, the city's religious elite consists of local people. Preachers, judges, religious intellectuals, etc. are all from Buraydah. Having a religious elite from the region helps them to act as brokers. In other words, while they act as agents of the state, they will also help in representing and channelling the region's interests. This function is lacking in other regions, which have externally appointed elites.

In Qatif the economic, educational, and religious factors created different dynamics in terms of allowing the city to reproduce its regional elite. The fact that it is close to the oil industry serves it in two ways. First, it has provided its population with the opportunity to find work without leaving their town. Workers from other regions need to leave their homes and live in workers' camps, or, later, in the new emerging cities of Khobar and Dammam. This situation has allowed the city to keep an important segment of its population in town, part of which became politicized and played an important role in the labour movement in the 1950s and 1960s. They were thus able to mobilize their community to provide shelter, food, and support for workers who went on strike.[17] Second, although Qatif was close to the oil industry, it was not as close as other oil cities such as Dammam and Khobar. This relative distance made it a less attractive destination for migrant workers to settle. Instead, these workers settled in the oil cities. This situation allows Qatif to at least partially sustain its demographic homogeneity.

The same thing applies to education. While there is no university in Qatif, the universities in nearby Dammam and Dhahran allow Qatifis the opportunity to get an education without leaving their region. In 1963 the College of Petroleum and Minerals was opened in Dhahran. Its purpose was to provide Aramco with Saudi engineers and administrators. In 1975 the college became a university, and in 1987 it became King Fahd University for Petroleum and Minerals. The university only admits men, and is considered the most prestigious university in Saudi Arabia. In 1975 another university, King Faisal University, was founded in the Eastern Region. It has branches in Dammam and Hasa. In 2009 the Dammam branches were separated and combined to form a new university called the University of Dammam. These universities helped the Qatifi population to continue their education in most of the major disciplines without needing to leave their home towns. As with the oil industry, the fact that these universities were located in Dammam, Dhahran, and Hasa meant that the students from regions outside the Eastern Province seek residence in these towns and avoid Qatif.[18]

The final aspect is the issue of religion. While the Saudi state sent Sunni scholars, preachers, and judges, who are predominantly from the central region, to Sunni areas, non-Sunni regions, such as Qatif, Najran, and parts of Hasa, were allowed to continue relying on their own regional religious elite. This means that the preachers, scholars, and judges in these regions will be local. For most of its history, the Shi'i court in Qatif has taken responsibility for civil affairs, endowments, and property matters for the Shi'a population of Qatif. The huge demand for religious experts caused some of the Qatifi people to travel to the Shi'i religious educational centres in Iraq and Iran. Among these religious experts are leading Qatifi opposition figures such as Hassan al-Saffar, who studied in Kuwait and became a preacher in one of Qatif's mosques.

Prospects for Trans-Regional Alliance?

This chapter has emphasized the role of regional identity in influencing the outbreak of protests in Saudi Arabia. It did that by moving beyond what it characterized as a 'two sectarian worlds' paradigm that made it difficult to identify and explain why some cities in Saudi Arabia are sites of protest and others are quiet. Relying on a modified version of Timur Kuran's rationalist theory on revolution, the chapter was able to suggest one theory that explains the incidence of protest in both Qatif and Buraydah. It shows why some Saudi regions have more powerful regional identities than others. Moreover, it provides two factors that allow regional identities to motivate protest.

While the theory suggests that it is highly unlikely for a nationwide protest to occur in Saudi Arabia, I would like to conclude with a few remarks on the prospects of trans-regional alliance. By this, I mean some kind of coordinated actions between regional protesters acting on separate regional agendas. An example of such trans-regional solidarity is when Qatifi women protested in support of Buraydah's women on 6 March 2013.[19] Sometimes protest action in one region can influence that in another region without leading to a trans-regional alliance. For example, Buraydah's protesters use the phrase 'A lion on me, and an ostrich in Qatif'. The original phrase is a part of a poem by a seventh-century Arab poet who mocked the brutal Umayyad ruler of Iraq al-Hajjaj ibn Yusuf for being harsh on him but a coward in the battlefield. The original phrase says 'A lion on me and an ostrich in war'. The lion and the ostrich are used as metaphors for bravery and cowardice, respectively. Buraydah's protesters use a modified version of the phrase to claim that the government adopts harsh oppressive policies against them, while being more lenient in Qatif. Moreover, Buraydah's activists usually compare what they have gained from their protests with gains by Qatifi activists. Sometimes this comparison takes a competitive form, in which Buraydah's activists ask their regional brethren to be better than Qatif in their struggle.[20] These forms of Qatifi influence in Buraydah do not contain any potential for trans-regional alliance. This is because Qatif's activism is mentioned in the following style: 'Hey X Buraydah's activists, how come these Shi'a protesters in Qatif were able to gain Y while you could not?' In other words, the sectarian element that is an important component in both regional identities reduces the degree of trust that is a crucial element in any attempt at a trans-regional alliance. The above examples show that there are different forms of trans-regional influence that can, in one form, lead to an alliance, and, in another, do not. It is worth further investigation to understand how regional actors see each other, and how, what, and through what means do they learn from each other. The basic aim of this chapter is to highlight the importance of regionalism in understanding Saudi politics, and how this could take us beyond dominant frameworks.

5

FROM HASM TO HAZM

SAUDI FEMINISM BEYOND PATRIARCHAL BARGAINING

Nora Doaiji

In studies of the Arab world, women are portrayed as either being trapped by religion and society or as inescapably tools of legitimization for authoritarian states. Such an understanding is even more prevalent of Saudi Arabia, where a lack of democracy and a perceived abundance of traditionalism have led to an assumed absence of feminist movements altogether, particularly those that operate beyond the state. This is furthered by the assumption that 'citizen women need authoritarian states more than men do'.[1]

The aim of this chapter will be to problematize these assumptions. It will argue that Saudi feminists posed contentions within 'movement moments' in which they increasingly promoted a Saudi feminism beyond state feminism and in rejection of patriarchal bargaining. This chapter will not attempt to argue this through simply holding up 'successful' Saudi women activists to counter such limiting narratives, which ultimately only asserts a sort of 'exceptionalism'. Instead, through careful analysis, and a heavy reliance on primary sources, it will consider Saudi women as situated within a feminist activist framework, inspired by social movement theory, particularly Zakia Salime's concept of 'movement moments'. And, in doing so, it will situate, rather than exceptionalize, trends in Saudi feminism as part of a complex fabric of Saudi political action in the forms of activism, alliances, mobilizations, and within movement moments.

In arguing that their feminism grew increasingly beyond the state, this chapter will consider how, during the recent period of the Arab Spring and the rise of social media in Saudi Arabia, these Saudi feminist activists created and promoted an 'activist' womanhood that included feminist activism beyond the state. In the Arab Spring and Hasm[2] movement moment, this meant doing so under relatively fluid identifying categories of *nashitat*, *hasmawiyyat*, or *huquqiyyat*,[3] and 'female youth'. These later all intersected in a campaign which occurs in the subsequent Hazm[4] movement moment under the identifying categories of 'feminists' and 'activists', which became, tellingly, interchangeable. Again, these feminists firmly established their 'activist' womanhood; this time, against challenges of a new state womanhood: Hazm-inspired 'nationalists', in addition to challenging other womanhoods of the state, such as 'pious' and 'cosmopolitan' womanhoods. However, one symptom of the Hazm movement moment, among other factors, is that a category of women active during the Arab Spring found it essentially impossible to partake in this 'activist' womanhood: the Islamist-leaning women who were involved in the political prisoners' campaign. Due to constraints of space, they will not be discussed in this chapter.

Thus, this chapter will show that their feminism was also increasingly beyond patriarchal bargaining with the state. Rather than then simply calling on the state to 'save' them, these feminists increasingly used this framing to focus on how the state is not their 'saviour'. In this way, although they are ultimately referring to the state in their demands, as any other movement must, I argue that they increasingly seek to do so on their *own* terms, rather than those of the state.

Past Studies on Saudi Women and Chosen Analytical Framework

The first trend within the literature on Saudi women is the statist approach.[5] It reduces Saudi feminism to feminism espoused by the state, in defiance of society.

118

Another trend is based on an Orientalist and modernist approach. It either comes to the shallow[6] conclusion that Saudi feminism is entirely absent, either because of Saudi Arabia's ISIS-like state and society or due to the state regarding societal divisions over Saudi women as among its 'survival skills'.[7] This has been challenged by competing, subalternist literature, particularly from anthropologists who drew attention to Saudi women's social and familial lives[8] and their writings.[9] A noticeable theme among these is that their approach is often executed along the very modernist lines that they critique.[10]

This chapter will build on this trend in drawing on Madawi Al-Rasheed's work[11] that counters both the statist and Orientalist approach and argues that the state formed a 'religious nationalism', followed by a more 'cosmopolitan' image, which represented Saudi 'womanhoods' as 'pious' or 'modern' subjects and the source of 'Saudi exceptionalism'.[12] It will also draw on Le Renard's work[13] within this trend that focused on 'everyday feminisms' of urban, middle-class Saudi women. It moved away from modernist lines and adopted a more Foucauldian approach that feminist transformations 'signify shifting power relations and ways of governing',[14] and it is this aspect that this chapter aims to build on.[15] This will be in combination with a more recent work[16] which focuses on Saudi activism, specifically Hasm, during the Arab Spring. It will attempt to fill a gap in the literature by considering a growing group of 'activist' Saudi feminisms that emerged in 2011.[17] In turning to how it emerged 'from below', it will counter accusations that Saudi feminism might be understood as consistently one-directional, where the state 'allows', 'permits', and 'uses' it from above and that it is bound by its function as state feminism, which 'seems to satisfy the leadership'.[18]

This chapter will rely on a methodology of data collection, including structured and semi-structured interviews, as well as discourse analysis and media research, predominantly of the 'new' social media. Second, it will utilize 'theoretical extension' to draw on Zakia Salime's theory of movement moments.[19] While her theory was related to women's movements in Morocco, it is nonetheless relevant as holding both theoretical explanatory power as an analytical framework and applicability as a study of women's movements under a monarchical system. Specifically, it has two main characteristics which this chapter will utilize. The first characteristic is a focus on interdependent trajectories and fluid identifications among Islamist and feminist movements, where she studied them relationally rather than comparatively. The second characteristic is a focus on movement moments that incorporate historical, cultural, and political contingencies and signify 'turning points'[20] in non-linear, contradictory trajectories. This chapter will similarly study interdependency and dialectical exchanges resulting in mutually influenced movements across various 'moments', in this case Hasm and the Arab Spring, followed by Hazm. This will serve to critique binaries and dichotomies between Saudi feminism and Saudi political activism, and thus the assumed equivalence of Saudi feminism with state feminism. This will also counter social movement theory (SMT) literature's tendency to reduce mobilization to structural opportunities and constraints existing outside the movements themselves.[21] Instead, it draws on emerging directions in SMT which adopt more nuanced approaches of 'orienting devices', such as the concept of contention and a valuing of informal and interpersonal networks as central to mobilization.[22]

Saudi Arabia, Hasm, and the Arab Spring

Although it is difficult to determine what precisely the term 'Arab Spring' means, it can be said that the Saudi government has not only taken note of it, but has also realized that, whatever it may mean, it has imposed its presence on the country. The Arab Spring was appealed to as a dazzling event with which both direct and indirect members of the government wanted to be associated, because its force as a positive rhetorical tool could not be avoided. In an interview with the Charlie Rose Show, Prince Turki ibn Faysal, former ambassador to the USA, stated:[23] 'I think Saudi Arabia over the past eighty years has been going through an Arab Spring.' And Prince Khalid ibn Faysal, a self-proclaimed poet, told[24] an audience of students at their graduation ceremony, 'You started the Saudi Spring eighty-two years ago. The miracle is you always surpass others ... you proved that there is a miracle in this land, called the Saudi man.'[25]

For Saudi women, the Arab Spring meant an emerging Saudi feminist movement and activist networks, which produced campaigns for women's driving and voting, as well as the mobilization of previously apolitical women in the form of university protests. Crucially, it also meant an intersection with other activist movements such as Hasm. In what follows, the categories of *nashitat*, *huquqiyyat*,[26] and *hasmawiyyat*[27] as new emerging variations of 'activist' Saudi womanhood will be considered within the Arab Spring and Hasm movement moment. These womanhoods found definition and legitimacy in ways they had not done before, and all while forming and operating beyond the state, its feminisms, and 'acceptable' Saudi womanhoods. Additionally, Saudi feminism posited by actors of these categories will be shown as not only increasingly forgoing their bargaining position with the state, but also questioning and objecting to the very terms on which the relationship between the state and Saudi female citizens were based.

I. *Nashitat*: Women's Driving Campaigns, the Arab Spring, and Hasm

The start of the Saudi feminist movement beyond the state began following the release of Manal al-Sharif and the start of the Women2Drive campaign on 17 June 2011.[28] While it began in mid-2011, this shift heightened over the campaign's second year in 2012 and with the subsequent October 26 campaign during 2013–14. Specifically, from its first manifestation (2011–12) to its second (2013–14), the diagnostic framing of grievance shifted to the state rather than society or Islam, whether in the campaign's founding statements or more broadly in its general rhetoric and framings, as well as increased intersection with and influence from Hasm. This signified an increased tendency to promote a rejection of patriarchal bargaining as a means of achieving feminist aims.

A main source of this shift was the responsiveness of the campaign to public critique online. For instance, during its timid start, critics framed the campaign's focus on women's driving as mistakenly blaming society, as well as being narrow and frivolous in focus. It was often contrasted with legal reform for Saudi divorcees and widows, who were framed as experiencing the 'real' hardships of women's lack of rights in Saudi Arabia. To counter this, the Women2Drive campaign sought to reframe their cause in a way that would resonate as more meaningful. In

September 2011 the campaign announced that the women's driving campaign was from that time just one campaign within a larger movement, now named My Right to Dignity, or Right2Dignity.[29] Manal al-Sharif included the hashtag #SaudiWomenSpring with her announcement, indicating that the initiative had not departed from its inspiration in the Arab Spring. Similarly, the movement's name itself, with its emphasis on rights and dignity, also evoked Arab Spring norms and reflected this movement moment.

On the other hand, Women2Drive's first identifying documents under the auspices of the new movement on 25 September 2011 was entitled 'Our Identity and our Names', and stated: 'We strive to end all discrimination against women and restore their rights that have been bound by societal customs that contradict with Islamic Sharia. We do not condone this fact to be used for any other political or personal goals.'[30] Alongside this founding statement, the campaigners repeatedly distributed a 2005 statement by Prince Nayif, then the minister of interior, in which he stated that women's driving was 'a societal issue that is for society to decide'.[31] In its timidity towards 'political ideological classifications' or 'political agendas', its touting of official statements, and its emphasis on the social in its diagnostic framing, it may have appeared that this campaign simply represented a continuation of similar methods used in the earlier women's driving campaign of 2007–9. Such earlier attempts did not always appear distinct from state feminism in how they related, as activists, to the state. This was particularly obvious in how its main member, al-Sharif, often also framed the ban on driving as a social taboo to be broken, aside from being a state-sanctioned ban. Such tactics placed the campaign firmly within the framework of state feminism, in which the state is the benevolent grantor of rights denied by social norms.

However, it is a mistake to stop at this conclusion. Instead, such tactics ought to be understood as different from the previous campaign of the early 2000s in that they were only an opening gambit to avoid repercussions, rather than a static ideological commitment. This is because such activism was considered suspect at its beginning in 2011, before non-state 'activist' womanhood had risen to prominence as an alternative to the 'acceptable' state version.

Evidence of this loose ideological commitment is the way the campaign then shifted away from such rhetoric, showing again its responsiveness to context. This was signified first in the activists' willingness to forgo the demand for women to be permitted to drive, which was deemed apolitical, and adopt a larger political project concerned with the political status of women in Saudi Arabia, i.e. their relationship with the state, the public sphere, and the nature of female citizenship. Additionally, this resulted in the campaign being subjected to continuous pressures to be more expansive in its concerns and, as we will see, led to a political turn in both the members and the movement. Furthermore, the campaign shifted after the activists' own learning experiences of repeated repressive reactions from the state, rather than the religious and social spheres. For instance, the campaign's second statement, issued only days after its founding one, was dedicated to condemning the security services' targeting of its members and other women who attempted to drive. It also boldly criticized the Ministry of Interior and encouraged women to reject investigation, demand a lawyer, and publicize any physical or legal harassment by arguing that challenging the state with 'publication is the best remedy to end these harassments'.[32]

Thus, a nascent movement beyond state feminism is observable at these beginnings of the Right2Dignity movement and the Women2Drive campaign of 2011–12. It clearly continued and increased when compared to the subsequent October 26 driving campaign of 2013–14. In this campaign's identifying document, which was in the form of a petition as its website had been blocked by the Saudi state, it stated first its rejection of the previous focus on the social aspect and a demand for state accountability: 'If the state refuses to lift the current ban on women driving, we demand that it provide citizens justification for its refusal, and not to transfer responsibility for such a decision to a societal consensus as an alternative justification.'[33] The statement then turned to a highly political demand: 'In the event that the government does not lift the ban on women driving, and does not provide justification for its continued refusal, we demand that it provides a mechanism to enable "society" to express what they want.' In evoking the fact that society is not even asked its opinion on issues, the campaign turned the focus on the social sphere on its head to critique the state and its governance, and hinted at demanding an altered political system with a more participatory form of governance. Finally, the petition concluded with a feminist rejection of the 'patriarchal bargaining' most often characteristic of Saudi feminism: 'We ask for this because we cannot find any justification for the government's opposition to women driving their cars. The state is not a parent and citizens are not children or minors.'[34]

This rhetoric was not restricted to the petition. Instead, it was promoted consistently by the campaigners, and rivalled the dominant framings of the issue. What is also most noteworthy is that this line of reasoning from the October 26 campaign also appeared in the activism of Hasm. Specifically, it echoed a September 2011 interview on al-Hurra with Mohammad al-Qahtani, a Hasm co-founder, who addressed[35] the association's stance on the women's driving campaign.[36]

It is not surprising that this later showed up in the petition of the October 26 campaign, as part of its context was influenced by Hasm, in terms of both ideology and mobilization, and some of its members were among the unofficial supporters of Hasm. The very fact of this intersection also serves as evidence of this shift in Saudi feminism away from state feminism. This is because the Hasm movement was clearly externally understood and internally designated as political in its members, demands, and the movement itself in relation to the state. In combination with the Arab Spring of this movement moment, it was facilitative and formative of this new trend of a Saudi feminism beyond state feminism.

Through an extensive process of mapping activist networks, as well as tracking their public and private support and efforts, it became clear that numerous activists of both women's driving campaigns had many links with Hasm at two levels: both in terms of actual alliances and of the diffusion of political ideas. Aside from some well-known or predictable intersections, such as Maha al-Qahtani or Aziza al-Yousef, there were also some surprising ones that demonstrated the strength of this movement moment in facilitating such shifts and intersections.

An example is Loujain al-Hathloul. While she acted as an independent feminist activist, Eman al-Nafjan, a co-founder of the October 26 campaign and unofficial supporter of Hasm, explained in a post how Loujain al-Hathloul's relationship with the campaign was welcomed from its start in October 2013, as al-Hathloul was chosen as the face of the campaign and presented its first public announcement in a video online.[37] Her most prominent and public intersection with Hasm was in the form of a high-profile 'letter' to then-King 'Abdullah on 22 August 2013. In a letter-like, twenty-six-tweet statement, al-Hathloul recounted Hasm's history as an association and its demands for an end to arbitrary arrests and corruption and for an elected parliament. She then likened its goals to the Declaration of Human Rights.[38] What makes this surprising is that al-Hathloul was first known to the Saudi public simply for her rejection of the veil in a short video posted on Keek,[39] after which she initially mainly focused on public critiques of the social constraints on Saudi women. This shows how al-Hathloul herself independently underwent the same shift that is traced here as happening more broadly in the campaign itself.

Even more surprising is that Manal al-Sharif participated in such signs of support for Hasm, although at a much lesser rate. This can be seen in how she drew a connection between the mutual struggle and trial of feminist activists Wajeha al-Huwaider and Fawziyah al-Owaini and the trial of Hasm members. She exclaimed on 16 June 2013: 'I washed my hands since the days of the trial of Hasm, but I convinced myself that there was a "scrap" of hope and kept wishing [for a positive response from the state]. Today [after the trial of the feminist activists] I wash my hands with Clorox.'[40] This is surprising given her ideational stance[41] as one of the more classically liberal members of the campaigns, like Saudi women activists of the 1990s. In other words, she held a slight bias towards favouring state feminist methods in focusing on the social aspect,[42] and showed unease about fully accepting political activism or reformist efforts that intersected with Tanwiri trends of thought. However, what is clear from this is that, like al-Hathloul, this shift in al-Sharif mirrored a broader shift in her own Right2Dignity movement. Thus, these examples reveal how a shift in the campaigns' strategies and rhetoric was also reflected at the ideological level of these mobilized activists.

These exchanges and diffusions did not occur without internal negotiations, however. In describing a dispute that happened between Hasm and some of these women activists who were more ideologically liberal leaning and had more direct alliances with Hasm, rather than mainly public supporters, Maha al-Qahtani explained in an interview with the author: 'The *ithniniyya* [*diwaniyya* or meeting held regularly on Mondays] were started and recorded so that Hasm could disseminate its political ideas and goals online. The women's section disputed it as unfair since women were not allowed to attend, but the reason was fearing for them and because the *ithniniyya* was open to the public and many *mabahith* (secret police) were always in attendance.' One way that this was resolved was by convening alternate meetings held by women, for other women to attend. It was also only semi-public, and entry was predicated on an existing member deeming a newcomer to be 'safe' to join in. Aziza al-Yousef describes other internal negotiations in regard to the driving campaign's relationship with Hasm as follows: 'As for the women activists, some of them were interested and supported Hasm. Others were scared at first, they feared Hasm's project was a repressive one. But currently I think the picture is much clearer to everyone.'

II. *Huquqiyat or Hasmawiyyat*: Women's Involvement with Hasm and Support for the Political Prisoners' Campaign

Maha al-Qahtani also explained in her interview that the involvement with Hasm among women, while including a few affiliates of the driving campaign, also extended largely to Saudi women who were not members of that campaign. She elaborated:

> Hasm was not against women's rights, they saw political reform as the main goal and the foundation of any political system that served the people. After the Arab Spring, there was a clear and felt interest from Saudi women, and at daring degrees, in political activism. They joined and helped the members of Hasm in writing, publicizing, and in-person meetings with women relatives of political prisoners and helped them with raising the issues of their relatives for mobilization of public support.

She acknowledged the necessity of these women's contributions to Hasm, saying that these activities 'lifted the burden or workload [that had been] solely on the Hasm members'. This marks further evidence of a trend towards a Saudi feminism beyond the confines of state feminism.

An example of their involvement came during the first[43] semi-public trial[44] of Hasm's most prominent founding members, Mohammad al-Qahtani and Abdullah al-Hamid, which began on 3 September 2012. Numerous Saudi women activists began to write blogs, post tweets,

126

and speak to international media, as well as to international human rights organizations such as Amnesty and Human Rights Watch. They also started hashtag campaigns, updated and translated Wikipedia pages, wrote posts in English for other websites—all in support of Hasm and its call for civil and political rights, as well as for democratic reform in Saudi Arabia.

Through such activities these activists reproduced a Saudi feminism that was beyond state feminism, as an extension of the Arab Spring, and held such political activism as inextricable from their own aspirations as women activists. This represented a trend, and many of these women began to call themselves *huquqiyyat*, or 'female rights activists', as distinguished from 'women's rights activists'. To a lesser extent they were sometimes also called *hasmawiyyat*, after the rights organization's name, Hasm. Ideologically they were largely a mix of the following groups: previously non-political youth, leftists, Arabists, Tanwiris, and liberals prepared to work alongside activists with slight Islamic ideational tendencies.

In addition to focusing on Hasm itself, they also began to work within the campaign for political prisoners' rights, which Hasm had taken on. One particular instance of this is Nofah Abdulaziz. She was among the most prominent younger activists, and worked tirelessly on following Hasm's work and assisting in its involvement in the political prisoners' campaign. She also worked to promote the Arab Spring-themed concepts, disseminated further by Hasm, such as the right to protest, to a fair trial, freedom of expression, to elected government, and the like. She was among the first to use the well-known campaign hashtag e3teqal, and according to some reports[45] was its creator. She used this as early as 2011 to promote and mobilize for these concepts and to disseminate information about the campaign's protests and arrests online. She even held hunger strikes for many of these political cases. This same hashtag would later form the e3teqal Twitter account, which was responsible for essentially running the political prisoners' virtual campaign and its many physical protests, up until 2013.

Another example of *huquqiyya* supporters of the political prisoners' campaign is Leila al-Nahdi, a Saudi woman who was led to activism following the Jeddah floods of 2009. Al-Nahdi had a very public marriage to Asem al-Ghamdi, who became a prominent Saudi reporter for al-Jazeera with a presence in the Saudi Twittersphere. Both had attended and participated in Tanwiri or Islamist reformist conferences in Qatar that focus on active citizenship as a form of *nahda*, or Arab Spring-like change. Their attendance at one of these conferences, along with the very prominent Essam al-Zamil, was recorded and, in the recorded video, al-Nahdi is holding a microphone and describing her contribution and campaigning efforts for the political prisoners' movement in Saudi Arabia. Following the designation of the Muslim Brotherhood as a terrorist group, with the promulgation of two new laws against terrorism and cybercrime,[46] this trend of supporters were no longer able to mobilize for this campaign. Not only that, al-Nahdi herself had to lessen her online presence and activism at this point, as recordings of their attendance at the conference were disseminated online and they were framed as 'Ikhwani revolutionaries' who were being 'trained' in Qatar to cause 'incitement' and public unrest in Saudi Arabia.

Aside from considering such examples, it is also of interest to investigate how some *huquqiyyat* related to their *nashitat* counterparts within this movement moment. This is possible by turning to the work of the 'consciousness-raising group', which was initiated by *huquqiyyat* at the start of the semi-public Hasm trials in October 2012 and remained active until January 2015. The group explained that it focused on 'spreading political and rights awareness in Saudi Arabia in an impartial manner' and promised to 'document what we are used to being forgotten ... spreading and learning from these [activist] experiences'.[47] The group covered the histories of each Hasm co-founder, their trials, and all other the concepts and causes embraced by the association.

Besides this, what is most relevant is that the group was also careful to focus equally on 'the feminist movement in Saudi Arabia', and featured this on both its Twitter account and main website. It did so by following both 'liberal' activists and 'Islamist' women activists. This was possibly motivated by the emphasis on impartiality by the consciousness-raising group in its founding statement and social media accounts. More broadly, it stemmed from a priority among *huquqiyyat* or *hasmawiyyat* women, as they tended to contrast their own impartiality with their view of other women activists, and considered them to be partial to their causes, whether liberal or Islamist. For instance, the *huquqiyyat* often criticized the 'feminist silence on the arrests of women for political prisoners, under the claim that they are women with extremist ideas' which they held as comparable to 'conservative women, which make up most the women relatives of political prisoners, attack women who call for driving or elections, under the claim that they are liberal ideas'.[48] However, the complaint[49] from these *huquqiyyat* against feminists might fit some, but such an assertion about all *nashitat* can be problematized given the existing intersections between even the liberal-leaning activists of the driving campaigns and Hasm, as previously examined.

III. 'Young Women': University Protests and the Arab Spring

Considering Saudi women in university protests highlights an important example of grassroots, youth efforts that tapped into the emergent activist Saudi womanhood promoted by these more networked Saudi feminists. Additionally, this shows how 'everyday' feminisms began to take hints from these new feminist trends, rather than the established example of state feminism.

In March 2012 hundreds of students participated in organized protests at King Khalid University, in the southern city of Abha. These protests were started by female students, soon followed by students in the male sections of the university. Online Saudi commentary helped to frame the protest as an example of 'peaceful protest' and compared them to those students who had participated in the start of numerous revolutions of the Arab Spring. This was perhaps the only visible protest to occur in Saudi Arabia during the Arab Spring to be followed by a government response that included real gains and demands met— namely, the ouster of the head of the university. It was followed by female student protests at Qassim University in Buraydah, as well as Tabuk University in the northern city of Tabuk. None of these students shied away from using both social media and traditional media, such as the *Ya Hala* show on the Rotana Khalijia TV channel, to publicize their cause. This is noteworthy for previously non-political actors, given the risks of doing so, since protests are illegal in Saudi Arabia and such stances can easily be interpreted as opposition to the state.

Their combination of rights rhetoric, evoking the Arab Spring, and a willingness to engage in public, even given the risk of losing 'patriarchal bargaining power' with the state, arguably indicates these women as a budding instance of something beyond Saudi state feminism. It also shows how Saudi feminists were emboldened and affected, like all else, by the Arab Spring and its popularization of the social category of youth, which increased the public and self-perception of this group as a legitimate actor with unheard, public, positions and demands, often in opposition to the state. This sense of legitimacy as an actor remained constant, and emerged more forcefully in the following movement moment, when many previously non-political youths would participate in various ways and degrees in the campaign against the state's male guardianship system.

Saudi Arabia, Hazm, and the Yemen War

In this movement moment, starting most prominently by the end of 2014, a renewed incorporation of the Saudi state's early gendered project of religious nationalism occurred within the context of broader geopolitical and sectarian rivalry in the region and a new king's desire to surpass his predecessor's legacy. However, while equally masculine, this version of religious nationalism was modified in two aspects.

On the one hand, unlike the early religious nationalism, in which King Faysal's state incorporated religiosity both externally and internally, this Hazm nationalism, although beginning as religious in nature in both spheres,[50] dramatically decreased as such internally, probably as part of a strategy to counter ISIS, while being maintained externally, probably to gain an advantage in dealings with Iran. While this gradual decrease might be interpreted as similar to the way in which King Faysal's form of religious nationalism used modernism to counter Nasserism, although in this case it would be to project an anti-ISIS image, this new form of nationalism is nonetheless increasingly taking on a distinctly counter-religious nature in a way that did not occur as part of the early 'religious nationalism' and is more so than the previous king's purported modernism following 9/11.

On the other hand, this Hazm nationalism grew more representative of a new masculine Saudi exceptionalism, in the form of an unprecedented militarization of the idea of Saudi nationhood. The name for this moment itself reflected this emphasis on a masculine nationalism with a militaristic rather than religious focus: *hazm* (meaning 'decisive') stemmed from Operation Decisive Storm, the state's name for its war in Yemen, and the state and its supporters began to promote the term as a symbol of the decisiveness, strength, and machismo of the new king's era. For instance, the king was increasingly called the 'King of Hazm', in contrast to the previous king's unofficial title as the King of Humanism. Such militaristic and 'decisive' sentiments were initially largely adopted by Saudi society due to the sectarian regional context, and arguably remain thanks to international discursive trends such as Islamophobia, which also had the effect of encouraging an equally 'rally around the flag' atmosphere.

For Saudi women and men, the increased masculinization of the Saudi state and the militarization of the idea of the Saudi nation has meant changed, Hazm-inspired gendered constructs of both Saudi masculinity and femininity or womanhoods within the Saudi nation. It is in this context that unorthodox Saudi womanhoods were able to emerge under King Salman's idea of the nation, but only to the extent that they furthered valuation of the military and acted as new Hazm state feminisms. For, 'precarious and treacherous as it may be, the war zone is not merely a wasteland for young women, but at times may also be a field ripe with possibilities for upwards social and economic mobility'.[51] And while the notion of Saudi women was promoted to symbolize the need for militant protection, other 'acceptable' Saudi womanhoods also emerged as militarized state feminisms within this new idea of nationhood.

One notable example of these new, 'acceptable', womanhoods is a Saudi female journalist, Haifa al-Zahrani, who gained recognition by adopting this Hazm state feminism throughout her coverage of Operation Decisive Storm in Yemen at the frontlines of the conflict. Al-Zahrani was featured in Saudi media, and was photographed wearing a military-style helmet and vest, even posing inside a military tank. Playing into the militarized idea of the nation and her 'masculine' feminist position in it, she argued publicly that she did not want to be 'treated as a girl' and 'on the ground, she demanded to be treated like a man'. In asserting her Hazm state feminism, she declared that this was not because she was brave, but because she was 'fulfilling a duty to the nation'.[52]

What is interesting to note here is that al-Zahrani was previously a feminist activist, supported Manal al-Sharif, and was a member of the Right2Dignity movement and its Women2Drive campaign of 2011. However, in a recent interview for this research she backtracked from this and stated:

> I was not a member in the sense of being a 'member'; rather, I was only of those that supported this campaign. The Arab Spring had no effect. ... [And anyone] who critiques the government holds no allegiance to the country. ... The best feminist efforts are in accordance with government laws and the worst is thinking they can force the government by outside organizations to grant their wishes.

Additionally, she asserted:

> Hasm is a traitor to the country and humanity and it does not deserve any support and I don't see any Saudi women supporting them. ... I don't see any issue between the feminist movement and the government, but rather between the feminist movement and society. The state fully supports women, even at varying times. What is more of a problem is societal acceptance.

The example of al-Zahrani shows not only how Hazm womanhoods were constituted during this moment by the state, but also how some feminist activists returned to bargaining with the state.[53]

In contrast, the popularized activist womanhood of the Hasm and the Arab Spring moment remained low profile, with only timid adoptions occurring. This is because the 'decisive' nature of the militarized national narrative implied that it would be likely to deem their non-state-sanctioned activity as traitorous to the nation, particularly following the start of King Salman's Operation Decisive Storm in Yemen.[54] This was reflected in the perspective of activists of Hasm and the Arab Spring movement moment, such as Maha al-Qahtani, who maintained a less than favourable stance towards the state, as stated in an interview with the author: 'I don't predict anything new in the current state of things, except maybe worse, because the current mentality is entirely authoritarian.'

Some activists perceived the situation as repressive but nonetheless sought to find a way to project 'balanced' or mediated activism. Tamador al-Yami, a member of the October 26 movement, stated cautiously that 'activism continues now through safer ways ... not movements out in the streets'. When asked specifically about the Hazm moment, al-Yami explained:

> Female activists were more hesitant than before after what happened to Loujain and Maysa and also the destabilization of the region made activists, females I mean, aware that when the country needs them to calm down, they will calm down. When the country has priorities and border issues to deal with and the country needs to focus on protecting its existence and national security, those activists will not do something crazy to jeopardize the security of their countries at such a time.

Furthermore, reflecting on the previously discussed trends among Saudi feminist activists, she stated:

> I don't think Saudi feminism is linked to Hasm whatsoever, or in any way. They are two different things. That one was a political movement asking for political rights. Feminism is not political, at all. It is just a women's rights movement, which is not aiming to change the status quo of any states, not even our government. It does not ask for much, except for the right to drive. So, it is simple, it's clear, it's straightforward, it doesn't have any other agendas except driving and it shouldn't be compared to any other movement, whether political or any other agenda except the rights of women.

The safer forms of activism that al-Yami mentioned seem to include those that focused on utilizing opportunities of this moment, such as Hatoon al-Fassi and Rasha Hefzi's work towards women entering municipal elections and participating in municipal councils, and Lama al-Suleiman, who resigned from her elected position after being denied her seat by some of the men on the municipal council.[55] On the other hand, Saudi feminist activists such as Halah al-Dosari of the October 26 campaign left the country altogether, for the time being at least.

In this way, the specific example of former activist al-Zahrani, the changed reactions of current feminist activists, the timid use of opportunity spaces, and, in sum, the general shift from Hasm to Hazm in Saudi Arabia brings up significant questions regarding the Saudi feminism of movement moments during the periods of greater repression and less conciliatory rhetoric, tactics, and alliances that the Arab Spring moment provided, most notably in Hasm. How do we understand these tensions between activists on methods and positions which have emerged, particularly in terms of their relationship to the political?

How do Saudi women pose an 'activist' womanhood now, beyond being subsumed into notions of state feminism and its 'acceptable' womanhoods? As we shall see, the next segment of this Hazm movement moment begins to offer some answers to these questions.

Saudi Arabia, Hazm, and Vision 2030

Cracks in this Hazm moment effect began to emerge under three circumstances. The first was the lengthy engagement in Yemen. Although Saudis did not feel its effects generally, except along the remote border in Najran, it was no longer a source of legitimacy for the state, since it had simply become a routine, long engagement, rather than a quick, victorious triumph for Saudi society to witness. Second, the Saudi public was beginning to feel the financial strains of the depressed oil market and the war in Yemen. Third, part of the Hazm moment's effect was that both the Saudi public and activists lay low in anticipation of Vision 2030,[56] as a sort of 'breath-holding' or 'pause' during that time. Upon its official release in April 2016, it put an end to speculation on its content and began the next stage of public consideration and critique.

Coinciding with Vision 2030, on 17 July 2016 Human Rights Watch released its report on the male guardianship system in Saudi Arabia,[57] which was the product of a one-year collaborative effort with Saudi feminists. It was introduced along with a coordinated Twitter hashtag #TogetherToEndMaleGuardianship to launch a budding campaign against the male guardianship system. This was mainly started by previously active women, particularly from the October 26 campaign, who also issued a petition calling for the end of the male guardianship system a month later.

The initial hashtag was used for a week, but after that the women who had started the campaign lost their control over it.[58] This was rhetorically marked by the change in the campaign's official hashtags to #StopEnslavingSaudiWomen, with a corresponding Arabic hashtag, 'Saudi Women Demand the Fall of the Guardianship', which ended in a number that changed each day of the campaign.

It was at this point that the campaign morphed into a much broader campaign that mobilized diverse circles and groups of women and men alike. Specifically, it included the previous categories of *nashitat*, *huquqiyyat*, and *hasmawiyyat*, and previously non-political youth of the Hasm and Arab Spring moment. The campaign was so forceful in its popularity and mobilization that it also brought state feminists into its fold: liberal-leaning columnists, women of the Shura Council, and other *nashitat* who had found a home in the state since their previous bouts of activism.

The most interesting aspect of this was the growth of the category of 'female youth' who had not previously been active, and had only participated in the Arab Spring during university protests. They grew in numbers as well as in diversity of ideology and sense of identity. Some who gained prominence even included Saudi female atheists, often also identified by highly specific gender and sexual orientations, and a growing network of *muhajirat*, Saudi women who had recently fled the country for various reasons, both religious and familial. It was as though they had sought to go beyond the state in a literal sense, whether beyond its religion or its borders.

As the campaign went on, these varied categories increasingly identified themselves as *niswiyyat* (feminists) and identified this as interchangeable with *huquqiyyat*. In this way, aside from young women, the previous projects by women's activists (*nashitat*) and female rights activists (*huquqiyyat* and *hasmawiyyat*) had merged. This is impressively evidenced by how even the *hasmawiyyat*, who had previously distrusted feminism as a theory or cause and preferred to campaign for human rights instead, were now fully identifying with this category and with the campaign.

Overall, the campaign went through many stages, faced nuanced discussions, and had fascinating dynamics. All of this, to varying degrees, was evidence of a Saudi feminism persistently beyond bargaining with the state and any adoption of its womanhoods. In what follows, the ways in which the campaign promoted this 'activist' womanhood against state feminists within the Hazm movement moment will be explored.

I. Saudi Feminists Utilizing Hazm-Style Masculine Nationalism for Hasm-Based Citizenship and the Reintroduction of the Arab Spring Activist Womanhood

Before the campaign turned its attention to state feminists, this Hazm movement moment's emphasis on nationhood, and Vision 2030's emphasis on citizens' rights and obligations to economic development, led the campaigners to communicate their positions within the nation. However, they did so by turning to an emphasis on Hasm-like citizenship; in other words, a concept based on engagement and rights of citizens in the political sphere. This was achieved mainly through utilization of the state's rhetoric and its new technological advances and tools of this period—specifically, its new e-governance programmes, such as YESSER in 2005, which were part of its efforts[59] to combat terrorism.[60]

For Saudi women this shift towards e-governance has meant that the guardianship system has found new life through such technological tools. Where it was previously open to possibly being overlooked in personal interactions with the state, it now became institutionalized and its requirements automated through such technologies. Amélie Le Renard traced gendered segregation in Saudi Arabia to 'modern means' such as technology and the discovery of oil wealth, and the further institutionalization of the guardianship system can be traced to similar modern means such as this move towards e-governance in the country.[61]

In combination with the opening of women-only sections of government offices, this led to some unexpected consequences for the state, which were taken advantage of by the campaign. For example, it has allowed Saudi women to become more involved, aware of their position as citizens in their increased experience of these services, while also heightening the visibility of restrictions that they find increasingly objectionable.

Such sentiments were incorporated into the campaigners' tactics, as they co-opted these technological intrusions by the state into citizens' lives to their advantage. For instance, they began to assert their position as 'true' Saudi citizens by posting online proof that they were Saudi women, in the form of pictures of themselves along with their new, digitized Saudi IDs, their Saudi passports, often alongside a protest sign with a written message deploring male guardianship or alongside their cellphones with their Twitter profiles showing onscreen. This tactic had not been used to this degree in previous campaigns, as women had been less willing to risk showing their identities so openly.

Another tactic came on Saudi Arabia's national day, as activists encouraged supporters to send telegrams directly to the king. While this strategy had been used before, what was novel this time is that it was accompanied by rhetorical framing that focused heavily on citizenship. Its supporters were reminded that they had a right to participate in such forms of protest against guardianship, and that they ought not fear any rumours of its illegality,[62] since they were simply exercising their right to engage as citizens. For the timid, they pointed out that telegrams could even be sent via government websites, also a co-optation of the move towards e-governance.

This also appeared in the way the campaign utilized how such moves towards e-governance made it easier to object through simply highlighting aspects revealed by e-governance improvements and referencing them[63] within online campaigns,[64] often through widely disseminated screenshots of government websites and forms. For instance, one campaigner named Nouf stated: 'On the automated list of claims that a guardian can raise in the Ministry of Justice's website is "deliver a woman to her *mahram*". She sounds like a bag of rice, not a human!'[65]

Thus, in their use of government advances such as e-governance and assertions of the campaign's Saudi identity, they were ultimately tapping into the rise in nationalist rhetoric of the Hazm movement moment. At the same time, this allowed them to also begin to reference citizenship, the right to protest rather than remaining passive, and their objections to restrictions on their freedom to do so. In doing so, they were pushing against the Hazm movement moment's more masculinist, nationalist beginnings to promote a more engaged Hasm or Arab Spring-like citizenship and to practise, once again, the 'activist' womanhood which it had been previously difficult to do within this movement moment's rhetorical frameworks.

II. Challenging the Saudi State's Pious, Cosmopolitan, and Hazm Womanhoods

Following this, the campaign turned its attention to the state-sanctioned and officially promoted Saudi womanhoods, whether 'religious' and 'pious' or 'cosmopolitan' and 'modern'.[66] Later it also turned its focus to countering the aforementioned Hazm womanhood, or Hazm state feminism, like that of al-Zahrani.

These images of Saudi womanhood were challenged through what is perhaps most unique to this campaign: the concept of a 'shame list'.

137

Within these shame lists[67] many opponents and perceived opponents of the campaign were challenged through interrogation of their stance on male guardianship, and how they aligned with state images of Saudi womanhood. This was often done through incessant commentary and screenshots. Each interrogation was disseminated in an organized fashion within master shame lists by a select few campaigners and then repeated in countless independent posts by readers of these lists and supporters of the campaign. Previously, this had never been done in such an organized fashion or with a focus on non-religious women. Instead, particularly during the driving campaigns, many supporters had reserved this kind of critique for religious figures.

It is important to note that all of the examples in this section were not brief episodes online, but rather were extensive critiques, some lasting for days. They were then repeated later in other stages or contexts of the campaign, and thus incorporated into the campaign's 'memory'[68] and rhetorical tools of persuasion. Just as Hasm attempted to create 'virtual forms'[69] of their trials, the campaigners essentially created a series of virtual trials of whomever they deemed as state-sanctioned womanhoods who objected to the campaign, its aims of removing the guardianship system, and its activist method of criticizing the state.

i) 'Pious' Womanhood

Much of the critical characterizations of such opponents dipped heavily into psychoanalysis.[70] The 'pious' womanhood was critiqued in the abstract, more than through attention to specific examples.[71] 'Pious' women who were against the campaign's demand to end the male guardianship system were deemed as either non-elite 'brainwashed, pitiful women' who were against their fellow women's rights or elite 'privileged, beneficiaries of the status quo'.

The non-elites were often labelled *durar*, hinting at a term given to 'respectable women' in Saudi religious rhetoric, and typically targeted non-elite women whom the campaigners deemed in need of feminist 'consciousness-raising' efforts[72] to awaken them from their 'psychological and patriarchic enslavement'. The elites were seen as conservative, privileged women who benefited from the country remaining as it was.

Those elite opponents who were not conservative themselves, but nonetheless represented the state's 'pious' womanhood against the campaign were labelled *mustashrifin*.[73] This label meant that they sought to present conservative or at least pro-conservative moral positions, but were not moral themselves in a pious or conservative sense. An example of how the campaigners critiqued women such as this is Rawda al-Yousef, known for her 2009 campaign My Guardian Knows What's Best for Me. Essentially, the campaigners framed these women as being willing instruments of the state in exchange for their bargaining position as elites, as evidence of the state's modern and cosmopolitan nature, while at the same time espousing the necessity for pious forms of womanhood, even if they themselves did not embrace such a lifestyle. In this way, the activists often framed these women as acting with a duplicity only matched by that of the state itself, which promoted both womanhoods simultaneously, in accordance with its own prerogatives, and while denying recognition to any other dissenting forms of womanhoods.

ii) 'Cosmopolitan' Womanhood

Those opponents who represented the state's 'cosmopolitan' womanhoods and did not promote piety were often labelled *ananiyyat*, or selfish women. These were not viewed as in need of consciousness raising, as they were considered knowledgeable about women's rights and feminism. Instead, the campaigners depicted opponents identified as such privileged, cosmopolitan women either as wanting to maintain their special status as privileged women for themselves and afraid of losing it, or as abstaining from or criticizing the campaign in order to enjoy the approval of Saudi men. More importantly, they were characterized as having rational or calculated reasons for their opposition, rather than psychological ones. In other words, they were seen as seeking to obtain or maintain a bargaining position with the state, or as more concerned with the political image of Saudi Arabia than with the status of its women.

An example of this was Adwa al-Dakheel, an upper-class 'modern' Saudi woman, popular social media personality, and MiSK affiliate.[74] In an al-Arabiyya interview, when asked to name a right that Saudi women needed, she replied with an abrupt 'No,' followed by 'Don't give me problems!' and finally: 'Saudi women need freedom, but not liberation.' While this may have been simply a fumbling of words due to al-Dakheel's surprise at the question itself, her desire to evade 'problems' made her heavily criticized online, including by activists such as Loujain al-Hathloul.[75] Al-Dakheel responded by stating: 'Liberation is to throw away your passport ... to feel the need to yell all the time. ... No one works more than I do in the name of Saudi women and the Saudi state.' Her use of the terms 'liberation' and 'yelling' reflects how al-Dakheel sought to contrast her own position in relation to the state with the unacceptable, 'activist' Saudi womanhood of the campaigners. Furthermore, the ways in which she was aware of her role as the state's 'proofs of modernity' is clear in her clinging to 'not throwing away your passports', as well as in her bold proclamation to the campaigners that her cosmopolitan lifestyle and modern persona, rather than being evidence of her privileged status or obligation to act, were, to the contrary, crucial, and that she operated 'in the name of' Saudi women and the state. What is important to note is the ways in which the campaigners fiercely rejected any such justification of cosmopolitan women's state feminism.[76]

iii) Hazm Womanhood

This privileged class of cosmopolitan Saudi women had not been subject to activists' critiques previously, or not to this extent. In response, they often began to evoke the new Hazm womanhood as a source of their legitimacy, as a form of pushback against these campaigners who represented a dissenting activist womanhood and an increasingly non-bargaining form of Saudi feminism. The activists of the campaign tended to focus their responses in three ways.

The first was by critiquing the ways in which these state feminists began to promote a 'society, not state' narrative around Saudi feminism, which represented the traditional representation by state feminists[77] of the state as Saudi women's 'saviour'. The second was by condemning bargaining methods of activism promoted by state feminists. Finally, rejecting such methods also entailed rejecting the state feminists' promotion of Hazm womanhoods and Hazm nationalism; in particular, rejecting those womanhoods that did not also allow for Arab Spring and Hasm-inspired state–citizen relationships or forms of governance. In other words, they focused on any that were unlike the co-opted Hazm nationalism that the feminists attempted to promote at the start of the campaign with their reintroduction of 'activism' through Vision 2030 and other means.

Ultimately, the result of these tactics is that the activists who challenged these Hazm womanhoods were shaping their campaign within this Hazm movement moment as one that posed, time and time again, a Saudi feminism that insisted on being beyond bargaining and distinct from state feminism. In doing so, they also displayed a constant theme throughout their activism, namely, Hasm and Arab Spring-themed critique of governance and citizen–state relations. To showcase this, this section will conclude with illustrative examples of how the last two tactics played out throughout the campaign, whether the tactic of condemning bargaining methods of activism promoted by state feminists or rejecting such methods also entailed rejecting the state feminists' promotion of Hazm womanhoods and Hazm nationalism.

III. Rejecting Hazm State Feminism and Its Promotion of Bargaining-Based Activism

In previous campaigns, both within and without the campaign itself, feminists were often torn between two positions: the liberal-leaning Lamya al-Suwailem's critique of 'Women Activists with Male Priorities!'[78] and Eman al-Quwaifli's defence of 'The Fairness of Bending the State's Arm'.[79] While the former critiqued a focus on activism that could be deemed 'political' in nature, a veiled criticism of women with Hasm or Arab Spring-themed goals as risking women-centric goals achievable through the state, the latter defended these, along with activism aimed at the state itself. In this campaign, however, activists promoted rhetoric in which the former position in this debate was virtually instantly delegitimized and the latter stance taken as a given.

A clear example of how this played out in exchanges with cosmopolitan women who adopted the bargaining method or a less accommodating Hazm nationalist stance towards activism is the example of a few defections by key liberal-leaning participants of the campaign,[80] such as Hailah al-Mashweh.[81] Despite having continuously promoted the campaign for months, they would suddenly announce their defection from it. Their justifications were often dependent on notions of patriotism that evoked the rhetorical framework of the Hazm movement moment, but, in this case, to disadvantage the campaign.

Ultimately, these defections were presented as following their 'discovery' of 'unacceptable' womanhoods in the campaign, in the form of activists who were critical of the state or against patriarchal bargaining with it. Al-Mashweh publicly announced her own defection as follows: 'This is the truth. [The campaign] is just a woman tweeting from outside the country, cursing the government, and you are all following her naively. It is my duty to point this out, for I know their tactics.'[82] She called for 'being less abrasive'[83] and described this approach in her next column. In it, she explained: 'I was active in this campaign … until al-Johara al-Otaibi turned my attention to the fact that it was being diverted from its cause.'

The 'unacceptable' feminist who troubled her was al-Anoud al-Tamimi. Within the campaign al-Tamimi represented one of the most prominent voices to openly identify with the previously analysed group of *hasmawiyyat* (female rights activists). She reflects how such women[84] merged with the cause of feminism in terms of ideology and mobilization, as reflected in the anti-male guardianship campaign. She explained this merge as such: 'Blaming feminism for supporting authoritarian[ism] is not fair. … For me, HASM is my cause, before all else. Nonetheless, it is ridiculous for anyone to demand women focus on being against authoritarianism [only] when they can't even get a passport by themselves.'[85] She often used the hashtags #WeAreAllHasm and #GetToKnowHasm[86] to promote ideas concerning democracy, freedom of speech, and political rights. At a time when many were not comfortable writing directly about Hasm, she did so with widely disseminated posts.[87] She was also among those who promoted and participated in hashtag campaigns such as #SaudiArabiaWithoutIllegalDetentions.[88]

Following her initial defection, Hailah al-Mashweh, along with al-Johara al-Otaibi, began to distinguish themselves from the campaign's activists with a new label and hashtag entitled *niswiyyat wataniyyat* or 'patriotic feminists', which they explained as beyond 'people with agendas … against the nation'[89] and indicating 'we work *with* the state

... and refused to have our causes used to incite against it'.[90] In doing so, they were evoking the previously discussed Hazm state feminism.

They also attempted to support their decision to defect by delegitimizing the campaigners. It was using this line of reasoning that al-Mashweh tended to refer to them as 'teenagers' and al-Otaibi contrasted them with examples, such as Latifa al-Shalaan of the Shura Council, as the 'right' kind of Saudi feminist, one who received praise from the state and served her country. Similarly, they began to evoke the state's 'pious' womanhood by asking: 'How can a Muslim, conservative society like Saudi Arabia's have homosexuals and atheists speaking for its women's rights? And those that approve external interference? Do they not have any sense of social strategies?'[91]

In response to al-Mashweh and al-Otaibi the campaigners again rejected such Hazm state feminisms, framed their *wataniyya* as a sign of blind patronage, and began to critique the very state-sanctioned womanhoods these women evoked by promoting the activist womanhood and the campaigners' version of Saudi feminism. For instance, Nouf, a visible activist of the campaign, responded by stating: 'Suddenly promoting the cause concerns you now? Suddenly you care who the demands are by, whether atheists, homosexuals, Christians, or rock-worshippers? I thought Haila used to critique the Sahwa!'[92] Here, she implied that these defectors were simply using Sahwist rhetoric (i.e. evoking the 'pious' womanhood) in their objections to delegitimize the activist Saudi feminists, even though they were liberal-leaning women who typically dedicated their time to critiquing the memory and effects of the Sahwa. Similarly, al-Anoud al-Tamimi, the prominent new activist of the campaign whom these defectors had deemed a 'dissident', responded: 'Whether atheist, homosexual, heretic, pro-outside interference, bald, wears pants, wears an Islamic *abaya* or a colored one, basic rights and just laws are for all these women.'[93]

Conclusion

This chapter has tried to show a Saudi feminism that is not synonymous with state feminism, and that this has taken the form of an increasing reluctance towards a citizen–state relationship marked by patriarchal bargaining with the state. Additionally, that Saudi feminists have increasingly promoted their own 'activist' womanhood, as distinct from 'acceptable' state womanhoods. However, this is not to say that such developments constitute inevitable progress. Instead, this chapter has used the concept of 'movement moments' that incorporate historical, cultural, and political contingencies and signify 'turning points' in non-linear, interdependent, and possibly contradictory trajectories. In using such a concept, I have sought to show how such moments translated into varying, often contradictory, trajectories for Saudi feminisms—whether in its shifting from the Arab Spring and Hasm to Hazm, or between statist and non-statist variants.

Ultimately, the importance and significance of this analysis is that it illustrates how Saudi feminist activism is not explainable by the prevalent understanding of Arab women as trapped by religion and society on the one hand, or as tools of legitimization for authoritarian states on the other. Such conclusions and findings hold particularly important implications given that this understanding is even more prevalent in the context of Saudi Arabia, where a lack of democracy and a perceived abundance of traditionalism have led to an assumed absence of feminist movements altogether. Or, an assumption that, in such a context, feminism could only be that of the state since 'citizen women need authoritarian states more than men do'[94] and thus they would never act beyond being inescapably a function of the state, whether as legitimizers, distractions, or patriarchal bargainers.

PART II

SAUDI ARABIA
AND TRANSNATIONAL SALAFIYYA

6

PRODUCING SALAFISM

FROM INVENTED TRADITION TO STATE AGITPROP

Andrew Hammond

Salafism has pressed its case in recent years as the expression of normative Sunni Islam in both belief and practice. The term has made its way
into public discourse in English since the 9/11 attacks, when its nov-
elty was such that there was no convention on how to spell the word,[1]
but in time it spurred considerable scholarly interest, at first in the
expanding field of 'transnational Salafism', but latterly in the origins of
the designation itself and the ideology it claims to represent.[2] Its trajectory in Arabic discourse, while of longer duration than its elaboration
in other languages, remains rather vexed. In this chapter I offer a diachronic analysis that attempts to bring out some problems in Salafism's
genealogy, its contested set of meanings, and its role in the Islamization
of Saudi foreign policy, looking at the little-studied example of its
engagement with Turkey.

The Iranian revolution in 1979 signalled an important shift in
Western discourse on Islam. Modernization theory's rejection of reli-

gion as an organizing force in society, which still retained currency at that time in scholarly discussion of the Islamic world, was overtaken by the notion of radical alterity and new attention to cultural difference. Discussion of the Islamic across various disciplines (and in media and policy discourse) began to reflect this new essentialism, ranging from the reduction of Islam to unsalvageable fundamentals (neo-conservative scholars such as Daniel Pipes) to the search for an Islamic liberalism (e.g. Leonard Binder's *Islamic Liberalism*). The essentialism works on two levels: treating Islam as the 'key' to understanding society and culture; and distilling elemental constitutive parts to this Islam.[3] With the entry of 'Salafism' into public discourse, Islam's domination of the social and political *imaginaire* in relation to all things Arab/Islamic/ Middle East has found new focus. Salafism vies to become the paradigm *du jour* for understanding Islam in the twenty-first century, aligning with traditional Orientalist scholars' conception of a monolithic Islamic civilization reducible to early (Arab) generations and immutable divine texts, 'after which the authenticity of the original article is progressively corrupted', as Shahab Ahmed writes.[4] The rise of the ISIS caliphate in Syria and Iraq has only accentuated the trend. Salafism's semantic victory in defining the West's constitution of Islam, to use Joseph Massad's phrase, is not yet assured.[5] Ideological and political disputes between different trends within Islamic politics broadly understood are complicating the process. But in the dialectic between policy makers and the commentariat, 'Salafism' looms as the West's essentialist Islam—literalist and legalistic, puritan and suitably Other—and academia is inevitably impacted by this.

Defining Salafism

The terms 'Salafi' and 'Salafism' derive from the Arabic term *al-salaf al-salih* (the pious predecessors), a phrase understood by today's Salafis to indicate the first three generations of Muslims who are imagined to have lived in an exemplary manner since they had first-hand experience of the Prophet or lived by the standards of those who did. But 'Salafi' is of a different genus: rather than describing the first Muslims, it came to be deployed as a referent for those claiming adherence to a complex of jurisprudential and theological positions, using the Salaf as an ordering principle[6] and Salafiyya as an abstract noun describing their ideology *in toto*. When it entered Arabic discourse in the early twentieth century Salafism brought together three streams of thinking: the writings of Ibn Taymiyya (1263–1328) and his Hanbali critique of Ash'ari theology as filtered through the beliefs and practices of the Wahhabi movement; the trend which developed the ideas of figures such as Shah Waliullah (1703–62) and Muhammad al-Shawkani (d. 1834), rejecting the practice of *taqlid* within the four Sunni legal schools (*madhhabs*) for an unmediated interpretation (*ijtihad*) of the scriptural sources of Qur'an and prophetic hadith that reaches back to an imagined purer pre-school tradition;[7] and the revivalist modernism of intellectuals Jamal al-Din al-Afghani (1838–97) and Muhammad 'Abduh (1849–1905). Mainly through writings in *al-Manar*, Rashid Rida (1865–1935), a disciple of 'Abduh, attempted a synthesis of all three as an Arab-oriented revivalism that would enable Islamic culture to meet the challenge of Europe, with 'Abduh and Ibn Taymiyya configured as its pivotal figures.[8] Yet while all appealed to the Salaf in their discourse, none of the three groups originally called themselves Salafis or described themselves as adherents of an ideology called Salafiyya.[9]

This very broad notion of 'Salafism' underwent considerable ideological and semantic transformation in subsequent decades. At the Muslim Brotherhood's fifth general conference in 1938 Hasan al-Banna was able to define the organization as 'a Salafiyya message, a Sunni way, a Sufi truth',[10] but by the 1980s the term had become the province of Wahhabiyya, such that today political scientists tend to define the Brotherhood and its peers as 'Islamist', distinct from the Salafists.[11] In the meantime, and in line with the Islamic policy of Faysal as Saudi crown prince and king, Saudi Arabia from the 1960s had become the site for elaborations of Salafism shorn of the modernist legacy and centred on an alignment of Wahhabiyya and the anti-*taqlid* faction, who together shared perhaps more commitment to upending what Jonathan Brown calls the 'late Sunni traditionalism' of the *madhhabs* and their ordering of social and religious life.[12] Salafism's third stage comes in the 1990s in the context of globalization and the communications revolution, through which these trends merge into what Olivier Roy calls a deterritorialized, transnational ideology imagining an Islamic nation 'beyond ethnicity, race, language and culture'.[13] This ideology is interested neither in fostering 'Muslim culture' nor in local Islams, and it easily adapts to processes of individualization, consumerism, and the free market.

Three general elements are usually adduced in Western scholarship (though Salafis themselves have more complex groups and sub-groups),[14] based on a typology developed by Quintan Wiktorowicz: jihadi Salafism, political Salafism, and quietist Salafism.[15] The first, jihadi Salafism, channels Wahhabi thinking on how to manage Muslims and Muslim-run entities failing to make the grade as regards faith, but is influenced by Muslim Brotherhood thinker Sayyid Qutb's ideas on the apostasy of post-colonial Muslim rulers. The second, sometimes termed *al-salafiyya al-tanzimiyya* (organized/activist Salafism), supports some level of involvement in national political processes (as seen in Kuwait, Bahrain, and Egypt). The third, often termed *al-salafiyya al-'ilmiyya* (scholastic Salafism), is 'quietist'[16] in that it rejects participation in processes of political contestation and advocates obedience to rulers as long as they ensure the writ of shari'a through empowerment of its guardians, the *'ulama'*.[17] While useful, this classification offers a model for understanding transnational Salafism as contemporary practice rather than as a historically shifting set of beliefs, reflecting the influence on various disciplines (plus media) of policy-oriented Security Studies.[18]

Meijer's volume offers a model for predicting the spread of Salafism that considers its chances weak where the population is strongly embedded in local practices and engaged in an ethnic–nationalist struggle. 'It can only succeed in making inroads when its quietist current can find a niche or the nationalist movement has failed and the national struggle can be linked with a larger global struggle, or it fits into the politics of identity in Western Europe,' he writes.[19] By this standard it has not been successful among Palestinians, despite a stream of Wahhabi influence through Palestinian students who attended Saudi universities from the 1970s,[20] but has had varying fortunes in Yemen, where there exists something of a historical base,[21] Indonesia, where it is regarded as more of a Saudi import,[22] and France, where it has spoken to immigrant disaffection with the state.[23] In most if not all cases there is a connection of some nature to the post-1960s Saudi milieu.

Salafism in Saudi Arabia

Salafism's trajectory in the Saudi orbit began with Rida. Attracted by Saudi–Wahhabi state-building successes and the manner in which 'Abd al-'Aziz (Ibn Saud) managed the colonial powers, he would often write forewords to Wahhabi texts that 'Abd al-'Aziz sought to publish in *al-Manar* or wrote his own articles,[24] while Wahhabi material was also published in his colleague Muhibb al-Din al-Khatib's journal *al-Majalla al-Salafiyya*. 'Wahhabi' was often used as a term of abuse by detractors of both modernists such as 'Abduh and the anti-*taqlid* group around Jamal al-Din al-Qasimi.[25] Although both trends regarded Wahhabism as an extremity too far,[26] Rida's work offered the Saudi–Wahhabi state an avenue for normalizing a religious movement that had been in an antagonistic relationship with Istanbul and other regional centres for over a century. In a speech delivered in 1929 'Abd al-'Aziz took the opportunity to reject the Wahhabi appellation through emphasizing repeatedly that in following the *al-salaf al-salih* the Saudi scholars did not represent a new school (*madhhab*) in itself: Ibn 'Abd al-Wahhab was a renewer (*mujaddid*), not an innovator. Yet while this does appear to be an attempt to attach Wahhabiyya to the Salafi wave, it is only tangentially done, in that he avoided using Salafi/Salafiyya as an adjective/abstract noun of self-designation while asserting before the Hijazi Hanafis Wahhabiyya's respect for the imams of all four legal schools.[27] Nabil Mouline notes that the term *al-tariqa al-salafiyya* (the Salafi path) is used by 'Abd Allah Ibn Qasim in his anthology of Wahhabi material *al-Durar al-Saniyya* (1934), but here again the word is positioned as an adjective whose referent is the Salaf themselves, not contemporary movements who deploy the Salaf in their discourse.[28] At the same time, Redissi notes that, despite 'Abd al-'Aziz's rebuke, Wahhabiyya was in fact embraced during this period by many Wahhabi scholars as a badge of honour after its long history as a means to disparage.[29]

Salafism as an ideological trademark only really takes off in Islamic discourse in 1960s Saudi Arabia, in the context of the government's nascent projection of an Islamic foreign policy and the activism of Syrian anti-*taqlid* hadith scholar Nasir al-Din al-Albani (1914–99).[30] Al-Albani introduced the term to the Saudi sphere in 1960s, arguing that it was necessary for a Muslim, freed from the constraints of an elaborate, unnecessary, and diverting tradition of *fiqh* schools, to declare his *manhaj* as Salafi, even suggesting that Ibn 'Abd al-Wahhab wasn't fully 'Salafi' because while his theological positions were sound (the literalism of Ibn Taymiyya) he followed the Hanbali school in law.[31] This tension between al-Albani's views and Wahhabism's commitment to the methodology of the schools, and preference for the Hanbali among them, produced a tension that has put limits to this day on the Saudi state and its scholars' use of Salafi/Salafiyya as labels of self-definition. Albani's influence was felt institutionally in two ways: through the Islamic University of Medina where he taught briefly from its inception in 1962 and al-Jama'a al-Salafiyya al-Muhtasiba (the Salafi Hisba Group, or Salafi Group for Promoting Virtue and Preventing Vice) established by disciples of al-Albani in 1966. In his account of membership in the Salafi Hisba Group, a faction of which under Juhayman al-'Utaybi in 1979 led a failed insurrection in Mecca, Nasir al-Huzaymi recounts how Salafism was the touchstone of the movement: he was made familiar with the work of al-Albani, visited the Salafi community in Kuwait, and learned that being Salafi meant rejecting the intellectual tradition of the schools (including the dominant Ash'ari theology).[32] Al-Albani's position inspired many students who passed through Saudi Arabia,[33] helped by his closeness to senior *'alim* 'Abd al-'Aziz Bin Baz (1910–99) and his opposition to the political activism of the Muslim Brotherhood, despite the fact that he was forced out of the country in 1963 and only able to visit intermittently over the following two decades.[34] Similar to the Damascus *'ulama'*, who objected to al-Qasimi's group several decades before, the official *'ulama'* in Saudi Arabia felt threatened by the notion of excavating a pre-school *fiqh*.[35]

It was from the milieu of 1960s and 1970s Saudi Arabia that the discourse of Salafism began to mutate, expanding to encompass numerous factions crossing various taxonomical and geographical boundaries, including the Muslim Brotherhood, state Wahhabism, and various anti-*taqlid* groups. Yet still the relative reserve in adopting the terms Salafi/Salafiyya as an ideological marker is striking, given how ubiquitous their use is today. Ottoman Turkish hadith scholar Mehmed Zahid Kevseri (1879–1952), writing in Arabic in 1940s Cairo, denounced the anti-*taqlid* group as advocating *la-madhhabiyya* ('no-schoolism'), resisting their efforts to appropriate the term Salafism for themselves.[36] Sayyid Qutb, neither a Wahhabi nor an anti-schools ideologue, makes barely any mention of the Salaf in *Ma'alim fi al-Tariq* (1964) and other works; Brotherhood Supreme Guide Hassan al-Hudaybi cites the Salaf twice in his response to Qutb, *Du'ah La Qudah* (1977); 'Abd al-Salam Farag, leader of the Islamic Jihad group that assassinated Anwar Sadat, cites the Salaf four times in *al-Farida al-Gha'iba* (c. 1980/1), where he does extensively cite Ibn Taymiyya.[37]

However, Abu Muhammad al-Maqdisi, an associate of the Juhayman group who sought opinions from al-Albani in Jordan,[38] deploys the notion of Salafiyya in a more systematic manner in *Millat Ibrahim* (1983). He describes leading Wahhabi scholars as *'a'immat al-da'wa al-najdiyya al-salafiyya* (imams of the Salafi Najdi call)[39] and warns of government clerics who adopt the label Salafiyya to give themselves an aura of respectability,[40] while in *al-Kawashif al-Jaliyya fi Kufr al-Dawla al-Sa'udiyya* (1989) he condemns what he calls 'government Salafism' (*al-salafiyya al-hukumiyya*).[41] Syrian *'alim* Said Ramadan al-Buti (1929–2013) published two refutations of the al-Albani position, *al-Lamadh-habiyya: Akhtar Bid'a Tuhaddid al-Shari'a al-Islamiyya* (1969) and *al-Salafi-yya: Marhala Zamaniyya Mubaraka La Madhhab Islami* (1988),[42] in which *la-madhhabiyya* in the first becomes Salafiyya in the second.[43] But when in 1989 the Egyptian *'alim* Muhammad al-Ghazali (1971–96) ridiculed those who 'fight the *fiqh* tradition for the sake of an alleged Salafism' (*yuharibun al-fiqh al-madhhabi li hisab salafiyya maz'uma*) as engaging in 'childish *ijtihad*' (*al-ijtihad al-subyani*),[44] he provoked a vigorous response from many in the Salafi–Wahhabi scene beyond al-Albani, with some support from Saudi print media, because he was also attacking the literalism of their theology.[45] 'Salafism' had acquired a degree of identitarian value in Wahhabi circles beyond the anti-*taqlid* group.

On the whole, in the period up to the 1990s when Salafism in its third stage takes on its transnational character in the context of globalization, Wahhabiyya maintained an ambiguous position, with many *'ulama'* advocating freedom to choose between the options in *fiqh* over allegiance to one particular school, but rejecting the extreme position of unmediated access to divine texts. Nabil Mouline also identifies a desire among the Saudi *'ulama'* to establish themselves as heirs of the pre-Wahhabi Hanbali tradition, 'to establish a clear line of descent from it and also appropriate it', which may also have put brakes on the use of Salafi/Salafism: between 1960 and 2000 more than three hundred classic Hanbali works were edited and published.[46] Senior scholars embrace the term, but not with enthusiasm. With al-Albani's radical position rejected, it becomes a Wahhabi stand-in for Sunni Islam itself, but a rather superfluous one. The Permanent Fatwa Committee under Bin Baz stated simply in response to a questioner that 'the meaning advanced to include those who follow the way of the Salaf'.[47] Salih al-Fawzan said that 'the terminology of *salafiyya* is okay [*la ba's bihi*], if it's used properly', while asserting that not only Mu'tazila but Ash'aris too are not considered as part of *ahl al-sunna*.[48] The Mecca-based Muslim World League's Islamic Fiqh Council went further, issuing a statement in 1987 that took the by now familiar view condemning *al-ta'assub al-madhhabi* (schools' fanaticism) and accepting diversity in *fiqh* (as opposed to the Salafi–Wahhabi canonical requirement regarding *'aqida*), but condemned the extreme anti-schools position exemplified in al-Albani's *la-madhhabiyya* as a 'hateful method' (*uslub baghid*) that misleads and divides.[49] This decision was reissued in the Council's journal in 2005.

Islam and Saudi Foreign Policy

Saudi foreign policy did not begin to play with Islamic themes until the 1960s. Wary of any scheme of meaningful integration, 'Abd al-'Aziz saw the projection of Islamic power as merely a means to impress foreigners, 'by invoking his status, however self-proclaimed, as guardian of the holy places, to make it seem that his influence reached beyond his own frontiers'.[50] But as Faysal asserted himself, formally seizing power in 1964, and with Nasserist Egypt weakened, the regime came to see possibilities in a limited deployment of Islam as a tool of foreign policy. To that end the Muslim World League was established in 1962, and, following a 1969 summit in Rabat, the Organization of the Islamic Conference (OIC) was established in 1972 as 'a permanent institution through which the Saudis could express their views and emphasize their special role in the Islamic world'.[51] Since only indirect benefit accrued to the Saudi regime through the largesse bestowed upon these institutions, as well as governments and organizations within countries,[52] Piscatori, writing in 1983, was able to wonder 'whether Islam plays as much of a role in Saudi foreign policy as is customarily thought', indeed if there was such a thing as an Islamic foreign policy at all.[53]

Islamization of foreign policy responded not only to the challenge of external ideologies but to problematic sectors at home as well. Al-Yassini argues that as the state expanded, one of the underlying policies of the ruling clique was to keep the *'ulama'* outside the political realm of decision making; alongside the bureaucratization of the priestly class seen in the 1960s and 1970s, Islam in foreign policy fitted that purpose. The World Assembly of Muslim Youth (WAMY) was established in 1972 with internationalist aims of supporting Muslim youth and student organizations around the world, 'spreading *tawhid*' (unicity), building mosques and schools, sending preachers to Muslim communities, and distributing religious material. In 1979, shortly before Juhayman's revolt in Mecca, a new drive towards 'Islamic cohesion' (*al-tamasuk al-islami*) was launched on the occasion of the fourteenth Islamic century; administrative material laid out plans for new institutions serving 'the whole Islamic nation, across national, racial, linguistic and other borders that now divide the Islamic community'.[54]

This impulse to view the Muslim exterior as an arena for managing both domestic and foreign antagonists was renewed in light of the Mecca insurrection, the Soviet bolstering of its leftist allies in Afghanistan and elsewhere, and Iranian revolutionary ideology. In its first response the government used the Muslim World League, the Muslim Brotherhood, and Pakistani Jamaat-i Islami and Ahl-i Hadith networks (which had intermingled through the Islamic University of Medina) to funnel people and cash to the Mujahidin fighting the Soviet-backed Afghan regime.[55] Olivier Roy makes the point that this disparate alliance was broken by the 1990–1 Gulf crisis, when most Islamic groups condemned the US troop presence in Saudi Arabia as Western imperial aggression.[56] The second major response the Saudi regime adopted was the expansion of its global proselytization effort. After taking power in 1982 King Fahd sponsored a new edition of the Qur'an for mass distribution through the King Fahd Complex for Printing the Holy Qur'an, the first such undertaking since al-Azhar published its version in 1926 following the dissolution of the Ottoman caliphate. Power was shifting from the old centres of Islamic learning to Saudi Arabia; interpretation of the text was passing to 'Salafi' Wahhabiyya.[57]

The expansion project of Fahd marks the beginning of a new phase in which the domestic and the foreign are fused in pressing Saudi claims to represent normative Sunni Islam. Funding for the coercive morality apparatus (Hay'at al-Amr bi-l-Ma'ruf wa Nahy 'an al-Munkar) rises from SR85.7 million in 1979 to more than SR203 million in 1985, and in 1994, after domestic legitimacy was rendered vulnerable through the political demands of the Sahwa 'ulama', the organization launched a journal, Majallat al-Hisba.[58] It is from this time that political science scholars began to rethink Islamic themes in Saudi foreign policy. In his 1992 study The Failure of Political Islam Olivier Roy discusses Salafiyya solely in the context of the early twentieth-century reform movement.[59] In examining what he calls the 're-Islamization' of the 1980s and 1990s he avoids the term 'Salafi', preferring 'neo-fundamentalism', by which he intends the tradition of disengagement from political processes which was fostered by 'ulama' in the Saudi orbit. However, in Globalized Islam: The Search for a New Ummah, published a decade later, Roy embraces Salafiyya to describe this movement, acknowledging the semantic shift that has taken place. Similarly, the original 2003 edition of Raymond Hinnebusch's study The International Politics of the Middle East, a standard work in the field, contains almost no discussion of Saudi deployment of Islam internationally,[60] while the 2015 imprint notes the Islamization of foreign policy, citing support for Salafi networks in Egypt and Syria in the context of geopolitical conflict with Iran.[61]

From a theoretical perspective, Saudi Arabia embraced 'Salafism' in its regional conflicts with Iran and Sunni political Islam. The constructivist model in international relations theory argues that discourses of culture and identity can delineate, direct, and restrain the political choices of regimes. This helped produce the notion of an Arab public sphere that is created through satellite television, the internet, and, latterly, social media.[62] It could be argued that despite the limits on the use of Salafi nomenclature in the domestic sphere, Salafism offers a means to balance against some of the challenges to regime interests; in other words, it is effective against what Lawrence Rubin calls the 'ideational security dilemma' presented by Iran since 1979 and political Islam since 2011.[63]

PRODUCING SALAFISM

Turkish Salafism and Saudi Arabia

Turkey has been largely absent from the growing literature on the phenomenon of transnational Salafism. Salafism is a fringe strand of Turkish Islam that evolved in the context of the state's effort in the 1980s to recalibrate religion as a complement to Turkish nationalism. Although Salafism became a topic of discussion in media and scholarly writing in Turkish religious studies faculties, a continued lack of orthographic stability (variously, *Selefiye, Selefiyye, Selefilik,*[64] *Selefçilik,*[65] *Selefiyyecilik, Selefizm*)[66] gives an indication both of the denial of its relevance to Turkey and the success of republican secularism in clearing religion from public discourse. Yet since the 1980s Salafi preachers trained in Saudi Arabia have been able to find a niche through publishing houses that have endeavoured to translate Arabic texts from the Saudi Salafi scene in an attempt to change the discursive landscape of Turkish Islam. With the implication of Turkish citizens and the Justice and Development Party (AKP) government in Syria's civil war, public discussion began to question the narrative of Salafism as a phenomenon alien to Turkey.[67]

Salafism becomes an observable element of religious discourse in Turkey in the context of the military regime's attempt to outmanoeuvre movements emerging as a challenge to the Kemalist secular order, namely the left, Necmettin Erbakan's Islamism, Kurdish nationalism, and Iran. Through the Turkish–Islamic Synthesis (*Türk İslam Sentezi*), the scientific positivism that had been the guiding principle of the republic since 1923 was modified to make room for Islam as a central element of Turkish national culture. The military authorities oversaw an increase of more than 50 per cent in the budget of the religious affairs administration (known as Diyanet), expanding it from 50,000 employees in 1979 to 85,000 in 1989.[68] Pursuing closer ties with Saudi Arabia, Turkey involved itself in a more meaningful manner in the pan-Islamic institutions under Saudi tutelage, and Diyanet received Muslim World League funding to send officials to Europe to develop outreach activities in Turkish immigrant communities.[69] A network of commercial and cultural links was established with Saudi businesses and institutions in banking and financial services, publishing houses, newspapers, magazines, and children's books.[70]

Preachers who had studied at the Islamic University of Medina, and applied the Salafi designation, also established publishing houses and charity organizations (*dernek*).[71] Subject to periodic harassment and arrest by security forces, particularly in the early years of AKP rule, they adopted markedly more public profiles with AKP ascendancy over the military following a resounding electoral victory in 2007.[72] The Turkish Salafis became active on YouTube, Twitter, and Facebook, complementing websites for their publishing enterprises. Saudi-based scholars such as Bin Baz, al-Albani, Salih al-Fawzan (b. 1933), and Muhammad ibn al-'Uthaymin (1925–2001) form the core of their references, while they avoid contemporary *'ulama'* associated with the Muslim Brotherhood such as Yusuf al-Qaradawi (b. 1926), an Egyptian scholar based in Qatar. Turkish is their prime language of communication, but Arabic is prominent in special sections on websites, Arabic-language Salafi texts in their bookshops, and heavy use of Arabic terminology in their Turkish texts.

The most well-established among them is Abdullah Yolcu (b. 1958), whose work will be discussed in detail here.[73] A Turkmen from Kirkuk in Iraq, Yolcu speaks fluent Arabic and publishes in Arabic and Turkish. Before issuing his books in Turkish he published extensively in Saudi Arabia using his full Arabic name, 'Abd Allah ibn 'Abd al-Hamid al-Athari, sometimes adding al-Iraqi to indicate Iraqi origin. His Turkish works are published under the name Abdullah Yolcu or Abdullah b. Abdulhamid el-Eseri.[74] After settling in Turkey in 1986, Yolcu established the Guraba publishing house in Istanbul in 1992 with what Guraba describes as the aim of countering a century of Westernization, extreme Sufism (*aşırı tasavvuf*), and the prevalence of Shi'i and Christian practices.[75] An arm of Izmir-based charity İlim Der, Guraba publishes Turkish translations of Bin Baz, al-'Uthaymin, al-Albani, and al-Fawzan, and from 2005 began to draw on a pool of Yolcu's work in Arabic for presentation to a Turkish audience in Turkish.[76] With his bookstore in the Sultanahmet district of Istanbul, the heart of government in the Ottoman period and the location of many of its most important mosques, Yolcu has positioned himself as the face of apolitical Salafism, often appearing in the gold-rimmed black cloak and white headdress of Saudi *'ulama'*.[77] His books avoid political issues such as the invasion of Iraq, the war in Syria, or direct intervention in Turkey's domestic politics, and are careful when engaging Salafi positions on *takfir* and jihad.[78] This studied moderation helps present Salafi Wahhabism as the summation of the four schools of Sunni *fiqh* with the most sound creed.

Guraba lists nine of Yolcu's Turkish-language books for sale, but he has many other titles from Saudi publishers in Arabic. They reflect the archetypal themes of the Wahhabi tradition: the danger to the Muslim's faith of engaging, even unwittingly, in over-friendly relations with non-Muslims, partaking in non-Muslim festivities and customs, indulging in the temptations of modern music, slipping into the laxity that is the condition of many if not most Muslims in post-shari'a states. Declaring that the *shahada*, the Muslim profession of faith, is not enough, and insisting in the face of argumentation on forsaking the Ramadan fast, or prayer, or any other of the main commands of the shari'a tradition, is apostasy.[79] Other actions that put one's Islam in jeopardy include use of saint figures as intermediaries (a polytheistic dilution of the focused worship of God alone), compromising the absolute authority of shari'a, dabbling in sorcery (addressing entities other than God), denigrating any elements of Islam, or suggesting that it is an incomplete system.[80]

Yolcu has made choices regarding which of his works to translate into Turkish and which to republish in Arabic from Saudi originals, what additions to make and what to omit. Nonchalance towards rituals and disregard for doctrinal questions, on the one hand, and the cultural–historical reach of Sufi practices, on the other, make Turkey a prime target for Salafi proselytization. His keynote works *Selef-i Salihin Akidesi* (Belief of the pious ancestors) and *Ehl-i Sünnet ve'l-Cemaat'e Göre İman* (Faith according to the Sunni tradition), both previously published in Arabic in Saudi Arabia, seek to define Sunnism in Salafi Wahhabi terms, and put that claim to a Turkish audience. *Selef-i Salihin Akidesi* was published by the Saudi Ministry of Religious Affairs in 2002 with an endorsement from the minister at the time.[81] It was issued in Turkish in 2013, with the addition of a series of forewords by twenty scholars from a number of countries; eleven of them are based in Saudi Arabia and one is from Turkey.[82] Defining *Selefilik*, he says it expresses the idea that Muslims who follow the Qur'an, the Prophet's sunna, and the example of the early Muslims are the most correct. Such Muslims are the guardians of Islam from unbelief and innovation; the Salafi way is pure *tawhid* (Turk. *tevhid*) and the furthest from *shirk* (polytheistic practice).[83] In the second title, first published in Saudi Arabia in 2003,[84] Yolcu acknowledges an Islamic awakening (*İslami uyanış*) across Muslim societies since the collapse of Arab nationalism, but says that youth must be aware of shari'a rules to protect their faith, in particular observing prayer.[85]

Yolcu discusses *taqlid* at length, condemning the dogmatic adherence of an *'alim* to a school or an unschooled believer to a particular scholar, while warning the believer against shopping around for views that suit one's desires (Hanbali scholars still dominate his citations and references).[86] It is imitation of the scholars that has led Muslims towards practices that put their faith at risk, such as visiting shrines and indulging music and singing. Music is productive of destructive atheistic practices such as mixing of the sexes and bodily adornment, and thus destructive for the moral fabric of the Muslim community.[87] He lists fatwas on the topic from Saudi scholars, including al-Fawzan's refutation of al-Qaradawi's argument that music was forbidden only in the context of alcohol and other sins;[88] he also reproduces a fatwa from 2000 issued by the permanent fatwa committee of the Council of Senior 'Ulama' in Saudi Arabia declaring music and song to be impermissible.[89] Since *ghina'* is understood by Salafis as poetry and rhyming prose, only the voice without instrumental musical accompaniment is legitimate, while the voice the believer hears should not be that of an unrelated adult woman (his one concession is that tambourines may be used among women at weddings).[90] Music is integral to the sin of Sufism. He faults *dhikr* rituals for clapping, shouting and 'acrobatic movements like people who drink alcohol', mixing of genders, singing that 'alights love and desire and excites the senses', and forms of song that have 'invented new forms of invoking God [*zikir*]', an innovation in Yolcu's reading rejected by the four Sunni legal traditions and in particular by Ibn Taymiyya.[91]

In these discussions on Sufism, shrines, and music the subtle crafting of Arabic texts into a Turkish discourse for Turkish audiences reveals itself most clearly. Yolcu's critique is easily understood to refer to Alevi practices in his reference to Sufi *sema* in Turkish, while his Arabic discussion of *sama'* does not convey Alevism at all.[92] Similarly, in discussing shrines he writes that 'the Shi'a and some Sunnis regard travelling to graves or mosques built upon them, known as *türbe*, as a form of pilgrimage', but the Turkish text carries a footnote, not present in the Arabic version, which gives the example of visitors to Mevlana's tomb in Konya and the mosque of Eyüp Sultan in Istanbul.[93] While the frequent use of Rawafid/Rafida would be understood by Arabic readers as references to Arab or Iranian Shi'a, Rafiziler can intimate Alevis to readers of the Turkish text. This becomes relevant again in his discussion of *takfir*. The rules of *takfir* should be followed scrupulously in order not to wrong a believer, he says; but while those who were never Muslim, such as Christians, Jews, polytheists, Zoroastrians, and philosophers, will go to hell, among Muslims it is the Batıniler and *aşırı* Rafiziler (extreme Shi'a) who may suffer the same fate, according to the specific innovations they engage in.[94] The term Batıniler, from the Arabic Batiniyya, denoting Isma'ili Shi'a and others who believe in esoteric knowledge, carries the semantic hint in Turkish of Sufi/Alevi practice. The overall message, however nuanced, is that Turkey is a nominally Muslim society on the edge of *kufr* because Muslims in their ignorance fail to live by the standards of the Prophet's sunna.[95]

So while Turkey has been outside the discussion on transnational Salafism, Meijer's observation that Salafism may succeed 'when its quietist current can find a niche or the nationalist movement has failed' seems to speak surprisingly well to the Turkish case.[96] In figures such as Yolcu such a current found a place from which to attempt the production of a Turkish Salafism from Arabic texts. Translation, as theorists Susan Bassnett and André Lefevere argue in *Translation, History and Culture* (1990), is never innocent: 'There is always a context in which the translation takes place, always a history from which a text emerges and into which a text is transposed',[97] it is a form of writing that involves 'the shaping power of one culture upon another in which the source language can wield a force of authority in the translated context'.[98] Yolcu does this in taking Arabic-language texts from Saudi Arabia and feeding them into the Turkish *ecumene* where they speak through articulation in Turkish to the historical experience of secular materialism and its production of a post-shari'a society. His project to introduce a shari'a sensitivity to Islamic practice in Turkey is radical in that it implies a rejection of the entire tradition of Ottoman–Turkish Islam with its extensive Sufi networks and legal-theological system: indeed, he dismisses the majority of republican Islamic scholars, intellectuals, and politicians for compromises to 'nationalism' (*qawmiyya*) and 'rationalism' (*'aqlaniyya*) and acceptance of the post-shari'a state.[99]

Conclusion

It could be said that in a general sense Salafism is appropriate as a term to define the Islam constituted by Orientalism. A number of scholars have noted the odd ideological alliance of the traditional *'ulama'*/ Islamist thinkers and modern Western scholarship on Islam/'the East' (from the era of high Orientalist writing in the nineteenth century to public discourse today) in their shared interest in producing fixed knowledge from divine texts.[100] Scripturalism was at one with the rationalist imperative of the high imperial age when Islam and Hinduism[101] were narrated and explicated by European scholars of the non-European as comparable and comprehensible 'world religions'. A Salafization of Islamic historiography took hold which privileges notions of decline (the fall of Baghdad, the rise of the Ottomans, the prevalence of Sufism, the intellectual culture of the Sunni legal schools) and, as Khaled El-Rouayheb has argued, idealizes Ibn Taymiyya as the leader of a counter-cultural revolt that eventually returns legal and theological order to the Islamic whole.[102] Even the modernists among Rashid Rida's 'Salafis' shared the broad outlines of this critique, although 'Abduh did not see Ibn Taymiyya as the central figure Rida wished.[103] A default position established itself in both Islamic and Western scholarship that places law rather than the practice of theological reasoning (*kalam*), or philosophy, or logic, or other sidelined disciplines, at the heart of what is described as 'Islam'.[104]

Recent thinking has moved to reject this notion of what El-Rouayheb calls 'timeless Salafism'[105] and shown that Salafism was in essence an invented tradition of the early twentieth century, an amalgamation of several trends that did not themselves use the Salafi designation as a marker of self-identity. I would argue that the elaboration of Salafiyya in contemporary understanding is perhaps of even more recent provenance than thought. In this research on the topic, Henri Lauzière has attempted to rescue the term for the anti-*taqlid* group of Damascus and Baghdad scholars, suggesting they are the true Salafis, with more rights to the term than the modernists and the Wahhabis.[106] This claim should rather be seen as a reflection of this group's proactive adoption of the appellation in the milieu of 1960s Saudi Arabia, from which point Salafi nomenclature begins to metamorphose into the field of meanings familiar today. State Wahhabism was never fully at ease with this group or the terminology, which operates discursively outside Saudi control, but one of its advantages has been in the propagation of Wahhabiyya as intrinsic to new understandings of normative Sunni Islam and in the branding of Islamic themes in Saudi foreign policy. Whether the Turkish Salafis are regular beneficiaries of Saudi state funding or not is a moot point, but that they should be interpreted as an emanation of the Saudi Islamic imaginary is clear.

7

TRANSNATIONAL RELIGIOUS COMMUNITY
AND THE SALAFI MISSION

Michael Farquhar

This chapter considers the forms of transnational religious community at stake in modern Salafism, by way of a discussion of the Islamic University of Medina (IUM) and the networks of migrant students that have grown up around it. As a missionary project founded by the Saudi state in 1961, the IUM was intended to support the worldwide promotion of a Salafi interpretation of Islam, broadly aligned with the Wahhabi tradition which represents officially sanctioned orthodoxy within the kingdom. It was to do so by offering fully funded religious education to mostly non-Saudi young men. Over the decades that followed, students came to the IUM from across the globe and formed a diverse collective on its Medina campus, brought together from divergent backgrounds in the shared pursuit of religious knowledge within a Salafi framework. The IUM initiative in its early years dovetailed with a growing emphasis on pan-Islamist commitments in Saudi official discourse, which was in turn bound up with an effort on the part of the

Saudi regime and religious establishment to situate themselves in a position of political and spiritual leadership over a worldwide community of believers. In these senses, the university's missionary endeavour was both predicated on and over time contributed to fostering particular conceptions of border-spanning religious solidarity. However, exploring the workings of this project and the networks that have grown up around it serves to illustrate the complexities, ambivalences, and contestation that characterize the notions of cross-border religious community at stake.

Considering these themes affords a perspective on recent debates concerning the status and nature of border-spanning forms of Islamic identity and solidarity in the modern period, and the shape that these take within Salafism in particular. On the one hand, it has been suggested that followers of modern Salafism tend to identify closely with a vision of a universal *umma*, which is said to have become a key locus of social identity and action as globalization has eroded the importance of local and national communities. On the other hand, and in part as a response to this kind of analysis, modern Salafism has been conceptualized as a transnational 'new social movement'. In this picture, Salafis do not conceive of political community or projects of social transformation primarily with reference to the nation, but neither are they said to lend their primary loyalty to a universal *umma*. Rather, like those involved in many other kinds of new social movements, they pursue normative projects in everyday social contexts whilst being bound together across borders by a loosely shared set of aspirations and discourses.

In what follows, I suggest that the kinds of transnational religious solidarities to be found in the networks that have grown up around the IUM encompass multiple layers of identification and attachment. Notions of a universal Muslim *umma* are certainly one dimension at stake here, and may be given concrete reality in the experience of life as part of the university's diverse student body. However, this does not mean that such forms of attachment necessarily replace or displace students' rootedness in local or national communities. Rather, these different layers of identification and attachment may coexist and intertwine, and the actors involved may undertake socially engaged action in an array of local, national, and transnational spheres. At the same time, rather than seeking to capture these dynamics with reference to an idea of new social movements, I suggest thinking of them instead in terms of a process whereby actors are drawn into a transnational Salafi 'community of discourse'. This way of thinking about things, I suggest, is better suited to emphasizing the dynamics of divergent interpretation and debate which contribute to constituting the form of transnational religious community at stake. This, in turn, is an important step towards appreciating that the ways in which Saudi actors have sought to insert themselves into the heart of a border-spanning Salafi community through projects such as the IUM have exposed their views and actions to far-reaching dynamics of debate and critique.

Transnational Salafi Solidarities

In the half-century since it was first established, the generous scholarships for religious study that have been made available through the IUM have attracted students from nearly every country around the world. Those who have enrolled in its programmes have included large numbers from Muslim-majority states and Muslim-minority communities from West Africa to South-East Asia, and more recently smaller but growing numbers from diaspora communities in the Global North.[1] Those who see out the duration of their degrees remain in Medina for many years, usually starting out with Arabic language training before progressing to undergraduate instruction in fields including shari'a, da'wa (religious mission), Qur'anic studies, and hadith studies.[2] A minority are then able to enrol in postgraduate programmes, at Master's or Ph.D. level. During their time in Medina, most students live in residences on campus, with the option of returning to their home countries for the duration of the main annual vacation. By the early 2000s well over 11,000 non-Saudi students had departed the IUM with undergraduate qualifications.[3] It is rare for graduates to be able to stay on in Saudi Arabia beyond the completion of their degrees, and at that point in their trajectories most either return to their countries of origin or settle elsewhere.

In so far as it draws together young men from all over the world within the ambit of a religious project, the IUM offers a useful case study for thinking about the nature and status of border-spanning forms of Islamic identity and community. It is an especially important case for thinking about religious solidarities within modern Salafism. From its earliest years, instruction at the IUM was grounded in syllabuses which were clearly Salafi in their framing and content, including in the key areas of creed and jurisprudence.[4] It is also the case that student recruitment has long operated in part through Salafi networks beyond Saudi Arabia, and thus brings in young men who may in one way or another already identify with a Salafi understanding of Islam. At the same time, other students come from backgrounds rooted in a diverse range of non-Salafi expressions of Islam in their home communities.[5] It is not necessarily the case that, on leaving Medina, all IUM graduates self-identify as Salafi. In this sense, in keeping with its missionary goals, the university operates as a kind of Salafi outpost even as it is situated within a country whose regime claims allegiance to the Salafi creed; while many of those who move in its orbit are already part of the Salafi community or become so as a result of their time in Medina, some others may remain on the margins of this community, or may even distance themselves from it. Exploring the networks that have grown up around the IUM thus offers a window not only onto the forms of transnational solidarity and identity at stake in modern Salafism but also onto the dynamics that play out at the borders of this far-reaching religious community.

Translocal forms of religious solidarity and identity date back to the earliest period of Islam. While this has always included understandings of Muslims worldwide as constituting a common community, denoted as the *umma*, it has also long included more narrowly delimited forms of identity associated with particular religious traditions. Forms of border-spanning Islamic identity have provided a foundation for and have simultaneously been given substance by material long-distance connections. These have been forged through phenomena including scholarly networks; circulations of migrant students, teachers, activists, and pilgrims who grew up around mosques, madrasas, and Sufi lodges; flows of funds and texts; and border-spanning institutional structures such as Sufi orders.[6] In more recent history, they have also encompassed activist networks, charities and advocacy groups, and religious formations forged in the diaspora.[7] While the existence of such border-spanning connections, identities, and understandings of community is not in itself novel, in recent years debates have emerged about how their status and role in social life should be understood in the modern period; and important contributions to this debate have paid considerable attention to notions of religious community within contemporary Salafism in particular.

One line of inquiry in this regard is associated with Olivier Roy, who situates contemporary Salafism as the archetypal expression of 'neo-fundamentalism', a distinctively modern mode of religiosity that he suggests has been produced as Islam has been swept up by the tide of cultural globalization.[8] According to Roy, the status of neo-fundamentalism as 'both a product and an agent of globalisation'[9] is reflected in its adherents' rejection of integration into local and national communities; their hostility towards particularistic cultural traditions, be they 'folk customs' such as celebration of the *mawlid*[10] or expressions of youth culture like *rai* music or hip hop;[11] and their drive to recast Islam as 'a decontextualized set of norms, [which] can be adapted to any society, precisely because it has severed its links with a given culture'.[12] These features are in turn bound up with a special emphasis on loyalty to an *umma* conceived in 'global and abstract'[13] terms—'an imaginary *ummah*, beyond ethnicity, race, language and culture, one that is no longer embedded in a specific territory'.[14] On the one hand, the neo-fundamentalists' alleged rejection of political action and social reform within the terms of national and local communities directs them to focus on individual moral reform and atomized patterns of religious consumption, in keeping with 'modern models of individualisation and the free market'.[15] On the other hand, they simultaneously 'strive to construct, from a collection of individual born-again Muslims, a true *ummah*—that is, a homogeneous community of equals, delinked from their natural milieu and devoted to the sole aim of practising a true Islam'.[16] In a world in which local and national communities and cultures are said to be undergoing a process of erosion by the forces of globalization, neo-fundamentalists are thus understood to take refuge in 'a sort of virtual, deterritorialised community', 'decoupled from real societies'.[17] In this understanding, then, Salafis—as the key exemplars of neo-fundamentalism—characteristically aspire to establish a new kind of religious community suited to life in a globalized world; and they look upon globalization as 'a good opportunity to rebuild the Muslim *ummah* on a purely religious basis'.[18]

It is worth noting that when Roy lists individual figureheads who are representative of the kind of neo-fundamentalist Salafism that he has in mind, he includes numerous scholars who have at one time or another held posts at the IUM. They include the Albanian-born hadith specialist Nasir al-Din al-Albani, the Mauritanian Muhammad al-Amin al-Shinq-iti, the Algerian Jabir Abu Bakr al-Jaza'iri, and the Saudis 'Abd al-'Aziz Bin Baz and Rabi' ibn Hadi al-Madkhali.[19]

Roy's arguments offer a constructive rejoinder to those who would see pious Muslims pitted in a hostile, zero-sum clash with the forces of globalization.[20] Rather than understanding Islam and globalization as two incompatible social and cultural forces at loggerheads, he offers ways of thinking about how globalization may in fact operate within and through existing religious frameworks.[21] In this picture, globalization and forms of religiosity such as Salafism are not fundamentally opposed but are in fact in a certain sense mutually constitutive. At the same time, I will argue, this approach risks overstating the role of an imagined global *umma* as a principal locus of identity and aspirations to community, even among Salafis who may put special emphasis on such ideas in their public discourse. It also tends to neglect complexities that arise when such universal forms of identification come to coexist and intertwine with—rather than supplanting—locally and nationally delineated forms of community.

In contrast, others have sought to understand the forms of identity and solidarity at stake in modern Salafism not with reference to a notion of globalization but rather through the lens of transnationalism. In doing so, they have drawn attention to the ways in which invocation of a universal *umma* may intertwine in Salafi discourse with attachments to more particularistic histories and social formations, such as tribal gene-alogies and local intellectual traditions.[22] Adopting a transnational perspective, one approach has been to treat Salafism as a kind of border-spanning social movement. It is in this vein that Peter Mandaville has argued 'against the idea that the *umma* has come to constitute a primary referent in contemporary Muslim debates about identity'.[23] He instead suggests thinking of trends such as 'global neo-Salafism' as akin to 'new social movements'. This way of thinking is intended to draw attention to the ways in which members of such movements may pursue projects of social engagement primarily in the context of everyday spheres of life, rather than through more obviously political efforts to capture or transform national state frameworks. While such movements may encompass a great deal of diversity and conflicting goals, they nonetheless in this picture remain bound together by transnational solidarities in so far as their members' varying forms of social engagement are rooted in 'shared values or cultural systems'.[24] It is not that all members hold the same goals; however, even in the absence of consensus on matters of detail, such movements are 'built around a loosely shared normative core and a movement "frame" that thematises, but does not concretise, the purposes of collective action'.[25] Mandaville locates the transnational solidarities at stake in Salafism in just such 'Islamic aspirations that cross national borders', rather than in any primary loyalty to a universal *umma*; in fact, he suggests that neo-Salafism 'resists positing the *umma* as a desired form of social collective'. Rather than supplanting local and national forms of community, then, 'transnational Muslim solidarities represent an intermediate space of affiliation and socio-political mobilisation that exists alongside and in an ambivalent relationship with the nation-state'.[26]

In what follows, I draw on elements of Mandaville's approach as a way of thinking about the status of the transnational Salafi solidarities that are at stake in the networks that have grown up around the IUM. Thinking transnationally can help to capture the ways in which those who move in these circuits, rather than appealing to universal religious solidarities at the expense of more particularistic forms of attachment, may in fact be bound up in multiple forms of social solidarity, at the local, national, and global levels. However, I seek to move beyond the appeal to notions of 'collective action' and shared aspirations as a basis for thinking about transnational Salafi solidarities. Instead, I argue in favour of an understanding of Salafism as constituting a transnational 'discursive community' forged through shared participation in debates which play out with reference to an overlapping set of past referents.

Saudi Arabia, the *Umma,* and the Salafi *Da'wa*

The Wahhabi form of Salafism that predominates in Saudi Arabia has long been bound up with many different kinds of attachments, from the universal to the particularistic. On one hand, the Wahhabi mission from its origins in the eighteenth century rested on just the kind of drive to establish a universal community of true believers that Roy attributes to later instantiations of modern neo-fundamentalism. This universalism is reflected in terms that have been used by Wahhabis to identify themselves and their school of belief and praxis, including *al-tariqa al-Muhammadiyya* (the way of the Prophet Muhammad) and even simply *al-da'wa al-Islamiyya* (the Islamic call).[27] On the other hand, membership in the Wahhabi scholarly community was to a significant extent structured by parochial ties, including genealogical links to Muhammad ibn 'Abd al-Wahhab. Its adherents also sometimes self-identified in more self-consciously localized terms, as proponents of *al-da'wa al-Najdiyya* (the Najdi call).[278]

In the twentieth century, Wahhabism also came to be interwoven with efforts to construct a new, delimited sense of Saudi national identity, which in official discourse was situated ambivalently as a constitutive element of a universal Islamic *umma*.[28] The 1960s and 1970s saw a growing emphasis on pan-Islamism in Saudi political discourse, particularly under King Faysal.[30] Rather than stemming naturally from any particular religious inclination, however, pan-Islamism as an element of foreign policy served national and regime interests; it offered a way of framing alliances with the governments of other Muslim-majority states and a basis for efforts to forge a position of international leadership distinct from that built by the Saudis' rival Gamal 'Abd al-Nasser through pan-Arabism.[31] Nevertheless, it also coincided with a growing recognition on the part of the mainstream Wahhabi establishment of non-Wahhabi Muslims as fellow believers rather than infidels to be spurned and fought, and helped to foster a grassroots pan-Islamist movement centred in the Hijaz.[32]

The consolidation of the IUM in the 1960s and its expansion with the oil boom of the early 1970s was one concrete manifestation of this new official emphasis on pan-Islamic solidarity. It played out alongside the founding of several other Saudi state-backed missionary endeavours, including the Muslim World League (1962) and the World Assembly of Muslim Youth (1972). Alongside their efforts to extend influence and dispatch resources outwards to locations around the world, these various initiatives were also bound up with pan-Islamism in so far as they brought together a diverse array of Islamic activist figures within the kingdom. These included migrant scholars, members of non-Saudi Salafi movements, and political exiles associated with movements such as the Muslim Brotherhood from across the Arabic-speaking world and beyond, who took up advisory roles and paid employment at the IUM and other comparable projects.[33] The university also came to be connected in certain ways with key pan-Islamist causes, including the insurgency fought against the Soviet occupation of Afghanistan in the 1980s. In the early years of the conflict, the IUM along with the Muslim World League dispatched delegations to assess its humanitarian fallout.[34] According to one graduate, students were also free to involve themselves directly: 'If you wanted to go and you were a student, they would say "Okay, you can go and we won't suspend you, we won't kick you out. If you come back, you resume your studies." And if anything happened to the student … they just send your family back home.'[35]

The IUM project itself, framed in terms of service to a global *umma*, was marked by the same ambivalent juxtaposition of Saudi political community and religious universalism that was a feature of Saudi official discourse more generally. Syllabuses included general content on 'the present situation in the Islamic world', while this in turn included instruction on 'the efforts of the Kingdom of Saudi Arabia in the service of Islam and the Muslims'.[36] The university journal carried articles invoking understandings of universal religious community in keeping with the official and grassroots emphasis on pan-Islamism. Their authors appealed to a notion of a universal Muslim *umma*, as a social and political community in need of practical support, and especially moral guidance, in order for it to be restored to its rightful place in the world. The *umma* was depicted as being beset by enemies without and within, who were weakening its standing in the world by maliciously undermining its moral foundations.[37] The solution to this dilemma tended to be framed in terms of a project of moral and spiritual reform. This was to involve not only individual moral cultivation but also socially engaged *da'wa*, or religious mission. In this sense, a universal conception of Muslim solidarity was advanced as a locus of attachment and a proper sphere of moral and social action. Indeed, transnational religious solidarity and a universal project of moral and spiritual reform were depicted as being mutually reinforcing. As the university journal's editor 'Ali ibn Muhammad ibn Naser al-Fuqayhi put it in an article in the early 1980s, 'the unity of the *umma* is the way of salvation'.[38] Yet these ideas were advanced alongside acknowledgement of the enduring importance and legitimacy of social relations organized within and between nation-states.

The discursive emphasis on a notion of a universal *umma* was matched by practical steps that appear to have been intended to foster a sense of community among students from different backgrounds at the IUM. The fact that all students received advanced instruction in Arabic provided a lingua franca by means of which they could communicate with each other during their time in Medina, whatever their native language. The campus set-up of the university brought them together into a single shared space, in and outside the classroom. Within the campus setting, students from different countries were placed together in shared accommodation in order to push them to develop their Arabic language skills.[39] They were also encouraged to take part in joint extra-curricular activities, including discussion seminars, off-campus trips, and student societies.[40] Such arrangements and activities were clearly meant to bring students into interaction with one another in one social space, governed by a 'correct Islamic atmosphere'.[41] Through such activities, one student suggested, university staff 'really try to make you feel that you are one *umma*, one community'.[42]

Many former IUM students speak in positive terms about this dimension of their experience of life in Medina. In the words of one, 'It opens up your mind and you interact with all these different students from all these different countries and you learn a lot about where they come from and their background.'[43] He goes on to note:

> I lived in a dormitory with three other students. ... My roommate was someone from France, there was a student from Sri Lanka, and there was a student from Indonesia. ... And—*alhamdulillah*—it was a great experience to learn about where they came from and, you know, their backgrounds and what Islam was like in those countries.[44]

Another observes that he and his classmates used to refer to themselves as 'the United Nations class' because they came from so many different countries: '*Wallahi* sometimes you would hear someone who is from a country that you have never heard [of]. ... We had students from all over the world. .... *Alhamdulillah*, we became very strong brothers and *mashallah* we worked together as a team.'[45]

At the same time, appreciating this emphasis on border-spanning religious solidarity should not distract from recognizing the enduring importance of more particularistic forms of identity and attachment. It is not only that the politics of pan-Islamism in the Saudi context were themselves very much bound up with questions of national interest and regime goals. It is also that local and national attachments can remain relevant for students themselves, even as they may aspire to act as part of a universal Islamic community.

One example of this is to be found in the ways in which some students speak of the culture shock associated with moving from their communities of origin to take up their studies in Saudi Arabia. As one British graduate from a South Asian family background puts it:

> You're going to a different country, it's like a different planet. The people are different, the way they speak is different, the language is different, the culture is different, the food is different, the weather is different, the whole environment is different. The lifestyle is different, everything is different. It's like, many of us are from Asia. We go back to Pakistan and we stay there for two or three weeks and we have enough, we want to come back—and we're supposed to be Pakistani. ... So it's difficult, it's not easy. And imagine going to Saudi Arabia. We have no link to Saudi Arabia. You know, we're not originally Arab; so it's difficult, it's not easy.[46]

Such testimonies, particularly in their emphasis on questions of lifestyle, culture, and ethnicity, begin to suggest that aspirations to universal religious solidarity exist alongside more particularistic forms of community, rather than filling a vacuum left by the latter's erosion in the face of globalization.

Some students also note that national, or even racial, identity continues to be an element in structuring social interactions on and around campus. One British graduate recalled that, when it came to studying and socializing in the Prophet's Mosque outside university hours, students of different nationalities tended to congregate together in different parts of the building.[47] Another British graduate from a South Asian family background spoke of his perception that Saudis living in the vicinity of the university looked down on its non-Saudi students, and that comparable dynamics played out within the university's international student body.[48] One graduate from a West African background emphasized that he didn't consider racism to be as big a problem in Saudi Arabia as it is in some other countries; yet he recalled that the presence of students from many different backgrounds led some Saudi youth to refer to the IUM as 'the zoo'. Similarly, another West African graduate noted that in his perception, students from Africa were looked down upon and stigmatized in the IUM context as being poor, compared to more 'advanced' Europeans.[49]

None of this is to suggest that life on the IUM campus is uniquely riven by such divides and tensions; nor is it to call into question the idea that some students, in part as a result of their experiences at the university, see themselves as part of a universal Muslim community. All forms of community have their own internal divisions and tensions, without that in itself being a reason to question the integrity of the community and the forms of identity associated with it. The point is only to suggest that alternative forms of identity do not simply evaporate in the face of aspirations to universal Islamic solidarity.

Local and national attachments may also intertwine with and contribute to structuring how students think and speak about their motivations for studying in Medina, and the choices they make about how to apply what they have learned there in their own *da'wa* after graduation. Discussing the issue of high drop-out rates at the IUM, one graduate notes that 'every one of us that went there, we had an *amana* on our shoulders, a trust on our shoulders, that we would go there and we would study, and we would come back and we would benefit our communities'.[50] The phrasing here suggests an understanding of multiple, more particularistic forms of community existing alongside any understanding of universal Islamic community, and remaining legitimate spheres of action and engagement. This also comes through in testimony from an American graduate, discussing his decision to return to the United States after leaving Medina and to take up a post at an Islamic centre there. He frames this choice by saying: 'I really care a lot about my people, the people from my country, the American people and I really want to see that the message of Islam reaches to them.'[51] Such statements are not in tension with any sense of loyalty to the global Muslim community; certainly, the two may coexist at the level of individual students, in the same way that official Saudi discourse has long juxtaposed notions of Saudi political community with universal religious community, and has posited one as being compatible with and in the service of the other. What they do again suggest is that any sense of universal religious solidarity does not necessarily supplant other forms of identity and community. This in turn implies that, to the extent that forms of universal religious identity and community come to be a concern for those who pass through the IUM's campus, these are best understood according to a transnational picture, in which they may well coexist and intersect with enduring forms of attachment to local and national communities.

After leaving Medina, those who have studied at the IUM engage in a variety of different kinds of socio-political projects. Some, like the Egyptian 'Abd al-Rahman 'Abd al-Khaliq, have taken an interest in formal politics. Often seen as a key figure who has fused Muslim Brotherhood-style activism with Salafi religiosity, 'Abd al-Khaliq settled in Kuwait after his graduation from the IUM in the 1960s and advocated for Salafi involvement in party politics. He became a key figurehead of the Society for the Revival of Islamic Heritage, which in the 1980s offered Salafis in Kuwait 'an institutional framework for engaging in the political process'.[52] Others have established formally organized, border-spanning *da'wa* projects—such as AlKauthar Institute, led by the IUM graduate Tawfique Chowdhury—which provide for coordination of religious instruction to large numbers of people in multiple countries. Many others have simply dispersed into workaday struggles to find employment and provide for families. To the extent that they undertake socially engaged religious activities, they do so in the context of mosques, Islamic centres, and through informal modes of preaching in the communities in which they live and work.[53] In this sense, IUM graduates have become involved in projects of moral, social, or political reform structured at a range of levels, from the local to the national and the transnational.

It is relevant in this context to consider how the valences of projects pursued by IUM graduates may differ, not only in their form but also in their content. Some such forms of diversity may be quite subtle. On the issue of jurisprudence, for example, the IUM teaches a comparative approach to Islamic law; students are invited to consider the rulings of all of the mainstream Sunni schools of law on any given issue, and to make a judgement on which is most legitimate with reference to proof texts from the Qur'an and the sunna. However, this has left scope for some to find ways of accommodating elements of their religious backgrounds into this framework. One graduate from a West African background, for example, noted how IUM graduates from Cameroon often remain 'diehard Malikis' but had come to reframe their affinity with the Maliki school of jurisprudence, which has long been a defining feature of religious practice in West Africa, by putting a special emphasis on seeking to justify Maliki legal rulings on any given issue with reference to proof texts from the Qur'an and the sunna. In this way, the universalizing principles taught at the IUM do not necessarily obliterate the significance of a sense of geographically situated, West African Maliki community; rather, they come to be bound up with a process whereby the meaning of that community is recast.

Other divergences are much more dramatic, particularly on issues of politics. Many graduates, for example, look quite favourably on the Saudi regime and will speak publicly in its defence.[54] Others, however, have been vocally critical of the Saudi regime and its policies.[55] Differing stances on other key issues, such as the legitimacy of engagement in party politics, have led to fierce disputes between figures who have moved in the orbit of the IUM. The IUM scholar al-Madkhali, for example, known for his forceful stance against engagement in opposition politics, has insisted on the need to refuse all engagement with the Society for the Revival of Islamic Heritage led by IUM graduate 'Abd al-Khaliq in Kuwait, on the grounds that any cooperation with them would inevitably be corrupting.[56] Similarly, 'Abd al-Khaliq's political engagement was condemned by the former IUM scholar al-Albani.[57] Such splits have also played out on a more everyday basis, among students on the IUM campus. Particularly in the 1990s, life at the IUM and in the networks surrounding it was strongly influenced by the thinking of scholars—such as al-Madkhali and the Ethiopian Muhammad Aman al-Jami—whose followers have a reputation for taking an especially strident, exclusivist stance in relation to other Muslims whose creed or praxis they understand to be flawed. Such influences have fed a dynamic whereby some IUM students would see others as falling outside a correct understanding of Islam, to the extent that they would refuse engagement with them in everyday social life and would go out of their way to 'refute' them as followers of the true Salafi creed and path. For many graduates, the experience of being faced with such splits is an enduring memory of their time in Medina.[58]

The sharp disparities involved in some of these splits and the depth of feeling associated with them is arguably sufficient to raise questions about the utility of thinking of those who move in the orbit of the IUM—or indeed Salafis more generally—as engaged in 'collective action' within the terms of something equivalent to a new social movement. While this way of thinking certainly makes room for diversity in the specific goals and worldviews of members of such a movement, there is arguably a risk that it tends to overplay the coherence and shared direction of their thinking and action. An alternative way of thinking, in terms of Salafis as bound together as members of a discursive community, may do more to emphasize the role of the kinds of divergences, debate, and disputation highlighted here, not only as features of the Salafi community but as being central to the processes by which it is constituted.

While the notion of a community of discourse is borrowed from linguistics,[59] it has been used previously by John Voll as a basis for thinking about Islam as a border-spanning social formation. Adapting ideas from world systems theory but distancing himself from its emphasis on material exchange, Voll uses the idea of a 'community of discourse' to capture Islam as a 'global [network] of human relations based more on discourse and exchange of ideas than on … economic relations'.[60] Focusing on common imbrication in this exchange of ideas, Voll suggests, makes it possible to speak of 'diverse communities as [having been] part of the "the Islamic world"' at points in history where it is not obvious that they were otherwise bound together by such phenomena as trade.[61] For Voll, it is through attention to a common 'pattern of communication or discourse' that the Islamic world becomes identifiable 'as a social system or human group possessing boundaries, structures, coherence and rules of legitimation'.[62]

Such ideas may be developed further with reference to Talal Asad's conception of Islam as a discursive tradition—a constellation of elements including texts, modes of argument, practices, and norms, which evolve as they are continually applied to new circumstances but which maintain coherence and continuity as pious Muslims seek to legitimize their new interpretations of the tradition through reference to its past.[63] If one understands Salafism as a subsidiary tradition within the broader Islamic tradition, then this suggests understanding its coherence with reference to the ways in which contemporary Salafis seek to develop and legitimize responses to contemporary concerns by appealing not only to the foundational Islamic texts but also to a more restricted, overlapping set of past referents. What is significant is that the process of appealing to an overlapping set of past referents draws Salafis into debate with one another. For, as Asad himself argues, it is not to be expected that all adherents of a given discursive tradition will arrive at the same conclusions in their efforts to bring that tradition to bear on contemporary circumstances. Rather, Islam and Salafism, in common with any other tradition, are inevitably marked by 'argument and conflict', as adherents contest each other's interpretation of the tradition.[64]

It is in a comparable way, I suggest, that Salafis may be understood as an identifiable transnational religious community. A point of departure for such thinking is available in accounts of the rise of modern nationalism which locate this process in the ways in which previously dispersed actors came to be connected in part through their common engagement in disputation and competition within new social spaces forged by the emergence of markets for print capitalism or the imposition of post-colonial state bureaucracies.[65] In such accounts, actors are drawn together into new forms of community and collective identity not necessarily on the basis of any pre-existing commonalities but partly through contestatory mutual engagement within these new shared spaces. In the same way, those who move in the orbit of the IUM are brought not only into the physical space of its campus but also into a broader shared space of debate encompassing actors in far-flung locations. In being introduced to texts from the Salafi canon and principles from the past Salafi tradition, they enter into debates about how lessons drawn from these precedents ought to be applied to matters of contemporary concern, in spheres of life from personal pious practice to politics. These debates may give rise to shared values, and they may also give rise to explicit discourses of universal community; but they can and do equally give rise to fierce splits. Regardless, they generate a thick web of direct and indirect interactions—in forums from scholarly works to study circles, pamphlets, and internet chat rooms—which are ultimately what make it meaningful to speak of Salafis as a transnational religious community. At the same time, as membership in this community is forged through shared participation in debates that arise as the tradition itself is applied to circumstances that present themselves at the local and national levels, as well as at the global level, it by no means necessarily supplants the relevance of those various levels of identification and attachment. As with the case of West African students recasting their attachment to Maliki traditions in a Salafi legal vocabulary, participation in these transnational debates may well leave room for the persistence of more localized forms of community, religious and otherwise.

Conclusion

As with modern Salafism more broadly, discourses at stake in the IUM context and in the networks that have grown up around it have featured a concept of a universal Muslim *umma*. The university's Salafi missionary project was one manifestation of an emphasis on pan-Islamism in Saudi official discourse and foreign policy in the period after it was founded, and it was also the case that the nature of the project—bringing together scholars and young students from across the world within the ambit of a shared endeavour—stood to foster a certain sense of border-spanning religious solidarities amongst those involved. However, this discourse of *umma* identity should not be isolated and allowed to distract attention from the other forms of local and national attachment which those involved may continue to feel. These are not necessarily in tension with universal religious solidarities; rather, it is important to consider how these different levels of attachment and community may coexist and intersect in such Salafi contexts.

As a way of understanding the forms of transnational solidarity and community at stake in modern Salafism, I have suggested thinking of Salafis as a community of discourse. In this understanding, while members of such a community may hold shared values and aspirations, whether they do or not is a matter of contingency. What is more fundamental is that, through their reference to an overlapping set of past practices, principles, and texts at stake in the Salafi tradition, Salafis are drawn together into a shared space of debate about how lessons drawn from those precedents ought to be applied to contemporary conditions, in the contexts in which they live their lives. It is the proliferation of direct and indirect relations produced by these debates that makes it meaningful to speak of Salafis around the world as being part of a single community. This also draws attention to the fact that, through efforts to place themselves at the heart of this community by means of missionary projects such as the IUM, Saudi political and religious actors place themselves at the heart of those debates; as a result, while they may find values and aspirations in common with many other members of this community, their views and actions equally become subject to scrutiny and critique.

8

WAHHABISM, SAUDI ARABIA, AND THE ISLAMIC STATE

'ABDULLAH IBN JIBRIN AND TURKI AL-BIN 'ALI

Cole Bunzel

On 13 July 2009, Shaykh 'Abdullah ibn Jibrin, at the age of about seventy-six, died of natural causes at the King Faysal Specialist Hospital in Riyadh. At the time of his death he was among the most senior members of the Wahhabi religious establishment. Indeed, along with Grand Mufti 'Abd al-'Aziz Bin Baz (d. 1999) and Council of Senior 'Ulama' member Muhammad al-'Uthaymin (d. 2001), Ibn Jibrin was one of the best-known Wahhabi scholars of the later twentieth century. He was, however, somewhat different from these two peers. Further removed from the official religious establishment of the kingdom, he embodied a harsher version of Wahhabism than the establishment had come to allow, one approximating to the ideology of Jihadi Salafism associated with such groups al-Qaeda and the Islamic State and making him, on his death in the summer of 2009, something of a contested figure.

Ibn Jibrin's demise was widely mourned in Saudi Arabia, and as is customary on such occasions members of the Saudi royal family telephoned his family to express their condolences. Among those to call were King 'Abdullah (d. 2015), Crown Prince Sultan (d. 2011), and Prince Salman, the governor of Riyadh, who would ascend the throne several years later, in 2015. According to Ibn Jibrin's son, 'Abdullah described Ibn Jibrin's death as a 'catastrophe.'[1] Elsewhere Salman would write that he had known Ibn Jibrin personally and had carried on a close personal relationship with him.[2]

But the Saudi royals were not the only ones mourning Ibn Jibrin's loss that day. Far afield, in the world of Jihadi Salafism, there was also an elegiac mood. Within days there appeared an online eulogy by a certain Turki al-Bin'ali, a young jihadi firebrand from Bahrain.[3] It was published on the website of the Jordanian–Palestinian jihadi ideologue Abu Muhammad al-Maqdisi. The twenty-five-year-old author, writing at the time under the pseudonym Abu Humam al-Athari, had been a student of Ibn Jibrin's in Riyadh. In just a few years he would become one of the leading scholars in the Islamic State group, living somewhere in the 'caliphate' between Syria and Iraq. Al-Bin'ali also considered Ibn Jibrin's death a catastrophe, but for other reasons. Ibn Jibrin, he stated, was a scholar who had promoted jihad, tutoring countless young men who went on to fight across the globe, including Saudis fighting the Saudi government. Evidently, Ibn Jibrin's legacy was disputed. Was he a quietist, pro-Saudi scholar, as the Saudi eulogies would suggest? Or was he a philo-jihadi, as al-Bin'ali claimed?

Herein lies a puzzle. How is it possible that the same Wahhabi scholar could be eulogized by a Saudi royal and a jihadi radical—no less than the current king of Saudi Arabia and one of the most senior religious authorities in the Islamic State group until his death in May 2017? That is the question that this short chapter addresses. The answer lies in understanding both Ibn Jibrin and what he represents—something of the more hardline Wahhabism of old—and al-Bin'ali and what he represents—a jihadi ideology increasingly oriented around the same hardline Wahhabism. As will be seen, this question has implications for the present and future of Saudi Arabia's fight against extremism.

Ibn Jibrin and the Trajectory of Wahhabism

'Abdullah ibn 'Abd al-Rahman ibn Jibrin was born in 1933/4 (1352 *hijri*) in the provincial town of al-Quway'iyya, located some 180 kilometres west of Riyadh, and grew up in the nearby town al-Rayn.[4] His birth came soon after the official establishment of the Kingdom of Saudi Arabia in 1932, an event that marked the completion of the process of restoring Saudi–Wahhabi authority in the Arabian Peninsula.

The Saudi–Wahhabi restoration—the rise of the third Saudi state—had begun in 1902 with the capture of Riyadh by 'Abd al-'Aziz ibn Saud from Rashidi control. The leading Wahhabi scholars of central Arabia quickly took up the cause of the new Saudi state, seeing in it a revival of what they deemed the paradigmatic model of the Islamic state: the first Saudi state. Founded in mid-eighteenth-century Najd, the first Saudi state was an expansionary polity that aggressively promulgated Wahhabism, the exclusivist creed formulated by preacher Muhammad ibn 'Abd al-Wahhab (d. 1792). According to the early Wahhabis, most of the world's professed Muslims had fallen into polytheism by failing to direct their worship to God alone. Their error was the perceived giving of partners to God that came with worshipping at the tombs and shrines of saints and prophets. The Wahhabis set out to eradicate such practices and to impose on society their uncompromising understanding of monotheism, or *tawhid* (God's oneness). As the early Saudi state developed, it prosecuted offensive jihad against its Muslim neighbours on the grounds of bringing true Islam to lands dominated by polytheism. Soon after seizing Mecca and Medina, however, the young state would succumb to a grim fate at the hands of the forces of Muhammad 'Ali. In 1818 it was crushed, its leaders and scholars killed or deported, and its capital razed to the ground. A second Saudi state would be formed in 1824, aiming to reunite Saudi political power with Wahhabi religious authority and reconquer the Arabian Peninsula. But it never grew to the size of the original, and in 1891 met its demise amid internal political turmoil. When Ibn Saud launched the third Saudi state in 1902, it was also on the model of the original Saudi–Wahhabi statebuilding project. The state's expansion was considered justified offensive jihad to spread the true faith among lapsed Muslims. In the decades preceding Ibn Jibrin's birth, the Wahhabi scholars wrote fatwas authorizing jihad in just such terms.[5]

But by the early 1930s the first Saudi state as a political model was fast going out of fashion. Ibn Saud had made the conscious decision to abandon that model in favour of establishing a kingdom that would function as a mere nation-state within the world nation-state system. Meanwhile, the Wahhabi scholars, who had so cheered the coming of a new Saudi state on the original model, saw their position severely undermined as partners of the Al Saud. 'After 1930', as one Western scholar has put it, 'the ulama's political position was finally reduced to one of a junior partner. ...The scholars were no longer able to shape important policy decisions.'[6] One reason for the decline of their influence was the suppression in 1929–30 of the Ikhwan revolt. In the 1920s the Ikhwan ('brethren'), a collection of sedentarized Bedouin tribal forces, rebelled against the perceived religious moderation of Ibn Saud, hoping to continue the jihad against their neighbours. The Wahhabi scholars, while sympathetic to the Ikhwan's more uncompromising vision of a proper Wahhabi polity, supported Ibn Saud in putting down the rebellion. But the loss of the zealous Ikhwan meant a decline in their influence. One indication of such a decline in these years was Ibn Saud's response to the scholars' recommendation, in 1927, to convert or expel the Shi'a from the Eastern Province: he ignored it.[7] Ibn Saud also ignored their many complaints about the presence of non-Muslim foreigners—namely European and American Christians—residing and working in Arabia.[8]

The co-author of one such complaint before 1930 was a young, up-and-coming scholar named Muhammad ibn Ibrahim Al al-Shaykh, later the kingdom's grand mufti. His complaint stated plainly that the presence of these foreigners was 'prohibited; the shari'a does not permit it'.[9] While in later life Ibn Ibrahim chose 'negotiation and compromise' with the political authorities[10] over confrontation—he oversaw the efforts to institutionalize the Wahhabi religious establishment in committees, organizations, courts, and periodicals[11]—he would still be remembered for an especially hardline Wahhabism. His 1960 essay on the illegality of man-made law, an implicit challenge to the government at the time, was a case in point. When he died in 1969, his successor as head of the religious establishment, Bin Baz, took the spirit of compromise to a whole new level. In 1990 he and the other members of the Council of Senior 'Ulama' (Hay'at Kibar al-'Ulama') approved the government's decision to invite US troops to enter the kingdom in the face of a belligerent Iraq. This deeply unpopular move was the final act of 'the Wahhabi ulama's evolution from guardians of an activist ideology to state servants'.[12]

When Ibn Jibrin moved to Riyadh in 1954/5 to begin his official studies, the education system he encountered had been deeply shaped by Ibn Ibrahim. He enrolled in one of the religious institutes founded by Ibn Ibrahim, the Ma'had Imam al-Da'wa al-'Ilmi, graduating in 1961/2. Ibn Ibrahim was one of his teachers. Thereafter he obtained a Master's degree from the Higher Institute of the Magistracy (al-Ma'had al-'Ali lil-Qada') in 1971, and a Ph.D. from the Faculty of Shari'a (Kulliyyat al-Shari'a) in 1986/7.[13] Ibn Jibrin also began to teach during this period, and came to hold a position, beginning in 1981/2, as a member of the official fatwa-issuing body, the General Presidency for Administration of Scholarly Research, Fatwas, Preaching, and Guidance (al-Ri'asa al-'Amma li-Idarat al-Buhuth al-'Ilmiyya wa'l-Ifta' wa'l-Da'wa wa'l-Irshad), more commonly known as the Dar al-Ifta'. His membership in this body continued till 1997.

What separated Ibn Jibrin from his scholarly peers, and what limited his career advancement, was the lack of deference he tended to display towards political authority. While never outright challenging the legitimacy of the Saudi government, he was unafraid to espouse views at odds with its wishes. In some ways he was thus a holdout against the scholars' evolution into pliant state servants.

His first act of dissent came in the early 1990s, a period of unrest in Saudi Arabia that saw the opposition movement known as the Sahwa ('Awakening') come to the fore. The Sahwa, an assembly of mostly younger Wahhabi scholars and religious intellectuals, was riding the wave of popular discontent that attended the arrival of American troops on Saudi soil, pushing a series of reforms. The intended reforms included, among other things, the establishment of an independent 'advisory council' and 'religious committees' to enforce greater conformity of laws and policies with the shari'a.[14] In January 1991 these reforms were set down in the well-known Letter of Demands (*Khitab al-Matalib*), a short document that would be revised in much longer form as the Memorandum of Advice (*Mudhakkirat al-Nasiha*) in mid-1992. Ibn Jibrin was one of 110 signatories of the latter document, being one of only three senior

Wahhabi scholars to add his imprimatur. These three men—the other two being Humud al-Shu'aybi and 'Abdullah al-Mas'ari—were known as the 'supporters' (*munasirun*), a term indicating the few Sawha-aligned scholars of the Wahhabi establishment.[15]

Ibn Jibrin was part of a very small group that was unafraid to voice its displeasure with the direction in which the kingdom was heading. When the Council of Senior 'Ulama' produced a fatwa refuting the Memorandum of Advice, the three *munasirun* returned fire with a stinging counter-refutation.[16] Ibn Jibrin showed himself willing to criticize the government and its most loyal scholars in a public setting. Soon afterwards he became one of six founding members of the Committee for the Defence of Legitimate Rights (CDLR; Lajnat al-Difa' 'an al-Huquq al-Shar'iyya), an opposition group established in May 1993 that later moved its operations to London. Ibn Jibrin would ultimately bend to government pressure and withdraw from the CDLR, but his reputation for outspokenness and dissent had been made, and would endure.[17]

Another issue on which Ibn Jibrin spoke out was the Shi'a. Wahhabi scholars had long looked upon Shi'ism as a heretical sect, as witnessed by their attempt to have the Shi'a deported or converted in the 1920s. Yet in the later twentieth century, as the scholars embraced the Shi'a, however reluctantly, as fellow citizens of the state, there emerged a noted tendency to distinguish between the Shi'i laity and their clergy. The laymen could be excused being born into Shi'ism, but the clerics could not. The question, in other words, was whether individual, ordinary Shi'i Muslims were to be counted as heretics deserving of death. The question would be noted by Turki al-Bin'ali, who wrote that among his teachers were those who excommunicated the Shi'a as individuals and those who excommunicated only the genus of Shi'ism.[18] Ibn Jibrin, as one can see from his writings, belonged to the former group of scholars: he deemed the individuals among the Shi'i masses to be apostates. In one place he wrote that 'perhaps eighty years ago they [the Shi'a] could be excused' their theological errors, but 'today they have no excuse' considering the proliferation of refutations against them.[19] Elsewhere he described them as 'deserving to be killed' for their flawed beliefs.[20] A related fatwa of his states that it is wrong to support the Lebanese militant group Hizballah, since this is a Shi'i group and 'the Shi'a have always harbored hostility toward the Sunnis'.[21]

Yet it was not Ibn Jibrin's willingness to defy the Saudi government, nor his harsh stance on the Shi'a, that al-Bin'ali chose to celebrate in his July 2009 eulogy. Rather, it was his support for jihad. According to al-Bin'ali, Ibn Jibrin spoke fondly of Osama Bin Laden and those waging jihad across the world. 'How often', he wrote, 'did I see him with my own eyes and hear him with my own ears ... expressing support for those waging jihad in all parts of the world and beseeching God on their behalf, after practically every meeting.'[22] 'The theatres of fighting and jihad' were mourning his loss, for the battlefields had been 'watered ... by the blood of the students of our shaykh Ibn Jibrin'.[23] Al-Bin'ali put his feelings into verse:

> The theatres of jihad and their lions mourn you,
>   every sword and spear mourns you.
> The army of truth mourns you, not the army of those
>   who deserve chastisement and loss.[24]

Ibn Jibrin, al-Bin'ali related, preached that the Sunni armed resistance to the American occupation of Iraq was a legitimate jihad.[25] And indeed, Ibn Jibrin has a fatwa to this effect, stating that it was an individual duty (*fard 'ayn*) for Iraq's Sunnis to take up arms against the Americans, considered an invading infidel enemy.[26] In another fatwa he defended the jihadi groups fighting the Americans, criticizing those scholars who would speak ill of them.[27] Al-Bin'ali further claimed that Ibn Jibrin supported the violence of the al-Qaeda jihadis in Iraq. Asked whether he approved of the way Abu Mus'ab al-Zarqawi executed the American Nicholas Berg in a filmed beheading in May 2004, Ibn Jibrin drew his finger across his throat in approbation.[28]

Another jihadi connection to which al-Bin'ali alluded concerns al-Qaeda in the Arabian Peninsula (AQAP), which led a domestic insurgency in Saudi Arabia beginning in 2003. AQAP's chief religious authority, its judge (*qadi*), was a Saudi named 'Isa al-'Awshan, who was not only a student of Ibn Jibrin's but also his son-in-law. Other AQAP members, al-Bin'ali proudly related, were Ibn Jibrin's students as well; he recalled walking past a poster in Riyadh featuring the faces of several wanted men, nearly all of whom were students of Ibn Jibrin.[29]

There is, to be sure, an element of exaggeration in these words painting Ibn Jibrin as a supporter of all things jihad. For example, while Ibn Jibrin praised Osama Bin Laden, he also criticized Bin Laden's position on the Saudi kingdom and condemned the 9/11 attacks. As for Iraq, he wrote that those intending to wage jihad there needed the permission of their parents and of the Saudi government, a position at odds with the jihadis. And he spoke out strongly against AQAP's uprising in Saudi Arabia.[30] Most importantly, unlike the jihadis, he never questioned the legitimacy of the Saudi state.

Yet despite the hyperbole in al-Bin'ali's eulogy, the fact remains that Ibn Jibrin was different. To a large degree he was a relic of the more hardline Wahhabism of old—politically engaged, doctrinally exclusivist, and favourably disposed to jihad—that the Saudi kingdom had sought to distance itself from, and that al-Bin'ali and his allies had come to embrace as their own.

Al-Bin'ali and the Trajectory of Jihadi Salafism

According to a short biography by one of his students, Turki ibn Mubarak al-Bin'ali, also known by the teknonym Abu Sufyan al-Sulami, was born in Bahrain in early September 1984.[31] He grew up in al-Muharraq, a heavily Sunni city in the north of the Shi'a-majority country, and took his early education at local religious schools. His curriculum vitae, in terms of official education, could be described as modest. The young man spent a year and a half at the College of Islamic and Arabic Studies in Dubai, before being arrested and deported for his political views. Thereafter he moved to Lebanon and enrolled there in the Imam al-Awza'i College in Beirut, from which he obtained a 'licence' (*lisans*), the equivalent of a Bachelor's degree, in August 2009.[32] He then returned to Bahrain, earning a graduate certificate (*shahadat takharruj*) from the Bahrain Institute for Shari'a Sciences in May 2011.[33]

But this was only formal education. As the biography goes on to note, al-Bin'ali had a number of prominent Salafi and Jihadi Salafi scholars among his teachers. The second named is Ibn Jibrin. The first is Abu Muhammad al-Maqdisi, the Jordanian jihadi ideologue of Palestinian origin.

The influence of al-Maqdisi on al-Bin'ali's intellectual formation cannot be overstated. According to one of his childhood friends, al-Bin'ali's entry onto the Jihadi Salafi scene began in the early 2000s when a fellow Bahraini regaled him with stories of 'the *mujahidin*' and introduced him to some of al-Maqdisi's books.[34] Al-Bin'ali never actually met al-Maqdisi, but they got to know each other via email and phone. By the late 2000s al-Bin'ali had become a contributor to the senior ideologue's website, Minbar al-Tawhid wa'l-Jihad (The pulpit of monotheism and jihad).[35] Most of his contributions were made under the pseudonym Abu Humam al-Athari, one of several pseudonyms he used at the time.[36] In April 2009 al-Maqdisi provided al-Bin'ali with a general *ijaza*, or teaching certificate, praising his pupil's 'zeal' for knowledge and authorizing him to teach 'all of my writings'. He spoke of al-Bin'ali in glowing terms:

> I authorized him to teach all of my writings, knowing that he has read most, nay, all of my writings, and because of what I saw in him of extraordinary passion and support for the religion, for God's unity (*tawhid*), for jihad, and for the *mujahidin*. Such passion as this ought not to be met but with backing and support and encouragement. If a shaykh has the right to take pride in any of his students, I am proud of this beloved brother.[37]

The affection was no doubt mutual. In 2009 al-Bin'ali wrote an entire book in praise and defence of his teacher.[38] It was also in 2009 that al-Maqdisi set up a shari'a council on his website to answer questions from a Jihadi Salafi perspective, giving Abu Humam al-Athari a leading role.[39] Over the course of several years al-Bin'ali would produce more than 200 fatwas for the council, in addition to penning dozens of essays and books on numerous subjects for the website.[40]

That al-Bin'ali acquired jihadi ideology directly from al-Maqdisi's works is significant, for it means that he imbibed Jihadi Salafism at what has been called 'the end point of the school's development'.[41] Jihadi Salafism (*al-salafiyya al-jihadiyya*) developed over the course of several decades, beginning with the radical ideas of Sayyid Qutb and later incorporating certain tenets of Wahhabism (usually termed Salafism by its adherents). No one did more to bring Wahhabi ideas into jihadism than al-Maqdisi. His highly influential book *Millat Ibrahim* (The religion of Abraham), published in 1984, calls for revolutionary jihad in the idiom of militant Wahhabism; it was a conscious effort to Wahhabize jihadi thinking.[42] The 'end point' of the Jihadi Salafi school's development was the point at which Wahhabi ideas came to prevail, and Jihadi

Salafi 'doctrine no longer made explicit reference to Qutb'.[43] Thus a scholar like al-Bin'ali will be found, in his books, essays, and fatwas, grounding nearly all of his ideas in the religious heritage of Wahhabism. So great indeed was al-Bin'ali's commitment to the Wahhabi heritage that, influenced by traditional Wahhabi views, he initially believed the earth to be flat.[44]

According to the same childhood friend, what drew al-Bin'ali to jihadism was first his exposure to al-Maqdisi's books, and second his experience studying in Riyadh with Ibn Jibrin. Al-Bin'ali's study tour in Riyadh began in either late 2003 or early 2004 and lasted about a year.[45] In a short memoir, al-Bin'ali described his studies and relationship with Ibn Jibrin at length.[46] He claimed to have attended some sixty lessons with Ibn Jibrin per week on a variety of Islamic subjects; to have grown close to him during walks to and from lessons; and to have received several books from him as gifts. Overall, al-Bin'ali said, Ibn Jibrin had a 'great influence' (*athar 'azim*) on him. There is also some evidence that Ibn Jibrin thought highly of his pupil. In April 2004 he wrote al-Bin'ali a letter of recommendation for the Islamic University of Medina, praising his student's 'commitment to knowledge'.[47]

Perhaps just as influential for al-Bin'ali's development as a jihadi thinker was the educational environment of Riyadh. Al-Bin'ali spent most of his time in al-Suwaydi, a suburb of western Riyadh that was known for its jihadi sympathies, and was also where Ibn Jibrin lived and taught. In his eulogy al-Bin'ali said that this area was known as 'the Tora Bora quarter' of Riyadh, which was to say that support for al-Qaeda and its ideology ran deep there.[48] A late 2004 article in one of Saudi Arabia's leading newspapers, *al-Sharq al-Awsat*, conveyed the same impression. It noted that al-Suwaydi had come to be known as 'the Falluja quarter' of Riyadh, having recently witnessed some of the key battles between AQAP and Saudi security forces. The quarter had contributed numerous fighters to the jihad in Afghanistan in the 1980s, was a centre of support for the Sahwa in the 1990s, and was a key battleground in the fight against AQAP. Ibn Jibrin, the article noted, was among the quarter's best-known scholars.[49]

From al-Maqdisi's works al-Bin'ali had acquired the increasingly Wahhabized form of jihadism. His study tour, and his pupillage under Ibn Jibrin, only seem to have strengthened his convictions. There would also appear to be a symbolic significance in al-Bin'ali's claiming Ibn Jibrin as a teacher. In Ibn Jibrin, al-Bin'ali had found a direct link to the Wahhabi scholarly heritage of which he saw himself as the true heir. He had studied under the last of the great Wahhabis.

The Islamic State

The Islamic State group, from its founding in 2006, had long been representative of the general shift in jihadi ideology towards Wahhabi—or Salafi—ideas at the expense of the radical discourse of Muslim Brotherhood thinkers.[50] Abu Mus'ab al-Zarqawi and his al-Qaeda in Iraq group, founded in 2004, were also representative of this trend. Their greater willingness to engage in *takfir*, or excommunication, of large numbers of perceived heretics owed much to the increasing doctrinal influence of Wahhabism. The al-Qaeda old guard, for their part, while to some extent also caught up in the Wahhabizing trend, were intent on maintaining a more pan-Islamic approach to jihadism, being less disposed to engage in *takfir* of those Muslims deemed to hold inadequate beliefs. The distinction between the al-Qaeda view and the Islamic State view is well captured by Zarqawi's insistence in the mid-2000s on targeting Shi'a civilians in Iraq, and Aymen al-Zawahiri's objection that the Shi'a masses are not legitimate targets.

The Islamic State had thus appealed to the Wahhabi heritage for many years. Yet such appeals grew much stronger from 2013, when the Islamic State emerged as the leading group in the global jihad and as a plausible state—indeed, with the June 2014 caliphate declaration, as the restored Islamic caliphate. So critical has Wahhabism been to the Islamic State's religious ideology that it can fairly be described as a Wahhabi state.[51] After setting up a printing press in Mosul in 2014, many of the group's official publications were the key works of the Wahhabi canon, including several by Muhammad ibn 'Abd al-Wahhab. The anonymous editors of these works made the purpose of these publications clear. The Islamic State was laying claim to the mantle of Wahhabism, arguing that it was the heir of the Wahhabi mission, not the kingdom of Saudi Arabia and its 'court scholars'. As the editor's introduction to one of Ibn 'Abd al-Wahhab's printed works wrote: '[The court scholars] know perfectly well that the Islamic State, its mission, and its jihad are an extension and embodiment of the mission of *tawhid* and jihad begun by the Messenger of God and his companions, and renewed by Ibn 'Abd al-Wahhab and his descendants.'[52] Such sentiments would also be found on streets and in training camps. Preaching vans in Islamic State territory, for example, would be seen carrying posters of the theological catechisms of Ibn 'Abd al-Wahhab.[53]

Al-Bin'ali himself gave voice to the Wahhabi claims of the Islamic State. His connection to the group ran deep. In 2003 he travelled to Iraq around the time of the US-led war, and there got to know some of the men who would found al-Qaeda in Iraq and later the Islamic State. He would show marked partiality to the Islamic State from an early date. In 2007, according to his own testimony, he wrote a passionate defence of what was then the Islamic State of Iraq.[54] He wrote again in its favour after two major leaders were killed in 2010.[55] Finally, in 2013, when the Islamic State expanded to Syria and al-Qaeda objected, al-Bin'ali led the charge in support of the Islamic State and its new leader, Abu Bakr al-Baghdadi, against al-Qaeda. In August that year he released a treatise urging all Muslims in Syria and Iraq to give Baghdadi *bay'a*, or allegiance.[56] And he proved himself to be no armchair jihadi, travelling to Syria that year and meeting with the Islamic State's leadership.[57] In early 2014 he returned to Syria, this time settling in Islamic State territory for good.[58]

Al-Bin'ali had quickly become the most prominent and prolific advocate for the Islamic State, writing numerous essays online, including attacks on the group's detractors. The last thing he wrote during this period was a highly personal refutation of his former teacher, al-Maqdisi, who had come out against the Islamic State, sticking by al-Qaeda. Fittingly, al-Bin'ali compared al-Maqdisi to an early detractor of Ibn 'Abd al-Wahhab.[59]

Yet shortly after this, in mid-2014, al-Bin'ali fell silent. His public profile would recede, probably as part of the Islamic State's policy against allowing a cult of personality to grow up around any one scholar. On 31 May, 2017, he was killed in an airstrike in eastern Syria carried out by the US-led coalition. US Central Command's statement on the operation described al-Bin'ali as the Islamic State's 'chief cleric'.[60] His official position at the time of his death, however, as internal communications show, was head of the group's Office of Research and Studies (Maktab al-Buhuth wa'l-Dirasat).[61] In this capacity, as a journalist's interviews from 2015 with several defectors from the group's scholarly ranks show, he remained instrumental. The defectors noted that he was responsible for preparing the religious manuals used at Islamic State training camps and authoring fatwas, among other duties.[62] The most important of these manuals was a précis of Wahhabi creed (*Muqarrar fi 'l-tawhid*) setting out the mandatory beliefs of a Muslim living in Islamic State territory.[63] It is mostly a collection of statements by traditional Wahhabi scholars from the eighteenth to the twentieth centuries. It even quotes from as late an authority as Muhammad ibn Ibrahim, the former grand mufti, on the subject of man-made laws.

That such an important Islamic State document—very likely written by al-Bin'ali—quotes a major Saudi scholar of the mid-twentieth century might seem peculiar in light of the fact that the Islamic State, along with al-Qaeda, considers Saudi Arabia an illegitimate state whose rulers are unbelievers. An earlier fatwa by al-Bin'ali explains how this is possible. Responding to a question about Ibn Ibrahim's stance on the Al Saud, al-Bin'ali was apologetic. He wrote that perhaps the mufti supposed there was an excuse ('*udhr*) for the rulers' un-Islamic behaviour, or did not know the extent of their wrongdoing. In any event, he said, what matters is the substance of his views and how they apply to the Saudi state as we know it today. And one should also remember that before 9/11 very few scholars in the Jihadi Salafi movement deemed the rulers of Saudi Arabia to be unbelievers.[64]

The once ambiguous approach of the jihadis to Saudi Arabia has of course since changed. Both al-Qaeda and the Islamic State call for its immediate overthrow. Between 2003 and 2006 al-Qaeda led a failed uprising in the kingdom, and beginning in 2014 the Islamic State launched its own undertaking to destabilize the country. In November that year Abu Bakr al-Baghdadi announced the establishment of an official presence in Saudi Arabia, and soon afterward a series of terrorist attacks took place across the country, the main targets of which were the Shi'a minority in the Eastern Province and the Saudi security forces. In the span of a year there were at least sixteen security incidents involving the Islamic State and nearly a hundred people were killed.[65] The attacks ranged from assassinations to the murder of family members working for the security services to suicide bombings. The deadliest attacks were two suicide bombings, the first against a Shiʻi mosque in the Eastern Province in May 2015, which killed twenty-one, the second against a mosque belonging to the security forces in ʻAsir in August 2015, which killed fifteen. Attacks since then have been smaller and episodic, suggesting that a security crackdown has been largely successful in disrupting the group's networks. An important development seems to have been the arrest in May 2016 of a Saudi militant believed to have been the main link with the group's leadership in Iraq and Syria.[66]

The Islamic State's campaign in Saudi Arabia may have lost momentum. The group is hopeful, however, that the intended reforms of Deputy Crown Prince Muhammad ibn Salman can revive it, turning the country's religious conservatives against the government. In a speech from November 2016, Baghdadi decried the Al Saud's efforts 'to secularize the country' (*ʻalmanat al-bilad*) and called on Saudis to step up attacks, especially against the security forces.[67] As the Islamic State adopts a decidedly Wahhabi posture, and as the kingdom tries to move further away from the hardline Wahhabism of its origin, the potential for jihadi unrest in Saudi Arabia continues to loom large.

9

PARRICIDE IN THE KINGDOM

GENEALOGY, NATIONALISM, AND THE ISLAMIC STATE CHALLENGE

Nadav Samin

Saudi Arabia is today challenged by the revolutionary Islamic State movement (ISIS), which seeks to topple the Saudi monarchy and impose a new governing order in the heart of the Arabian Peninsula. One aspect of Islamic State's strategy emerged in March 2015, when a Saudi commander with the movement called on fellow Saudis to kill relatives employed by the state's security services. While religious in its justification, this parricidal call and its bloody response by a small yet significant subset of Saudi youth is, I argue, motivated by deeper resentments and pathologies that derive from the particular nature of the Saudi political system. A crucial yet poorly understood aspect of that system is the politics of genealogy.

Genealogy serves two roles in the Saudi system of governance. It is both an instrument of domination and a basis for an idiomatic nationalism. The structuring of politics around genealogical ideas and mechanisms accentuates the patriarchy, ageism, and state paternalism that constitute the dominant modes of Saudi social and political life. Yet a genealogical politics also produces the foundation for an authentically Arabian concept of nationhood, one that works to bind Saudis together around a sense of shared destiny. I call this latter phenomenon kinship nationalism, which is a form of nationalism that prevails in countries such as Kyrgyzstan and Saudi Arabia,[1] one that draws heavily from pre-modern conceptions of clan and tribe, yet repurposes them for the contemporary political space. Genealogy is thus the distinctive quality of Saudi domination, at once a resonant nationalist discourse and a technology of power, raising people up while cutting them down. This duality in the kingdom's genealogical politics explains the impetus behind the Islamic State's parricidal campaign, but also its failure.

God, Kin, and Parricide

In a March 2015 video address, a Saudi commander with ISIS enjoined his countrymen to attack and kill members of their own families who worked for the state's security services. Enacting this edict is the only pious course of action, he insisted, the means by which to eliminate injustice in Saudi Arabia and precipitate the monarchy's overthrow. Since that address, Islamic State sympathizers in the kingdom have responded with acts of extreme violence against their family members, among them: a group of cousins including a doctor and an engineer executed another cousin by firearm 100 metres from a busy Saudi highway; a dreamy-eyed Instagram enthusiast killed his officer uncle and later blew himself up in his vehicle outside a prison; two brothers kidnapped their soldier cousin and filmed themselves shooting him to death in the desert; and twin brothers stabbed their parents and brother to death in their home in a wealthy section of north Riyadh.

Parricide as a political strategy does not originate with ISIS. The act of killing one's parents or close relatives finds expression in the realm of political philosophy and the historical practice of states in a range of interesting ways. The earliest call to eviscerate a kinship-based civic order comes to us from Plato. In his *Laws*, Plato suggests that the ideal polity or political system is one in which the family unit (or private patriarchal domain) has been dissolved and a system of communal property instituted. While parricide is not here directly contemplated, Plato's vision of a radically communal polity enacted through the coercive authority of an elite class of guardians represents an important model for social engineering in subsequent ages.[2] Machiavelli contemplates parricide more explicitly. He blames the Catholic Church for the perpetual instability of Italian politics in the sixteenth century, and faults Cesare Borgia for failing to assassinate his father, the pope, seeing this action as the virtuous route towards a new non-ecclesiastical order.[3] Modern regimes from North Korea to the Cambodian Khmer Rouge have made political sport of ripping families apart on ideological grounds. ISIS has built on this dubious multi-confessional legacy and adapted it for an Arabian and Islamic milieu.

ISIS's parricidal campaign, conducted through subterfuge and viral video, is meant to drive a wedge through the Saudi family unit, which Article 9 of the Saudi Basic Law proclaims to be 'the nucleus of Saudi society'. It is also an assault on the broader ideological architecture of the state, according to which a particular family, the Al Saud, governs on behalf of the kingdom's many kinship collectives. The campaign rests on a bloodthirsty transmuting of a core Islamic ethic, the notion that it is the obligation of Muslims to intervene in the lives of other Muslims if the latter are perceived to be behaving unethically—to 'command right and forbid wrong', in Michael Cook's foundational rendering.[4] More specifically, it derives from a statement popularly attributed to the Prophet Muhammad and interpreted in idiosyncratic terms by ISIS to mean that 'one's relatives are the most appropriate [address] for encouraging ethical behavior' (al-aqribun awla bi-l-ma'ruf). Atop this edifice is asserted another religious ethic, that of loyalty and disavowal (al-wala wa-l-bara'), or loyalty to true Muslims and disavowal of those hostile to Islam.[5] Because of their support for the Saudi regime, disavowal of one's relatives must be absolute, the militant explains, and can include killing them.

While justified or even impelled by these two related religious injunctions, ISIS's parricidal campaign responds to pathologies and resentments that exceed the dimensions of this religious discourse. In his address the Saudi militant quickly shifts to a more mundane argument for why the targeting of one's own kin is necessary for destroying the Saudi regime: 'By God, the Saudi royal family could not rule the Arabian Peninsula without the tribes.' His position was later echoed by the kingdom's de facto ruler, Muhammad ibn Salman, in comments made to Thomas Friedman for the *New York Times*: 'People misunderstand our monarchy. It is not like Europe. It is a tribal form of monarchy, with many tribes and subtribes and regions connecting to the top.'[6]

The resilience of the Saudi system, and the nature of ISIS's challenge to it, cannot be understood without attention to how kinship works in the kingdom. By 'kinship' is not meant an atavistic principle assumed to constitute the bedrock of consciousness and political organization in Arabia—the tribal model. In the modern Gulf states genealogy has been transposed as a locally resonant discourse of nationalism,[7] and, just as important, as a technique of governance and control. While oil wealth and Wahhabism are the stuff of fixation for most observers, the intimate, ubiquitous, and opaque world of kinship and tribal politics lies at the heart of the kingdom's social contract.

The Saudi tribe is today a shell of its former self. The state now performs what were once its core functions, the provisioning of economic goods and physical security. Tribal identity is largely a symbolic virtue, and, for those who lack tribal affiliation, a normative aspiration. The aspiration to claim a prestigious lineage is reinforced by the glorification of family rule that forms a core element of the ideology of the ruling regime. Being a respectable Saudi means mimicking the prestige of the royal lineage in miniature—for example, by producing a family tree. Yet there are more profound and significant ways in which genealogy and kinship factor into the techniques of governance and control that prevail in the kingdom, and in turn into the shaping of citizen identities and practices.

Though a powerful centralized state, Saudi Arabia is still no model of Weberian order. Informal networks of power and patronage remain central to the workings of the Saudi system. In highly significant ways, however, the state has bureaucratized its native milieu, formalizing kinship mechanisms for the purposes of domination and control. A key argument of my book *Of Sand or Soil* is that the Saudi state has structured politics in such a way that the process of what I call lineal authentication is at the heart of almost all sub-state political action.[8] By lineal authentication is meant a practice of verifying clan or tribal affiliation for the purposes of criminal justice or broader political and social control. The state's fastest access point to drug smugglers and jihadists is through their families and kinship groups—and that is by design.

Out of this system has emerged a new class of quasi-political actors: lineal authenticators. Lineal authenticators include prominent scholarly authorities such as the genealogist Hamad al-Jasir (d. 2000), who over the course of his lifetime fielded thousands of queries from Saudis wishing to affirm their lineal origins, but also quasi-governmental officials known as *mu'arrifun*, who are paid to police their kinship collectives on behalf of the Interior Ministry. These classes of individuals exist alongside a range of other lineal authentication committees and bodies, all of which help structure and order Saudi society beyond the limits of formal state control. Authenticators have also come to play important roles in the new Saudi economy, from the validation of citizenship claims, to the distribution of state subsidies, to the facilitation of foreign-labour-import schemes.

In October 2015 King Salman decreed that tribal leaders and authenticators would henceforth receive regular monthly stipends from the Interior Ministry.[9] This major new entitlement programme, announced at a time of severe economic contraction, was the culmination of a process many decades in the making, namely, the formalizing of long-emergent systems of governance, control, and domination specific to the Saudi system. In a state characterized by a deep concentration of power and a weakness of comprehensive vision, authentication is one of the few political functions that demand delegation to semi-autonomous agents. In a country governed by a genealogical principle that permits no meaningful vehicles for political engagement, politics can only be about religious exhortation or lineal affirmation.

Kinship politics in Saudi Arabia works as an instrument of domination meant to further fragment a politically underdeveloped polity. Yet it also has an affirmative lining, as a basis for asserting a distinctive Arabian address in the age of ethno-linguistic nation-states. The genealogical discourse tacitly or actively promoted by the Saudi state has helped to lay the groundwork for an idiomatically Gulf Arab kinship nationalism, one rooted in ideas of lineal purity, and underpinned by a sense of the kingdom's unique providence in having been endowed as the linchpin of the fossil-fuel economy and the birthplace of Islam.

How do ideas of genealogical relatedness work as a component of nationalism in the broader Middle East? They don't always, in fact. We might recall here Sayf al-Islam Gaddafi's televised late-night plea to the Libyan people in February 2011, as the country ruled by his father was beginning to disintegrate. 'Libya is not Tunisia or Egypt,' he insisted. '*Libiya qaba'il wa 'asha'ir*' (Libya is tribes and clans).[10] The experience of Libya hints at a significant problem with any kinship-based nationalism. By glorifying the idea of ascriptive attachments, kinship nationalism breathes life into potentially adversarial micro-collectives, thus encouraging fractiousness and weak citizen ties. Yet for authoritarian regimes, kinship-based nationalism has great utility. When you are tribes and clans, you tend not to also be revolutionary republicans. For the Saudi regime, a kinship-based nationalism keeps the cauldron of tribal and/or clan pride boiling, without bubbling over into mass insurrection.

To understand how, we might consider the meaning of Saudi kinship in Toquevillian terms, as a form of civic association. Few meaningful forms of civic association are permissible in Saudi Arabia. Political parties, labour unions, and syndicates, those vanguards of the Arab Spring uprisings, do not exist there in any meaningful capacity.[11] Public gatherings of a political nature are prohibited. Khalid al-Juhani learned this last fact the hard way on 11 March 2011, when he was arrested and jailed after responding to an anonymous Facebook call for public protest in Riyadh against the Saudi regime. He was quite literally the only person who showed up to the demonstration site in downtown Riyadh on that day.

What remains by way of civic association in the kingdom is the kinship group, extended family, or tribe. Since the turn of the century, members of historically nomadic tribal confederations have gathered in the tens of thousands for sometimes month-long competitive camel and vernacular poetry festivals called *mazayin al-ibl*. As a participant at the massive 'Utayba festival observed to me, 'the quantity of meat served there could have fed all of the starving people in Somalia'. It is notable that the Saudi regime decided in 2007 to outlaw such gatherings, promoting in their stead more generically Bedouin, state-sponsored cultural and camel festivals (for example, Umm Ruqayba), which are intended to foster kinship nationalism minus its subversive corollary, *'asabiyya* or tribal chauvinism. Meanwhile, Saudis of sedentary origin (*hadar*) are in the grip of their own genealogical obsession, the pageantry of which recalls sixteenth-century Seville, when the exogenous shock of New World gold produced opportunities for social mobility through the fabrication of pure (that is, non-Jewish or non-Muslim) lineages.[12]

From intimate family ties to the most grandiose expressions of Saudi nationalism, the Saudi kinship unit is the essential glue that binds the kingdom's disparate populations together, while at the same time preventing them from mobilizing collectively for radical political change. The form of revolutionary violence enacted by ISIS against this arrangement is motivated only in part by religious conviction. It is just as much about overthrowing the signature Saudi modes of domination: patriarchy, ageism, and state paternalism. This revolutionary violence, I would also like to suggest, is not generic to repressive states, but is rather an idiomatic response to the distinctive Saudi system of politics. In making this claim, I reconsider the nature of Saudi exceptionalism as a substantive reality originating in Saudi Arabia's unique relationship with colonialism.

The Revolt against Paternalism

'I began to realize that even the practices of my father were not part of Islam,' the rural Moroccan notable Hajj 'Abd ar-Rahman explained to Dale Eickelman in 1976.[13] The universal drama of intergenerational conflict, of fathers and sons, is certainly exacerbated in Saudi Arabia, a society in which both private and public culture, that of the *majlis* (private gathering space) and that of *nasab* (lineage) and *hasab* (inherited reputation), are structured around kinship dynamics and hierarchies. When nephews turn guns on their uncles, or sons on their fathers, they are indicting that fuzzy space between private and public patriarchy that constitutes the forming grounds of citizen identity in Saudi Arabia.

July 2015 marked the first macabre enactment of ISIS's viral campaign in the kingdom. In that month, a young unemployed man, 'Abdallah Fahd al-Rushayd, killed his maternal uncle, a Ministry of Interior officer named Rashid Ibrahim al-Sufyan, before blowing himself up at a vehicle checkpoint near the notorious al-Ha'ir prison in south Riyadh. Both 'Abdallah al-Rushayd and his uncle were active on social media. We are thus afforded a useful comparative snapshot of the lives, worldviews, and attitudes of intimately related regime supporters and opponents.

Rashid al-Sufyan's Twitter feed features the standard repertoire of Saudi national loyalties and avocations: love of homeland, king, and his predecessors; deference to the religious guidance of establishment scholars; passion for soccer. His social media profile reflects a sense of fastidious regularity, even a banality. It is peppered with bourgeoisie pious affirmations that are not much different from Hallmark greetings or self-help aphorisms. Al-Sufyan's religious preoccupations are magnanimous and this-worldly: 'God, please bring warm weather to Syria.'[14] He displays no particular affection for matters of tribal identity. Yet that is just as well. To be a Saudi patriot is to be attached to one's kin identity, to one degree or another. Kinship, at least in Najd, is the air al-Sufyan breathed.

His nephew 'Abdallah al-Rushayd's Instagram account, by contrast, reflects the life of a religious activist youth, of an identity in formation. Whereas his uncle's social media religiosity is of an anodyne variety, al-Rushayd's feed includes a great number of brusque and demonstrative pietistic statements and anti-liberal quotations. The majority of al-Rushayd's Instagram posts from the last few months of his life consist of short videos of the young man performing religious exhortations (wa't) in the fashion of an activist religious scholar. Two images from al-Rushayd's account stand out. The first is a portrait of the Saudi-born jihadist commander Khattab. The second is a diptych featuring a Saudi youth with long, unkempt hair and pants falling off of his waist, alongside an old black-and-white image of a hunter in traditional Arabian clothes holding a gun and the body of a big cat, over which is superimposed in block letters the word 'Ancestors'.[15]

Patriarchy and ageism, meaning domination by elders, serve as intensifiers of militant challenges by Saudi youth to the system in which they have been reared. Whereas earlier generations of Saudi jihadists including Osama Bin Laden paid rhetorical fealty to elders such as the late Wahhabi mufti Bin Baz,[16] ISIS shatters this normative framework, along with everything else in its path. The revolt against elder authority can also be read in terms of the extreme age disparities within many Saudi families. Western popular culture reshapes attitudes towards

Figure 1: Image from 'Abdallah al-Rushayd's Instagram feed. His caption reads, 'God damn some people'.

patriarchy and respect for elders, a shift that is now compounded by ISIS's prodding. Yet as a form of revolutionary parricide, ISIS's campaign is more than a revolt against the Saudi family structure. It is also an effort to overthrow what we might term the stifling paternalism of modern Saudi life.

In a society of cradle-to-grave subsidies, where politics is personalized through networks of patronage, and citizens are constrained from asserting an economic, social, or political will that is independent from that of the state, resistance takes a distinctive texture and form. The challenge for the average citizen was captured viscerally by Khalid al-Juhani, the 11 March protester:

> I was frightened, and held my tongue, until I exploded. Enough! What is there to be afraid of anymore? [The princes say that their doors are open], but if you had a request, and you came on a Saturday, they would say to you, 'The prince … isn't here today, come back on such-and-such date'—in a thousand years. I am a son of this country. I need [state services] to be provided to me without having to beg for them.[17]

Al-Juhani was imprisoned for his public disparaging of the Saudi regime and the failed promise of state paternalism.

'Abd al-'Aziz al-Muqrin, founder of al-Qaeda in the Arabian Peninsula (AQAP), was killed in 2004 for his violent defiance of that very order. Before his fiery demise, al-Muqrin captured the frustrations engendered by state paternalism:

> Recently, people have begun to imagine that making a living can only be accomplished by securing a government job. This is a vulgar notion that the apostate traitorous rulers have planted in people's heads. They also planted in their minds the notion that you will not be able to eat or drink until they control you and you become their employee. Praise God, the people have begun returning to commerce and relying on themselves, after economic difficulties beset them.[18]

Saudi jihadism, like its liberal activist corollary, is at its core a campaign to cast off the immobilizing effects of state paternalism. It is about reclaiming a martial spirit that was abandoned with Saudi Arabia's emergence as the slow-moving custodian of the world's energy supplies, a martial spirit that is also a key dimension of ethno-nationhood in the modern world. In light of this understanding, the poetical pronouncements of Muhannad al-Shihri, a 9/11 hijacker from the marginal Saudi south, take on newfound meaning: 'So forge the passports, and oppose all who bootlick, and whoever finds a way, should come to us. Light a fire in the infidels, to raise from us the shame, don't fear or be afraid, but say "I am rough."'

'Asib al-Ra's: Poetical Contests of Renewed Consequence

ISIS's parricidal campaign distills the tension between kinship and religious bonds that is at the heart of modern Saudi citizen identity. This tension has arguably existed since the birth of Islam,[19] yet it takes an acute form in modern Saudi Arabia. On the one hand is a religious tradition, Wahhabism, that demands complete fealty to its status-levelling imperatives and thus the dissolving of greater kinship attachments. On the other is a modern state and a residual nomadic culture that affirm the enduring value of greater kinship associations and social hierarchies, albeit for differing reasons. In working to sever those bonds of kinship at their root and forge new solidarities and bases of camaraderie, ISIS takes the logic of that religious tradition to extreme ends. The story of its Saudi herald Sa'd al-Shatiri and the poetical contest he helped instigate personifies this tension in compelling fashion.

Like many young Saudis, Sa'd al-Shatiri's life has been lived out to a significant degree online. In 2008 the future poet of ISIS was a pious-minded employee of the Saudi religious police, known informally as the Hay'a. Al-Shatiri even composed a praise poem honouring the Hay'a's successes in disrupting Saudi moonshine operations. '*Wallahi*, the efforts of the Hay'a cannot be denied (*yinkir*)', a melodic reciter of his poem intones in an online music video, as images of plastic alcohol barrels being overturned or hacked apart pass grainily across the screen.[20]

Sa'd is the second or third of four brothers. In 2012 two of his siblings left for Syria to join the militant group Jabhat al-Nusra (now one part of Tahrir al-Sham) in its fight against the Syrian regime. A short-lived Twitter account created by Sa'd in November 2012 underscores his religious convictions and commonality of view with his siblings. '[I repent] to He who possesses the keys to good things and the locks against evil things,' he declares in his first tweet, perhaps signalling his readiness to join the battle.[21] The account conveys Sa'd's angst over the Saudi regime's ambivalent policy toward the Syria conflict. It also captures the moment when Sa'd learns of the death of his older brother Fahd in combat on the Syrian border, in a phone call from his younger brother Ahmad. By mid-December the Twitter account goes dark. Sa'd was probably already on his way to Syria, where he would join the emergent Islamic State movement in July 2013.

On 1 January 2014, in the midst of their lightning expansion, Islamic State militants posted a video of a celebratory *'arda* dance performed in the halls of an Iraqi mansion. Clutching a microphone in the background and belting out pulsating verse is Sa'd al-Shatiri. The poem in question, titled 'Ya 'Asib al-Ra's, Waynak' [O turbanned one, where are you?], would go on to ignite a raging poetical contest that pitted Islamic State militants against a multitude of Saudi tribal subgroups and freelance poets. The story of 'Asib al-Ra's thus distills some of the key tensions in the relationship between genealogy and politics in Saudi Arabia.

Both in form and in content, the 'Asib al-Ra's battle is a quintessentially twenty-first-century Arabian literary phenomenon. Drawing from the tradition of duelling poets known as *riddiyya*,[22] yet updated for the asynchronous battle spaces of social media, the poetical contests for and against Islamic State's legitimacy have attracted scores of Saudi participants and millions of YouTube viewers. Referencing in its title the headgear favoured by modern jihadists, Sa'd al-Shatiri's 'Asib al-Ra's was engineered as a tool to attract potential Saudi recruits to the movement. Pitched at disaffected Bedouin-origin youth in particular,[23] Sa'd's infectious chant urges Bedouin 'dune skidders' (ta's) to abandon their aimless and oppressive life and join Islamic State's revivalist project:

> You sing, while your era is like a tin can, tossed away, lost, and lowly.
> O turbanned one, where are you?
>
> You sing of glory in the midst of affliction, but that is not my aim[24]
> O turbanned one, where are you?
>
> We, we are the men of war, so hey dune skidder,[25] are you with us?
> O turbanned one, where are you?
>
> You have yet to join Abu Bakr [al-Baghdadi], who founded the State on [this] land.
> O turbanned one, where are you?
>
> You poor guy, it's the lineage of the Prophet that has changed the regime of maps (nizam al-kharita).
> O turbanned one, where are you?
>
> We are the men of creed, bringing back the glory of the Prophet's Companions.
> O turbanned one, where are you?[26]

In the months that followed al-Shatiri's viral videos, a host of response poems composed by Saudis using the same meter and rhythm (though with a modified refrain) began cropping up on YouTube.[27] While premeditated in the manner of a qasida or formal poem, these versified responses have an air of improvisation to them, with the poets glancing down from the camera towards their phones or papers between each recited line.

Most of the responses were composed in the name of specific tribes or tribal subgroups, and many by associates of the Saudi Special Forces and other Interior Ministry security units, both officers and soldiers.[28] A group of Harb youth, perhaps the first to post their 'Asib al-Ra's response poem on YouTube, were awarded a prize of tens of thousands of dollars by Muhammad ibn Nayif and (formerly) his Interior Ministry for the superior quality of their verse. The criteria for the award were perhaps truly nationalistic, since, unlike the other response poems, these youth did not call attention to their lineage. Yet the prominent place afforded to kin identity by the vast majority of responding poets underscores the significance of kinship nationalism in the Saudi political balance. Against ISIS's revolutionary boasts, Saudi tribal pride is in no short supply, as the following selections from the response poems reveal:

In the ancient lands of Harb, we will set you ablaze.[29]
O turbanned one, woe onto you (*waylak*)!

It is simply impossible, for you to win the support of all the tribes.
O turbanned one, woe onto you (*waylak*)!

Without the Haram and Medina, life is not precious.
O turbanned one, woe onto you!

O good ones from all of the tribes, we do not single out Ha'il.
O turbanned one, woe onto you!

A greeting of peace from us to Shammar, in whose lands are good fruits.
O turbanned one, woe onto you![30]

The noble Wa'ili ancestry,[31] is my response to the Da'ish phenomenon.
O turbanned one, woe onto you!

In front of us the army stands, and the National Guard, and the soldiers of Nayif.
O turbanned one, woe onto you![32]

We terminate rivals, *wallah* you fool, we are Juhayna.
O turbanned one, woe onto you![33]

We are the people of Abu Mit'ib,[34] while you wander around and grow weary (*tit'ab*).
O turbanned one, woe onto you!

We are the ancient Sulaym, and by God, [we will set you] ablaze.
O turbanned one, woe onto you!

We are the kings of the Peninsula, and you have no rightful territory.
O turbanned one, woe onto you![35]

We are 'Utayba, O Da'ish, stomping on the dim-witted insects.
O turbanned one, where are you?

We are the defenders of our nation, you are incapable of violating it.
O turbanned one, where are you?[36]

I am 'Utaybi, through both lines (*muraddad*), while you are a doggie driver (*chalbin yuqawwad*).[37]
O turbanned one, where are you?[38]

In September 2015 two Bedouin-origin Saudi teenagers kidnapped their soldier cousin, took him to the desert, and filmed themselves shooting him, while declaring their loyalty to ISIS and its parricidal injunctions. Shortly after this event, which sent shock waves through Saudi society due to its raw subversiveness and violence, Saʿd al-Shatiri appeared in a clip with a newly composed poem addressing the killing. Saʿd and his featured companion framed the poem implicitly as a defence of the parricide strategy. No matter how frequently the kingdom's rulers and their worthless (*sarabit*) soldiers fast or pray, the poet recited, they are infidels whose proper treatment is slaughter in the manner of an animal (*mudhakka*). The only ones who are immune from this judgement, his companion insisted haltingly, are 'the son of my brother, the son of Islam, the son of the Islamic State'.[39] Saʿd al-Shatiri's repudiation of the Saudi system and its underlying bases is undeniable. Yet it should not be lost upon us that the kinship ties that he and his comrades have demanded be severed are also those that helped lead him to Syria in the footsteps of his brothers, towards alternate yet not altogether unfamiliar forms of solidarity.

Exceptionalism and the Nature of the Saudi State

Is Saudi kinship nationalism of the sort disparaged by Saʿd al-Shatiri and affirmed by his poetical respondents purely transactional in nature? Is the tribal nationhood trumpeted by Muhammad ibn Salman simply a rehashed Orientalist construct, a reappropriation of the primordial persona ascribed to Arabian peoples?[40] Or is the entwined glorification of *nasab* and homeland built out of a substance that is retrievable from Arabia's pre-modern past? A good place to begin considering these questions is in the legal architecture of the Saudi state. In lieu of a constitution, Saudi Arabia has a Basic Law. Article 9 of that Law reads:

> The family is the nucleus of Saudi society. Its members shall be raised and adhere to the Islamic creed which calls for obedience to god, his messenger and those of the nation who are charged with authority; for the respect and enforcement of law and order; and for love of the motherland and taking pride in its glorious history.[41]

Thumbing its nose at liberalism, Article 9 embraces a kinship-based or non-individualistic ethos of nationhood. The purposeful rejection of the individual as the basic unit of value in the Saudi political system moves in harmony with the Saudi state's discourse concerning its exceptional nature and origins, 'in which Saudi Arabia is a blessed land, an island of stability and harmonious family'.[42] This notion of exceptionalism has been challenged by Jones, who considers it a 'veneer' masking Saudi Arabia's formation after the fashion of most other developing states in the twentieth century.[43] For Ménoret as well, the idea of Saudi exceptionalism is 'almost entirely fictitious', an invention of Western consultants.[44] Like Louis Dumont's *Homo Hierarchicus*, the notion of Saudi exceptionalism has been rendered all but extinct in academic discourse.[45]

Taking a long (i.e. historical) view, however, we might note at least one measure by which Saudi Arabia is exceptional: its relationship to colonialism. It is in the company of only a handful of other non-Western states to have collectively avoided the experience of colonial rule. Najd, the Saudi–Wahhabi heartland, saw no British administration or system of order superimposed atop its own. The post-war US–Saudi alliance undoubtedly drove many aspects of the kingdom's development trajectory, but the deep structures of the state, its kinship and religious culture, were shaped in more opaque ways than would be predicted by the terms of that relationship.

Scholars with post-colonial orientations are too quick to dismiss the idiomatic mix of social and political processes that have shaped modern Saudi Arabia. By choosing not to organize politics and social life along republican lines, by granting coercive power to religious authorities and institutions, and by making kinship the root matter of citizen legal and social identity, Saudi Arabia's rulers engendered an exceptional political system, one that cannot be explained with reference to post-colonial social and political paradigms alone.

In dismantling the Saudi discourse of exceptionalism, scholars risk diminishing the staying power of locally specific forms of knowledge and social valuation. As I argue in *Of Sand or Soil*, pre-modern ethno-kinship hierarchies in the Arabian Peninsula served as the sociological basis on which new structures of hierarchy and control were formed in the modern state period.[46] Without understanding the dynamic underpinnings of social hierarchies and tribal affiliations in pre-modern central Arabia, we may fail to grasp the scope and significance of oil-age social and political transformation in the kingdom.

The challenge for us as scholars of Saudi history, politics, and culture is to avoid paying excessive deference to the ghosts of Foucault and his successors, or to be fearful of demolishing their inputs when they prove ill suited to the phenomenon in question. In this chapter I have sought to demonstrate how narratives of kin and faith emerge, combine, and clash in Saudi Arabia, with little explicit reference to our dominant categories. We are right to be shocked by ISIS's lust for parricide. 'As Machiavelli repeatedly emphasizes ... the very act of founding or reforming [political orders] requires horrifying deeds.'[47] Yet we should not be shocked by the manner of its unfolding, or sputtering, within the particular context of Saudi political life.

Appendix: 'Ya 'Asib al-Ra's Waynak?'

We are at the summit's peak, [so] I have nothing but blame for you.
O turbanned one, where are you?

You sing, while your era is like a tin can, tossed away, lost, and lowly.
O turbanned one, where are you?

You sing of glory in the midst of affliction, but that is not my aim.
O turbanned one, where are you?

See us in al-Nujayfi palace, in their lands we take hospitality.
O turbanned one, where are you?

We, we are the men of war, so hey dune skidder, are you with us?
O turbanned one, where are you?

Living in cowardice and humiliation, with no sword to unsheathe.
O turbanned one, where are you?

You have raised up an apostate ruler, who seduces you with laws.
O turbanned one, where are you?

They incline toward the Christians, [while] you are a bustard's pudendum.[48]
O turbanned one, where are you?

We are the soldiers of the Caliphate, usurping the press corps.
O turbanned one, where are you?

You have yet to join Abu Bakr [al-Baghdadi], who founded the State on [this] land.
O turbanned one, where are you?

PARRICIDE IN THE KINGDOM

You poor guy, it's the lineage of the Prophet that has changed the regime of maps (*nizam al-kharita*).
O turbanned one, where are you?

Expanding out toward you, and yet you call this my shame?![49]
O turbanned one, where are you?

O you who are beloved by the Westerner, you count for nothing, this age will forget you.
O turbanned one, where are you?

We are the cure for the Rafidites, poison for every single Rejectionist.
O turbanned one, where are you?

We are the men of creed, bringing back the glory of the Prophet's Companions.
O turbanned one, where are you?

[The State] is enduring and expanding, none who belong to it are hesitating.
O turbanned one, where are you?

PART III

FOREIGN RELATIONS

10

SAUDI ARABIA AND THE COLD WAR

Toby Matthiesen[1]

If you could find a communist in Saudi Arabia, I will hand you his head.

Ibn Saud in conversation with Brigadier General Edwin M. Day,
the commanding general of Dhahran airfield, 1951[2]

The United States has borne the responsibility of stopping the Communist advance in the countries of Asia and Africa. It has done this by extending a helpful hand to the various states and by participating in economic development and raising the standard of living in the countries which stand against the Communist current which we combat on religious grounds and which you combat for doctrinaire reasons. Our aims are the same in this matter. It is my belief that the Communist elements in the Middle Eastern area regard it as only a part of the broad scale Communist plan for establishing bases for itself in the various parts of the world in order to spread out therefrom to carry out its aims and to realize its intentions.

In view of the many ties and the traditional friendship which bind our two countries, I take the liberty of exchanging views with Your Excellency in order to coordinate our joint efforts aiming at putting an end to the spread of Communism in the world as a first step toward eliminating it.

Letter from King Faysal to President Lyndon B. Johnson,
16 February 1966[3]

We did not use East—West arguments or America's anti-communism, we used
religion. We said 'the Communists are atheists, they don't believe in religion and
we are fighting them for religious reasons.' We galvanized the Muslim world
behind us, which fitted perfectly into Reagan's strategy for fighting the Soviet
Union in an area where they could not influence it in a way that we could.

Prince Bandar ibn Sultan Al Saud[4]

Saudi Arabia is best known for its oil wealth, its sponsorship of
Wahhabi Islam, and for being home to the two holy places of Islam,
Mecca and Medina. Its regional and international position as a key US
ally is often analysed in terms of America's thirst for Saudi oil. Only
rarely is this alliance studied in the context of recent Cold War scholarship, such as the notion of the Global Cold War, which seeks to refocus
the power struggle between the US and the Soviet Union away from
Europe and the nuclear arms race towards what was once called the
Third World.[5] But the alliance with the USA was sealed in 1945, at the
outset of the Cold War, and Saudi Arabia became a key sponsor of anti-
communist causes across the world, in particular in the last two
decades of the Cold War.

The recasting of Saudi Arabia as both a Cold War actor and an arena
in which Cold War struggles were played out allows a fresh look at the
history of the country and the Arabian Peninsula and Persian Gulf
region in the wider Cold War.[6] It also encourages us to look at domestic politics in the country through a new lens, seeing domestic developments as part of broader Cold War struggles. A re-thinking of the
impact of leftist and Arab nationalist movements, not least on the
threat perception of Saudi decision makers, needs to go hand in hand
with a reassessment of the Saudi role in the Global Cold War.

The US—Saudi Alliance, Oil, and Petrodollar Recycling

The Soviet Union had been the first country to recognize Saudi Arabia
in 1926 after Ibn Saud had conquered the Hijaz, initially seeing him as
an anti-imperialist leader, but only maintained diplomatic personnel
there until 1938. Thereafter, Saudi Arabia did not revitalize diplomatic
relations with the Soviet Union or states of the socialist bloc until

1990.[7] Ibn Saud had had important contacts with imperial powers, above all with Britain and the Ottoman Empire, since the early twentieth century. The US–Saudi alliance was then sealed in 1945. After the Yalta conference, at which US president Franklin D. Roosevelt, British prime minister Winston Churchill, and Soviet leader Josef Stalin agreed on the future of post-Second World War Europe, Roosevelt made a stop-over at the Suez Canal, where he met Ibn Saud, King Farouk of Egypt, and Haile Selassie of Ethiopia.[8]

Little noticed at the time, the meeting was crucial for US–Saudi relations, and was apparently spurred by Ibn Saud's decision to pivot towards the USA and hedge against Britain, which dominated the Persian Gulf region and controlled oil resources in most Gulf countries at the time. The origin of the US–Saudi relationship is thus firmly located at the outset of the Cold War, for, only a few months after the historic meeting, tensions between the United States and the Soviet Union mounted in Europe and Azerbaijan, effectively starting what was later termed the Cold War. This reaffirmed the strategic importance of Central Asia and the Middle East, and in particular of oil-rich countries such as Iran, Iraq, and Saudi Arabia to the future of the wider Cold War.[9]

The first decade of the Cold War saw a profound shift in global energy consumption, with oil overtaking coal as the key strategic global energy resource.[10] The rapid increase in oil production in the Gulf countries in the 1950s and 1960s went hand in hand with this, and fuelled the rise of the United States-led global economic order.

Aramco, owned by a consortium of the largest American oil companies, was a key actor in US–Saudi relations, and became the single largest US overseas asset.[11] In this context control over Gulf oil was not so much about providing cheap energy to the USA or its allies in Europe or Asia, although that did play a role. It was rather America and Britain's ability to control and, in the case of war, deny the flow of oil to adversaries, during the Cold War, primarily the Soviet Union, which spurred America's long-term diplomatic and military presence in the Gulf.[12]

At the same time, in particular after 1973, the massive influx of revenues from oil turned Saudi Arabia and other oil-producing countries into key creditors for international financial markets. 'Petrodollar

recycling', both in the form of investments in the West and the purchasing of Western products, in particular arms, thus became increasingly important for the neoliberal economic and financial system
largely set up, shaped, and dominated by the USA.[13]

After the 1973 oil embargo had driven oil prices to previously
unthinkable levels, the United States sold government debt to allies
around the world, including to oil-producing countries, with a substantial amount being bought by Saudi Arabia.[14] Saudi Arabia was given
preferential treatment, and its buying of US bonds was kept secret at
the request of King Faysal.[15]

Oil and the recycling of petrodollars were thus key factors for the
US–Saudi alliance. But Saudi Arabia's strategic location was also key.
The USA maintained an airfield in eastern Saudi Arabia (Dhahran) from
1952 to 1996, located less than a thousand miles from the Soviet
Union. The airfield served as an important logistics hub, not least in the
Afghan campaign and the First Gulf War.[16] The third, and equally cru-
cial, aspect of Saudi Arabia's position in the Cold War as a US ally lay in
the realm of ideas.

Islam as Anti-Communism

The role and use of religion during the Cold War, in particular as anti-
communism, has recently received some scholarly attention.[17] Indeed,
religion, particularly Christianity and Islam (in the Middle East, Central
Asia, South and South East Asia) were seen as two very powerful anti-
communist belief systems. At the start of the Cold War the United States
government saw the Middle East as a strategically important region in
its rivalry with the Soviet Union, and identified the role of religion as
one of its key features—and possible assets for the USA—in that part
of the world.[18] A National Security Council report in 1952 identified
the centrality of the Middle East to the attitudes of peoples in the
'greater Islamic world stretching from Morocco to the Philippines'.

> The reactions of the peoples in this area to United States policy will be
> reflected in the reactions of Jews and Moslems throughout the world. The
> three monotheistic religions in the area have in common a repugnance to
> the atheism of communist doctrine and this factor could become an
> important asset in promoting Western objectives in the area.[19]

The view of Saudi Arabia as a leader of the Islamic world increased its importance in the eyes of the Americans. The missionaries' son later turned secret agent William A. Eddy, who after the war worked with Aramco in Saudi Arabia, advocated Christian–Muslim cooperation against communism. He wrote that 'there have been very few signs that the Western Powers place any value upon Muslims and from the point of view of psychological warfare alone, we need desperately some common ground to which we welcome the Muslims and the Arabs as respected and valued friend'. He argued that Ibn Saud, 'as head of the puritanical Wahhabi movement to restore the pure faith and practices of Islam', was 'without any doubt the most representative and influential Muslim in the world today'.[20]

When President Dwight D. Eisenhower gave John Foster Dulles letters of introduction for the latter's tour of the Middle East, the letter to Ibn Saud referred to a shared interest in fighting 'godless communism'. Earlier, Ibn Saud had indicated to the Americans that his religion dictated an anti-communist stance.[21] The Truman administration then expanded security assistance and other ties with Saudi Arabia, partly because of the Saudi leaders' staunch anti-communism.[22]

When Ibn Saud's eldest son and designated successor, Prince Saud, told an American official in 1952 that he had plans for a pan-Islamic movement led by Saudi Arabia, he was told that the US 'would welcome such a movement under his leadership because we could be sure that it would be friendly and wisely led'.[23] Indeed, the Americans hoped that Saud, who succeeded his father in 1953, could become an anti-Nasser with religious legitimacy. At times, he was hopefully described as an 'Islamic pope'. But they eventually came to the conclusion that Saud lacked the charisma and political instincts to successfully challenge Arab nationalism and communism in the region and keep Saudi domestic politics under control.[24]

Saudi Arabia was also an arena in which American anti-communist propaganda was spread (in coordination with British anti-communist and anti-Nasserist propaganda, which was produced in Lebanon and spread across the Gulf region as well as Oman and Yemen).[25] American anti-communist propaganda, sometimes containing religious elements, was placed in Saudi newspapers and broadcast on Radio Jidda.[26] At the same time, Saudi Arabia, the Saudi kings and Saudi Arabia's version of

Islam were discussed in stereotypical and Orientalizing, but overwhelmingly positive, ways in the American print media.[27] King Faysal's Islamic institution building, most notably the Muslim World League in 1962 and the Organization of Islamic Conference (OIC) in 1969, is much invoked. But their precise influence, and Faysal's legacy, in particular also through his tours across Africa, the Middle East, South and South East Asia, is still not fully appreciated, in particular not with reference to the Cold War.[28] And the use of Islam as anti-communism continued throughout the Cold War. As late as 1986, an inter-agency meeting of Reagan officials urged the highlighting of the opposition between Islam and communism as a key public diplomacy strategy, in particular to undermine the People's Democratic Republic of Yemen (PDRY).[29]

Interpenetration of Domestic and Regional Politics during the Arab Cold War

The Middle East experienced its own particular version of the Cold War. From the early 1950s to 1967 the Arab world was split in what became known as the 'Arab Cold War', with conservative monarchies such as Saudi Arabia backed by the United States on the one side, against revolutionary military regimes with the support of the Soviet Union on the other.[30] Arab nationalists such as Gamal 'Abd al-Nasser were the most popular leaders in the Arab world, while communist parties and Marxist movements by and large played a rather subordinate role.

In the 1960s Yemen became the 'hot' arena of this regional cold war. After the revolution that led to the overthrow of the Imam in Sana'a in 1962, a five-year civil war pitted Saudi-backed royalists against Nasser's republican allies.[31]

One of the main objectives for Nasser that drove his decision to intervene in Yemen with thousands of Egyptian soldiers was his rivalry with Saudi Arabia. Egypt carried out air and sea attacks on Saudi targets in early November 1962, and in January 1963, just shortly after the USA had recognized the Yemen Arab Republic (YAR) in the North, again conducted air raids on southern Saudi Arabia. Egypt also performed an air drop of weapons and ammunition inside Saudi Arabia destined for Saudi dissidents north of Jeddah.[32] This threat to Saudi

Arabia reinforced Washington's commitment to the Saudi ruling family, although this was initially mitigated by American interests in a working relationship with Nasser, who the Americans feared would be pushed fully into the Soviet sphere of influence if they were too critical of him or were to cut off aid. After all, Nasser was staunchly anti-communist, viciously persecuting Egyptian and other Arab communists, and thus at times seen somewhat favourably in Washington.[33] The Six-Day War with Israel in 1967 heralded the end of Egypt as a regional superpower, and forced Nasser to withdraw the remaining Egyptian soldiers from Yemen between September and December 1967.

Developments within Saudi Arabia during this period, in particular the labour movement in the Eastern Province, the establishment of leftist and nationalist underground organizations, the rivalry between King Saud and Crown Prince Faysal, and the appointment of 'progressive' officials to key positions in the bureaucracy, also have to be studied in the context of the Arab Cold War.

Ibn Saud, the founder of modern Saudi Arabia, had chosen Saud to become king after his death in 1953, and in the period from 1953 to 1964, when Saud was forced to abdicate in favour of Faysal, politics in the country was dominated by the rivalry between the two men and their shifting power bases. Saud occasionally sought to ally himself with progressive officials, including a group of Arab nationalist-oriented princes called the Free Princes around Prince Talal, and at times refused to follow British and American policies in the region. He for example refused to join the British-sponsored Baghdad Pact, and sometimes toyed with a non-aligned stance.[34]

The Saudi communists, since the 1950s organized in the National Liberation Front (Jabhat al-Taharrur al-Watani, NLF), supported King Saud's reforms, and in particular the appointment of 'progressives' to the 1960 cabinet.[35] The cabinet was led by the so-called 'Red Prince', Talal ibn 'Abd al-Aziz, and included Abdallah al-Tariqi, a progressive Saudi oil official, who went on to co-found the Organization of Petroleum Exporting Countries (OPEC) in 1960. It also included the communist Mustafa Hafiz Wahba as deputy minister of finance in 1960. But Wahba was dismissed alongside other progressive officials in 1962 when Crown Prince Faysal strengthened his position. Faysal had his power base amongst the *'ulama'*, the clerical elite, and it was they who eventually publicly urged Saud to leave matters of state to Faysal in 1964.[36] On 2 November 1964 Saud was forced to abdicate by the Council of Ministers and was replaced as king by Faysal. Interestingly, despite its close alliance with the United States, Saudi Arabia was also a founding member of the Non-Aligned Movement (NAM), and Faysal reiterated in his accession speech that Saudi Arabia would stand by the decisions taken at Bandung, the founding conference of the NAM, in 1955.[37]

In mid-December 1966 Nasser invited the former King Saud to reside in Cairo. While Nasser was commonly perceived to have lost the Arab Cold War, his former rival Saud had effectively defected to his side, living in Cairo for a while, which added an ironic twist to the whole story.[38]

As part of its efforts to strengthen the Saudi monarchy, and ensure that the pro-American branches of the ruling family would remain in power, the USA helped to build up the internal Saudi security services. Repression against left-wing underground political organizations was particularly fierce. Communists were at the forefront of the labour mobilization in the Eastern Province from 1953 to 1956. Many were either expelled or jailed. Aramco was at that time still an American-owned company with its own security officials, some of whom were undercover agents of the CIA. They were thus directly involved in the suppression of the labour movement. Further waves of repression occurred throughout the 1950s and 1960s. In addition, American diplomats and CIA agents probably played a role in foiling some of the coup plots between 1967 and 1970. This led to the arrests of hundreds of activists and dealt a blow to all the Saudi opposition organizations.[39] The USA thus also played a key role in supporting the suppression of secular opposition forces in the domestic politics of Saudi Arabia. At the same time, particularly under Faysal, arms sales to Saudi Arabia increased dramatically.[40]

The repression and cooptation of leftists and left-leaning Arab nationalists went hand in hand with an increase in funding for Islamist groups and the adoption of Islam as a counter-ideology both at home and abroad. Islam was, for example, used to undermine the Dhofar rebels and the South Yemeni regime, as well as Marxism and Arab nationalism more broadly. This coincided with crackdowns on Islamists in Egypt, Syria, and elsewhere in the region. These Islamists then found a safe haven in the Gulf states, where in particular members of the Muslim Brotherhood came to staff many of the newly founded educational and charitable institutions. Gulf leaders such as King Faysal embraced a more Islamic approach to foreign policy, including foreign aid for Islamic countries and causes.

When the British were driven out of Yemen in 1967, the newly founded PDRY in the south soon became a base for leftist revolutionaries from the whole region. PDRY-supported guerrillas in the Omani province of Dhofar sought to liberate the whole of the Arabian Peninsula and the upper Gulf states. Particularly in its early years, the PDRY adopted a radically anti-Saudi stance.[41]

Saudi decision makers such as King Faysal were very worried about Marxist subversion from the PDRY. Indeed, it is clear from the archival record that the PDRY and communism dominated much of Saudi leaders' threat perceptions until the Iranian revolution of 1979. King Faysal himself saw communism as a global conspiracy in alliance with Zionism, against which he vowed to fight by all means. His frequent elaborations of this theory, some of them during state visits to the USA, caused some embarrassment to US officials.[42]

A number of Saudi leftists and nationalists used Aden, the capital of the PDRY, as a base, and some also fought with the Dhofari rebels. When a distant relative assassinated Faysal on 25 March 1975 and Khalid succeeded him on the throne, a general amnesty was issued to release the remaining political prisoners from left-wing movements and allow those abroad to return. Many Saudi leftists and Arab nationalists took up this offer. Those leftists who continued to be active politically, including some who had profited from the amnesty, became organized in two underground parties, al-Hizb al-Shuyu'i fi al-Su'udiyya (the Communist Party of Saudi Arabia, CPSA) and Hizb al-'Amal al-Ishtiraki fi al-Jazira al-'Arabiyya (Socialist Action Party in the Arabian Peninsula). But most became integrated into the burgeoning patronage networks of the post-1973 Saudi state.[43]

Kamal Adham and the Establishment of Saudi Intelligence

A key Saudi Cold Warrior was Kamal Adham, the younger brother of Iffat bint Ahmad al-Thunayan, the third wife of King Faysal and mother of Princes Turki and Saud ibn Faysal. Adham played a role in ensuring that Faysal would ascend to the throne,[44] and was then appointed the first head of the General Intelligence Directorate (GID) in 1965, a position he held until 1979, when he was replaced by his nephew Turki ibn Faysal. In this position, Adham played a crucial role in the wider region, as did Turki ibn Faysal, the latter in particular with regard to Afghanistan.[45]

Adham's best-known Cold War success was Egypt. King Faysal sent him on a secret mission to President Anwar al-Sadat to encourage him to lessen his dependence on the Soviet Union. Adham had known Sadat since the early 1950s, and the two had become friends. In 1955 Sadat apparently stood witness at Adham's wedding. After Nasser's death in 1970, Sadat became president and Adham a frequent visitor to Egypt. According to several accounts, he distributed money in Egypt, including to Sadat, paving the way for Egypt's spectacular about-turn from the Soviet to the American side of the Cold War in 1972, when Sadat expelled Soviet advisers and severed relations with the Soviet Union.[46] Saudi Arabia thus effectively won the Arab Cold War and was eventually instrumental in getting the most populous Arab country to switch sides during the Cold War. Thereafter, Saudi Arabia and Egypt cooperated on many regional issues, for example on countering Soviet influence in the YAR.[47]

In the early 1970s Adham also became a key figure in the BCCI bank, which was involved in a global money-laundering scheme through which parts of the Afghan jihad were financed. This involvement later put him into the spotlight in the USA, where he became the subject of an investigation, although he managed to settle on a negotiated deal with the prosecution.[48]

The Safari Club

After the Watergate scandal, President Jimmy Carter was keen to avoid too direct US and CIA involvement in anti-communist covert operations across the world, and instead preferred to rely on proxies.[49] In Africa, American anti-communist priorities often pitted the USA against African liberation movements, which exacerbated its domestic racial tensions.[50] The USA's Middle Eastern and African allies thus came to play a key role. Africa, and particularly the Horn of Africa, became a focus of Saudi anti-communist and anti-Soviet activities. Iran also had a special interest in Africa, in particular through its close alliance with South Africa's apartheid regime. Reza Shah had been in exile in South Africa, and the Pahlavi family had large investments in the country, which was seen by Cold Warriors as a bastion against Marxist advances in Africa.[51] From the mid-1970s onwards Africa became a major theatre of the Cold War. The conflict in Angola became internationalized, the war over Namibia, Africa's last remaining colony, gained traction, and the anti-apartheid movement in South Africa garnered increasing international support.[52]

Saudi Arabia was a key member of an intelligence alliance that carried out anti-communist operations in Africa in the 1970s. The other members of the so-called Safari Club were Iran, Egypt, Morocco, and France. In many ways the Safari Club built on long-standing alliances. Kamal Adham had, for example, been key in providing a Saudi loan for Moroccan purchases of US weapons in 1974.[53] Egypt was also buying arms from France with Saudi money, including Mirages 2000. France also maintained extensive military presences in former colonies such as Congo and Chad, and French (and Belgian) interests in national resources in Africa remained substantial.

The mastermind behind the group was the head of the French external intelligence service, the Service de Documentation Extérieure et de Contre-Espionnage (SDECE), Count Alexandre de Marenches. Saudi Arabia's role was apparently mainly in financing the operations.[54] De Marenches coined the term 'Safari Club' 'as a sort of joke' but with a 'deadly serious' aim.[55]

A charter was signed on 1 September 1976 by the heads of the external intelligence services of the five member countries, including Saudi Arabia's GID head, Kamal Adham. The agreement started as follows: 'Recent events in Angola and other parts of Africa have demonstrated the continent's role as a theatre for revolutionary wars prompted and conducted by the Soviet Union, which utilizes individuals or organizations sympathetic to, or controlled by, Marxist ideology.' The agreement stated that Soviet aims in Africa were firstly control over the continent's raw materials, 'and thus over the industry and economic life of Europe and the Third World'; secondly control over sea routes around Africa; and thirdly to manipulate client states. The response would therefore have to be 'global in conception'. The alliance was going to be headquartered in Cairo with a secretariat, a planning section, and an operations branch. The Egyptians were asked to prepare office space and accommodation for the Club's members, while France was supplying technical equipment for communications. The Club's members met frequently, either at the Centre in Cairo or in Saudi Arabia, Paris, or Casablanca, and the chair of the Club was held for one year by each member state in turn.[56]

Its first major operation was to be in the Congo (later Zaire), where Moroccan and Egyptian troops, aided by French air transport and logistical support, came to the rescue of President Mobutu Sese Seko, who was threatened by a dissident general, General Bomba. Heikal alleges that Mobutu and the mining companies in Congo appealed to the Club for help.[57]

Given the proximity to Saudi Arabia and Egypt, and its strategic location at the intersection of international shipping lanes, in particular on the path of Gulf oil shipments through the Suez Canal to Europe, the Horn of Africa became a major focus of Cold War confrontations, and thus also of the Safari Club.[58] The Soviet Union and its allies did indeed see the Horn of Africa as a major opportunity to expand their sphere of influence in their rivalry with the USA over the future of the Third World.[59]

The PDRY, Saudi Arabia's nemesis on the Arabian Peninsula, also supported Marxist movements and governments in the Horn of Africa, in particular Ethiopia, in the late 1970s.[60] President Carter's former national security adviser Zbigniew Brzezinski had pointed out that 'if Ethiopia and South Yemen become Soviet associates ... there will be a serious and direct political threat to Saudi Arabia. This is something we simply cannot ignore.'[61]

Mohamed Siad Barre had become president of Somalia in October 1969, and sought to unite the territories where Somalis live outside Somalia. Besides former British, Italian, and French Somaliland, this included a part of Kenya and the Ogaden, an Ethiopian province. The Russians supported him, which alarmed the Americans.[62]

In 1974 a revolution took place in Ethiopia, and the Russians also started supporting the new leader, Mengistu Haile Mariam.[63] Somalia under Siad Barre was thus looking for new allies, and this is where the Safari Club stepped in. If Siad Barre would expel the Russians, then the Club would supply him with arms. The Shah was very enthusiastic about this, and Saudi Arabia paid for $75 million of Soviet arms that Egypt no longer needed to be sent to Somalia. But the 1977–8 conflict between Somalia under Siad Barre and Ethiopia soon became too hot to handle for the Club. Russia and Cuba increased military support to Ethiopia with the help of regional allies such as the PDRY, which strengthened Ethiopia considerably. Eventually, a superpower deal by which the Soviets did not get involved in Rhodesia while the USA ceased support for the Somali campaign in Ogaden decided the matter.[64] Saudi support for Somalia was partly seen through the prism of a 'Muslim Somalia against Marxist Ethiopia'.[65] The Saudis urged Britain and the USA to provide military assistance to Siad Barre, but they refused to provide substantial aid.[66]

Another focus for the Safari Club was North Africa, where Colonel Muammar al-Gaddafi had emerged as a new 'radical' anti-Saudi leader after coming to power in a coup in 1969. Saudi Arabia and its allies were soon engaged in a serious rivalry with Gaddafi in Africa. Gaddafi had sent troops to Chad in 1980. Saudi Arabia in turn paid the Chadian army to repel Libyan forces in the northern border region of Chad.[67] At the same time, Saudi Arabia increased aid to Sudan, which helped the Nimeiry government fend off challenges by leftist forces in the country.[68] Saudi Arabia also opened Islamic banks in Sudan and supported Islamic organizations and institutions directly.

Members of the Safari Club, which kept US and Israeli intelligence informed on its activities, probably also played a role in paving the way for the 1979 peace treaty between Egypt and Israel.[69] Adham certainly visited Egypt frequently, both because of the activities of the Safari Club and to liaise with Sadat, throughout the 1970s.[70]

While the Safari Club is interesting in and of itself, and remains little researched, it is crucial because it was in many ways a precursor of the largest Saudi Cold War operation, the support for the jihad in Afghanistan. On the Saudi side, 1979 saw the replacement of Kamal Adham by Turki ibn Faysal, who would become the key figure in the Saudi financing of the Afghan war. The example provided by the Safari Club, where Saudi Arabia financed anti-communist operations by other countries' intelligence agencies and armies with some success, was thus emulated in Afghanistan.

Saudi Arabia and the wider 'Third World'

In the 1970s and 1980s Saudi Arabia also gave aid and cash to Syria, Jordan, the PLO, North Yemen, Angola, Sudan, Somalia, Djibouti, Uganda, Mali, Nigeria, Zaire, Guinea, Pakistan, Bangladesh, South Korea, Malaysia, Taiwan, and the Philippines, amongst others, to further its foreign policy and broader Cold War objectives. Throughout the 1980s the remaining members of the Safari Club continued their activities in Africa, often successfully. Saudi Arabia became one of the key sponsors of the UNITA rebels fighting the Angolan government and continued its involvement in the Horn of Africa.[71]

Saudi Arabia also contributed funds to the Contras in Nicaragua who were fighting against the Sandinista government. National Security Adviser Robert McFarlane met with Prince Bandar several times in 1984 and 1985, obtaining $8 million at a rate of $1 million a month from May 1984 onwards for this cause. Saudi Arabia was then again asked to increase its contributions in February 1985, when it contributed an additional $24 million to the Contras, meaning that the Saudi contribution totalled $32 million between June 1984 and March 1985.[72] Saudi Arabia may also have funded efforts to counter 'Eurocommunism', in particular in Italy.[73] As Bronson put it, 'Saudi aid went to anti-Communist, pro-Islamic, and pro-Palestinian causes. Aid was at its most forthcoming when all three justifications overlapped.'[74] It is important to note that while Saudi Arabia indeed funded pro-Palestinian causes, one of its key aims was to weaken the leftist elements within the Palestinian national movement, in particular the Popular Front for the Liberation of Palestine (PFLP) and the other leftist currents in the PLO. Funding thus often went directly to Fatah. This strategy was eventually successful. This was also vital for Saudi Arabia since the Movement of Arab Nationalists and the Palestinian left were involved in attempts at spreading revolution on the Arabian Peninsula, in particular through Dhofar and South Yemen, where two movements that originated in the Movement of Arab Nationalists sought to establish a new popular order.[75]

Afghanistan

The most dramatic episode of the Cold War collusion between the USA and Saudi Arabia was to take place in Afghanistan. In 1978 a communist regime came to power, and a few months later (but, in contrast to claims at the time, before the deployment of Soviet troops to Afghanistan in 1979) President Carter authorized covert aid to the rebels. The war was presented as a battle against a brutal regime that was trying to apply alien communist ideas onto a 'Moslem' society. And so the 'Moslems' were naturally supposed to rise up against the 'communists'. The networks and ideologies that had previously been used in the Arab Cold War and the Safari Club were now used against the Soviet Union. The key to this story is the relationship between the USA, in particular the CIA, and Saudi and Pakistani intelligence (as well as Egypt). Together, they supported those who came to be known as the Mujahidin with money and arms. The networks of the Safari Club also played a key role, despite the fact that one of its core members, Pahlavi Iran, had just been overthrown. The remaining members, in particular Sadat's Egypt and Saudi Arabia, were very concerned about Afghanistan. Sadat saw support for the Afghan Mujahidin as a way of bolstering his Islamic credentials and deflecting the attention of the Muslim Brotherhood and al-Azhar, both of whom supported the Afghan resistance. The idea that Egyptian Islamists would travel abroad to fight rather than cause trouble at home was also popular at the time. Egypt's large stockpile of Warsaw Pact weapons was shipped en masse to Afghanistan, paid for by the US and Saudi Arabia. Many of the clerics and leaders of the Afghan resistance had been students at al-Azhar, so significant religious networks were already in place.[76]

Saudi Arabia famously matched US funding, channelled through the CIA, 'dollar by the dollar', while Pakistan handled logistics. Several billion dollars were thus funnelled to the Mujahidin in Afghanistan.[77]

The Gulf Crisis and the End of the Cold War

Despite the lack of official diplomatic relations, negotiations between the Soviet Union and Saudi Arabia occasionally took place, particularly throughout the 1980s. Secret talks took place in 1985 in Kuwait.[78] In 1988 representatives from the Soviet Ministry of Foreign Affairs visited the Saudi deputy prime minister and foreign minister in Riyadh.[79] In 1988 Saudi Arabia also bought ballistic missiles from China, without having full diplomatic relations with the country and without informing the Americans, who were furious about this.[80] This deal brought to the public eye a secret relationship that had existed for years and was going to take on a significant economic dimension after the end of the Cold War. Saudi Arabia's strong relations with Taiwan, however, and its self-perception as the spiritual home of Muslims in China, set clear limits to Saudi–Chinese relations.[81]

Saudi Arabia only formally established diplomatic relations with China in 1990, and re-established them with the soon to be dissolved Soviet Union in the same year. Saudi Arabia and other Gulf governments then granted the Russians a $3 billion loan package.[82] Saudi–Syrian relations improved dramatically, as the Syrian Ba'ath regime, the Iraqi Ba'ath's arch enemy, cooperated in the international coalition to liberate Kuwait. As a result, some of the few Saudi communists in Damascus moved to London, and the party and its successor organizations ceased to exist by 1993.[83] The PDRY, the only Arab Marxist state and a key sponsor of leftists in the region, ceased to exist, and on 22 May 1990 North and South Yemen united to form the Republic of Yemen. The end of the Cold War thus eliminated the perceived threat of communism in Saudi eyes, but the mass deployment of American troops to the country for the 'liberation' of Kuwait had its own consequences, leading to a broad-based Islamic opposition to the regime.[84]

Conclusion

A reappraisal of the Saudi role in the Cold War can provide new light on the second half of the Cold War, in particular in the Global South. Saudi Arabia underwrote American and French-led anti-communist intelligence and military operations, some of which might not have been funded otherwise because of restrictions on the funding of covert operations. In addition, religion, and in particular conservative Sunni Islam, was a crucial ideological weapon throughout the Cold War. In this ideological battle Saudi Arabia was again key. One should not overstate Saudi agency in all this, as the broader outlines of Cold War policy were drawn up in the USA and in some instances in the UK (Southern

Yemen and the Gulf) and France (Africa). In that context, these global powers took the lead in anti-communist activities, and decided on the broader policies, with regional allies playing a secondary role. In the Middle East and Central Asia, Israel and Iran were until 1979 the leading American allies.[85] The Safari Club continued to operate throughout the 1980s, with Saudi Arabia taking on a more important role after the collapse of the Pahlavi regime in Iran. And the security alliances that were bolstered throughout the 1970s continued to be of great importance throughout the 1980s and into the post-Cold War era. The US–Saudi alliance and the broader position of the GCC states in the global neoliberal economic and political order dominated by the United States thus has to be understood with reference to the origins of this alliance in the Cold War.

11

KING SALMAN AND HIS SON

WINNING THE USA, LOSING THE REST

Madawi Al-Rasheed

With the appointment of Muhammad ibn Salman as crown prince in June 2017, Saudi foreign policy has become the subject of wide-ranging speculation. Although at the time of writing King Salman is still in office, we can assume that his son Muhammad had been the de facto orchestrator of Saudi foreign policy even before he was confirmed in his new role. In terms of relations with the USA, Muhammad ibn Salman succeeded in establishing a momentary strong rapport with President Donald Trump and his administration, thanks to serious investment in public relations companies, lobbyists in Washington, and the promise to inject funds into the US economy. Relations with Europe look as if they had entered a cooling-off period, with European leaders still unsure about how to assess the young prince. Many are nevertheless keen to win him over with the prospect of financial rewards and stronger military ties for economic, strategic, and security

235

reasons. In the Arab region, the young Saudi prince has already cemented new, albeit shaky, partnerships with countries such as Egypt and the United Arab Emirates (UAE) in order to further isolate his arch-enemy, Iran, and, more recently, Qatar.

This chapter assesses the prospects for new directions in Saudi foreign policy, highlighting its continuities and discontinuities under the new leadership of King Salman and Crown Prince Muhammad. It draws tentative conclusions that, amidst a series of foreign policy failures, winning the favour of the USA under Trump has been the major achievement of the new Saudi leadership. However, Saudi foreign policy in Europe has—as ever—taken a back seat, and today in several European capitals there is serious doubt as to the merit of the assertive and interventionist Saudi regional policy, considered in some European circles to be destabilizing the Arab world. With the USA secured as the old Saudi patron and ally, King Salman and his son will pay little attention to Europe, but will continue with an erratic—and probably ultimately unsuccessful—bid to gain decisive power within the Middle East and emerge as a regional power on a par with Iran, Turkey, and Israel.

Within the Gulf, Saudi policies have fractured the Gulf Cooperation Council (GCC), with two countries—Oman and Qatar—choosing to break ranks with Saudi Arabia over several issues, from Iran to the role of Islamist movements in the Arab world. This latest episode in Saudi regional assertiveness will no doubt embarrass its international partners, who will eventually be expected to choose sides in this new Gulf conflict that may not correspond with their own national interests. The new young prince is swift in rewarding allies and punishing those reluctant to support him in each of his foreign policy initiatives.

The chapter concludes with the observation that King Salman and his son have proved to be reckless, unwilling to extinguish the many fires that are currently raging across the Arab world. In fact, their foreign policy is based on a single doctrine: establishing the supremacy of Saudi Arabia in order to make it the sole arbiter of Arab affairs and the main point of entry for all international powers into the region. Saudi Arabia under King Salman seems determined to pursue this objective even if it contributes to greater insecurity and upheaval in the Arab world, with serious humanitarian, social, and political consequences beyond this troubled region.

236

Muhammad ibn Salman and Trump: A Successful Momentary Symbiosis

Young Prince Muhammad ibn Salman is preparing to inherit the throne, provided that no further succession changes take place during the king's lifetime. Saudi Arabia's international relations may follow new directions with the USA, Europe and the region.

Before his promotion to crown prince, Muhammad ibn Salman visited America several times with a view to making himself known in Washington[1] and promoting himself at the expense of his cousin Muhammad ibn Nayif, who had maintained close contacts with the US intelligence and defence community as a result of his involvement in War on Terror efforts since 9/11.[2] Immediately after Donald Trump was elected US president in November 2016, the young prince rushed to court him, promising greater Saudi investment.

During his election campaign, Trump frequently declared that America would not continue to support its traditional partners in Europe, Asia, and the Middle East unless all of them committed greater financial resources to cement the military partnerships that the USA had helped to forge since the Second World War. He did not hesitate to describe Gulf countries, including Saudi Arabia, as void of everything except money. Trump's repeated attempts to ban Muslims from travelling to the USA and his anti-Muslim rhetoric did not detract from the new opportunities that both he and Muhammad ibn Salman anticipated to inaugurate a new era of close cooperation between their two countries. It seemed that both leaders were determined to go back to the *status quo ante*—before the election of Barack Obama—when Saudi Arabia and the USA had enjoyed a close and unchallenged partnership.

A short-lived period of troubled relations with the USA occurred during Barack Obama's presidency. The relationship reached a nadir as Obama declined to indulge Saudi Arabia and accede to its constant requests to bomb its arch-enemy, Iran, or topple Bashar al-Assad of Syria. The Saudis made the first request in 2008, and the second after the outbreak of the Syrian uprising in 2011. Saudi Arabia considered the Iran Nuclear Deal that Obama and several European leaders signed in 2013 a potent threat, signalling that the USA was determined to end four decades of Iranian isolation and diversify its interlocutors in the Middle East after having relied on Saudi Arabia, Turkey, Egypt, the

Gulf, and Israel as its main partners in the region. Despite this, under the Obama administration the USA sold more than $115 billion of arms to Saudi Arabia.[3]

While Trump did not fully acquiesce to the Saudi requests regarding Iran and Syria, he made enough vague noises to encourage the Saudi leadership and restore the troubled relations to their pre-Obama harmony. Trump's anti-Iranian rhetoric—which he immediately ramped up once elected—his repeated threats to reconsider and perhaps abandon the Nuclear Deal, his willingness to impose new sanctions on Iran, and his description of Iran as a terrorist state pleased the Saudis and paved the way for his historic visit to Riyadh. On Syria, immediately after he became president, Trump authorized limited air strikes that barely affected the balance of power against al-Assad. Nevertheless, such a swift move was enough of a positive signal for Riyadh to think that Trump was on their side and would pursue regime change in Syria.

On 20 May 2017 Trump arrived in Riyadh, accompanied by a large entourage of family advisers, consultants, and businessmen, and was welcomed with great fanfare and pomp. The Saudis offered Trump much-needed affirmation, not only inside Saudi Arabia but across the Muslim world. Muhammad ibn Salman assembled over fifty Muslim leaders for a Muslim summit and gave the president the opportunity to address them in a historic speech.[4] This speech was meant to counter Obama's famous Cairo speech in 2009 when he emphasized the USA's commitment to democracy and human rights in the world and its respect for Islam as a religion. Obama called on history to show that Islam is an integral part of America by drawing on his mixed parentage, especially his Muslim Kenyan father. In contrast, Trump announced in Riyadh that:

> We signed historic agreements with the Kingdom that will invest almost $400 billion in our two countries and create many thousands of jobs in America and Saudi Arabia. It should increasingly become one of the great global centers of commerce and opportunity. This region should not be a place from which refugees flee, but to which newcomers flock.[5]

While Muhammad ibn Salman was pleased that Trump emphasized economic ties, he was more eager to hear a denunciation of Iran, so he must have been thrilled when he heard Trump pointing to Iran's disruptive role in the region:

For decades, Iran has fuelled the fires of sectarian conflict and terror. It is a government that speaks openly of mass murder, vowing the destruction of Israel, death to America, and ruin for many leaders and nations in this room. ... Until the Iranian regime is willing to be a partner for peace, all nations of conscience must work together to isolate Iran, deny it funding for terrorism, and pray for the day when the Iranian people have the just and righteous government they deserve.[6]

Saudi Arabia urgently wanted Trump to absolve it from any responsibility for the deadliest crisis to have befallen the Arab world, namely terrorist-plagued sectarian conflict. There was no mention of how, like Iran, Saudi Arabia had resorted to sectarianism as a counter-revolutionary force to derail the 2011 Arab uprisings in Bahrain, Syria, and, most recently, in Yemen. Its religious ideology, known as Wahhabism, has appeared indistinguishable from that adopted by ISIS, with the latter incorporating Saudi religious texts into the Raqqa school curriculum and enforcing a social and sectarian policy very similar to that practised in Saudi Arabia. Sex segregation, anti-Shi'a rhetoric, and beheading point to a common ideological affinity between the religious ideology of ISIS and Wahhabism.

Furthermore, Trump refrained from mentioning the role played by Saudi Arabia in spreading this radical version of Islam around the globe. The Saudi role had been criticized since 9/11, but Trump absolved the kingdom from any responsibility for the expansion of a global jihadi trend that it had initially promoted together with several Western governments, notably during the Reagan and Thatcher years in the 1980s as an antidote to Soviet communism and the occupation of Afghanistan. The promotion of Saudi Wahhabism was a project conceived during the Cold War, during which the country was elevated to the status of global player in the Muslim world; but it was specifically useful in Afghanistan when it was expected to contribute ideologically, financially, and personally to the country's liberation from Soviet occupation. Trump was not interested in a deeper understanding of the roots of the global jihadi menace, which would implicate both the USA and Saudi Arabia in addition to many partners in both the West and the Muslim world. Both Muhammad ibn Salman and Donald Trump felt comfortable turning the page and sinking into historical amnesia. From now on, the Saudi–US relationship is set to reinstate itself as a pragmatic marriage of convenience, void of any ideological underpinnings such as concerns over human rights, democracy, or any other terminology that makes Riyadh uncomfortable. Vague incremental social and political reform rather than military intervention or promotion of democracy is Riyadh's preferred option.

It is important to understand how the two leaders managed to strike an alliance, though it may well prove to be temporary, set as it is against a background of tension and animosity. Like Muhammad ibn Salman, Trump is unpredictable, and the two men may fall out over minor differences in the future. However, they will keep the facade of agreement on main issues and maintain a traditional, albeit revived, bargain: the Americans shall continue to offer unconditional and unequivocal support to Saudi Arabia while the latter continues to pay for the privilege of remaining the main US ally after Israel in the region. This bargain had until recently appeared shaken, and perhaps lacking in enthusiasm on the American side. However, Trump and Ibn Salman share a common belief that 'money talks', and so their common outlook is based on the assumption that in both business and politics only this cherished currency has the potential to solve almost all problems, from terrorism to failing economies. Both lack any deeper understanding of the current challenges of the Arab world, and they share a disdain for any 'deep thinking' and an insatiable appetite for public relations companies, lobbyists, and the pomp that comes with the sudden acquisition of power. So far, the two leaders appear to be in lockstep at least over a number of key issues, from Syria to Yemen, but deep down the administration around Trump does not seem to share his overt enthusiasm for Saudi regional policies. In Yemen, Syria, and Qatar, the three hot spots in 2017, both the Pentagon and the US State Department tempered Trump's hasty announcements, thus indicating that contradictions exist within his administration, parts of which are prepared to force climb-downs from the president, at least with regard to brash announcements like those he made when visiting Riyadh, where his comments were understood at the time to fully endorse Muhammad ibn Salman's regional wars and interventionist policies.

However, while Ibn Salman may have won over Trump, he still faces uncertain votes in the House of Representatives and the Senate. In the past, American presidents with clear majorities were able to get both houses to approve important arms sales to Saudi Arabia. Since the 1990s Saudi Aramco has continued to sell US refineries' crude oil at a discount price, often cheaper than that sold in Asia. The discount policy resulted in a reallocation of contributions toward members of congressional committees that reviewed bills of interest to Saudi Arabia. This is only one way in which Saudi Arabia influences Congress in Washington.[7] Other means include threatening to withhold intelligence, and think-tank lobbying.

But after 9/11 the legislature's unequivocal support could no longer be taken for granted. Having alienated the Saudis when he called them 'free riders' in his famous *Atlantic* interview,[8] Obama tried to mend the relationship in his last months in office. In September 2016 both the House of Representatives and the Senate overwhelmingly rejected his bid to veto the Justice Against Sponsors of Terrorism Act (JASTA), which allows family members of 9/11 victims to sue Saudi Arabia in American courts.[9] This law will prove a serious obstacle to further US–Saudi partnerships should it be put in motion.

Tension between the American president, this time Donald Trump, and Congress resurfaced in 2017 over arms sales to Saudi Arabia. Immediately after Trump's return from Riyadh, he narrowly escaped a Senate veto on a $500 million deal to sell Saudi Arabia precision-guided munitions. With Saudi Arabia's erratic air strikes killing many civilians in Yemen and the conflict reaching a stalemate almost three years after it started, opposition to arms sales may continue to grow in the US Congress. While this is not necessarily a reflection of Congress or the Senate being opposed to Saudi Arabia, their position should be understood as a reflection of the tension between Trump, the Republicans, and the Democrats within America itself.

Trump wants to capture a historical moment in which Saudi Arabia is set to transition to a bright neoliberal economy open to global trade, accompanied by a minimalist welfare state weaned off oil. Privatization, diversification, and Saudization are the backbone of Muhammad ibn Salman's Vision 2030—an economic blueprint to deliver economic prosperity at times of falling oil prices and budget deficits. The expansion of the private sector and most importantly the announced partial privatization of the Saudi oil company Aramco offer new economic opportunities that both leaders want to promote and benefit from.

Should the national interest of the USA coincide with that of Muhammad ibn Salman, the two leaders hope to closely cooperate in the future. However, both can be erratic and capable of making ad hoc decisions that may backfire.

Salman's Son and Europe: Secondary Partnerships

Having secured the support, however fleeting, of Donald Trump, does Muhammad ibn Salman have the time or inclination to seek further partnerships with European countries beyond the historical alliances that have more recently become rooted in trade, arms sales, and security concerns?

Since the Second World War, Saudi relations with leading European countries—specifically Britain, France, and Germany—have been secondary to the project of greater military and security integration with the USA. Many European countries, especially France and Britain, saw a window of opportunity to seek greater cooperation with the Saudis after 9/11 when they assumed that America would be unwilling to continue its unconditional support for the kingdom after it became known that fifteen of the hijackers who attacked New York were Saudis. This proved to be a good moment to endear themselves to the Saudis by selling them arms denied to them by the US Congress, and by positioning Europe as the old ally who genuinely understood Saudi Arabia, its history and leadership more than the American neophytes. Saudi Arabia, meanwhile, was seeking to diversify its arms sources, and leapt at the opportunity to buy more weapons from Europe.

Under the Conservative government of David Cameron, Britain's arms sales to Saudi Arabia reached almost £6 billion.[10] Britain needed to boost its trade with the Gulf in general and Saudi Arabia in particular immediately after the financial crisis of 2008. Under pressure from Saudi Arabia and the UAE, in April 2014 David Cameron, the British prime minister, ordered an investigation into the Muslim Brotherhood in Britain with a view to banning the Islamist movement and limiting its global outreach. Saudi Arabia, keen to reverse the Brotherhood's success in Egypt after the uprising of 2011, had banned the movement in Saudi Arabia itself. The investigation, led by ex-ambassador to Saudi Arabia John Jenkins, found no clear links to terrorism. The Muslim

Brotherhood continues to organize in Britain. It took the British government several months to release the information gathered during the consultation period, and Saudi Arabia was not pleased with the findings of the report.

The drive to seek closer ties with Saudi Arabia became more urgent after the British referendum of 2016, when it became certain that the British economy would face the possibility of shrinking after its exit from the European Union. Prime Minister Theresa May honoured her pledge to continue to be a friend of the Saudis and refrained from taking any measures or making any statements that would embarrass them in the international arena. Like other European leaders, she rushed to visit the Saudis as part of a Gulf tour. In April 2017 she arrived in Riyadh (before Trump), and sought to strengthen trade relations with Saudi Arabia.

More recently, Theresa May continues to block the publication of an internal Home Office report investigating Saudi sponsorship of radical religious ideology in Britain. The enquiry was commissioned by the Conservative–Liberal Democrat coalition government. It is believed that Theresa May is still resisting any exposure of Saudi Arabia to more criticism both in Britain and Europe. The release of the report may undermine relations with Riyadh at a critical moment for Britain when it is seeking new trade partners to compensate for its expected losses after Brexit.

Since 2015, when Saudi Arabia began air strikes on Yemen, Britain has come under mounting pressure from parliamentary committees and civil society organizations that oppose arms sales to countries that do not respect human rights and violate international law through illegal military interventions abroad. Human rights organizations accused Muhammad ibn Salman of using British cluster bombs and other banned weapons. Civilian deaths in Yemen, estimated at over 10,000, and the humanitarian crisis pushed British public opinion against arms sale but the logic of the British government remains constant: 'if we don't sell arms to the Saudis, the French will'.

Like Britain, France and Saudi became interconnected after 9/11 through a series of arms deals that boosted the French economy and offered Saudi Arabia a sense of security—especially as France continued to be a staunch critic of Iran's policy in the region, particularly in

Lebanon, Syria, and Iraq. Saudi military aid to Lebanon was conditional on the purchase of equipment from France, a deal negotiated by then-president François Hollande. Saudi Arabia, however, cancelled this gift to Lebanon to put pressure on Iranian-backed Hizbollah, but pledged to compensate France for its losses.

Saudi Arabia looked to France for support in its bid to oust Syrian president Bashar al-Assad and strengthen the Syrian opposition to his regime. It also expected France not to normalize relations with Iran after the Nuclear Deal and to remain critical of its regional policy. France honoured the bargain in order to maintain its lucrative military trade with Saudi Arabia and neighbouring Gulf countries. However, more recently, the policy to oust Bashar al-Assad has proved unsuccessful, and both Saudi Arabia and France—in fact, most European interested parties—are currently facing serious defeat in Syria. As the objective was regime change, rather than mediation in the Syrian crisis with the hope of attaining peaceful coexistence between the regime and the many opposition groups, some of which are violent radical Islamists and jihadists, a resolution in Syria was delayed until it became impossible to achieve. In a country where foreign policy has been the sole prerogative of the president since the times of General de Gaulle, France may continue to seek closer ties with Saudi Arabia after the French elections of 2017. But the Syrian debacle and the failure to resolve the crisis continue to haunt both countries.

Added to that is the new Saudi–Qatari crisis, which started in May 2017. Muhammad ibn Salman expects France and other European countries to accept the Saudi narrative about Qatar's sponsorship of terrorism, including its support for Hamas and the Muslim Brotherhood, who are both believed to destabilize the region, and the media policies of the pan-Arab al-Jazeera channel. The newly elected French president Emmanuel Macron may be put under pressure to back the Saudis against Qatar, a move that would undermine France's greater economic and military interests in this small but rich Gulf state.[11]

With its wide-ranging economic and military ties to Saudi Arabia, Germany was less than enthusiastic about the sudden rise of the young Muhammad ibn Salman to power. A 2015 leaked German intelligence report was damning about the prince.[12] The report considered his rise cause for concern because of his 'regional destabilising impact'.[13] While it is very unusual for the German intelligence services to disseminate such reports, the leak was perhaps a deliberate warning signal intended for the international community in general, and Germany's European partners in particular. Neither King Salman nor his son attended the annual G20 Summit in Hamburg in July 2017, though this may have been due to their preoccupation with the escalating Qatar crisis. Perhaps Saudi Arabia did not want to face additional pressure from the G20 members to resolve the crisis and seek negotiation, rather than the path—which they chose—of confrontation with the small emirate. The king and his son avoided further questioning by sending a technocrat to the G20 meeting. Another reason may be related to the abrupt sacking of Muhammad ibn Nayif and his alleged house arrest, both of which would signal a difficult and uncertain moment for the king, given that he must have alienated a large number of aspiring princes, some of whom are older and more experienced than his young son.

Saudi Arabia, however, cherishes economic relations with Germany in addition to the training opportunities it offers Saudi youth.[14] In 2016 Saudi Arabia invited Germany to send a representative to be a guest of honour at the annual National Guard al-Janadiriyya festival. However, even with over half a billion euros worth of weapons exported to Saudi Arabia, Germany was dismissed as a future military trading partner following its criticism of the Saudi-led war in Yemen. Chancellor Angela Merkel expressed alarm at the high level of civilian casualties and insisted that military action was not a solution to the conflict in Yemen. Saudi Arabia immediately responded by rejecting any future arms deals, which had long been lucrative but controversial in Germany.[15]

Notwithstanding the existing close ties between Saudi Arabia and the aforementioned European countries, the new Saudi crown prince does not seem to have time for Europe at the moment. For him it remains merely a source of any weapons that he cannot get from the USA and a network of support for his regional policies, especially his rivalry with Iran and his interventionist agenda. This has resulted in competition among European arms manufacturers and governments for the attention of the young prince, even if it comes to undermining their own national interest by continuing uncritical support for Saudi Arabia. A more fruitful European policy would push Saudi Arabia towards greater dialogue with Iran and a *modus vivendi* with this formidable regional power, rather than simply and unequivocally taking the Saudi side lest lucrative arms deals are diverted elsewhere.

Furthermore, the national interests of Saudi Arabia's European allies would better be served by encouraging the Saudis to seek mediation and conflict resolution in their regional battles, from Damascus to Sana'a. As with Iranian interventions in Syria, Iraq, Lebanon, and Yemen, Saudi meddling in the internal affairs of Arab countries has had devastating effects, prolonging conflicts, militarizing the Arab uprisings, and precipitating sectarian conflicts, humanitarian disasters, and an unprecedented influx of refugees to European countries. Saudi Arabia's role in spreading radical religious ideology is still a taboo topic in many European capitals, where governments remain silent, preferring not to confront Riyadh with clear evidence of its involvement in radicalizing a troubled European Muslim population.

Europe may have lost its favourite Saudi candidate, deposed Crown Prince Muhammad ibn Nayif, who had established a good rapport with Western intelligence services as he was seen as a key player in the fight against terrorism. Counter-terrorism dominates European policy agendas from London and Paris to Berlin and beyond.

Losing the Regional Struggle: Saudi Arabia, Turkey, Iran, and the Elephant in the Room

Muhammad ibn Salman is currently struggling to establish Saudi Arabia as a serious regional power on a par with Turkey, Iran, and Israel. All are currently flexing their muscles in a bid to emerge as the dominant force dictating the outcome of several conflicts in the Arab world. In this heated regional struggle, new alliances are formed and old ones are reversed.

The young Saudi prince has continued the anti-Iranian rhetoric that dates back to the reign of King 'Abdullah (2005–15). Unexpectedly, in May 2017 he announced that he is determined to bring the fight to the Iranian heartland, a statement tantamount to a declaration of war. Turki ibn Faysal, a Saudi prince and the ex-director of the Intelligence Services, attended two conferences held by the Iranian opposition abroad; notable amongst them were the Mujahideen-e Khalq.[16] Under King Salman, the proxy war between Saudi Arabia and Iran has continued without a resolution in sight. The latest battleground was Yemen in 2015, where Saudi Arabia accused the Iranians of backing the Houthi rebellion.

Saudi's relations with Iran deteriorated after the American occupation of Iraq in 2003. At the time the Saudis accused the USA of removing Saddam Hussein from power only to hand the country to the Iranians. The occupation led to the further expansion of Iranian influence in the Arab world, a threat that the Saudis had warned of. Today it is in Iraq where the king and his son are desperately trying to reach out to Iran, the backer of both the Baghdad government and the various militias—most prominently al-Hashd al-Sha'bi (Popular Mobilization Forces), which it has armed and supported since 2014 to fight ISIS. Recently, for purely internal reasons, the Iraqi government of Haidar al-Abadi has proven more responsive to the new Saudi advances than former prime minister Nouri al-Maliki. Three Saudi state visits to Iraq promised to herald a new era of Saudi–Iraqi relations. Foreign minister Adil al-Jubair visited Baghdad on 25 February 2017, followed by Prime Minister al-Abadi arriving in Riyadh in June to meet the king. A meeting with the Iraqi oil minister followed.

However, Saudi Arabia went further by inviting the controversial Shi'i cleric Muqtada al-Sadr to Riyadh. The Iraqi government welcomed Saudi advances to gain Arab support and undermine any accusations of being motivated by Shi'i sectarian politics. This was especially urgent after the liberation of Mosul, where a Sunni population has been struggling to find political space in Iraq in a post-ISIS era. In the battle of Mosul, word of atrocities committed by official and para military Shi'i Iraqi troops and militias spread across the Arab world. Al-Abadi has tried to recast himself as a leader for all Iraqis rather than just the Shi'a, and good relations with the Saudis could go some way towards improving his image.

On the Saudi side, there is a belated understanding that their previous policy of ostracizing Iraq in the post-2003 era has merely intensified the country's estrangement from its Arab neighbours, precipitating its steady drift toward the Iranian orbit. But without Iran's approval, Saudi Arabia will find it difficult to 'reconcile' with Iraq, especially after several decades of media wars, terrorism blamed on Saudi Arabia, sectarianization, and general hostility. Iran's militias operating on Iraqi soil

SALMAN'S LEGACY

and the pro-Iranian position of its leading political party, Hizb al-Daʻwa, threaten any genuine future reconciliation between the two countries. Moreover, Riyadh's erratic foreign policy under Muhammad ibn Salman is a further obstacle to any regional *détente* between the two estranged neighbours. It is unlikely that Saudi–Iraqi relations will return to any kind of normality before the forthcoming Iraqi elections in 2018. Even if Riyadh seeks genuine cooperation with Baghdad, Iran's approval and sanctions will remain crucial for further normalization, let alone cooperation.

Turkey, considered a close Saudi partner during the Syrian civil war, sided with Qatar in the Saudi–Qatari crisis that began in May 2017 when the small Gulf emirate was subjected to sanctions by Saudi Arabia, the UAE, Bahrain, and Egypt. Turkey is currently strengthening its military presence in Qatar, stationing several thousand soldiers there in preparation for any threat to the small emirate. In an unprecedented move, Saudi Arabia exacerbated the conflict with Qatar when it tried to promote a member of Qatar's Al Thani royal family as an alternative amir, thus deepening an already near-intractable rift. This recent episode in inter-Gulf relations has proven to seriously undermine cooperation and unity. More importantly, as with other regional conflicts in the Arab world, regional powers Turkey, Iran, and Israel have taken the opportunity to become involved. Israel backed Saudi Arabia and its allies when it announced that it would close al-Jazeera's Jerusalem bureau in July 2017.

Muhammad ibn Salman may have made considerable progress with the elephant in the room, Israel—now jokingly dubbed the newest Sunni state—in his bid to form a pan-Islamic and international alliance against both Iran and Qatar. He has continued to clandestinely cooperate with Israel on security and economic matters.[17] In July 2016 a delegation of Saudi academics and businessmen visited Israel with a view to establishing discreet relations, aimed at strengthening Saudi Arabia's military capabilities and enlisting Israel in any armed confrontation with Iran. Saudi Arabia also has a new geographical and strategic link to Israel after Egypt offered to cede the two Red Sea islands of Sanafir and Tiran to Saudi Arabia. Both islands sit on the Straits of Tiran, Israel's only access to the Red Sea, and they may in the future serve as launching pads from which to enhance military and security cooperation between Israel and Saudi Arabia. The Saudi public is being prepared for greater cooperation with Israel, especially through Saudi-sponsored media, now much more willing to permit articles that do not overtly criticize the Israeli occupation and its treatment of Palestinians in the West Bank and Gaza. Saudi Arabia has also criticized Qatar for supporting the Palestinian group Hamas, now designated as a terrorist organization. Muhammad ibn Salman has certainly pleased the Israelis by doing so, and assured them of his willingness to foster greater cooperation. However, we shouldn't expect an Israeli flag to be raised in Riyadh soon. This will take some preparation and coordination, and the stakes in such a controversial move are high for the aspiring young prince.

Conclusion

Salman's kingdom is being shaped amid real challenges domestically, regionally, and internationally. The newly appointed crown prince Muhammad ibn Salman is not a capable fire-fighter or a tactical statesman. He is confident that, equipped with nothing more than money and unconditional US support, he can surmount any obstacles to his imminent accession. So far he has succeeded in marginalizing his rival cousin Muhammad ibn Nayif and enlisting Donald Trump as an ally, albeit temporarily. He is unlikely to turn his attention to Europe as he considers the USA the only superpower that can guarantee his survival, despite the recent broadening of the search for international partners.

However, Muhammad ibn Salman's command of a rich economy—despite falling oil prices—and recent loud US support have not enabled him to claim victories in the various wars and conflicts he has entered into. The most obvious setback is in Yemen, where over two years of Saudi air strikes have failed to end the local power struggle between multiple factions. His relations with Qatar are bound to deteriorate as the conflict has already reached a stalemate. By July 2017 the Saudis had already tempered their list of demands imposed on Qatar a month earlier as preconditions for lifting the boycott and sanctions. His rivalry with Iran is currently being fought through several proxy wars. As long as he continues to secure Mr Trump's approval and support, Muhammad ibn Salman is more likely to light further regional fires than extinguish existing ones.

King Salman and his son have decisively shifted Saudi foreign policy from cautious diplomacy and behind-the-scenes manoeuvring to a more interventionist doctrine. Under the future kingship of the young prince, Saudi Arabia will continue to attempt to become an undisputed Arab regional power even if this requires greater shifting alliances, for example closer cooperation and partnership with Israel. The domestic consequences of such a provocative policy may backfire and lead to future internal upheaval. Saudi Arabia has been set on an unknown future path, and its aggressive foreign policy is above all a reflection of domestic political and economic uncertainty that has prevailed since Salman became king.

12

CHINA'S RISE IN THE GULF

A SAUDI PERSPECTIVE

Naser al-Tamimi

The 'rise' of China as a global power may be inevitable and could have significant implications for the Middle East and beyond. China had overtaken the USA as the largest economy in purchasing power parity (PPP) terms by the end of 2014, and in market exchange-rate terms is projected to overtake the USA by 2030. Saudi officials increasingly see the writing on the wall: China will be their biggest oil market in the future, making it absolutely vital to cultivate strategic relations with this rising power.

- Economically, China is the world's most populous country, with the second-largest economy. It could surpass the USA by the end of the next decade to become the world's largest economy.
- In terms of energy, China is the world's largest energy consumer and second-largest oil importer. It is already on the point of overtaking the United States as the world's largest crude-oil importer.

- Militarily, China has the world's largest army; it is a nuclear power and has the second-largest military budget after the United States. Under the present climate, the fact remains that many Chinese weapons are less technologically sophisticated than those of the Western military powers. However, China is expected to close the gap over the next two decades.
- Politically, China is a permanent member of the UN Security Council (UNSC), and its political influence will increase over time with its growing economic and military powers.

Meanwhile, the current unwritten security architecture ('oil for security') between Saudi Arabia and the USA has become complex and sometimes contradictory due to the emergence of several international, regional, and domestic factors. At the international level, the significance of the so-called shale boom may, some argue, for the first time in history give the USA the chance to abandon its dependence on oil imports from the Middle East once and for all. Regionally, the lifting of sanctions on Iran has made the country more strategically confident and regionally assertive. Finally, as the Saudi leaders take popular sentiments into account, it will become more difficult for the governments to disregard the reactions of domestic audiences on important economic and security issues in order to satisfy the policy demands of the West—in particular, those made by the USA.

All this raises more important questions: in the long term, will the shift in the geopolitics of energy bring with it a shift in political relations? Will Saudi Arabia's ties with China lead towards abandoning the strategic relations with the United States? Or will America scale back its military presence in the Middle East, giving room for other powers, especially China, to fill the 'vacuum'? These are important questions that must be answered in order to understand the great power realignment that is currently under way in the Middle East region.

Emerging Economic Power: New Opportunities

China, with a population of over 1.3 billion, has emerged as a major global economic and trade power. It is currently the world's biggest economy (in terms of PPP), manufacturer, exporter, merchandise trader, and holder of foreign-exchange reserves.[1] This impressive performance and rapid economic expansion has been achieved in a short period of time. Indeed, over the past two decades the global economic weight (its share of the world nominal gross domestic product) of China rose more than six-fold. It increased from less than 2.4 per cent in 1995 to almost 15.2 per cent by the end of 2016.[2] Importantly, China's economy accounts for one-third of global GDP growth, 14.6 per cent of global trade, and around 22 per cent of global oil demand growth in 2016.[3] However, the International Monetary Fund (IMF) anticipated lower growth over the next five years. The IMF has projected that China's real GDP growth will average around 6.0 per cent from 2017 to 2022.[4]

China's spectacular economic development has been accompanied by a sharp increase in oil demand. China's share in global oil consumption rose from less than 4 per cent in 1993 (since the country became an oil importer) to about 12.3 per cent by the end of 2016.[5] In the process, Saudi Arabia became the centre of gravity for Chinese economic activities in the Middle East, largely as a result of its enormous crude-oil reserves, production and export capacity, or as Chinese president Xi Jinping summarized it: 'An oil kingdom with huge oil and gas reserves, a country with time-honoured history which is the birthplace of Islam, and the magnificent setting sun against the vast expanse of the desert: these are the images that Saudi Arabia brings to our mind.'[6] Consequently, Saudi Arabia has been China's largest global supplier of crude oil since 2002. In 2013 China became Saudi Arabia's number one trade partner for the first time. Two-way trade reached nearly $70 billion in 2014, growing by 230 times since the establishment of diplomatic relations in 1990.[7]

Nevertheless, China–Saudi relations have been restricted mainly to energy exports (oil, petroleum products, and petrochemicals), Chinese manufacturing goods, and limited cross-investment. The decline in global oil prices has hit the trade between them very hard. The volume between the two countries dropped significantly to $42.8 billion in 2016, a decline of almost 18 per cent from the previous year and nearly 40 per cent since 2014, when the oil prices started to decline (see table 12.5).[8] Nevertheless, the relations between China and Saudi Arabia are expected to grow steadily and diversify over the coming years, so forces for further engagement will still be strong. The Chinese economy will get bigger; the Centre for Economics and Business Research (CEBR) predicts that China will overtake the USA as the world's largest economy by 2030 for the first time since 1890.[9]

In this context, several factors could play an important part in deepening the Chinese economic engagement in the Middle East. First, there is strong political will on both sides to improve their relations at all levels. During (then) Deputy Crown Prince Muhammad ibn Salman's visit to China in August 2016 the two countries signed seventeen cooperative agreements covering politics, security, energy, peaceful nuclear energy, finance, investment, housing, water resources, quality inspection, science, technology, and culture.[10] Importantly, King Salman during his visit to China on 16 March 2017 oversaw the signing of deals worth as much as $65 billion, involving everything from energy to space.[11] Second, in spite of increasing competition in global energy markets, the Gulf region will remain a strategic area, especially in terms of energy resources, regardless of the increase in production of other regions. Over the next two decades Chinese oil and gas imports are projected to rise significantly. Consequently, the importance of the Gulf countries will increase even with China's tireless efforts to diversify its oil imports from Africa, Russia, Central Asia, and South America. The surge in China's energy consumption will certainly open new opportunities for Saudi Arabia exports, particularly oil.

Aside from energy, more than 160 Chinese companies are operating in several sectors of the Saudi economy, and the number of Chinese projects in the kingdom reached around 175.[12] Increasing participation by Chinese contractors in Saudi Arabia's construction, communication, oil, gas, and petrochemical sectors is already becoming more evident. Perhaps one of the biggest success stories of Chinese companies is Huawei. The Chinese multinational networking, telecommunications equipment, and services company has administered communication support for the annual Hajj (pilgrimage) for ten consecutive years, providing communication services for 3 million Muslim pilgrims.[13] Importantly, Huawei has officially been licensed to carry out business in Saudi Arabia, making it the first Chinese company to obtain a 100 per cent commercial licence to invest in the kingdom and establish a centre for innovation.[14]

As per the China Global Investment Tracker, which measures China's investments and contracts worldwide, the Chinese have poured $28.46

billion into Saudi Arabia's economy, of which most went to the energy sector ($10.08 billion) and the rest was invested in several other sectors such as real estate, metals, transport, agriculture, and chemicals between 2005 and January 2017.[15] Meanwhile, Saudi investments in China have amounted to about $15 billion, almost all of them in the energy sector (refining and petrochemicals).[16] Looking forward, a recent report by BMI Research is expecting China to

> deepen its investment presence across the infrastructure spectrum of MENA [Middle East and North Africa] countries in the coming years for two primary reasons. On the one hand, the region will continue to be home to a wealth of such diversified, high value project opportunities; on the other, MENA features prominently in China's "Belt and Road" [or One Belt, One Road—OBOR] initiative.[17]

Banking and financial opportunities are other promising areas for both countries. Chinese banks are looking at global markets for growth, while the Saudi government and companies are set to borrow billions to fund the budget deficit and find new sources of financing, considering the scarcity of liquidity to be a result of declining oil prices. In this regard, USA-based Standard & Poor's (S&P) forecasts that Saudi Arabia will borrow as much as $180 billion by 2019.[18] Importantly, Beijing is working with the Jeddah-based Islamic Development Bank (IDB) for possible use of Islamic finance within the framework of the recently launched Asian Infrastructure Investment Bank (AIIB).[19] From the Saudi perspective, the future of China's currency, the yuan or renminbi (RMB), is also a very important issue. At the end of September 2016 Standard Chartered announced that it had started direct trading between RMB and Saudi Arabia's riyal, making it one of the first market-makers to trade Saudi currency in China's interbank market.[20]

Perhaps more important is the signing of the free-trade agreement (FTA) between China and the Gulf Cooperation Council (GCC), which could boost their economic relations. Between 2004 and January 2017 nine rounds of negotiations were held,[21] but these faltered over protectionist policies[22] as the GCC countries believe that China is trying to protect its petrochemical sector. However, in January 2016 Chinese president Xi Jinping during his visit to Saudi Arabia called for the speedy conclusion of an FTA between China and the GCC.[23]

Energy: The Engine of Interdependence

The growing importance of China represents a fundamental shift in the geopolitics of energy and provides Saudi Arabia with new and stable markets. Since China became a net oil importer its oil consumption rose dramatically to nearly quadruple in only twenty years, increasing from 2.9 mb/d in 1993 to 11.9 mb/d in 2016, and could jump to over 14.8 mb/d by 2030, almost 22.6 per cent.[24] Oil imports have therefore also rapidly increased, rising from zero in 1993 to more than 64 per cent of China's total oil supply[25] or over 7.6 mb/d in 2016 (see table 12.2).

The future also looks promising for Saudi Arabia. China's consumption of oil, gas, and petrochemical products will increase steadily in the next twenty years. Thus, it is logical to expect energy trade between Saudi Arabia and China to also grow. Estimates of China's oil consumption vary as a result of the uncertainty regarding the growth prospects of the Chinese economy, the development of indigenous sources, the use of alternative energy sources, and increased efficiency measures. However, all estimates seem to agree that China will still need to import large amounts of oil in the medium to long term.

For example, the International Energy Agency (IEA) forecasts global annual growth to average 1.2 per cent, propelling demand from 96.6 (mb/d) in 2016 to 103.8 (mb/d) in 2022, an increase of 7.2 mb/d.[26] China is expected to account for 1.8 (mb/d) by 2022. This equates to an average annual increase of around 300,000 barrels per day, although this is less than China's demand growth in recent years.[27] The IEA projects that China's demand will grow at an average annual rate of 2.4 per cent. This compares with 4.8 per cent a year in the five years to 2016 and 5.5 per cent a year in the five-year period ending in 2011.[28] In the long term, BP's latest forecast (Energy Outlook 2035) predicts that global liquids demand (oil, biofuels, and other liquid fuels) could increase by 15 mb/d, to reach 110 mb/d by 2035. Growth comes exclusively from emerging economies, with China accounting for half of it.[29] Meanwhile, China's oil-import dependence will rise from 64 per cent in 2016 to 79 per cent in 2035—higher than the USA at its peak in 2005.[30]

Chinese estimates are also in line with international projections. Taking into account the influence of the decline in Chinese oil production; alternative energy; rising demand by independent oil refiners, known as teapots; strategic or commercial reserves and re-export, China's domestic oil consumption could reach 12.5–13 mb/d and 14–14.5 mb/d in 2020 and 2030 respectively.[31] China has sought to diversify oil supplies and is developing its own resources, yet in 2016 nearly half of China's oil imports (7.6 mb/d) came from the Middle East (see table 12.2).[32] Fatih Birol, executive director of the IEA, told the *Financial Times* recently that 'the region [the Middle East] was expected to meet three-quarters of demand growth over the next two decades'.[33] Meanwhile, BP's Energy Outlook 2035 projects that OPEC is assumed to account for nearly 70 per cent of global supply growth, increasing by 9 mb/d to 48 mb/d by 2035.[34]

Beyond oil, China also offers important economic advantages to Saudi Arabia's downstream and petrochemicals sectors. Saudi Arabia Basic Industries Corporation (SABIC) already holds a 50 per cent stake in a polycarbonate complex in Tianjin with China Petroleum & Chemical Corporation (Sinopec Group) and Saudi Aramco holds 22.5 per cent of a refining and fuel marketing company in Fujian in south-east China.[35] Aramco is also in advanced negotiations with China National Petroleum Corporation (CNPC) to build the Yunnan refinery in south-west China.[36] SABIC also signed an agreement with Shenhua Ningxia Coal Industry Group in May 2016 to build a joint petrochemical complex in the Ningxia Hui region of China. Its coal-to-chemicals project will cost approximately $3–4 billion and is expected to be ready by 2020.[37] The chief executive of SABIC, Yousef Abdullah al-Benyan, said recently that the company investments in China amounted to about $6 billion, while SABIC sales in China reached $7 billion, or 30 per cent of SABIC's total sales.[38]

Another potential factor is the kingdom's own economic outlook. There is a growing push within Saudi Arabia to develop renewable energy and to reduce dependence on fossil-fuel consumption. In this area there are opportunities for Chinese companies in sectors such as solar energy, peaceful nuclear energy, and renewable energy. To be sure, Saudi Arabia has already set an initial target of generating 9.5 gigawatts of renewable energy by 2030.[39]

Yet despite this optimistic outlook there are significant challenges awaiting the development of Saudi Arabia–China relations in the medium and long term. Perhaps the main concern for Riyadh is the future trajectory of China's economy and the uncertainty over its oil demand amid growing risks of a financial crisis or a prolonged slow-down in growth.[40] In this context, the Economist Intelligence Unit (EIU) forecasts that China's economy will slow significantly in the coming years as the real GDP growth is forecast to average less than 5 per cent a year by 2017–21, a situation that will be perceived as a 'hard landing'.[41] From the Saudi perspective, the impact of any major Chinese economic slowdown could be especially severe. Certainly, the trade between Saudi Arabia and China is still transactional and vulner-able to potential shocks of price volatility.

One of the contentious issues that may arise is protectionist policies. As long as there is no free-trade agreement signed between the two sides, China's protectionist measures could present a problem for Saudi petrochemical producers in the future. Meanwhile, Chinese oversupply of steel, aluminium and electrical cables has caused concern among producers in GCC countries. Saudi Arabia's steel producers often called on their government to take urgent action to stop what they call 'Chinese dumping'.[42]

In this regard, several factors may also negatively affect Saudi petro-chemical producers: first, China's petrochemical capacity is projected to grow significantly over the coming years, which would inevitably reduce the country's reliance on imports. Second, as China's growth is slowing down, government policy is shifting to focus more on its domestic economy.[43] Importantly, the reduction of energy subsidies in Saudi Arabia could result in increasing the costs for the kingdom's petrochemicals producers,[44] or, as BMI Research noted, 'Saudi petro-chemicals production margins are set to come under increasing pres-sure as a result of reductions in the government's energy subsidies'.[45] Finally, a push to tap China's shale-gas potential could provide cheaper and more abundant feedstock over the long term.[46] BP's Energy Outlook 2035 expects that China will become the second-largest shale gas producer, after the USA, by 2035.[47]

Growing competition is also an emerging challenge for Riyadh. Saudi Arabia is now facing competition from Russia, Iraq, Iran, Venezuela, and even Oman for a share of the Chinese market. These countries have consistently increased their market share, while Saudi

Arabia's exports to China have been in stagnation in the last few years and its market share of Chinese crude imports has been declining since 2011 (see table 12.2). Certainly Russia in particular enjoys a significant geographical advantage over Saudi Arabia and is already usurping it as the top crude supplier to China in 2016 (see table 12.2). In response, Saudi Aramco is stepping up its marketing strategy in China by offering more cargoes at spot prices and flexible payment terms in addition to the company's long-term model. Importantly, Aramco has increased its crude-oil storage capacity of 6.29 million in Okinawa in Japan's southwest by nearly a third to help supply China's new buyers.[48]

Direct investments between the two countries are also still limited. Despite twenty-six years of trade between China and Saudi Arabia, a number of hurdles have inhibited Saudi investment; these have included language barriers, business attitudes, differences between Saudi and Chinese laws, and a lack of transparency in information and data on potential investment projects. Other difficulties have included a lack of suitable local partners, insufficient protection for intellectual property, and a complex and contradictory legal and regulatory system. In addition, there is a significant shortfall in the number of specialized companies that study and market opportunities.[49] The investment hurdles are highlighted by a World Bank survey which ranked China seventy-eighth and Saudi Arabia ninety-fourth globally in ease of doing business.[50]

Importantly, the perception in Saudi Arabia is that Chinese companies (except perhaps Huawei) lack advanced technology in comparison to their Western, Japanese, and South Korean competitors. Many Chinese companies still need more time in order to establish their presence and gain a good reputation in the Gulf—Saudi Arabia in particular. Sun Yi, a Chinese expert with the United Nations, recently wrote a revealing article urging Chinese companies to adapt in order to win respect in foreign deals; he gave an example from Saudi Arabia:

> China Railway Construction Corporation (CRCC) signed a contract in 2009 with the government of Saudi Arabia to build an 18 km light rail in the oil-rich country. The contract adopted an engineering, procurement, and construction mode, which means CRCC, the contractor, was made responsible for activities ranging from design and procurement to construction. But after having signed the agreement, the Saudi side

insisted on letting European companies make the design, citing the reason that the European standard is a prerequisite and making no secret of the Saudi Arabia side's higher opinion of Western companies than of the Chinese contractor.[51]

According to MEED's (Middle East Economic Digest) annual engineering, procurement, and construction (EPC) contractor survey for the hydrocarbons sector only, Chinese Sinopec picked up $1.367 billion worth of work between 1 July 2015 and 30 June 2016 on oil, gas, and petrochemicals projects across the Middle East and North Africa (MENA) (excluding Iran and Turkey). This was less than 4 per cent of nearly $34.83 billion, the total value of the top twenty contractors in the region.[52] Most the top twenty contractors in MENA were European and South Korean companies that have been successful in the MENA's energy sector for years.[53]

Above all, China's relations with Iran will remain a source of concern for the leadership of Saudi Arabia. Indeed, since King Salman ascended the throne in 2015 and Iran struck a nuclear deal with world powers, Saudi Arabia has adopted a more confrontational strategy to counter what it perceived as an expansion of Iranian influence in the Arab region, especially with regard to Syria, Iraq, Lebanon, and Yemen. Most notably, Riyadh has used its influence in the Islamic world to isolate Iran, by creating an Islamic coalition against terrorism without inviting Tehran to join.[54] Here perhaps we can say that it is not an improvement in political and economic relations between Tehran and Beijing that worries Riyadh, but rather the possibility of growing military ties between China and Iran, though Beijing has repeatedly declared that its relations with Tehran will not be at the expense of the Gulf states.[55]

Security Considerations: China's Growing Muscle

China's growing economic and technological power could eventually translate into increased military power and allow Beijing to pursue more assertive policies to achieve its strategic goals. In 2017 China announced another rise in its defence budget by 7.0 per cent to around $152 billion; the Chinese government stated, however, that this was the lowest rise in seven years.[56] Nevertheless, Stockholm International

Peace Research Institute (SIPRI) estimates that the real figure may be 30 per cent higher. According to SIPRI, China had by far the world's second-largest military expenditure, an estimated $215 billion, in 2016.[57] In contrast, the USA defence budget was $611 billion, or 36 per cent of global spending.[58]

China is also the world's second-biggest investor in research and development (R&D) with a forecast spending of $396.3 billion for 2016;[59] consequently, a large and strong economy will provide extra resources to enhance the capabilities of R&D. According to the Organization for Economic Co-operation and Development (OECD), China's R&D intensity—which accounted for 2.047 per cent of GDP—'increased sharply' from 0.57 per cent of GDP in 1998 and had caught up with the combined European Union expenditure of 1.97 per cent in 2012.[60] China is planning to increase its R&D spending to 2.5 per cent of its GDP,[61] and at the current rate the country is expected to surpass that of the USA by about 2023.[62] Importantly, according to the World Intellectual Property Organization (WIPO) in 2016, China ranked third after the USA and Japan for filing patents.[63] In this regard, the *Financial Times* noted recently that 'Chinese patenting applications surged 45 per cent in 2016 … placing the country on track to overtake Japan and the US to become the largest user of the international patent system within two years'.[64]

To close the technology gap with the West, China has in recent years been spending lavishly to develop its military capabilities.[65] China's ambitious defence industry included naval modernization; plans to build three more aircraft carriers by 2020 as part of its new 'blue-water' strategy; and a submarine force, including nuclear-powered ballistic missile submarines (SSBN).[66] Additionally, China continues to develop sophisticated integrated air defences including stealth fighters (J-20), a new generation of long-range bombers, unmanned aerial vehicles (UAV), and advanced long-range accurate conventional ballistic and cruise missiles, whilst also progressing with commercial and military robotics industries, intelligence systems, and foreign bases.[67]

One area in which China has made impressive progress is the navy. Jesse Karotkin, then-senior intelligence officer for China at the US Office of Naval intelligence (currently deputy national intelligence manager for East Asia Office of the Director of National Intelligence in

Washington, DC), in his recent testimony before the US–China Economic and Security Review Commission, described China's military development strategy thus:

> Beijing characterizes its military modernization effort as a 'three-step development strategy' that entails laying a 'solid foundation' by 2010, making 'major progress' by 2020, and being able to win 'information-ized wars by the mid-21st century'. Although the PLA (N) faces capability gaps in some key areas ... they have achieved their 'strong foundation' and are emerging as a well-equipped, competent, and more professional force.[68]

China's Thirteenth Five Year Plan (FYP, 2016–20), passed by the National People's Congress and released on 17 March 2016, declares that China will build itself into a 'maritime power', by means of creating a highly effective system for protecting overseas interests and safeguarding the legitimate overseas interests of Chinese citizens and legal persons, while simultaneously actively promoting the construction of strategic strong points for the '21st Century Maritime Silk Road'.[69] Chinese premier Li Keqiang recently provided an interesting insight regarding China's view as a maritime power:

> The traditional mentality that land outweighs sea must be abandoned, and great importance has to be attached to managing the seas and oceans and protecting maritime rights and interests. It is necessary for China to develop a modern maritime military force structure commensurate with its national security and development interests, safeguard its national sovereignty and maritime rights and interests, protect the security of strategic SLOCs [Sea Lines of Communication] and overseas interests, and participate in international maritime cooperation, so as to provide strategic support for building itself into a maritime power.[70]

Against this strategic backdrop, China's military ambitions will be curbed by a slowing economy and ageing population.[71] BMI Research noted in its 2016 defence and security report on China that '[the] Chinese economy is staggering from overcapacity, significant debt, falling profits and an ageing population. These factors will weigh on future economic growth and in turn could prove detrimental to the substantial growth military spending has so far been experiencing.'[72] The Chinese defence industry still also lags behind many Western arms manufacturers, in particular the USA, while its navy has also limitations and needs at least two decades, possibly more, to rival the US navy, according to some observers.[73] To be sure, China hasn't fought a war since 1979; this makes it difficult to assess the performance of the Chinese military through numbers, equipment, and technology alone.

However, from the Chinese perspective the new capabilities are not intended to rival the USA or to become militarily involved in the Middle East, but to secure China's crucial overseas supply lines (which are occasionally threatened by pirates or terrorist attacks), conduct humanitarian assistance and disaster relief, and, if the need arose, evacuate Chinese citizens working overseas.[74] Certainly China's interests at stake are enormous and cannot be ignored. In 2016 China's aggregate trade with Europe reached almost $679 billion,[75] reaching $214 billion with the Middle East and hitting over $150 billion with Africa. The three regions combined represent over 28 per cent of China's total trade with the world (see table 12.5).[76]

China's burgeoning trade with these areas further increases its dependence on sea lanes and maritime straits such as the Suez Canal, the Bab al-Mandeb, the Straits of Hormuz, and the Straits of Malacca. In addition to the strategic importance of these routes, China now obtains nearly half of its oil from the Middle East (see table 12.2).[77] Looking forward, China's dependence on Middle Eastern oil is likely to increase to 60 per cent or over 5 mb/d by 2022, according to the IEA. In the long term, China is expected to import around two-thirds of its needs from the region.[78]

As China's military capabilities keep growing, and with the country's dependence on oil from the Middle East being apt to rise significantly over time, Beijing is likely to use its navy to protect its vital interests in the Middle East and Africa in the coming years. China's Military Strategy, which was published on 26 May 2016, stated clearly that 'PLA Navy (PLAN) will gradually shift its focus from "offshore waters defence" to the combination of "offshore waters defence" with "open seas protection", and build a combined, multi-functional and efficient marine combat force structure'.[79]

To be sure, in 2016 China announced that construction of its first overseas military outpost (China officially calls it a logistics support base) in Djibouti had begun, and sent Guan Youfei, a senior official in the People's Liberation Army (PLA), to Syria where he promised to increase aid and training for Assad's forces.[80] In 2015 China started building its first home-made aircraft carrier, and had begun its first deterrent patrol by SSBN.[81] Importantly, a 2015 counter-terrorism law gave the PLA the ability (for the first time) to send Chinese troops abroad for combat missions without a UN mandate.[82] Marking the sixty-eighth anniversary of the founding of the Chinese navy on 23 April 2017, Xu Guangyu, a senior adviser to the China Arms Control and Disarmament Association, told the Chinese newspaper *Global Times*:

> In the long run, China needs to develop its own aircraft carrier battle teams, with at least six aircraft carriers, naval forces led by guided missile destroyers, as well as attack submarines ... China will build about 10 more bases for the six aircraft carriers. ... Hopefully, China could have bases in every continent, but that depends on countries which would like to cooperate with China.[83]

Looking Ahead: Are the Chinese Coming?

As China comes to rely more on energy imports from the Middle East, the US imports are shrinking as a result of the shale (tight-oil) boom. This situation, in addition to the American budgetary constraints, has prompted some to argue that the USA will be able to reduce or abandon its military presence in the region entirely. We would argue that it is highly unlikely that the USA would completely disengage from the Gulf region, at least in the medium term. American engagement in the Middle East is not simply about oil imports. After all, even before the shale boom, the Gulf region provided only about 10 per cent of total US oil supply.[84] Indeed, the USA still has strategic or 'core interests' in the region, such as securing the free flow of energy and commerce; nuclear non-proliferation; countering terrorism; confronting external aggression against US allies; economic opportunities and arms deals worth tens of billions of dollars. This is in addition to the military bases in the Arab Gulf states which are strategically positioned, cheap to maintain, and difficult to replace.[85]

Furthermore, the USA would still need to worry about the Gulf region, since oil prices are set globally. In the US Department of

Energy's reference case for 2040 (Annual Energy Outlook 2017), total US consumption of petroleum and other liquids, including fossil fuels, biofuels, and lease condensate will stay in the range of 19–20 mb/d between 2016 and 2050.[86] The bottom line: US oil and goods prices still depend on what happens abroad, not the source or quantity of US production or imports. In this regard, the executive director of the IEA, Fatih Birol, is sceptical about US energy independence; he told the *Financial Times* recently: 'US oil production will increase, but it is still an oil importer and will be for some time ... some have the view the rise of tight [shale] oil will sideline the Middle East. This view, I would never subscribe to.' Tony Blair, the former British prime minister, even went further to say:

> Whatever the long-term implications of the USA energy revolution, the world's dependence on the Middle East is not going to disappear any time soon. In any event, it has a determining effect on the price of oil; and thus, on the stability and working of the global economy.[87]

However, in the short and medium terms Saudi Arabia seems to have few viable options for pursuing a more independent and forthright foreign policy.[88] Robert Jordan, the former US ambassador to Riyadh, argues that there would be limits to any Arab Gulf state alliances with other powers: 'There is no country in the world more capable of providing the protection of their oil fields, and their economy, than the US, and they are aware of that. We're not going to see them jump out of that orbit.' Indeed, the Saudis and the Chinese recognize that, for at least until the next decade, the USA will remain the only country in the world capable of projecting substantial amounts of conventional military (and soft) power into the Gulf region. China's Foreign Minister Wang Yi told al-Jazeera TV in May 2016: 'From what we know about the country, the United States will probably remain the world's No. 1 for a fairly long time to come.'[89]

Given this strategic background, it is reasonable to expect that the foreign policy of Saudi Arabia will have several fundamental elements in the short and medium term. The most important one is strengthening the GCC's own military capabilities collectively or individually, including the formation of a 'united military command' of GCC forces, as previously suggested by Saudi Arabia.[90]

Saudi Arabia is unlikely now or in the immediate future to seek to use China as a military replacement (this, of course, if China agreed to it) for the United States. From the Saudi perspective, maintaining good relations with America remains the key foreign policy objective. The USA is still seen as a global power, so much so that Riyadh has signed an arms contract worth tens of billions; American companies still play an important role in the development of the local economy, particularly the energy sector, which is the lifeblood of Saudi Arabia. This is in addition to the United States still being the favourite destination for students from Saudi Arabia, where their numbers are estimated at eighty thousand in 2016,[91] in comparison to 650 Saudi students in China.[92]

Above all, the two countries are still bound together by some common interests such as the free flow of energy supplies from the Gulf, counter-terrorism cooperation, shared concerns over jihadist groups such as ISIS and al-Qaeda, opposing what they perceived as Iranian hegemony, and US logistical/intelligence support for the Saudi war in Yemen.[93] Importantly, President Trump's hostile attitude towards Iran, combined with his good relationship with the Egyptian president, Abdel Fattah al-Sisi, is already helping Riyadh in opening a new chapter with the new US administration.

Nevertheless, developing strategic relations with China is one of Riyadh's most important foreign policy goals in the coming years. In this context, China can play an important role in several issues that concern Saudi Arabia. Through Riyadh's lens, Beijing could be regarded as a valuable source of political support as Saudi Arabia continues a path of selective economic reforms whilst also seeking to deflect Western pressure in the area of political reforms. For example, in October 2016 China backed Saudi Arabia's sovereign immunity and criticized the USA's Justice Against Sponsors of Terrorism Act (JASTA).[94]

China may also play an important role in supplying the kingdom with weapons that the United States refuses to sell, such as long-range missiles, unmanned planes, and satellite and nuclear technology. There are several reports that Saudi Arabia has already bought new models of Chinese long-range missiles (DF-21 ballistic missiles) and unmanned (UAV) planes or drones.[95] Saudi Arabia and China have confirmed recently that one of the deals signed during King Salman's visit to China in March 2017 was a partnership to set up the first factory for Chinese unmanned aerial vehicles (UAVs) in the Middle East.[96]

Finally, Saudi Arabia will continue using all its economic and political tools to support countries such as Egypt, Bahrain, Jordan, Morocco, and its allies in Yemen, Syria, and Lebanon, to better coordinate Arab efforts in order to shape regional politics in their favour. Taken together, this suggests less Saudi Arabian reliance on the USA, but nothing like a significant break in its ties with Washington.[97] However, to what extent this policy is sustainable and successful remains to be seen.

In the long term, with China continuing to 'rise', there will be the potential for a comprehensive global power shift. China's persistence in actively securing energy resources and building strategic alliances is, and will remain, a source of direct competition to the USA. In this context, there are three scenarios regarding the Sino–US relationship predicted for the Gulf region.

(1) containment: the USA will see China's 'rise' in the Gulf as a threat which should be contained;
(2) unilateral approach: the USA will pursue its objectives in the Gulf while refusing to acknowledge or take into account Chinese interests;
(3) the USA will maintain the status quo and pursue its objectives in the Gulf while acknowledging or respecting Chinese interests.

With trade between China and the Middle East increasing rapidly, it is most likely that Beijing will become the main trading partner of all countries in the Gulf region (China is already the top trading partner of ten Arab countries, including Saudi Arabia in addition to Iran), possibly before the end of the current decade. Consequently, there is no question that China's high interdependence with the Middle East, Africa, and Europe will make it more challenging for the United States to successfully pursue its objectives and to follow through with unilateral action. While cooperation is the desirable outcome, it is difficult to predict the future; but what is certain is that China's interests in the Middle East will expand significantly in the future, and so will its role.

Although Beijing has so far shown no interest in challenging America's influence and strategic interests in the Gulf region, China cannot afford to ignore the so-called realpolitik, or as Mearsheimer straightforwardly put it: 'A powerful China is sure to have security interests around the globe, which will prompt it to develop the capability to project military power into regions far beyond Asia. The Gulf region will rank high on the new superpower's list of strategically important areas.'[98]

Conclusion

China is currently the largest importer of the Middle East's oil, and Saudi Arabia is the largest supplier from the region. Accordingly, the peace and stability of the Gulf region is of strategic interest to Chinese political calculations. Riyadh sees China as a superpower in the making and expects that the country will soon become the first destination for its oil exports. It would thus make sense to strengthen ties with this rising power.

Nevertheless, Saudi Arabia (or China) is unlikely, either now or in the immediate future, to seek to use China as a military replacement for the United States. Certainly, maintaining good relations with the USA remains a key foreign-policy objective for the kingdom. However, Riyadh is likely in the longer term to seriously consider multiple political–security arrangements if Washington was to put some distance between itself and the Middle East or if the rift developing between Saudi Arabia and the USA was to widen.

Table 12.1: China's Global Power (Selected Indicators, 2016)

	In Numbers	Ranking in 2016
Population	1.38 billion	1
Land size	9,706,961 km	3
GDP (Nominal)	$11.21 trillion	2
GDP based on purchasing power parity (PPP)	$21.29 trillion	1
Military expenditure	$215 billion	2
Exports	$2.098 trillion	1
Imports	$1.587 trillion	2
Trade	$3.685 trillion	1
Manufacturing	1	1
FDI (Inflows to mainland excluding Hong Kong)	$138 billion	3
Foreign-exchange reserves	$3.01 trillion	1

Sources: China's official data; IMF; SIPRI military expenditure database; and WTO.

Table 12.2: China Crude Imports (2010–2016, '000 B/D)

Region / Country	2010	2011	2012	2013	2014	2015	2016
Middle East	2,260	2,607	2,700	2,940	3,222	3,414	3,660
% of total	47.3%	51.5%	49.8%	52%	52.2%	50.8%	48.1%
Saudi Arabia	893	1,005	1,075	1,078	993	1,011	1,017
% of total	18.7%	19.9%	19.8%	19.1%	16.1%	15.1%	13.4%
Iraq	225	276	313	471	572	643	723
Iran	425	554	438	428	548	531	623
Oman	319	365	393	512	599	645	703
North Africa	455	385	273	237	221	237	161
Africa (ex-North Africa)	959	816	1,017	1,044	1,134	1,045	1,185
Americas	413	464	546	549	658	842	1,033
Venezuela	145	222	293	303	265	308	387
FSU/Europe	521	610	718	748	815	1,005	1,257
Russia	306	371	487	491	665	852	1,051
Total Imports	4,781	5,062	5,417	5,656	6,177	6,715	7,609

Sources: China Official data; *MEES*; and author calculations.

Table 12.3: Long-Term Oil Demand in the Reference Case (mb/d)

	Forecast					
	2015	2020	2025	2030	2035	2040
OECD	46.2	45.9	44.3	42.1	39.7	37.3
Latin America	5.6	6.0	6.4	6.7	7.0	7.3
Middle East & Africa	3.8	4.2	4.6	5.1	5.5	6.0
India	4.1	5.1	6.4	7.7	9.0	10.4
China	10.8	12.2	13.6	14.9	16.1	17.1
Other Asia	6.3	7.1	7.9	8.7	9.3	9.8
Russia	3.4	3.5	3.6	3.6	3.6	3.5
World	93.0	98.3	102.3	105.5	107.8	109.4

Source: OPEC, World Oil Outlook 2016, 8 Nov. 2016.

Table 12.4: Global Chinese Investments and Construction (2005–January 2017)

Country / Region	Investment Volume ($ bn)	% China Total
Global	1485.91	100%
Sub-Saharan Africa	252.61	17.0%
Europe	227.84	15.33%
East Asia	192.81	12.98%
United States	153.77	10.35%
Arab Middle East and North Africa	142.82	9.61%
Saudi Arabia	28.46	1.92%
South America	136.5	9.19%
Australia	92.84	6.25%
North America (excluding USA)	61.88	4.16%
Pakistan	44.4%	2.99%
Russia	40.71	2.74%
Iran	17.41	1.17%

Source: Compiled and calculated by the author from American Enterprise Institute, China Global Investment Tracker.

Table 12.5: China Trade with Main Regions (2016, $1,000)

	Exports	Imports	Total trade	% of China Total
World	2,118,980,582	1,588,695,867	3,707,676,449	100%
Europe	391,843,219	286,912,550	678,755,769	18.30%
(NAFTA)*	448,235,369	163,606,780	611,842,149	16.50%
(ASEAN)**	259,864,461	196,229,263	456,093,724	12.30%
Latin America and Caribbean	113,788,606	101,762,599	215,551,205	5.80%
Middle East	125,102,555	88,487,324	213,589,879	5.80%
Africa	93,489,370	56,827.399	150,316,769	4.1%
Russia	37,506,059	32,131,140	69,637,199	1.90%
Saudi Arabia	19,266,738	23,613,002	42,879,740	1.20%
Iran	16,578,741	14,952,884	31,531,625	0.90%
Turkey	16,807,503	2,775,455	19,582,958	0.50%

Source: Compiled and calculated by the author from International Trade Centre (ITC).
* North American Free Trade Agreement.
Association of South-East Asian Nations.

Figure 12.1: China: Top Trade Partners, 2016

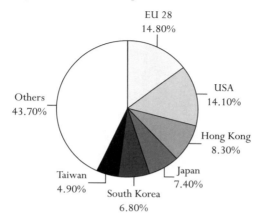

Source: IMF.

Figure 12.2: Saudi Arabia: Top Trade Partners, 2016

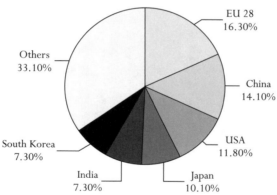

Source: IMF.

NOTES

INTRODUCTION: THE DILEMMAS OF A NEW ERA

1. Saud Al-Otaibi, 'The Resilience of Monarchy in the Middle East: A Case Study of Saudi Arabia', *Journal of King Saud University* 10 (1998); D. Long, *The Kingdom of Saudi Arabia*, Gainesville: University of Florida Press, 1997; Robert Lacey, *Inside the Kingdom: Kings, Clerics, Modernists, Terrorist, and the Struggle for Saudi Arabia*, London: Penguin, 2010; Sean Foley, 'When Collision Emerges as Unexpected Harmony: Saudi Responses to the Arab Spring', *Contemporary Review of the Middle East* 1, 1 (2014).

2. Fred Halliday, *Arabia without Sultans*, New York: Penguin, 1975; Said Aburish, *The Rise, Corruption and Coming Fall of the House of Saud*, London: Bloomsbury 1994; Christopher Davidson, *After the Sheikhs: The Coming Collapse of the Monarchies*, London: Hurst & Co./New York: Oxford University Press, 2013.

3. Elihugh Abner, 'The Collapse of Saudi Arabia and the Cataclysmic Power Shift in the Middle East', *Journal of International Affairs* 69, 2 (2016).

4. Ola Rifai, 'Online Mobilization for Civil and Political Rights in Saudi Arabia', *Asian Politics and Policy* 6, 3 (2014).

5. On state and gender see Madawi Al-Rasheed, *A Most Masculine State: Gender, Politics and Religion in Saudi Arabia*, Cambridge: Cambridge University Press, 2013; Amelie Le Renard, *A Society of Young Women: Opportunities of Place, Power, and Reform in Saudi Arabia*, Stanford: Stanford University Press, 2014. On more recent developments see Nora Doaiji in this volume.

6. Michael Cook, 'The Expansion of the First Saudi State: The Case of Washm', in C. Bosworth, C. Issawi, and A. Udovitch (eds.), *The Islamic World from Classical to Modern Times: Essays in Honor of Bernard Lewis*, Princeton: Darwin Press, 1988; Khalid al-Dakhil, *al-Wahhabiyya bayn al-*

Shirk wa Tasadu al-Qabila, Beirut: Arab Network for Research and Publishing, 2013. On the relationship between Wahhabiyya and the historiography of Saudi Arabia see Jorg Matthias Determann, *Historiography in Saudi Arabia: Globalization and the State in the Middle East*, London: I. B. Tauris, 2014.

7. For an overview of the work of local Saudi historians see Determann, *Historiography in Saudi Arabia*.

8. Philippe Pétriat, *Le Négoce des Lieux Saints: négociants hadramis de Djedda, 1850–1950*, Paris: Sorbonne, 2016.

9. Several volumes include discussion of Saudi religious and ideological outlook. See Paul Aarts and Gerd Nonneman (eds.), *Saudi Arabia in the Balance: Political Economy, Society, Foreign Affairs*, London: Hurst & Co., 2005; Bernard Haykel et al., *Saudi Arabia in Transition: Insights on Social, Political, Economic, and Religious Change*, Cambridge: Cambridge University Press, 2016; Mohammed Ayoub and Hasan Kosebalaban (eds.), *Religion and Politics in Saudi Arabia: Wahhabism and the State*, Boulder: Lynne Rienner, 2009; David Commins, *The Mission and the Kingdom: Wahhabi Power behind the Saudi Throne*, London: I. B. Tauris, 2006; Nabil Mouline, *The Clerics of Islam: Religious Authority and Political Power in Saudi Arabia*, New Haven: Yale University Press, 2014.

10. Most recently, this is discussed in Ben Rich and Ben MacQueen, 'The Saudi State as an Identity Racketeer', *Middle East Critique* 26 (February 2017), http://www.tandfonline.com/doi/full/10.1080/19436149.2017.1283753 (accessed 28 February 2017).

11. The most damning opinion on Wahhabiyya recently appeared in the *New York Times*. See Kamel Daoud, 'Saudi Arabia, an ISIS that has made it', *The New York Times*, 20 November 2015, http://www.nytimes.com/2015/11/21/opinion/saudi-arabia-an-isis-that-has-made-it.html (accessed 16 February 2017).

12. Natana DeLong-Bas, *Wahhabi Islam: From Revival and Reform to Global Jihad*, London: I. B. Tauris, 2004.

13. Madawi Al-Rasheed (ed.), *Kingdom without Borders: Saudi Arabia's Political, Religious and Media Frontiers*, London: Hurst & Co., 2008; Michael Farquhar, *Circuits of Faith: Migration, Education, and the Wahhabi Mission*, Stanford: Stanford University Press, 2017.

14. Khalid al-Mushawah, *al-Tayarat al-Diniyya fi al-Soudiyya*, Riyadh: al-Intishar al-Arabi, 2012; Muhammad al-Atawnah, *al-Islam al-Wahhabi fi Muwajahat Tahadiyat al-Hadatha*, Beirut: al-Shabakah al-Arabiyya lil-Abhath wa al-Nashr, 2014; Madawi Al-Rasheed, *Contesting the Saudi State: Islamic Voices from a New Generation*, Cambridge: Cambridge University Press, 2007; Mansoor al-Shamsi, *Islam and Political Reform in Saudi Arabia: The Quest for Political Change and Reform*, London:

Routledge, 2011; Stéphane Lacroix, *Awakening Islam: Religious Discourse in Contemporary Saudi Arabia*, Cambridge, MA: Harvard University Press, 2011; Thomas Hegghammer, *Jihad in Saudi Arabia: Violence and Pan-Islamism since 1979*, Cambridge: Cambridge University Press, 2010; F. Gregory Gause III, 'Kings for All Seasons: How the Middle East's Monarchies Survived the Arab Spring', Brookings Doha Center Analysis Paper no. 8, Doha: Brookings Doha Center, 2013, https://www.brookings.edu/research/kings-for-all-seasons-how-the-middle-easts-monarchies-survived-the-arab-spring/.

15. Robert Vitalis, *America's Kingdom: Myth Making on the Saudi Oil Frontier*, Stanford: Stanford University Press, 2007; Toby Matthiesen, 'Migration, Minorities and Radical Networks: Labour Movements and Opposition Groups in Saudi Arabia 1950–1975', *International Review of Social History* 59, 3 (2014).

16. See Toby Matthiesen's chapter in this volume.

17. Madawi Al-Rasheed, 'The Shi'a of Saudi Arabia: A Minority in Search of Cultural Authenticity,' *British Journal of Middle Eastern Studies* 25, 1 (1998); Madawi Al-Rasheed, 'Sectarianism as Counter-Revolution: Saudi Responses to the Arab Uprisings', in Nader Hashemi and Danny Postel (eds.), *Sectarianization: Mapping the New Politics of the Middle East*, London: Hurst & Co., 2017; Toby Matthiesen, *The Other Saudis: Shiism, Dissent, and Sectarianism*, Cambridge: Cambridge University Press, 2014.

18. See Sultan Alamer et al., *Fi Tarikh al-Ouroba*, Beirut: Jusour, 2016.

19. For a general survey of Saudi foreign policy see Neil Partrick (ed.), *Saudi Foreign Policy: Conflict and Cooperation*, London: I. B. Tauris, 2016. However, many studies become out-dated very quickly as King Salman and his son proved to be erratic in the way they handled regional foreign policy.

20. Most recent works on Saudi–Iranian relations include Simon Mabon, *Saudi Arabia and Iran: Power and Rivalry in the Middle East*, London: I. B. Tauris, 2016.

21. On how oil forged Saudi Arabia see Toby Craig Jones, *Desert Kingdom: How Oil and Water Forged Saudi Arabia*, Cambridge, MA: Harvard University Press, 2010; Steffen Hertog, *Princes, Brokers and Bureaucrats: Oil and the State in Saudi Arabia*, Ithaca: Cornell University Press, 2010.

22. For an assessment of the Saudi Vision 2030 see http://carnegieendowment.org/sada/64227 (accessed 29 November 2016).

23. Michael Herd, *All in the Family: Absolutism, Revolutions, and Democracy*, New York: State University of New York Press, 1999.

24. F. Gregory Gause III, 'Beyond Sectarianism: The New Middle East Cold War', Brookings Doha Center Analysis Paper no. 11, Doha:

Brookings Doha Center, July 2014, https://www.brookings.edu/wp-content/uploads/2016/06/English-PDF-1.pdf (accessed 18 December 2016).

25. 'Saudi Arabia Launches Military Exercise with 20 Countries', CNN, 15 February 2016, http://edition.cnn.com/2016/02/15/middleeast/saudi-arabia-military-exercises/ (accessed 15 February 2017).

26. The famous Saudi Islamist scholar Muhammad al-Araifi endorses the narrative about a Shi'a–Alawite takeover of Syria, the land of Sunni Islam. See http://www.raialyoum.com/?p=575612, 5 December 2016 (accessed 10 February 2017).

27. Toby Matthiesen, *Sectarian Gulf: Saudi Arabia and the Arab Spring That Wasn't*, Stanford: Stanford University Press, 2013.

28. Madawi Al-Rasheed, *Muted Modernists: The Struggle over Divine Politics in Saudi Arabia*, London: Hurst & Co., 2015, pp. 45–50.

29. Al-Rasheed, *Muted Modernists*.

30. Hegghammer, *Jihad in Saudi Arabia*.

31. Gassan al-Kibsi et al., *Saudi Arabia beyond Oil: The Investment and Productivity Transformation*, London/Dubai: McKinsey Global Institute, December 2015.

32. Madawi Al-Rasheed, 'Saudi Arabia: Running into the Sand', *Prospect Magazine*, 12 October 2016, http://www.prospectmagazine.co.uk/magazine/saudi-arabia-oil-price-running-into-the-sand (accessed 13 October 2016).

33. Madawi Al-Rasheed, 'Saudi Internal Dilemmas and Regional Responses to the Arab Spring', in Fawaz Gerges (ed.), *The New Middle East: Protest and Revolution in the Arab World*, Cambridge: Cambridge University Press, 2014.

34. Lacey, *Inside the Kingdom*, pp. ix.

35. Pascal Menoret, *L'Énigme saoudienne: les Saoudiens et le monde 1744–2003*, Paris: La Découverte, 2003.

36. See Al-Rasheed, *A Most Masculine State*.

37. Sebastian Maisel, 'The New Rise of Tribalism in Saudi Arabia', *Nomadic Peoples* 18, 2 (2014).

1. SAUDI REGIME STABILITY AND CHALLENGES

1. Paul Aarts and Carolien Roelants, *Saudi Arabia: A Kingdom in Peril*, London: Hurst & Co., 2015; Walter Russell Mead, 'The Specter of Saudi Instability', *The American Interest*, 4 October 2015, http://www.the-american-interest.com/2015/10/04/the-specter-of-saudi-instability/ (accessed 22 December 2016); John Hannah, 'It is Time for the United States to Start Worrying about a Saudi Collapse', *Foreign Policy*,

7 October 2015, http://foreignpolicy.com/2015/10/07/will-the-united-states-help-if-saudi-arabia-starts-to-fall-apart/ (accessed 22 December 2016).

2. Christopher Davidson, *After the Sheikhs: The Coming Collapse of the Gulf Monarchies*, New York: Oxford University Press, 2013.

3. Fred Halliday, *Arabia without Sultans*, New York: Penguin Books, 1974.

4. Victor Menaldo, 'The Middle East and North Africa's Resilient Monarchs', *Journal of Politics* 74, 3 (July 2012); Michael Herb, 'Monarchism Matters', *ForeignPolicy*, 26 November 2012, http://mideast.foreignpolicy.com/posts/2012/11/26/monarchism_matters (accessed 22 December 2016).

5. I examine these arguments in great detail in 'Kings for All Seasons: How the Middle East's Monarchies Survived the Arab Spring', Brookings Doha Center Analysis Paper no. 8, Doha: Brookings Doha Center, September 2013, https://www.brookings.edu/research/kings-for-all-seasons-how-the-middle-easts-monarchies-survived-the-arab-spring/ (accessed 22 December 2016).

6. Tribal affiliation is still extremely important in Saudi Arabia, to be sure. It is important socially. It creates networks for acquiring government jobs. It is a recruitment avenue into the National Guard. But the Al Saud have successfully broken tribal autonomy in their state. On the way in which tribalism plays into the state's bureaucracy see Steffen Hertog, *Princes, Brokers, and Bureaucrats: Oil and the State in Saudi Arabia*, Ithaca: Cornell University Press, 2010.

7. See http://www.tradingeconomics.com/saudi-arabia/government-debt-to-gdp (accessed 22 December 2016).

8. For a concise description of these various plans see 'Saudi Monarch Announces Billions in Handouts', al-Jazeera, 18 March 2011, http://www.aljazeera.com/news/middleeast/2011/03/2011318174117916648.html (accessed 22 December 2016); Jason Benham, 'Saudi King Orders More Handouts, Security Boost', Reuters, 18 March 2011, http://www.reuters.com/article/us-saudi-king-idUSTRE72H2UQ20110318 (accessed 22 December 2016).

9. Kiren Aziz Chaudhry, *The Price of Wealth: Economics and Institutions in the Middle East*, Ithaca: Cornell University Press, 1997, convincingly argues the case that the Al Saud were able to create a new Najdi business class with state patronage. She is less convincing when she argues that the existing merchant and business families in other parts of the kingdom were disadvantaged.

10. For accounts of the development of the official Saudi religious institutions see Ayman al-Yassini, *Religion and State in the Kingdom of Saudi Arabia*, Boulder, CO: Westview Press, 1985, and Nabile Mouline, *The

Clerics of Islam: Religious Authority and Political Power in Saudi Arabia, trans. Ethan S. Rundell, New Haven: Yale University Press, 2014.

11. I provide a number of examples in 'Official Wahhabism and the Sanctioning of Saudi–US Relations', in Mohammed Ayoob and Hasan Kosebalaban (eds.), *Religion and Politics in Saudi Arabia: Wahhabism and the State*, Boulder, CO: Lynne Rienner Publishers, 2009.

12. Thomas Hegghammer, *Jihad in Saudi Arabia: Violence and Pan-Islamism since 1979*, Cambridge: Cambridge University Press, 2010.

13. Stéphane Lacroix, *Awakening Islam: The Politics of Religious Dissent in Contemporary Saudi Arabia*, trans. George Holoch, Cambridge, MA: Harvard University Press, 2011.

14. On the post-9/11 reactions of Sahwa leaders Salman al-Awda and Safar al-Hawali see Gause, 'Official Wahhabism and the Sanctioning of Saudi–US Relations', pp. 142–3.

15. Steffen Hertog, 'Rentier Militaries in the Gulf: The Price of Coup-Proofing', *International Journal of Middle East Studies* 43, 3 (August 2011).

16. Jill Crystal explains how this change occurred in the extended Al Sabah family when Kuwait came into considerable oil money. See *Oil and Politics in the Gulf: Rulers and Merchants in Kuwait and Qatar*, Cambridge: Cambridge University Press, 1990, chap. 4.

17. On the Saud–Faysal struggle see Sarah Yisraeli, *The Remaking of Saudi Arabia: The Struggle between King Saud and Crown Prince Faysal, 1953–1962*, Dayan Center Papers 121, Tel Aviv: Moshe Dayan Center for Middle Eastern and African Studies, 1997.

18. For a critical account of an early period of tension and alliance management between Saudi Arabia and the United States see Robert Vitalis, *America's Kingdom: Mythmaking on the Saudi Oil Frontier*, Stanford: Stanford University Press, 2007.

19. See http://www.macrotrends.net/1369/crude-oil-price-history-chart (accessed 22 December 2016).

20. Ahmed Feteha and Zainab Fattah, 'Main Features of Saudi Arabia 2017 Budget, 2016 Performance', Bloomberg, 22 December 2016, https://www.bloomberg.com/news/articles/2016–12–22/main-features-of-saudi-arabia-s-2017-budget-2016-performance (accessed 31 March 2017).

21. Jadwa Investment, 'Saudi Arabia's 2016 Fiscal Budget', 28 December 2015, http://www.jadwa.com/en/researchsection/research/economic-research (accessed 22 December 2016).

22. National Commercial Bank, 'Saudi Economic Perspectives, 2016–17', June 2016, http://www.alahli.com/en-us/about-us/Documents/NCB-Saudi-Economic-Perspectives-2016–2017.pdf (accessed 22 December

2016); Jadwa Investment, 'The Saudi Economy in 2016', February 2016, http://www.jadwa.com/en/researchsection/research/economic-research (accessed 22 December 2016).

23. Karen E. Young, 'Saudi Arabia's Impeccable Timing in Debt Markets', Arab Gulf States Institute in Washington, 9 November 2016, http://www.agsiw.org/saudi-arabias-impeccable-timing-debt-markets/ (accessed 22 December 2016).

24. Nicolas Parasie, 'Saudi Government to Pay Money Owed to Private Companies by Year's End', *The Wall Street Journal*, 8 November 2016, http://www.wsj.com/articles/saudi-government-to-pay-money-owed-to-private-companies-by-years-end-1478596632 (accessed 22 December 2016).

25. Ahmed Feteha et al., 'A Quick Guide to the Saudi National Transformation Program', *Bloomberg News*, 6 June 2016, http://www.bloomberg.com/news/articles/2016-06-06/the-saudi-national-transformation-program-what-we-know-so-far (accessed 22 December 2016); Angus McDowell, 'Focus on Jobs at Heart of Saudi Reforms', Reuters, 7 June 2016, http://www.reuters.com/article/us-saudi-plan-employment-idUSKCN0YT1B5 (accessed 22 December 2016).

26. Ben Hubbard, 'Decline in Oil Prices Lands on Government Workers as Saudi Arabia Cuts Paychecks', *The New York Times*, 26 September 2016, http://www.nytimes.com/2016/09/27/world/middleeast/saudi-arabia-cuts-salaries-oil.html (accessed 22 December 2016).

27. Sewell Chan, 'Saudi Arabia Moves to Curb its Feared Religious Police', *New York Times*, 15 April 2016, http://www.nytimes.com/2016/04/16/world/middleeast/saudi-arabia-moves-to-curb-its-feared-religious-police.html (accessed 22 December 2016).

28. On the concept of 'dynastic monarchy' see Michael Herb, *All in the Family: Absolutism, Revolution and Democracy in the Middle East*, Albany: State University of New York Press, 1999.

29. Hugh Miles, 'Saudi Royal Calls for Regime Change in Riyadh', *The Guardian*, 28 September 2015, https://www.theguardian.com/world/2015/sep/28/saudi-royal-calls-regime-change-letters-leadership-king-salman (accessed 22 December 2016).

30. I obtained an English-language copy of this letter from an anonymous email source in the summer of 2015.

31. Jennifer Steinhauer, Mark Mazzetti, and Julie Hirschfeld Davis, 'Congress Votes to Override Obama Veto on 9/11 Victims Bill', *New York Times*, 28 September 2016, http://www.nytimes.com/2016/09/29/us/politics/senate-votes-to-override-obama-veto-on-9–11-victims-bill.html (accessed 22 December 2016).

2. MYSTIQUE OF MONARCHY: THE MAGIC OF ROYAL SUCCESSION IN SAUDI ARABIA

1. After the rise of Muhammad ibn Salman to power, commentators described him as Saudi Arabia's Gamal Mubarak, the son of deposed Egyptian president Husni Mubarak. See S. Cook, 'Saudi Arabia's Gamal Mubarak', New York: Council on Foreign Relations, 20 June 2015.

2. A. al-Shihabi, *The Saudi Kingdom: Between the Jihadi Hammer and the Iranian Anvil*, Princeton: Markus Wiener Publishers, 2016, p. 158.

3. D. Blair, 'Saudi Arabia's Quiet Revolution as King Salman Changes Royal Succession', *The Telegraph*, 29 April 2015, http://www.telegraph.co.uk/news/worldnews/middleeast/saudiarabia/11571482/Saudi-Arabias-quiet-revolution-as-King-Salman-changes-royal-succession.html (accessed 6 July 2016).

4. M. Al-Rasheed, *A History of Saudi Arabia*, Cambridge: Cambridge University Press, 2010, p. 257.

5. Percy Black develops these ideas in the context of understanding the survival of the British monarchy. See P. Black, *The Mystique of Modern Monarchy: With Special Reference to the British Commonwealth*, London: C. A. Watts & Co., 1954.

6. M. Al-Rasheed, 'Saudi Regime Resilience after the 2011 Arab Uprisings', *Contemporary Arab Affairs* 9, 1 (2016) and 'Modernizing Authoritarian Rule in Saudi Arabia', *Contemporary Arab Affairs* 2, 4 (2009).

7. F. Gregory Gause III, 'Kings for all Seasons: How the Middle East's Monarchies Survived the Arab Spring', Brookings Doha Center Analysis Paper no. 8, Doha: Brookings Doha Center, September 2013, https://www.brookings.edu/research/kings-for-all-seasons-how-the-middle-easts-monarchies-survived-the-arab-spring/; M. Lynch, 'Does Arab Monarchy Matter?' in *Arab Uprisings: The Arab Monarchy Debate*, POMEPS Briefings 16, Washington, DC: Project on Middle East Political Science, 2012, http://lynch.foreignpolicy.com/posts/2012/08/31/three_kings; E. Bellin, 'Reconsidering the Robustness of Authoritarianism in the Middle East: Lessons from the Arab Uprisings', *Comparative Politics* 44, 2 (2012); S. Heydemann, 'Upgrading Authoritarianism in the Arab World', Analysis Paper 13, Saban Center for Middle East Policy at Brookings Institution, October 2007; S. Yom and F. Gause III, 'Resilient Royals: How Arab Monarchies Hang On', *Journal of Democracy* 23, 4 (2012); M. Herd, *All in the Family: Absolutism, Revolution, and Democracy in the Middle East Monarchies*, New York: State University of New York Press, 1999.

8. E. La Boetie, *The Politics of Obedience: The Discourse of Voluntary Servitude*, Auburn, AL: Mises Institute, 1975.

9. N. Machiavelli, *The Prince*, trans. George Bull, London: Penguin, 2003 (repr.).
10. C. Jones, 'Seeing Like an Autocrat: Liberal Social Engineering in an Illiberal State', *Perspectives on Politics* 1, 13 (2015).
11. S. Kalberg, 'Max Weber's Types of Rationality: Cornerstones for the Analysis of Rationalization Process', *American Journal of Sociology* 85, 5 (1980).
12. Black, *The Mystique of Modern Monarchy*.
13. M. Al-Rasheed, *Politics in an Arabian Oasis: The Rashidis of Saudi Arabia*, London: I. B. Tauris, 1991, p. 29.
14. A. Bligh, *From Prince to King: Royal Succession to the House of Saud in the Twentieth Century*, New York: New York University Press, 1984; N. Mouline, 'Power and Generational Transition in Saudi Arabia', *Critique Internationale* 46 (2010); J. Kéchichian, *Succession in Saudi Arabia*, New York: Palgrave, 2001.
15. O. Ibn Bishr, *Unwan al-majd fi tarikh Najd*, 2 vols., Mecca: n.p., 1930; H. Ibn Ghanam, *Tarikh Najd*, 2 vols., Cairo: n.p., 1970.
16. Al-Rasheed, *Politics in an Arabian Oasis*, pp. 38–48.
17. A. Rihani, *Ibn Saud of Arabia*, London: Constable & Co., 1928; M. Al-Rasheed, *A Most Masculine State: Gender, Politics and Religion in Saudi Arabia*, Cambridge: Cambridge University Press, 2013, p. 62.
18. King 'Abdullah saw Saud's sons as potential allies against his powerful brothers Nayif, Sultan, and Salman. During his reign Saud's sons were granted greater visibility in the public sphere and some government jobs. They were allowed to revive the heritage of their father in publication and the heritage industry. King Saud established the first university in Riyadh in 1955 and named it after himself. However, Faysal renamed it Riyadh University. It remained so until King 'Abdullah allowed it to be renamed Saud University. One of Saud's sons, Sayf al-Islam, published a novel, revealing the inner dynamics and intrigues of palace life through narrating the life of his mother, a Baluchi slave woman in King Saud's harem. See Sayf al-Islam ibn Saud, *Qalb min bangalan*, Beirut: Dar al-Farabi, 2004. His second novel was even more provocative, as its historical context was the Saudi–Wahhabi realm. The two novels were initially banned in Saudi Arabia but they can be downloaded as pdfs. See Sayf al-Islam ibn Saud, *Tanin*, Beirut: Dar al-Farabi, 2006.
19. P. Dresch, 'The Significance of the Course Events Take in Segmentary Systems', *American Ethnologist* 13, 2 (1986).
20. D. Scott, 'The Saudi Paradox', *Foreign Affairs* 83, 1 (2004). Saudis also refer to the group as the Sudayris.
21. King Salman's other sons Faysal and Sultan are known to have received

Western educations at top universities in the USA and Britain. They have been marginalized in favour of his young son Muhammad, whose mother belongs to the Ajman tribe.

22. M. Al-Rasheed, *Contesting the Saudi State: Islamist Voices from a New Generation*, Cambridge: Cambridge University Press, 2007.

23. Saudi Arabia: Basic Law of Government, Saudi Embassy, 1991, available at https://www.saudiembassy.net/about/country-information/laws/The_Basic_Law_Of_Governance.aspx (accessed 9 July 2016).

24. R. Aba Namay, 'Constitutional Reforms: A Systematisation of Saudi Politics', *Journal of South Asian and Middle Eastern Studies* 16, 3 (1993); A. al-Fahad, 'Ornamental Constitutionalism: The Saudi Basic Law of Governance', *Yale Journal of International Law* 30 (2005).

25. M. Al-Rasheed, 'Circles of Power: Royals and Society in Saudi Arabia', in P. Aarts and G. Nonneman (eds.), *Saudi Arabia in the Balance: Political Economy, Society, Foreign Affairs*, London: Hurst & Co., 2005.

26. D. Coast and J. Fox, 'Rumour and Politics', *History Compass* 13, 5 (2015), p. 223.

27. J. Scott, *Weapons of the Weak: Everyday Forms of Peasant Resistance*, New Haven: Yale University Press, 1985, p. 282; J. Scott, *Domination and the Arts of Resistance*, New Haven: Yale University Press, 1990, p. 144.

28. Coast and Fox, 'Rumour and Politics', p. 231.

29. *Nathir ajil li kul Al Saoud*, letter circulated on 4 September 2015, https://docs.google.com/document/d/1VJC-PXbISm-iUCvUWpQb 5pZuETLvosq_9fHU1F6797Q/mobilebasic (accessed 11 October 2016).

30. *Idhahat* [Clarifications], 15 September 2015.

31. Hugh Miles, the son of a retired British diplomat and a Cairo-based freelance journalist, claims to have spoken to the author of the letter, but he is not named for security reasons. See H. Miles, 'Saudi Royal Calls for Regime Change in Riyadh', *The Guardian*, 28 September 2015. See also H. Miles, 'Saudi Prince Returned from Europe Against his Will, Say Staff', *The Guardian*, 29 March 2016.

32. The three princes stopped tweeting after the circulation of the two letters.

33. @SAUD_SAIFALNASR (accessed 12 September 2015).

34. International Arab and Western media excel in anticipating future Saudi reshuffles, with leading observers speculating about every decision that the king takes and volunteering sometimes unconvincing forecasts about future decisions. These speculations have grown into a cottage industry, with key analysts providing ample guesswork aimed at trying to 'read' the mind of the Saudi king. For a glimpse of this see an early example: S. Henderson, 'After King Fahd: Succession in Saudi

Arabia', Washington Institute Policy Paper 13, Washington: Institute for Near East Policy, 1994. See also C. Davidson, *After the Sheikhs: The Coming Collapse of the Gulf Monarchies*, London: Hurst & Co./New York: Oxford University Press, 2013. Currently, journalistic speculations are translated into Arabic and quickly reach Saudis on social media. Speculative articles find their way onto anonymous Saudi Facebook pages, blogs, and newsletters. For a critique of this literature see M. Al-Rasheed, 'Who is Next in Line for the Saudi Throne? Don't Ask', *al-Monitor*, 1 July 2016, http://www.al-monitor.com/pulse/originals/2016/07/saudi-arabia-succession-confusion-jail.html (accessed 2 July 2016).

35. @Mujtahidd and @mujtahidchannel
36. 'Mufti Abd al-Aziz al-Shaykh Warns against Lies and Dissent on Twitter', 28 January 2012, http://www.alarabiya.net/articles/2012/01/28/191001.html (accessed 11 July 2016).
37. R. Khalaf, 'Daring Saudi Tweets Fuel Political Debate', *The Financial Times*, 16 March 2012, http://www.ft.com/cms/s/0/1749888e-6f5e-11e1-b368-00144feab49a.html#axzz4DmuWr5K1 (accessed 16 May 2015).
38. Author interview with Mujtahid, 16 May 2016.
39. Author interview with Mujtahid, 17 May 2016.
40. Author interview with Mujtahid, 17 May 2016.
41. On this episode of opposition in Saudi Arabia see R. Vitalis, *America's Kingdom: Mythmaking on the Saudi Oil Frontier*, Stanford: Stanford University Press, 2007.
42. N. al-Said, *Tarikh Al Saud*, Beirut: n.p., 1981.
43. Interview and discussion with Nasir al-Said's wife, May 2010.
44. T. Hegghammer and S. Lacroix, 'Rejectionist Islamist in Saudi Arabia: The Story of Juhayman al-Utaybi Revisited', *International Journal of Middle East Studies* 39, 1 (2007).
45. M. Al-Rasheed, *Muted Modernists: The Struggle over Divine Politics in Saudi Arabia*, London: Hurst & Co./New York: Oxford University Press, 2015.
46. Riyadh-based Reuters journalist Andrew Hammond was expelled from Saudi Arabia after he reported that Prince Sultan was suffering from colon cancer. Personal communication.
47. Al-Shihabi, *The Saudi Kingdom*, p. 158.
48. Ex-wives of Kings 'Abdullah and Fahd, al-Anud al-Fayiz and Muna Harb respectively, both now in London, have contributed to spreading rumours about their ex-husbands. Al-Fayiz released information about how the king mistreated her daughters, while Harb went to court in London get her share of inheritance from King Fahd's fortune.

3. CHALLENGES TO THE SAUDI DISTRIBUTIONAL STATE IN THE AGE OF AUSTERITY

1. Steffen Hertog, *Princes, Brokers, and Bureaucrats: Oil and the State in Saudi Arabia*, Ithaca: Cornell University Press, 2010.
2. Ferdinand Eibl and Steffen Hertog, 'Why Are Some Oil Dictators Nice to their People?' draft paper, London, 2016.
3. Madawi Al-Rasheed, *A History of Saudi Arabia*, Cambridge: Cambridge University Press, 2002; Hertog, *Princes, Brokers, and Bureaucrats*; A. M. Vasil'ev, *The History of Saudi Arabia*, London: Saqi Books, 1997.
4. Hertog, *Princes, Brokers, and Bureaucrats*.
5. Hertog, *Princes, Brokers, and Bureaucrats*, p. 81.
6. Vasil'ev, *History of Saudi Arabia*, p. 339.
7. Vasil'ev, *History of Saudi Arabia*, p. 340.
8. Al-Rasheed, *A History of Saudi Arabia*, p. 112; Robert Lacey, *The Kingdom*, London: Hutchinson, 1981, p. 312; Gary Samuel Samore, *Royal Family Politics in Saudi Arabia (1953–1982)*, Ann Arbor: University Microfilms International, 1983, pp. 94f.
9. Vasil'ev, *History of Saudi Arabia*, p. 337.
10. Lacey, *The Kingdom*, p. 314.
11. David Holden, *The House of Saud*, London: Pan, 1982, p. 195; Lacey, *The Kingdom*, p. 317.
12. Vasil'ev, *History of Saudi Arabia*, p. 355; Sarah Yizraeli, *The Remaking of Saudi Arabia: The Struggle between King Saud and Crown Prince Faysal, 1953–1962*, Dayan Center Papers 121, Tel Aviv: Moshe Dayan Center for Middle Eastern and African Studies, Tel Aviv University, 1997.
13. Samore, *Royal Family Politics in Saudi Arabia*, pp. 104, 124f.
14. Samore, *Royal Family Politics in Saudi Arabia*, p. 125.
15. Vasil'ev, *History of Saudi Arabia*, p. 359; Robert Vitalis, *America's Kingdom: Mythmaking on the Saudi Oil Frontier*, Stanford: Stanford University Press, 2007.
16. British Embassy, Amman, to FO, 17 Aug. 1962, outlining Saudi press conference criticism of Nasser [FO 371/165355].
17. Lacey, *The Kingdom*, p. 341.
18. Lacey, *The Kingdom*, p. 342.
19. Secret memorandum of 15 Nov. 1962: 'Effects in the Persian Gulf of Developments in Yemen and Saudi Arabia', PM office to FO, 10 Dec. 1962 [FO371/162781].
20. Samore, *Royal Family Politics in Saudi Arabia*, p. 164; Vasil'ev, *History of Saudi Arabia*, p. 434.
21. Summary of 1963 budget, no provenance; Jeddah to DS, 16 April 63 [FO 371/168880].

22. S. Yizraeli, *Politics and Society in Saudi Arabia: The Crucial Years of Development, 1960–1982*, London: Hurst & Co., 2012.
23. Assessment of local governance, Jeddah to FS, 18 April 63 [FO371/168868].
24. Record of conversation between the Political Resident and the ruler of Dubai, 11 Dec. 1967; conversation between Political Agent and Shaikh Rashid, 2 Nov. 1967 [FCO 8/830].
25. Possible Change of Regime in SA (top secret), c. 30 Sept. 1964 [FO371/174671].
26. FO minute reporting attempted coup, 27 April 1965 [FO371/179878].
27. Lacey, *The Kingdom*, p. 381.
28. Samore, *Royal Family Politics in Saudi Arabia*, p. 177; Hertog, *Princes, Brokers, and Bureaucrats*, pp. 98f.
29. Vasil'ev, *History of Saudi Arabia*, p. 464.
30. Toby Matthiesen, 'Migration, Minorities, and Radical Networks: Labour Movements and Opposition Groups in Saudi Arabia, 1950–1975', *International Review of Social History* 59, 3 (2014), p. 502.
31. Steffen Hertog, 'Saudi Arabia's Political Demobilization in Regional Comparison: Monarchical Tortoise and Republican Hares', in Laura Guazzone and Daniela Pioppi (eds.), *The Arab State and Neo-Liberal Globalization: The Restructuring of State Power in the Middle East*, Reading: Ithaca Press.
32. Hertog, *Princes, Brokers, and Bureaucrats*, pp. 84–135.
33. Stéphane Lacroix, *Awakening Islam: The Politics of Religious Dissent in Contemporary Saudi Arabia*, trans. George Holoch, Cambridge, MA: Harvard University Press, 2011.
34. Hertog, 'Saudi Arabia's Political Demobilization'; Lacroix, *Awakening Islam*.
35. Ferdinand Eibl and Steffen Hertog, 'Political Subversion and Rentier State Building in the Gulf', draft paper, London, 2016.
36. Hertog, *Princes, Brokers, and Bureaucrats*.
37. Hertog, *Princes, Brokers, and Bureaucrats*, pp. 118–31.
38. International Monetary Fund, 'Energy Subsidy Reform: Lessons and Implications', Washington, DC: International Monetary Fund, 2013.
39. The Saudi shares are calculated as (government employed)/(all employed + 10 per cent unemployed), with all figures taken from labour-force surveys. The data for the other cases are from ILO (public employment) and World Bank (economically active population). Public enterprises are not included for any of the cases, so all figures are likely to be somewhat underestimated (possibly more so for Saudi Arabia, where important sectors such as mining, hydrocarbons, intercity transport and aviation, utilities, and heavy industry are still largely

in state hands). Non-Saudi cases include non-citizen employment, which could not be separated out but is unlikely to bias results strongly.

40. Giacomo Luciani, 'From Private Sector to National Bourgeoisie: Saudi Arabian Business', in Paul Aarts and Gerd Nonneman (eds.), *Saudi Arabia in the Balance: Political Economy, Society, Foreign Affairs*, New York: New York University Press, 2006.

41. Estimates based on data from Ministry of Finance budget statements, SAMA yearbooks, and Ministry of Labour yearbooks.

42. This direction of causality is also confirmed by recent IMF research (International Monetary Fund, 'Saudi Arabia: Selected Issues', IMF Country Report 16/327, 2016, pp. 56–60).

43. Steffen Hertog, 'Rent Distribution, Labour Markets and Development in High-Rent Countries', LSE Kuwait Programme paper series no. 40, 2014.

44. Madawi Al-Rasheed, 'Circles of Power: Royals and Society in Saudi Arabia', in Paul Aarts and Gerd Nonneman (eds.), *Saudi Arabia in the Balance: Political Economy, Society, Foreign Affairs*, New York: New York University Press, 2006; Michael Herb, *All in the Family: Absolutism, Revolution and Democracy in the Middle East*, Albany: State University of New York Press, 1999; Hertog, *Princes, Brokers, and Bureaucrats*.

45. Hertog, *Princes, Brokers, and Bureaucrats*, pp. 118–31.

46. International Monetary Fund, 'Saudi Arabia: Selected Issues', p. 57.

47. Hertog, 'Saudi Arabia's Political Demobilization in Regional Comparison'.

4. BEYOND SECTARIANISM AND IDEOLOGY: REGIONALISM AND COLLECTIVE POLITICAL ACTION IN SAUDI ARABIA

1. On the Qatif protests see Toby Matthiesen, *The Other Saudis: Shiism, Dissent and Sectarianism*, Cambridge: Cambridge University Press, 2014. On the Buraydah intifada see Stéphane Lacroix, *Awakening Islam: The Politics of Religious Dissent in Contemporary Saudi Arabia*, trans. George Holoch, Cambridge, MA: Harvard University Press, 2011. On the 2012 Buraydah protests see Wa'i Saudi political rights blog: https://w3iteam.wordpress.com.

2. Examples of such studies include: Jacob Goldberg, 'The Shi'i Minority in Saudi Arabia', in *Shi'ism and Social Protest*, eds., Juan Cole and Nikki Keddie (New Haven, CT: Yale University Press, 1986). Madawi Al-Rasheed, 'Sectarianism as Counter-Revolution: Saudi Responses to the Arab Spring', Studies in Ethnicity and Nationalism, vol. 11, no. 3 (December 2011), pp. 513–526. 3. Laurence Louer, Transnational Shia Politics: Religious and Political Networks in the Gulf, Series in

Comparative Politics and International Studies (New York: Columbia University Press, 2008). Frederic M. Wehrey, Sectarian Politics in the Gulf: From the Iraq War to the Arab Uprisings, Columbia Studies in Middle East Politics (New York: Columbia University Press, 2014). Matthiesen, Toby. *The other Saudis.*

3. Matthiesen, *The Other Saudis*, p. 13.

4. For example, when he talks about the term *Bahrani* he notes that it refers to people from Qatif and Bahrain and 'to a lesser extent al-Ahsa' (Matthiesen, *The Other Saudis*, p. 25). Also, when he describes the three conditions that define notable politics, he says that 'in the case of Qatif and to a lesser extent al-Ahsa ...' (p. 31). The last example is from the final chapter, where he describes the protest in al-Ahsa, saying that 'the largest protests yet were held on 4 March, both in Qatif, and for the first time also in al-Ahsa' (p. 201).

5. Timur Kuran, 'Now out of Never: The Element of Surprise in the East European Revolution of 1989', *World Politics* 44, 1 (1991); Timur Kuran, *Private Truths, Public Lies: The Social Consequences of Preference Falsification*, Cambridge, MA: Harvard University Press, 1997.

6. Nathan J. Brown, 'Constitutional Revolutions and the Public Sphere', in Marc Lynch (ed.), *The Arab Uprisings Explained: New Contentious Politics in the Middle East*, New York: Columbia University Press, 2014.

7. James C. Scott, John Tehranian, and Jeremy Mathias, 'The Production of Legal Identities Proper to States: The Case of the Permanent Family Surname', *Comparative Studies in Society and History* 44, 1 (2002).

8. Abdulaziz Al-Fahad, 'Rootless Trees: Genealogical Politics in Saudi Arabia', in Bernard Haykel, Thomas Hegghammer, and Stéphane Lacroix (eds.), *Saudi Arabia in Transition: Insights on Social, Political Economic and Religious Change*, Cambridge: Cambridge University Press, 2015.

9. For more details on this project see Jörg Matthias Determann, *Historiography in Saudi Arabia: Globalization and the State in the Middle East*, London: I. B. Tauris, 2014.

10. For more on the context of this work see Nadav Samin, *Of Sand or Soil: Genealogy and Tribal Belonging in Saudi Arabia*, Princeton: Princeton University Press, 2015.

11. See, for example, Toby Matthiesen, 'Shi'i Historians in a Wahhabi State: Identity Entrepreneurs and the Politics of Local Historiography in Saudi Arabia', *International Journal of Middle East Studies* 47, 1 (2015) and Determann, *Historiography in Saudi Arabia*.

12. Muhammad Sa'id al-Muslim, *Sahil al-Dhahab al-Aswad: Dirasa Tarikhiyya Insaniyya li-Mintaqat al-Khalij al-'Arabi*, 2nd edn., Beirut: Manshurat Dar Maktabat al-Haya, 1962.

13. Toby Matthiesen reports that the author was jailed because of the book's

'open discussion of the origins of and discrimination against the Shia of Eastern Arabia'. His source is Toby Jones, 'The Dogma of Development: Technopolitics and the Making of Saudi Arabia 1950–1980', Ph.D. thesis, Stanford University, 2006, which says that 'the Shi'a author Muhammad al-Muslim was imprisoned briefly for originally discussing the details of Shi'ism and oppression in the 1960s in his book on the Eastern Province. To secure his release al-Muslim edited out sensitive details in subsequent editions.' Jones does not provide a source for his claim. In 2011 the Saudi journalist Ahmed Adnan published a book about the biography of a well-known Arab nationalist, Mohammed Said Tayeb. The book is called *The Prisoner 32*. In this book, Adnan narrates the story of the first Faysal's crackdown on Arab nationalists and leftists in 1964. He lists al-Muslim among the people who were sentenced to ten years for their participation in opposition movements.

14. Mohammed Nasir al-Obodi, *al-Mu'ajam al-Joghraphy li Bilad al-Qasim*, Riyadh: Thulothia Publishing House, 1978.

15. Muhammad al-Rebdi, *Buraydah: Nomowoha al-Hadhari wa Alaqatuha al-Iqlimiah*, Buraydah: n.p., 1986.

16. Mai Yamani, *The Cradle of Islam: The Hijaz and the Quest for an Arabian Identity*, London: I. B. Tauris, 2004.

17. For more details on the labour movement see Robert Vitalis, *America's Kingdom: Mythmaking on the Saudi Oil Frontier*, Stanford: Stanford University Press, 2007. On how Qatif supported the labour movement see Toby Matthiesen, 'Migration, Minorities, and Radical Networks: Labour Movements and Opposition Groups in Saudi Arabia, 1950–1975', *International Review of Social History* 59, 3 (2014).

18. Some might argue that the lack of universities in Qatif is due to a deliberate discriminatory policy by the state. While this might be true, what I am interested in here is the outcome of this policy. This means that, regardless of its motivation, the outcome has enabled Qatif to keep reproducing its own local elite.

19. 'Awamyah: A Speech by Qatif's Women to Show Solidarity with Buraidah's Women', https://www.youtube.com/watch?v=65XVIMB Y9MI (accessed 27 March 2017).

20. See the blog http://a3lamona.blogspot.qa/, which covers and documents Buraydah's protest movement and how Qatif is often mentioned, comparing the state's behaviour in the two regions.

5. FROM HASM TO HAZM: SAUDI FEMINISM BEYOND PATRIARCHAL BARGAINING

1. Frances Hasso, *Consuming Desires: Family Crisis and the State in the Middle East*, Stanford: Stanford University Press, 2011, p. 14.

2. *Hasm* means steadfastness in Arabic, but is also the Arabic acronym for the Saudi Association for Civil and Political Rights (ACPRA), which was founded in 2009 and was prominent during the Arab Spring.

3. These terms can be translated as women's activists, pro-Hasm female activists, and female rights activists. Their distinctions and meanings will be drawn out further along in the chapter.

4. *Hazm* means decisiveness, but is also linked to the Saudi state's Operation Decisive Storm in Yemen, which began in 2015.

5. See Joseph Kéchichian, *Legal and Political Reforms in Saudi Arabia*, New York: Routledge, 2013. In this work he argues that episodes of state feminism occurred strictly at historical moments of state-initiated reforms for state-defined rights for women, as well as state-sanctioned, subordinated instances of Saudi women's public visibility, particularly when working within the state's development projects (p. 17).

6. See Simon Ross Valentine, *Force and Fanaticism: Wahhabism in Saudi Arabia and Beyond*, Oxford: Oxford University Press, 2015. A scholar of religion who taught English in Saudi Arabia for three years, Valentine sees it as 'dominated and controlled by men; with women invisible, clad from head to foot in long black robes, walking submissively and usually silently behind their husbands' (p. 1). He problematically asserts that 'there are considerable similarities between Wahhabism as practiced in Saudi Arabia and the beliefs and practices of ISIS' (p. 254).

7. See Karen Elliott House, *On Saudi Arabia: Its People, Past, Religion, Fault Lines, and Future*, New York: Alfred A. Knopf, 2012, written by a prominent journalist from the *Washington Post*. Despite a less hyperbolic view of the state, this source is not without outright Orientalism against Saudi women, such as the declaration that 'how diverse and divided are Saudi women beneath their public uniform of black, which makes all of them, regardless of age or physique, resemble flying crows' (p. 80).

8. See Saudi anthropologist Soraya al-Torki's *Women in Saudi Arabia: Ideology and Behavior among the Elite*, New York: Columbia University Press, 1986.

9. See Libyan anthropologist Saddeka Arebi's *Women and Words in Saudi Arabia: The Politics of Literary Discourse*, New York: Columbia University Press, 1994.

10. As al-Torki admitted, 'In retrospect, I believe that my choice to focus on urban society was partly a reaction to the stereotypical view of Saudi Arabia as a society of nomads and oil wells' (Soraya al-Torki and Camillia Fawzi El-Solh, *Arab Women in the Field: Studying your Own Society*, Syracuse: Syracuse University Press, 1988, p. 50).

11. See Madawi Al-Rasheed, *A Most Masculine State: Gender, Politics, and Religion in Saudi Arabia*, New York: Cambridge University Press, 2013.

12. At the same time, Al-Rasheed argued relevantly that 'women are not passive terrain on which secularizing states and religious groups vie to gain control' (Al-Rasheed, *A Most Masculine State*, p. 31). She highlighted this with examples of novelists, and was perhaps the first to also consider Islamist Saudi women and their feminist visions and actions (pp. 255, 271).

13. See French anthropologist Amélie Le Renard's *A Society of Young Women: Opportunities of Place, Power, and Reform in Saudi Arabia*, Stanford: Stanford University Press, 2014.

14. Le Renard, *A Society of Young Women*, p. 3. Specifically, Le Renard points to how 'reform discourse promotes new narratives and imaginings of what it means to be Saudi' (p. 5) and that 'women emancipate themselves from certain constraints and project themselves in new imaginings' even if these led to their adoption of other forms of constraints and norms (p. 9).

15. To a lesser degree, this chapter was also influenced by Le Renard's emphasis on public spaces and feminist displays as being 'like theatrical stages, on which each woman is simultaneously actress and spectator' (Le Renard, *A Society of Young* Women, p. 278), but differing in considering what such concepts mean and look like on such stages for 'activist' Saudi feminists.

16. Madawi Al-Rasheed, *Muted Modernists: The Struggle for Divine Politics in Saudi Arabia*, London: Hurst & Co./New York: Oxford University Press, 2015, which focused on the Saudi Association for Civil and Political Rights (ACPRA), also known, from its Arabic acronym, as Hasm. In this work she rightly described Hasm as 'a hybrid initiative that was conceived as going beyond the Islamist–liberal divide' (p. 57), with the goals of 'political representation, elected government, accountability, and respect for citizens' (p. 55). Additionally, through analysis of the association's textual sources, thinkers, and activism, she concluded that it 'fought two battles at the same time, one with the state institutions it held responsible for repression, and the other with the religious scholars who justified this repression in their fatwas or sentences in court' (p. 57).

17. This is particularly important given that the latter works were produced at the start of the Arab Spring and focused on earlier periods where *muthaqafat* and *multazimat* (Al-Rasheed, *A Most Masculine State*, p. 279), or the Islamist and liberal female intelligentsia of the state, were typically dominant in the Saudi public sphere and engaged in how 'debating gender has become a substitute for general political activism' (p. 153) and reflected how 'the state succeeded in putting gender issues on the agenda of most Saudis, thus diverting attention from calls for serious political reform' (p. 171).

18. See, e.g., Al-Rasheed, *A Most Masculine State*, pp. 171–2.
19. See Zakia Salime, *Between Feminism and Islam: Human Rights and Sharia Law in Morocco*, Minneapolis: Regents of University of Minneapolis, 2011.
20. Salime, *Between Feminism and Islam*, p. xix.
21. Salime, *Between Feminism and Islam*, p. xix.
22. Joel Beinin, 'Political Economy and Social Movement Theory Perspectives on the Tunisian and Egyptian Uprisings of 2011', LSE Middle East Centre Paper Series, 2016, http://eprints.lse.ac.uk/65291/, p. 8.
23. See Charlie Rose Show interview with Prince Turki ibn Faysal, available at SUSRIS, 'Confronting Tremendous Challenges: Prince Turki al-Faisal', Saudi–US Relations Information Service, 27 September 2012, http://susris.com/2012/09/27/confronting-tremendous-challenges-prince-turki-al-faisal/
24. See Prince Khalid ibn Faysal's participation in a graduation ceremony, quoted at http://okaz.com.sa/article/509464/الرأي/
25. Okaz, 'He Introduced a Technological University in Thahban and Debates Men of Business and Science: Khalid al-Faisal says Saudi Spring Started 82 Years Ago and you Proved a Miracle above the Sand', 26 September 2012, http://bit.ly/2l0BIs6.
26. Women's rights activists.
27. Pro-Hasm female rights activists.
28. A Saudi female activist named Manal al-Sharif began a campaign for women's driving in early May 2011 online, called 'Teach me How to Drive so I can Protect Myself'; she also released a video explaining that 17 June 2011 was set as the day on which women should start driving their cars. She began by driving herself prior to the campaign, filmed by veteran feminist activist Wajeha al-Huwaider, to encourage the mobilization of other women. However, this resulted in her arrest on 30 March at her home in the Eastern Province; she was released ten days later. Despite this, around sixty women still drove on 17 June 2011 and defiantly posted videos online.
29. As stated on al-Sharif's Twitter account: @Manal_AlSharif.
30. See quoted Right2Dignity founding statement at https://right2dignity.wordpress.com/2011/09/25/right2dignity/.
31. See quoted 2005 statement by Prince Nayif in Nora al-Huwaiti, 'Women's Driving Turns to a Public Decision', *al-Riyadh*, 29 December 2005, http://www.alriyadh.com/118992. See also quoted statement by Prince Nayif in Mohammed al-Ghonaim, 'Prince Nayef: Women's Driving is a Social Issue and Debating this is Pointless', *al-Riyadh*, 1 June 2005, http://www.alriyadh.com/69082.

32. See quoted second Right2Dignity statement entitled 'Right2Dignity Statement On Shaimaa's Unjust Sentence of 10 Lashes for Driving', at https://right2dignity.wordpress.com/2011/09/27/right2dignity-statement-on-shaimaas-unjust-sentence-of-10-lashes-for-driving/

33. As stated in the campaign's change.Org petition entitled 'Lift the Ban on Women Driving', 15 September 2014, at http://bit.ly/1Eai0eg.

34. As stated in the campaign's change.Org petition entitled 'Lift the Ban on Women Driving', 15 September 2014, at http://bit.ly/1Eai0eg.

35. Specifically, in this interview, al-Qahtani stated: 'Even in light of the Arab Spring, the state does not allow women to drive! I don't understand why the state is stubborn on issues that it claims are societal issues, and does not even offer the issue up to society. Doing so, in turn, requires political reform to allow women to discuss their issues in a parliament where they can reach such decisions. There is no source of authority to go back to assert such decisions otherwise.'

36. Author's translation of statements in Gulf Talks interview on al-Hurra with Mohammad al-Qahtani on 3 August 2011. Archived at https://youtu.be/dzaBhqP40dQ.

37. As stated in al-Nafjan's post entitled 'Loujain al-Hathloul', at https://saudiwoman.me/2013/11/09/loujain-al-hathloul/.

38. As stated by al-Hathloul in archived copy of now-deleted letter.

39. A more in-depth discussion of the case of Loujain al-Hathloul can be found in a Bil3afya post by Nora Abdulkarim entitled 'Saudi Feminism in the Social Realm: In Defense of Personal Revolutions', Bil3afya, February 2013, http://bil3afya.blogspot.com/2013/02/saudi-feminism-in-social-realm-in.html.

40. As stated on al-Sharif's Twitter account: @Manal_AlSharif.

41. See al-Sharif's stance in the prominent 'The Drive for Freedom' speech at the Oslo Freedom Forum on 12 May 2012, at https://youtu.be/0PXXNK-3zQ4.

42. This tendency is more extensively discussed in a Jadaliyya post by Nora Abdulkarim entitled 'Saudi Feminism: Between Mama Amreeka and Baba Abdullah', Jadaliyya, 14 May 2012, at http://www.jadaliyya.com/pages/index/5516/saudi-feminism_between-mama-amreeka-and-baba-abdul.

43. The first trial of a Hasm member as a member of Hasm occurred in 2011 with the arrest of Mohammad al-Bajadi for joining in the first organized protest by Saudi women on behalf of political prisoners at the start of the Arab Spring. However, the association had only just begun to be known more broadly by the Saudi public at that time, and al-Bajadi's trial was held in a secret court. It did not have the same visibility or influence as the later Hasm trials. Furthermore, the later trials were important for symbolic purposes.

44. An extensive account of the paramount importance of such trials is in Madawi Al-Rasheed's *Muted Modernists*, in which she describes it thus: 'New media offered the opportunity to create rhetorical space to debate issues around HASM founders, their initiative, trials, and later imprisonment. With each trial the audience became bigger, and the legal discussions spread across sections of society that might not necessarily be aware of the individual cases' (pp. 70–1).

45. As recounted by the w3i team activists at their website: w3iteam. wordpress.com.

46. Abdulmajid al-Buluwi, 'Saudi Anti-Terrorism Law Casts Wide Net', *al-Monitor*, 4 June 2014, http://www.al-monitor.com/pulse/origi-nals/2014/06/saudi-arabia-human-rights-activist-detained.html.

47. As stated in the w3i team website: w3iteam.wordpress.com.

48. As stated in the w3i team website: w3iteam.wordpress.com.

49. Similar anxious sentiments towards a perceived liberal-leaning 'femi-nist silence' were echoed in interviews with *huquqiyyat* who were also active protesters in the political prisoners' campaign. One participant, who also had two relatives who had been arbitrarily arrested, stated distrustfully: 'There is no connection at all between the political pris-oners' campaign and other campaigns for women's driving or elec-tions and the like.' Whereas in another interview, a participant with a more trusting view of the October 26 campaign in particular described *nashitat* more generally as follows: 'In terms of the feminist activists, I noticed they really cared about Hasm as Hasm, they liked it as a peaceful movement. But I don't think they all agreed that the prison-ers deserved a fair trial, at all.' This is in line with the aforementioned concerns shared by other *huquqiyyat* or female rights activists who were not active protesters.

50. Specifically, although the reign of King Salman had only just begun, many onlookers anticipated his affiliation with religious nationalist strands within the royal family, and felt that the king's first moves had confirmed their fears. In particular, he removed the 'reformist' head of the religious police, considered to have been sympathetic to wom-en's causes, and the female deputy minister of education, Norah al-Faiz, who had initially been appointed in 2009 by the late King 'Abdullah (Ahmed Al-Omran, 'Saudi Minister's Removal Spurs Fears among Women', *The Wall Street Journal*, 30 April 2015, https://www.wsj.com/articles/saudi-ministers-removal-spurs-fears-among-women-1430430015). However, this perception was tempered by views of Vision 2030 as a 'progressive' shift and how, later in the Hazm moment, women were again appointed to the new Shura Council, as in the previous king's era, an 'entertainment' ministry was launched,

and the religious police were greatly scaled back in terms of their legal powers, to a point that rendered them almost inactive, which held symbolic significance in terms of the level of religiosity of this new nationalism, at least from the perspective of those observing this new king's era.

51. Mats Utas, 'Victimcy, Girlfriending, Soldiering: Tactic Agency in a Young Woman's Social Navigation of the Liberian War Zone', *Anthropological Quarterly* 78, 2 (2005), p. 408, https://muse.jhu.edu/article/183227.

52. 'Haifa al-Zahrani: First Saudi Female Journalist on the Frontlines of "Decisive Storm"', *al-Sharq*, 2015, http://www.al-sharq.com/news/details/326394#.VUOUBc6przI.

53. When questioned further on her own involvement in feminist activism, al-Zahrani said: 'Yes, I stopped entirely out of my utter faith, and from personal experience that these campaigns are not sincere and they do not sit well with me in terms of their lacking national loyalty.' In terms of the relationship between her previous activism and current position as a prominent female journalist covering the war in Yemen, she explained: 'My work as a journalist is not a form of feminist activism. I told you, the state supports Saudi women, and proof of this is that I was the first female journalist to enter national security operation rooms in all military fields. I was the first female journalist to join Decisive Storm, to cover the lines of fire, and the first journalist to enter *mabahith* prisons, and others. ... This is proof that women can reach anywhere, as long as they don't challenge the state and its laws.' Her take on Saudi feminism and the Hazm moment was that 'the current state of Saudi feminism is, unfortunately, clearly challenging the state and some of it is betrayal of the country. Everything is possible to take with niceness, but force and challenge is pointless.'

54. See further commentary and interviews with anonymous activists on this in Aya Batrawy, 'Wartime Climate in Saudi Puts Calls for Reform on Hold', Associated Press, 19 April 2015, http://www.salon.com/2015/04/19/wartime_climate_in_saudi_puts_calls_for_reform_on_hold/.

55. For elaboration on the municipal elections of 2015 and the resignation of Lama al-Suleiman, see 'Female Saudi Councilor Resigns from Jeddah Council', Arabian Business, 17 March 2016, http://www.arabianbusiness.com/female-saudi-councillor-resigns-from-jeddah-council-625183.html.

56. That the Vision 2030 economic plan included 'market feminism', not unlike that which was used by the state during War on Terror efforts of the 2000s, is clear in its definition of Saudi women as 'yet another

great asset', with concern for their 'talents' and 'productive capabilities', and a desire to facilitate them to 'contribute to the development of our society and economy'. Previously the state's 'market feminism' had often necessitated a relationship between the state and its female citizenry in which the state had been the central 'progressive' actor, facilitating women's liberation from social and religious constraints. Essentially, it produced a feminism that amounted to state feminism. However, this did not play out in this campaign.

57. See Human Rights Watch, 'Boxed In: Women and Saudi Arabia's Male Guardianship System', https://www.hrw.org/sites/default/files/report_pdf/saudiarabia0716web.pdf.

58. @LoujainHathloul. Twitter, 18 July 2016, 3:42 a.m., twitter.com/LoujainHathloul/status/754944304280326144; @LoujainHathloul. Twitter, 18 July 2016, 3:45 a.m., twitter.com/LoujainHathloul/status/754945260539613184; @Hala_Aldosari. Twitter, 17 July 2016, 12:57 p.m., twitter.com/Hala_Aldosari/status/754721627376463872.

59. As stated in Saudi Ministry of Interior's 'National Information Center Strategy: 2014–2016', http://www.srec.org.sa/wps/wcm/connect/c3939a65-b01f-4204-b790–671c6bf21de9/NIC+Strategy+2014–2016_Publishing+Version_English.pdf?MOD=AJPERES.

60. This aim is further discussed in Bilal Khan, Muhammad Khurram Khan, and Khaled S. Alghathbar, 'Biometrics and Identity Management for Homeland Security Applications in Saudi Arabia', *African Journal of Business Management* 4, 15 (2010), http://www.academicjournals.org/article/article1380698656_Khan%20et%20al.pdf.

61. Amélie Le Renard, 'Only for Women: Women, the State, and Reform in Saudi Arabia', *Middle East Journal* 62, 4 (2008), p. 616, http://www.jstor.org/stable/25482571.

62. @hamssonosi. Twitter, 24 September 2016, 7:09 p.m., twitter.com/hamssonosi/status/779638971236253696; @hamssonosi. Twitter, 27 September 2016, 2:42 p.m., twitter.com/hamssonosi/status/780839958584123392.

63. @Ahmadooovich. Twitter, 23 October 2016, 3:23 a.m., twitter.com/Ahmadooovich/status/790091379112349696; @rema_dream. Twitter, 23 October 2016, 9:23 a.m., twitter.com/rema_dream/status/790181933343006720; @Fleeing_lifeing. Twitter, 24 October 2016, 2:21 p.m., twitter.com/Flee_life11/status/790619190386458624.

64. @MeshariGhamdi. Twitter, 25 October 2016, 6:58 a.m., twitter.com/MeshariGhamdi/status/790870146768396288; @Fleeing_lifeing. Twitter, 24 October 2016, 2:40 p.m., twitter.com/Flee_life11/status/790623902133260290.

65. @nouf_ahm_. Twitter, 19 October 2016, 4:34 a.m., twitter.com/nouf_allli_/status/788659632139034624.

66. Madawi Al-Rasheed argued that the state has promoted various womanhoods at various points in time: the state's early 'religious nationalist' womanhood, where the 'pious' Saudi woman is celebrated as the foundation of the nation and its 'exceptionalism', and the state's succeeding 'cosmopolitan modernist' womanhood, where, as part of state-driven War on Terror efforts, Saudi womanhood was reformulated as the nation's 'proof of modernity' and further 'acceptable' womanhoods began to emerge, particularly in the economic and professional fields: see Al-Rasheed, *A Most Masculine State*, pp. 281–2.

67. @J_mu001. Twitter, 9 September 2016, 1:09 a.m., twitter.com/J_mu001/status/774112424337084417; @Numy_Lumy. Twitter, September 2016, twitter.com/Numy_Lumy/status/759932312452681728; @mu____a1. Twitter, September 2016, twitter.com/mu____a1/status/771455993502900224.

68. @hebatia_ma. Twitter. 2016, twitter.com/hebatia_ma/status/762974746254405632; Al-Rasheed, *Muted Modernists*, p. 71.

69. Al-Rasheed, *Muted Modernists*, p. 71.

70. @mesfrah84. Twitter, 9 September 2016, 5:11 p.m., twitter.com/mesfrah84/status/774354468791922688; @dalsdas. Twitter, 6 February 2016, 11:51 p.m., twitter.com/dalsdas/status/69619447017439 2320.

71. While some of the activists of this campaign may have rejected identifying with a 'pious' form of womanhood, it ought not to be understood as synonymous with subordination. Refer to Saba Mahmoud's *Politics of Piety: The Islamic Revival and the Feminist Subject*, Princeton: Princeton University Press, 2004 for a more nuanced interpretation of pious women's agency.

72. @nouf_ahm_. Twitter, 2 October 2016, 3:43 p.m., twitter.com/nouf_allli_/status/782667264436895744; @s3eed_18. Twitter, 5 October. 2016, 2:25 a.m., twitter.com/s3eed_18/status/783553561363902464; @mesfrah84. Twitter, 22 September 2016, 1:36 a.m., twitter.com/mesfrah84/status/778830383009914880; @Sos123890. Twitter, October 2016, twitter.com/Sos123890/status/783654178920992768; @Fleeing_lifeing. Twitter, 5 October 2016, 1:50 p.m., twitter.com/Flee_life11/status/783726030544601088; @_mlllAKh. Twitter, 5 October 2016, 11:12 p.m., twitter.com/_mlllAKh/status/783867497741156352.

73. @J_mu001. Twitter, 9 September 2016, 1:09 a.m., twitter.com/J_mu001/status/774112424337084417.

74. MiSK is a philanthropic foundation (website: https://misk.org.sa/en/about-misk/) with the goal of encouraging leadership among Saudi youth. Its chairman is Prince Muhammad ibn Salman ibn 'Abd al-'Aziz.

It has numerous arms, such as MiSK schools and MiSK events. It also establishes its own programmes, sponsors local programmes, and partners with global programmes. Recently, it has also acted as a method of encouraging patronage to the state and increasing its influence on Saudi youth and social media actors that grew in prominence since 2011. This trend has become visible publicly in two primary events: the 'Saudi Tweeps' conference in March 2013, which focused on the Saudi Twittersphere, and the 'Shouf' conference in October 2013, which focused on new media in Saudi Arabia. These conferences are now held annually, which acts as a continued effort of maintaining the presence and influence of the state within such fields and on its actors.

75. @LoujainHathloul. Twitter, 23 October 2016, 1:35 a.m., twitter.com/LoujainHathloul/status/790064004685295616.

76. One commentator put it thus: 'Examples like Adwa al-Dakheel … and other virtual groups are taken in by semi-government philanthropic institutions. … They sell their principles … the state has dominated social media and philanthropic efforts through these methods and meetings [MiSK's Shouf Conference]. This world [social media] must remain independent from the state so that it can bear its fruits': https://twitter.com/mo8el/status/790163017476562944.

77. Examples in this campaign were the exchanges between Amani al-Ajlan and Aziza al-Yousef and Loujain al-Hathloul.

78. See Lamya al-Suwailem, 'Women Activists with Male Priorities!', Majalla, 12 October 2013, http://bit.ly/2kks4gr.

79. Eman al-Quwaifli's article was originally posted at https://medium.com/p/8ba559d663ca. Since then it was deleted, and one option to read portions of it is at https://twitter.com/manal_alsharif/status/392917779939995648.

80. Around three to five prominent examples occurred. Some were not explicit or consistent participants in the campaign prior to defecting, however. Instead, they publicly announced that they rejected being part of it.

81. Hailah al-Mashweh, 'A Fall of the Guardianship or a Fall of…?' Okaz, 22 November 2016, at http://bit.ly/2lohOVw.

82. @nouf_ahm_. Twitter, 6 December 2016, 11:00 a.m., twitter.com/nouf_ahm_/status/806166527271665664.

83. @hailahabdulah20. Twitter, 12 November 2016, 3:54 a.m., twitter.com/hailahabdulah20/status/797361805555273728.

84. The majority of other known and identifiable *hasmawiyyat* were observed to have made a similar ideological shift.

85. @nbaa2t. Twitter, 28 October 2016, 10:52 a.m., twitter.com/nbaa2t/status/792016091480489985; @nbaa2t. Twitter, 28 October 2016, twitter.com/nbaa2t/status/791995324806074368.

86. @nbaa2t. Twitter, 1 November 2016, 7:33 p.m., twitter.com/nbaa2t/status/793415625246908416.

87. @nbaa2t. Twitter, 7 August 2016, https://twitter.com/nbaa2t/status/707671109223710725.

88. @nbaa2t. Twitter, 12 October 2016, 12:11 p.m., twitter.com/nbaa2t/status/786237883988443136.

89. @aljo_oo. Twitter, 12 November 2016, 1:43 p.m., twitter.com/aljo_oo/status/797510024557957120.

90. @aljo_oo. Twitter, 12 November 2016, 2:06 p.m., twitter.com/aljo_oo/status/797515866099318784.

91. @aljo_oo. Twitter, 6 December 2016, 9:38 a.m., twitter.com/aljo_oo/status/806145741764837376.; @aljo_oo. Twitter, 6 December 2012, 9:24 a.m., twitter.com/aljo_oo/status/806142345213263872.

92. @nouf_ahm_. Twitter, 6 December 2016, 11:05 a.m., twitter.com/nouf_ahm_/status/806167699453788160.

93. @nbaa2t. Twitter, 6 December 2016, 11:31 a.m., twitter.com/nbaa2t/status/806174185731014656.

94. Hasso, *Consuming Desires*, p. 14.

6. PRODUCING SALAFISM: FROM INVENTED TRADITION TO STATE AGITPROP

1. For example, J. Hooper and B. Whitaker, 'Salafee Views Unite Terror Suspects: The Binding Tie', *The Guardian*, 26 October 2001.

2. Two major titles are Roel Meijer (ed.), *Global Salafism: Islam's New Religious Movement*, New York: Columbia University Press, 2009 and Olivier Roy, *Globalized Islam: The Search for a New Ummah*, New York: Columbia University Press, 2004.

3. A typical essentialist text, from the think-tank community, is Shadi Hamid's *Islamic Exceptionalism: How the Struggle over Islam is Reshaping the World*, New York: St Martin's Press, 2016.

4. Shahab Ahmed, *What is Islam? The Importance of Being Islamic*, Princeton: Princeton University Press, 2016, p. 219.

5. Joseph Massad, *Islam in Liberalism*, Chicago: University of Chicago Press, 2015. Edward Said's notion of much Western writing on the categories of 'the Arabs' and 'Islam' creating an ongoing discourse that exercises power in abstract and concrete ways over those caught in its remit remains in my view relevant.

6. Recent works on Salafism/Salafiyya as a neologism include Khaled El-Rouayheb, 'From Ibn Hajar al-Haytami (d. 1566) to Khayr al-Din al-Alusi (d. 1899): Changing Views of Ibn Taymiyya among non-Hanbali Sunni Scholars', in Yossef Rapoport and Shahab Ahmed (eds.), *Ibn*

Taymiyya and his Times, Karachi: Oxford University Press, 2010; Frank Griffel, 'What Do We Mean By "Salafi"? Connecting Muhammad 'Abduh with Egypt's Nur Party in Islam's Contemporary Intellectual History', *Die Welt des Islams* 55 (2015); and Henri Lauzière, 'The Construction of Salafiyya: Reconsidering Salafism from the Perspective of Conceptual History', *International Journal of Middle East Studies* 42 (2010).

7. For example, Mahmud Shukri al-Alusi (1856–1924), Shihab Mahmud al-Alusi (1802–54), and Jamal al-Din al-Qasimi (1866–1914). On *taqlid*, *ijtihad*, and the 'third way', *ittiba'*, favoured by the Wahhabis see Ahmed Fekry Ibrahim, 'Rethinking the Taqlid–Ijtihad Dichotomy: A Conceptual-Historical Approach', *Journal of the American Oriental Society,* 136, 2 (April–June 2016).

8. On religious revivalism and Arabism see David Commins, *Islamic Reform: Politics and Social Change in Late Ottoman Syria*, New York: Oxford University Press, 1990 and Itzchak Weismann, *Taste of Modernity: Sufism Salafiya, and Arabism in Late Ottoman Damascus*, Leiden: Brill, 2001.

9. The concept as an identity-marker-in-the-making is developed in 1908–13 correspondence between Mahmud Shukri al-Alusi and al-Qasimi: 1. They use *salafi* as an apparent alternative to *salaf*; 2. *Salaf* refers to Ibn Taymiyya and his followers; 3. *Salafi* is used as adjectivally to describe literalist Athari theology. See Muhammad bin Nasir al-'Ajmi, *al-Rasa'il al-Mutabadila*, Beirut: al-Basha'ir, 2001, pp. 47, 60, 74, 190. Al-Qasimi's group appear to have called themselves Jam'iyyat al-Mujtahidin; see Commins, *Islamic Reform*, pp. 50–5. Griffel points out that the Salafiyya Bookstore established by Rida's colleague Muhibb al-Din al-Khatib in Cairo in 1909 was committed to 'Abduh's intellectual project: see Griffel, 'What Do We Mean', p. 201.

10. *Risalat al-Mu'tamar al-Khamis*, Cairo: n.p., 1939, pp. 14–16, cited in Richard Mitchell, *The Society of the Muslim Brothers*, New York: Oxford University Press, 1993, p. 14.

11. Husam Tamam describes the 'Salafization' of the Brotherhood since the 1970s: see Husam Tamam, *Tasalluf al-Ikhwan: Ta'akul al-Utruha al-Ikhwaniyya wa Su'ud al-Salafiyya fi Jama'at al-Ikhwan al-Muslimin*, Alexandria: Bibliotheca Alexandrina/Future Studies Unit, 2010.

12. Jonathan Brown, *Hadith: Muhammad's Legacy in the Medieval and Modern World*, London: Oneworld, 2009, pp. 261–3. See also Ahmad Khan, 'Islamic Tradition in an Age of Print: Editing, Printing and Publishing the Classical Heritage', in Elisabeth Kendall and Ahmad Khan (eds.), *Reclaiming Islamic Tradition: Modern Interpretations of the Classical Heritage*, Edinburgh: Edinburgh University Press, 2016, pp. 56–8.

13. Roy, *Globalized Islam*, p. 272.

14. Yasir Qadhi lists seven: see Yasir Qadhi, 'On Salafi Islam', *Muslim Matters*, 22 April 2014, http://muslimmatters.org/2014/04/22/on-salafi-islam-dr-yasir-qadhi/5/ (accessed 7 November 2016).

15. Quintan Wiktorowicz, 'Anatomy of the Salafi Movement', *Studies in Conflict and Terrorism*, 29, 3 (2006). See Roel Meijer, 'Introduction', in Meijer (ed.), *Global Salafism*; and Bernard Haykel, 'On the Nature of Salafi Thought and Action', in Meijer (ed.), *Global Salafism*.

16. Note that no such term exists in Arabic.

17. Often referred to as the Madkhali school after Saudi scholar Rabi' al-Madkhali on account of his propagandistic pro-government positions in the 1990s; but, in its apoliticism, opposition to the Muslim Brotherhood, and doctrine of obedience to the ruler, this category includes his teacher al-Albani.

18. See Andrew Hammond, 'Rereading Jihadi Texts: Between Subalternity and Policy Discourse', in Noha Mellor and Khalil Rinnawi (eds.), *Political Islam and Global Media: The Boundaries of Religious Identity*, Abingdon: Routledge, 2016.

19. Meijer, 'Introduction', p. 29.

20. Khaled Hroub, 'Salafi Formations in Palestine', in Meijer (ed.), *Global Salafism*.

21. Laurent Bonnefoy, 'Salafism in Yemen: A "Saudisation"?' in Meijer (ed.), *Global Salafism*.

22. Nourhaidi Hasan, 'Ambivalent Doctrines and Conflicts in the Salafi Movement', in Meijer (ed.), *Global Salafism*, p. 187.

23. Mohamed-Ali Adraoui, 'Salafism in France: Ideology, Practices and Contradictions', in Meijer (ed.), *Global Salafism*, p. 369.

24. See Hamadi Redissi, 'The Refutation of Wahhabism in Arabic Sources, 1745–1932', in Madawi Al-Rasheed (ed.), *Kingdom without Borders: Saudi Political, Religious and Media Frontiers*, London: Hurst & Co., 2008.

25. The Ottoman government was suspicious of links between the Damascus group and Wahhabiyya; Rida was called 'Wahhabi' as an insult during a 1908 Damascus visit. See Commins, *Islamic Reform*, pp. 117, 130–1.

26. See Muhammad 'Abduh, *al-A'mal al-Kamila*, Beirut: al-Mu'assasa al-'Arabiyya, 1980, vol. 3, p. 532 and vol. 1, p. 869. Mahmud Shukri al-Alusi said they were excessive in use of *takfir*: see Mahmud Shukri al-Alusi, *Tarikh Najd*, Cairo: Madbouly, n.d., p. 94. On al-Qasimi see Mun'im Sirry, 'Jamal al-Din al-Qasimi and the Salafi Approach to Sufism', *Die Welt des Islams* 51, 1 (2011).

27. Printed in *Umm al-Qura*, 16 May 1929, front page. Griffel and Mouline's claim that this amounted to replacing Salafi for Wahhabi is not borne out by the speech as published.

28. Mouline says the term *salafiyya* was 'used by the 'ulama' of Najd throughout the nineteenth century' (Nabil Mouline, *The Clerics of Islam: Religious Authority and Political Power in Saudi Arabia*, trans. Ethan Rundell, New Haven: Yale University Press, 2014, p. 16, n. 46), but the references cited appear to refer to *al-salaf al-salih*, not contemporaries calling themselves Salafis who follow Salafiyya.

29. Redissi, 'The Refutation of Wahhabism', p. 176.

30. See Stéphane Lacroix, 'Between Revolution and Apoliticism: Nasir al-Din al-Albani and his Impact on the Shaping of Contemporary Salafism', in Meijer (ed.), *Global Salafism*.

31. 'Isam Musa Hadi, *al-Da'wa al-Salafiyya Ahdafha wa Mawqifha min al-Mukhalifin Laha*, Amman: n.p., 2013, collects his comments from cassettes regarding Salafiyya.

32. Nasir al-Huzaymi, *Ayyam ma' Juhayman: Kuntu ma' al-Jama'a al-Salafiyya al-Muhtasiba*, Beirut: Arab Network for Research and Publishing, 2011, pp. 14–15.

33. Al-Albani's student Muqbil al-Wadi'i took the Salafi banner with him to Yemen, where he is considered the father of the movement.

34. On al-Albani's influence in Saudi Arabia see Lacroix, 'Between Revolution and Apoliticism'. See also Qadhi, 'On Salafi Islam'.

35. For a critique of al-Albani's innovations see Christopher Melchert, 'Muhammad Nasir al-Din al-Albani and Traditional Hadith Criticism', in Kendall and Khan (eds.), *Reclaiming Islamic Tradition*.

36. Muhammad Zahid al-Kawthari, 'al-Lamadhhabiyya Qantarat al-Ladiniyya', in Muhammad Zahid al-Kawthari, *Maqalat al-Kawthari*, Cairo: al-Tawfikia Bookshop, 1953.

37. 'Abd al-Salam Farag, *al-Jihad: al-Farida al-Gha'iba*, Amman: n.p., 1982.

38. Al-Maqdisi related his experience in a 2009 statement regarding coeducation at the King Abdullah Science and Technology University: see English translation, 'Two Swords and a Palm Tree', October 2009, https://www.kalamullah.com/current-affairs20.html.

39. Abu Muhammad al-Maqdisi, *Millat Ibrahim wa Da'wat al-Anbiya' wa-l-Mursalin* (*c.* 1984), p. 27.

40. Al-Maqdisi, *Millat Ibrahim*, p. 33, n. 10.

41. Abu Muhammad al-Maqdisi, *al-Kawashif al-Jaliyya fi Kufr al-Dawla al-Sa'udiyya*, Amman: Minbar al-Tawhid wa-l-Jihad, 1989, p. 132.

42. See Andreas Christmann, 'Islamic Scholar and Religious Leader: A Portrait of Shaykh Muhammad Sa'id Ramadan al-Buti', *Islam and Christian–Muslim Relations*, 9, 2 (1998).

43. Said Ramadan al-Buti, *al-Lamadhhabiyya Akhtar Bid'a Tuhaddid al-Shari'a al-Islamiyya*, 2nd edn, Damascus: n.p., 1970, pp. 15–26. In the preface to the second edition in 1970 al-Buti recounts a meeting with al-Albani in which they argue over the concept of *la-madhhabiyya*.

44. Muhammad al-Ghazali, *al-Sunna al-Nabawiyya bayn Ahl al-Fiqh wa Ahl al-Hadith*, Cairo: Dar al-Shurouq, 1989, pp. 14–15.

45. See the responses of al-Albani, al-Wadi'i, and al-Madkhali in Abi 'Abd Allah Shakib al-Salafi (ed.), *Aqwal Ahl al-'Ilm fi Muhammad al-Ghazali al-Saqqa*, Riyadh: Sihab al-Salafiyya, n.d. Also Khaled Abou El Fadl, *The Great Theft: Wrestling Islam from the Extremists*, New York: Harper San Francisco, 2005, p. 93.

46. Mouline, *The Clerics of Islam*, p. 45.

47. See http://www.alsalafway.com/Sisters/showthread.php?p=92646 (accessed 25 January 2017).

48. See http://www.alfawzan.af.org.sa/node/2030 (accessed 25 January 2017).

49. 'Bi Sha'n al-Khilaf al-Fiqhi bayn al-Madhahib wa-l-Ta'assub al-Madh-habi', *Majallat al-Majma' al-Fiqhi al-Islami*, Year 4, 2nd edn (2005), pp. 383–6. The decision (*qarar*) was taken in its tenth session in Mecca, 17–21 October 1987.

50. James Piscatori, 'Islamic Values and National Interest: The Foreign Policy of Saudi Arabia', in Adeed Dawisha (ed.), *Islam in Foreign Policy*, Cambridge: Cambridge University Press, 1983, p. 37.

51. Piscatori, 'Islamic Values and National Interest', p. 41.

52. Grants and loans to OIC member states totalled $1.76 billion in 1975 and $1.99 billion in 1976, and Muslim World League spending in Africa on training imams, building mosques, printing Qur'an copies, etc. in the period 1975–81 was $2.6 million; Saudi Arabia also funded the Mecca-based Supreme World Council for Mosques. See Piscatori, 'Islamic Values and National Interest', p. 47.

53. Piscatori, 'Islamic Values and National Interest', p. 51.

54. Memorandum from the Islamic Academy in Riyadh to the Islamic General Secretariat organizing the celebrations; cited in Ayman al-Yassini, *al-Din wa-al-Dawla fi al-Mamlaka al-'Arabiyya al-Su'udiyya*, London: Saqi, 1990, p. 82.

55. For example, the PLO bureau in Riyadh was run by a former Brotherhood figure as a recruitment centre for the jihad; see Olivier Roy, *The Failure of Political Islam*, London: I. B. Tauris, 1994, p. 218, n. 7.

56. Hamas, Gulf chapters of the Brotherhood, and some of Tunisia's Ennahda stood with Saudi Arabia; Roy, *Globalized Islam*, p. 121.

57. Walid Saleh, 'The Politics of Quranic Hermeneutics: Royalties on Interpretation', public lecture, www.international.ucla.edu/cnes/podcasts/article.asp?parentid=110233. See also Franklin Foer, 'Moral Hazard', *New Republic*, 18 November 2002, www.tnr.com/article/moral-hazard.

58. Mouline, *The Clerics of Islam*, p. 213.

59. Roy, *The Failure of Political Islam*, London: I.B. Tauris, 1994 [1992].

60. Raymond Hinnebusch, *The International Politics of the Middle East*, Manchester: Manchester University Press, 2003, p. 122.

61. Hinnebusch, *The International Politics of the Middle East*, p. 84 (2nd edition, 2015).

62. Hinnebusch, *The International Politics of the Middle East* (2015 edn), pp. 2, 6–9.

63. Lawrence Rubin, *Islam in the Balance: Ideational Threats in Arab Politics*, Stanford: Stanford Security Studies, 2014.

64. Ali Bardakoğlu, 'Selefiliğin Geleceğine İlişkin Perspektifler', in Ahmet Kavas (ed.), *Tarihte ve Günümüzde Selefilik*, Istanbul: Ensar Neşriyat, 2014, p. 662. Bardakoğlu reprimands scholars for ignoring Salafism in Turkey.

65. Hayreddin Karaman, *Laik Düzende Dini Yaşamak*, vol. 1, Istanbul: İz Ayıncılık, 2002: see section 1, 'Selefiyye'den Kur'an Müslümanlığına', http://www.hayrettinkaraman.net/yazi/laikduzen/1/0043.htm (accessed 13 November 2016).

66. Presidency of Religious Affairs, *Daiş'in Temel Felsefesi ve Dini Referansları Raporu*, Ankara: Diyanet, 2015, p. 8. The state body defined the ideology as three groups: *Selefiyye*, *Selefilik*, and *Selefizm*.

67. In 2014 a number of print media writers began to discuss Salafism in Turkey. See Rüşen Çakır, 'Selefileri Beklerken', *Vatan*, 11 March 2014.

68. Eric Zürcher, 'The Importance of Being Secular: Islam in the Service of the National and Pre-National State', in Celia Kerslake, Kerem Öktem, and Philip Robins (eds.), *Turkey's Engagement with Modernity: Conflict and Change in the Twentieth Century*, London: Routledge Curzon, 2005, p. 65.

69. Feroz Ahmad, 'Islamic Reassertion in Turkey', *Third World Quarterly* 10, 2 (1988), p. 762. Also Feroz Ahmad, *The Turkish Experiment in Democracy 1950–1975*, London: Hurst & Co., 1977, p. 381.

70. Uğur Mumcu, *Rabıta*, Ankara: Tekin Yayınevi, 1987, p. 193.

71. For Turkish religious movements of the 1980s see Ruşen Çakır, *Ayet ve Slogan: Türkiye'de İslami Oluşumlar*, Istanbul: Metis Yayınları, 1991.

72. See Peköz, 'Selefiler—AKP kolkola' and Ismail Yaşa, 'Türkiyeli Selefiler Tekfirci mi?' *Tevhid Haber*, 24 July 2009, http://www.tevhidhaber.com/news_detail.php?id=60097 (accessed 30 October 2016). Yaşa is one of a number of AKP supporters/members who apply the Salafi label.

73. Others among them include Ubeydullah Arslan, Ebu Said Yarpuzi (aka Mehmet Balcıoğlu), Huseyin Abu Emre, Murat Gezenler, Murat Ekinci (aka Ebu Hafs), Ebu Hanzala Hoca (aka Halis Bayıncık), and Feyzullah Birışık.

pp. [158–160]   NOTES

74. For example, Abdullah al-Athari, *Islamic Beliefs: A Brief Introduction to the 'Aqidah of Ahl as-Sunnah wal-Jama'ah*, Riyadh: International Islamic Publishing House, 2004.
75. See http://www.guraba.com.tr/vitrin/hakkimizda.html (accessed 30 October 2016).
76. This site lists twenty-one titles: http://islamhouse.com/ar/author/6996/books/showall/1 (accessed 30 October 2016).
77. See the photograph on his Twitter page: https://twitter.com/AbdullaYolcu (accessed 30 October 2016).
78. He suggests that the laws of the secular state should not be obeyed, since removal of shari'a law is a form of apostasy: see Abdullah b. Abdulhamid el-Eseri, *Ehl-i Sünnet ve'l-Cemaat'e Göre İman: Hakikati, Onu Zedeleyen ve Bozan Şeyler*, trans. Ahmed İyibildiren, Istanbul: Guraba, 2014, p. 735.
79. Abdullah Yolcu, *Kur'an ve Sünnet'in Işığında İslam'ın Şartları*, Istanbul: Guraba, 2010, pp. 29–30, 62.
80. Yolcu, *Kur'an ve Sünnet'in Işığında İslam'ın Şartları*, pp. 81–95.
81. 'Abd Allah bin 'Abd al-Hamid al-Athari, *al-Wajiz fi 'Aqidat al-Salaf al-Salih*, Riyadh: Wizarat al-Shu'un al-Islamiyya, 2002. Guraba published it in Istanbul in Arabic in 1997.
82. Muhammed Raşid b. Halid Karaköylü, former imam of the Van Şerefiye mosque in eastern Turkey.
83. Abdullah Yolcu, *Selef-i Salihin Akidesi: Ehl-i Sünnet ve'l-Cemaat*, Istanbul: Guraba, 2014, pp. 59, 66, 69.
84. 'Abd Allah bin 'Abd al-Hamid al-Athari, *al-Iman: Haqiqatuhu, Khawarimuhu, Nawaqiduhu 'ind Ahl al-Sunna wa-l-Jama'a*, Riyadh: Madar al-Watan, 2003.
85. El-Eseri, *Ehl-i Sünnet ve'l-Cemaat'e Göre İman*, p. 44.
86. Abdullah b. Abdulhamid el-Eseri, *Meşru ve Gayrımeşru Tevessül*, trans. Ahmet İyibildiren and Mustafa Öztürk, Istanbul: Guraba, 2013, pp. 153–73, esp. pp. 155–6. He gives no comment on the juridical practice of *talfiq*, applied by Muhammad 'Abduh. The book was published in Arabic as 'Abd Allah bin 'Abd al-Hamid al-Athari, *al-Tawassul al-Mashru' wa-l-Mamnu': Anwa' wa Ahkam*, Istanbul: Guraba, 2013.
87. Abdullah b. Abdulhamid el-Eseri, *İslami Açıdan Müzik ve Teganni*, trans. Mustafa Öztürk, Istanbul: Guraba, 2013, pp. 17–18. Published in Arabic as 'Abd Allah bin 'Abd al-Hamid al-Athari, *al-Ghina' wa-l-Musiqa bayn al-Lahw wa-l-Wa'id*, Istanbul: Guraba, 2001.
88. al-Athari, *al-Ghina' wa-l-Musiqa*, p. 115.
89. al-Athari, *al-Ghina' wa-l-Musiqa*, pp. 118–24.
90. al-Athari, *al-Ghina' wa-l-Musiqa*, pp. 242–3.
91. al-Athari, *al-Ghina' wa-l-Musiqa*, pp. 141–2, 146–7.

304

92. al-Athari, *al-Ghina' wa-l-Musiqa*, pp. 140–70 (the section titled 'Sufi Sema'nin Hükmü'). For the Arabic see al-Athari, *al-Ghina' wa-l-Musiqa*, pp. 171–208.

93. El-Eseri, *Meşru ve Gayrımeşru Tevessül*, p. 244. For *türbe* the Arabic version uses the term *mashhad*; al-Athari, *al-Tawassul al-Mashru' wa-l-Mamnu'*, p. 283.

94. Yolcu, *Selef-i Salihin Akidesi*, pp. 168–9.

95. El-Eseri, *Ehl-i Sünnet ve'l-Cemaat'e Göre İman*, p. 762.

96. Meijer, 'Introduction', p. 29.

97. André Lefevere and Susan Bassnett (eds.), *Translation, History and Culture*, London: Pinter, 1990, p. 11.

98. André Lefevere, 'Translation: Its Genealogy in the West', in Lefevere and Bassnett (eds.), *Translation, History and Culture*, p. 24.

99. 'They are trying to reconcile Islam and the West; they rely on Sufism rather than the Qur'an and the sunna': interview (in Arabic), Istanbul, 26 March 2015.

100. Leonard Binder, *Islamic Liberalism: A Critique of Development Ideologies*, Chicago: University of Chicago Press, 1988, p. 96. See also Carool Kersten's comment on the critical thinkers Mohammed Arkoun (1928–2010) and Muhammad 'Abid al-Jabiri (1936–2010) in Carool Kersten, 'Critical Islam: Muslims and their Religion in a Post-Islamist World', *Singapore Middle East Papers* 10, 1 (2014), p. 119.

101. Christopher Bayly, *The Birth of the Modern World, 1780–1914: Global Connections and Comparisons*, Oxford: Blackwell, 2004, p. 4.

102. El-Rouayheb, 'From Ibn Hajar'. See also Khaled El-Rouayheb, *Islamic Intellectual History in the Seventeenth Century: Scholarly Currents in the Ottoman Empire and the Maghreb*, Cambridge: Cambridge University Press, 2015, p. 234.

103. Rida inserts footnotes in praise of Ibn Taymiyya in his edition of 'Abduh's *Risalat al-tawhid* (1885), faulting him for not mentioning the Damascus scholar.

104. See George Makdisi, 'Law and Traditionalism in the Institutions of Learning of Medieval Islam', in Gustave Grunebaum (ed.), *Theology and Law in Islam*, Wiesbaden: Harrassowitz, 1971 and Josef van Ess, 'The Logical Structure of Islamic Theology', in Gustave Grunebaum (ed.), *Logic in Classical Islamic Culture*, Wiesbaden: Harrassowitz, 1970. Both cited in El-Rouayheb, *Islamic Intellectual History*, pp. 88, 285.

105. El-Rouayheb, *Islamic Intellectual History*, pp. 15, 191. The idea of Salafism having deeper historical resonance is defended in Haykel, 'On the Nature of Salafi Thought and Action', esp. p. 38.

106. Lauzière, 'The Construction of Salafiyya'.

7. TRANSNATIONAL RELIGIOUS COMMUNITY AND THE SALAFI MISSION

1. Michael Farquhar, *Circuits of Faith: Migration, Education, and the Wahhabi Mission*, Stanford Studies in Middle Eastern and Islamic Societies and Cultures, Stanford: Stanford University Press, 2016, chap. 7.

2. More recently, the university has also established faculties of science, computer science, and engineering.

3. Farquhar, *Circuits of Faith*, p. 3.

4. Farquhar, *Circuits of Faith*, chap. 6.

5. Farquhar, *Circuits of Faith*, chap. 7.

6. Dale F. Eickelman and James P. Piscatori (eds.), *Muslim Travellers: Pilgrimage, Migration, and the Religious Imagination*, London: Routledge, 1990.

7. For an overview of such phenomena, see Mandaville, *Global Political Islam*, pp. 280–98.

8. Olivier Roy, *Globalized Islam: The Search for a New Ummah*, New York: Columbia University Press, 2004, chap. 6.

9. Roy, *Globalized Islam*, p. 258.

10. Roy, *Globalized Islam*, p. 259.

11. Roy, *Globalized Islam*, p. 264.

12. Roy, *Globalized Islam*, p. 270.

13. Roy, *Globalized Islam*, p. 238.

14. Roy, *Globalized Islam*, p. 272.

15. Roy, *Globalized Islam*, p. 270.

16. Roy, *Globalized Islam*, pp. 268–9.

17. Roy, *Globalized Islam*, p. 271.

18. Roy, *Globalized Islam*, p. 258.

19. Roy, *Globalized Islam*, p. 241.

20. Cf. Benjamin R. Barber, *Jihad vs. McWorld*, London: Corgi, 2003.

21. For comparable endeavours see also Timothy Mitchell, 'McJihad: Islam in the US Global Order', *Social Text* 20, 4 (2002); Mona Atia, *Building a House in Heaven: Pious Neoliberalism and Islamic Charity Egypt*, Minneapolis: University of Minnesota Press, 2013.

22. Madawi Al-Rasheed, 'The Local and the Global in Saudi Salafi–Jihadi Discourse', in Roel Meijer (ed.), *Global Salafism: Islam's New Religious Movement*, London: Hurst & Co., 2009; Laurent Bonnefoy, 'How Transnational is Salafism in Yemen?' in Roel Meijer (ed.), *Global Salafism: Islam's New Religious Movement*, London: Hurst & Co., 2009; Laurent Bonnefoy, *Salafism in Yemen: Transnationalism and Religious Identity*, London: Hurst & Co., 2011. For a treatment of the intersection of local, national, and transnational forms of identity among non-

Salafi Muslims see Hisham Aidi, 'Let us be Moors: Islam, Race and "Connected Histories"', *Middle East Report* 229 (1 December 2003).

23. Mandaville, Peter, 'Transnational Muslim Solidarities and Everyday Life', *Nations and Nationalism* 17, 1 (1 January 2011).

24. Mandaville, 'Transnational Muslim Solidarities and Everyday Life', p. 12.

25. Mandaville, 'Transnational Muslim Solidarities and Everyday Life', p. 15.

26. Mandaville, 'Transnational Muslim Solidarities and Everyday Life', p. 7.

27. Nabil Mouline, *The Clerics of Islam: Religious Authority and Political Power in Saudi Arabia*, New Haven: Yale University Press, 2014, p. 8.

28. Mouline, *The Clerics of Islam*, p. 8.

29. Madawi Al-Rasheed, *A History of Saudi Arabia*, 2nd edn, Cambridge: Cambridge University Press, 2010, chap. 7.

30. Abdullah M. Sindi, 'King Faisal and Pan-Islamism', in Willard A. Beling (ed.), *King Faisal and the Modernisation of Saudi Arabia*, London: Croom Helm, 1980.

31. Thomas Hegghammer, *Jihad in Saudi Arabia: Violence and Pan-Islamism since 1979*, Cambridge: Cambridge University Press, 2010, chap. 1.

32. Hegghammer, *Jihad in Saudi Arabia*, pp. 17–18.

33. Farquhar, *Circuits of Faith*, chap. 4.

34. Thomas Hegghammer, 'The Rise of Muslim Foreign Fighters: Islam and the Globalization of Jihad', *International Security* 35, 3 (Winter 2010), p. 85.

35. 'Memories from the Islamic University of Madinah—Sheikh Abu Usamah at-Thahabi', YouTube, https://www.youtube.com/watch?v=g7eg1swrbGo&feature=youtube_gdata_player, accessed 26 January 2015.

36. 'Abd Allah ibn Salih ibn 'Abd Allah al-'Abbud, *Juhud al-mamlaka al-'Arabiyya al-Su'udiyya fi al-da'wa ila Allah ta'ala fi al-kharij min khilal al-Jami'a al-Islamiyya*, al-Madina al-Munawwara: al-Jami'a al-Islamiyya, 2004, p. 554.

37. Muhi al-Din Ramadan, 'Wa-Lam Yazil A'da' al-Umma Yamkuruna', *Majallat al-Jami'a al-Islamiyya bi-l-Madina al-Munawwara* 10, 2 (September 1977).

38. 'Ali ibn Muhammad ibn Nasir al-Fuqayhi, 'Wahdat al-Umma Hiya Tariq al-Khalas', *Majallat al-Jami'a al-Islamiyya bi-l-Madina al-Munawwara* 58 (Rabi' al-Akhir-Jumada al-Akhira 1403 H).

39. Interview with IUM graduate, London, 18 January 2011; telephone interview with IUM graduate, 7 January 2017.

40. Farquhar, *Circuits of Faith*, pp. 121–2.

41. *Dalil al-Jami'a al-Islamiyya fi al-Madina al-Munawwara*, Medina: al-Jami'a al-Islamiyya, 1971, p. 11.

42. Telephone interview with IUM graduate, 7 January 2017.

43. 'Memories of Madinah: Life at the Islamic University of Madinah—Ustaadh Aqeel Mahmood', YouTube, https://www.youtube.com/watch?v=bTg_5xGgXRs&feature=youtube_gdata_player, accessed 26 January 2015.

44. 'Memories of Madinah: Life at the Islamic University of Madinah—Ustaadh Aqeel Mahmood'.

45. 'Memories from the Islamic University of Madinah—Sheikh Muhammad Ali', YouTube, https://www.youtube.com/watch?v=o70b7-VMPtg&feature=youtube_gdata_player, accessed 26 January 2015.

46. 'Memories of Madinah: Life at the Islamic University of Madinah—Ustaadh Aqeel Mahmood'.

47. Interview with IUM graduate, London, 18 January 2011.

48. Interview with IUM graduate, 14 July 2011.

49. Telephone interview with IUM graduate, 7 January 2017.

50. 'Memories from the Islamic University of Madinah—Dr Ahsan Hanif', YouTube, https://www.youtube.com/watch?v=KX233WNfGpw&feature=youtube_gdata_player, accessed 26 January 2015.

51. '"Life After Madinah" w/ Nick Pelletier', YouTube, https://www.youtube.com/watch?v=RrYhbLjE1aM, accessed 28 December 2016.

52. Zoltan Pall, 'Salafi Dynamics in Kuwait: Politics, Fragmentation and Change', in Francesco Cavatorta and Fabio Merone (eds.), *Salafism after the Arab Awakening: Contending with People's Power*, London: Hurst & Co., 2017.

53. Farquhar, *Circuits of Faith*, chap. 7.

54. See, for example, the following testimony, in which the speaker asserts that the Saudi royal family is not perfect but that it compares favourably to the governments of other Muslim-majority countries: 'Memories from the Islamic University of Madinah—Sheikh Abu Usamah at-Thahabi'.

55. See, for example, a YouTube video featuring a scathing attack on the Saudi regime by the US-based IUM graduate Ahmad Musa Jibril, discussed in Farquhar, *Circuits of Faith*, chap. 7.

56. Quintan Wiktorowicz, 'Anatomy of the Salafi Movement', *Studies in Conflict and Terrorism* 29, 3 (2006), p. 221.

57. Bjørn Olav Utvik, 'The Ikhwanization of the Salafis: Piety in the Politics of Egypt and Kuwait', *Middle East Critique* 23, 1 (2 January 2014), pp. 10–11.

58. For one example, couched in careful terms which avoid details or labelling of those involved, see 'My Journey to Madinah: Ep. 5: "Student Drama"', YouTube, https://www.youtube.com/watch?v=ePMEgDlrwus, accessed 28 December 2016.

59. John M. Swales, *Genre Analysis: English in Academic and Research Settings*, Cambridge: Cambridge University Press, 1990.

60. John Obert Voll, 'Islam as a Community of Discourse and a World System', in Akbar S. Ahmed and Tamara Sonn (eds.), *The Sage Handbook of Islamic Studies*, London: Sage, 2010, p. 4.

61. Voll, 'Islam as a Community of Discourse and a World System', p. 7.

62. Voll, 'Islam as a Community of Discourse and a World System', p. 8.

63. Talal Asad, *The Idea of an Anthropology of Islam*, Occasional Papers Series, Washington, DC: Georgetown University, Center for Contemporary Arab Studies, 1986.

64. Asad, *The Idea of an Anthropology of Islam*, pp. 15–16.

65. Sami Zubaida, 'The Fragments Imagine the Nation: The Case of Iraq', *International Journal of Middle East Studies* 34, 2 (2002); Benedict Anderson, *Imagined Communities: Reflections on the Origin and Spread of Nationalism*, rev. edn, London and New York: Verso, 2006.

8. WAHHABISM, SAUDI ARABIA, AND THE ISLAMIC STATE: 'ABDULLAH IBN JIBRIN AND TURKI AL-BIN 'ALI

1. 'Abd al-Rahman ibn 'Abdallah al-Jibrin, *U'jubat al-'Asr: Sirat Samahat al-Shaykh al-'Allama al-Imam 'Abdallah ibn 'Abd al-Rahman al-Jibrin*, Riyadh: Mu'assasat Ibn Jibrin al-Khayriyya, 2012, pp. 886–87.

2. al-Jibrin, *U'jubat al-'Asr*, p. 29.

3. Turki al-Bin'ali, *Jabr al-Rayn fi Ritha' al-Jibrin*, Minbar al-Tawhid wa'l-Jihad, July 2009, http://www.jihadica.com/wp-content/uploads/2016/11/jabr.pdf. All links cited in this chapter were last accessed on 20 September 2017.

4. The details of Ibn Jibrin's biography given here are drawn from 'Sirat al-Shaykh', Mawqi' Ibn Jibrin, http://www.ibn-jebreen.com/biography.html.

5. See, for example, the fatwa concerning jihad against the people of Ha'il in 'Abd al-Rahman ibn Qasim (ed.), *al-Durar al-Saniyya fi 'l-Ajwiba al-Najdiyya*, 8th edn, 16 vols., Riyadh: Warathat al-Shaykh 'Abd al-Rahman ibn Qasim, 2012), vol. 9, pp. 289–93.

6. Guido Steinberg, 'The Wahhabi Ulama and the Saudi State: 1745 to the Present', in Paul Aarts and Gerd Nonneman (eds.), *Saudi Arabia in the Balance: Political Economy, Society, Foreign Affairs*, New York: New York University Press, 2005, pp. 20, 24.

7. Guido Steinberg, 'The Wahhabiyya and Shi'ism, from 1744/45 to 2008', in Ofra Bengio and Meir Litvak (eds.), *The Sunna and Shi'a in History: Division and Ecumenism in the Muslim Middle East*, New York: Palgrave, 2011, pp. 172–3.

8. Steinberg, 'The Wahhabi Ulama and the Saudi State', pp. 24–5.

9. Ibn Qasim (ed.), *al-Durar al-Saniyya*, vol. 9, pp. 333–4.

10. Nabil Mouline, *The Clerics of Islam: Religious Authority and Political Power in Saudi Arabia*, trans. Ethan S. Rundell, New Haven: Yale University Press, 2014, p. 145.

11. Mouline, *The Clerics of Islam*, pp. 133–50.

12. Steinberg, 'The Wahhabi Ulama and the Saudi State', p. 30.

13. Mouline, *The Clerics of Islam*, pp. 137–8. These two institutions merged to become the Imam Muhammad ibn Saud University in 1974.

14. Stéphane Lacroix, *Awakening Islam: The Politics of Religious Dissent in Contemporary Saudi Arabia*, trans. George Holoch, Cambridge, MA: Harvard University Press, 2011, pp. 179–81.

15. Lacroix, *Awakening Islam*, pp. 186, 168–72.

16. Lacroix, *Awakening Islam*, pp. 187–8. The text of the counter-refutation (*al-bayan al-thalathi*) is available at http://www.al-oglaa.com/?section=subject&SubjectID=134.

17. Lacroix, *Awakening Islam*, pp. 189–91.

18. See, for example, Turki al-Bin'ali, *Majmu' Fatawa al-Shaykh Abi Humam al-Athari (al-Juz' al-Awwal)*, Shabakat al-Tahaddi al-Islami, 2011, http://www.jihadica.com/wp-content/uploads/2016/11/majmu-fatawa-1.doc, p. 23.

19. al-Jibrin, *U'jubat al-'Asr*, p. 746.

20. 'Abdallah ibn Jibrin, 'Hukm Dhaba'ih al-Rafidi wa-Mu'amalatihi' (fatwa 11092), http://www.ibn-jebreen.com/fatwa/vmasal-11092-.html.

21. al-Jibrin, *U'jubat al-'Asr*, pp. 266–72. For the original fatwa see 'Abdallah ibn Jibrin, 'Nusrat Hizballah al-Rafidi wa'l-Indiwa' Taht Imratihim wa'l-Du'a' Lahum bi'l-Nasr wa'l-Tamkin' (fatwa 4174), http://www.ibn-jebreen.com/fatwa/vmasal-4174-.html.

22. al-Bin'ali, *Jabr al-Rayn*, p. 2.

23. al-Bin'ali, *Jabr al-Rayn*, p. 1.

24. al-Bin'ali, *Jabr al-Rayn*, p. 2.

25. al-Bin'ali, *Jabr al-Rayn*, p. 2.

26. al-Jibrin, *U'jubat al-'Asr*, p. 774.

27. al-Jibrin, *U'jubat al-'Asr*, p. 772. Ibn Jibrin, it should be noted, was not the only Wahhabi scholar to defend the Sunni insurgency at this time; in December 2006 thirty-eight of them signed an open letter of support, for which see 'Nida' li-Ahl al-Sunna fi 'l-'Iraq wa-ma Yajibu 'ala 'l-Umma min Nusratihim', *al-Muslim*, 7 December 2006, http://www.almoslim.net/node/83656. For the story of this letter's composition see Nelly Lahoud et al., *Letters from Abbottabad: Bin Ladin Sidelined?* West Point, NY: Combating Terrorism Center, May 2012, pp. 24–6.

28. al-Bin'ali, *Jabr al-Rayn*, p. 2.
29. al-Bin'ali, *Jabr al-Rayn*, p. 1.
30. al-Jibrin, *U'jubat al-'Asr*, pp. 768–91.
31. For his biography see Abu Usama al-Gharib, *al-Mukhtasar al-Jali bi-Sirat Shaykhina Turki al-Bin'ali*, 2013, https://archive.org/download/almokhtasar.algali.high/almokhtasar.algali.high.pdf. See also, for pictures of al-Bin'ali's various certificates and *ijazas*, Abu Usama al-Gharib, *Minnat al-'Ali bi-Thabat Shaykina Turki al-Bin'ali*, 2013, https://ia601002.us.archive.org/15/items/minato.alali001/minato.alali001.pdf. Abu Usama al-Gharib is the assumed name of the Austrian jihadi Muhammad ibn Shawqi ibn Mahmud, on whom see Souad Mekhennet, 'Austrian Returns, Unrepentant, to Online Jihad', *The New York Times*, 15 November 2011, http://www.nytimes.com/2011/11/16/world/europe/austrian-returns-to-online-jihad.html. Since Mekhennet's article, Ibn Mahmud has left Europe to join the Islamic State group, where he married the group's official poetess, Ahlam al-Nasr. On this development see Robyn Cresswell and Bernard Haykel, 'Battle Lines', *The New Yorker*, 8–15 June 2015, http://www.newyorker.com/magazine/2015/06/08/battle-lines-jihad-creswell-and-haykel.
32. al-Gharib, *Minnat al-'Ali*, p. 41.
33. al-Gharib, *Minnat al-'Ali*, p. 42.
34. Interview with Ahmad al-Hamdan, Twitter, November 2016.
35. The url (now defunct) was www.tawhed.ws. Much of the content is still available at www.ilmway.com/site/maqdis/.
36. Others were Abu Hudhayfa al-Bahrayni and Abu Hazm al-Salafi. In 2014 al-Bin'ali acknowledged being behind the pseudonyms. See Turki al-Bin'ali, *Zubalat al-milal wa'l-nihal*, 4th edn, 12 April 2014, http://www.jihadica.com/wp-content/uploads/2015/06/B28.doc, pp. 2–4.
37. See the *ijaza* in al-Gharib, *Minnat al-'Ali*, p. 24.
38. See Turki al-Bin'ali, *al-Qawl al-Narjasi bi-'Adalat Shaykhina 'l-Maqdisi*, Majmu'at al-Ansar al-Baridiyya, 2009, https://ia802705.us.archive.org/9/items/elmqdsi/qaul.pdf.
39. On the council see Joas Wagemakers, 'Protecting Jihad: The Sharia Council of the Minbar al-Tawhid wa-l-Jihad', *Middle East Policy* 18, 2 (2011). Al-Bin'ali would later claim that al-Maqdisi had appointed him as head of the council. See Turki al-Bin'ali, *Shaykhi 'l-Asbaq: Hadha Firaq Bayni wa-Baynaka*, 31 May 2014, http://www.jihadica.com/wp-content/uploads/2015/06/B45.docx, p. 20.
40. His output for the website is now available at these two locations: http://www.ilmway.com/site/maqdis/MS_9367.html and http://www.ilmway.com/site/maqdis/MS_157.html.
41. Daniel Lav, *Radical Islam and the Revival of Medieval Theology*, Cambridge: Cambridge University Press, 2012, p. 169.

42. Joas Wagemakers, *A Quietist Jihadi: The Ideology and Influence of Abu Muhammad al-Maqdisi*, Cambridge: Cambridge University Press, 2012, pp. 36–8.

43. Lav, *Radical Islam*, p. 169.

44. Turki al-Bin'ali, *Mukhtasar al-Lafz fi Mas'alat Dawaran al-Ard*, 2nd edn, 15 April 2014, p. 20, www.jihadica.com/wp-content/uploads/2015/06/B31.doc. He was still of the view that the sun revolves around the earth.

45. Interview with Ahmad al-Hamdan.

46. Turki al-Bin'ali, 'Ma 'l-Tarjama al-'Ilmiyya lil-Shaykh Abi Humam Bakr ibn 'Abd al-'Aziz al-Athari Hafizahu 'llah?', Minbar al-Tawhid wa'l-Jihad, 19 April 2011, http://www.jihadica.com/wp-content/uploads/2016/11/tarjama-ilmiyya.pdf. A number of other Saudi scholars are mentioned here as part-time teachers, including Sa'id ibn Zu'ayr, 'Abdullah al-Sa'd, Sa'd al-Shathri, and Salman al-'Awda.

47. See the letter in al-Gharib, *Minnat al-'Ali*, p. 58.

48. al-Bin'ali, *Jabr al-Rayn*, pp. 1–2.

49. Shakir Abu Talib, 'al-Suwaydi Akthar min Hayy Sakani, Shahada 'l-Sahwa fi 'l-Thamaninat wa'l-Irhab Akhiran', *al-Sharq al-Awsat*, 14 December 2004, http://archive.aawsat.com/details.asp?issueno=9165&article=271180#.WH6RY5JgYqI.

50. Cole Bunzel, *From Paper State to Caliphate: The Ideology of the Islamic State*, Washington, DC: Brookings Institution, 2015.

51. See, for this general argument, Cole Bunzel, *The Kingdom and the Caliphate: Duel of the Islamic States*, Washington, DC: Carnegie Endowment for International Peace, 2016, pp. 8–9.

52. Muhammad ibn 'Abd al-Wahhab, *Kashf al-Shubuhat*, Mosul: Maktabat al-Himma, 2016, p. 5 n.1, http://www.jihadica.com/wp-content/uploads/2016/11/kashf-al-shubuhat.pdf.

53. See, for example, 'The Islamic State', *Vice News*, August 2014, https://news.vice.com/show/the-islamic-state.

54. al-Bin'ali, 'Ma 'l-Tarjama al-'Ilmiyya lil-Shaykh Abi Humam Bakr ibn 'Abd al-'Aziz al-Athari Hafizahu 'llah?'.

55. Turki al-Bin'ali, *'Abarat al-'Abir fi Ritha' Amir al-Mu'minin wa'l-Wazir*, Minbar al-Tawhid wa'l-Jihad, 25 April 2010, http://www.jihadica.com/wp-content/uploads/2016/11/abarat.pdf; Turki al-Bin'ali, *Waqafat wa-Khawatir ma' Dhikr Amir al-Mu'minin al-'Atir*, 1 May 2010, http://www.jihadica.com/wp-content/uploads/2016/11/waqafat-wa-khawatir.pdf.

56. Turki al-Bin'ali, *Madd al-Ayadi li-Bay'at al-Baghdadi*, Minbar al-Tawhid wa'l-Jihad, April 2013, http://www.jihadica.com/wp-content/uploads/2015/06/B01.pdf; subsequently published by the Islamic

State's Maktabat al-Himma, in abridged form, as *Muddu 'l-Ayadi li-Bay'at al-Baghdadi*.

57. Interview with Ahmad al-Hamdan.
58. For more on his activities during this period see Cole Bunzel, 'The Caliphate's Scholar-in-Arms', Jihadica, 9 July 2014, http://www.jihadica.com/the-caliphate%E2%80%99s-scholar-in-arms/; Cole Bunzel, 'Bin'ali Leaks', Jihadica, 15 June 2015, http://www.jihadica.com/binali-leaks/.
59. al-Bin'ali, *Shaykhi 'l-Asbaq*, pp. 11–12.
60. 'Coalition Forces Kill Turki al-Bin' ali', US Central Command, 20 June 2017, www.centcom.mil/MEDIA/PRESS-RELEASES/Press-Release-View/Article/1220221/coalition-forces-killed-turki-al-bin-ali/.
61. See his letter to the Delegated Committee (al-Lajna al-Mufawwada), dated 19 May 2017, at http://www.jihadica.com/wp-content/uploads/2017/09/Binali-letter.pdf. This was part of a theological controversy over *takfir* in which al-Bin'ali's views ultimately prevailed, but not till some months after his death.
62. Bunzel, 'Bin'ali Leaks'.
63. Turki al-Bin'ali, *Muqarrar fi 'l-tawhid*, Hay'at al-Buhuth wa'l-Ifta', 2014/15, http://www.aymennjawad.org/17633/islamic-state-training-camp-textbook-course-in.
64. al-Bin'ali, *Majmu' Fatawa al-Shaykh Abi Humam al-Athari*, pp. 191–4.
65. Bunzel, *The Kingdom and the Caliphate*, p. 12.
66. Munira al-Hudayb, 'al-Dakhiliyya Tuqallis Qa'imat Matlubiha bi''tiqal 'Iqab', *al-Hayat*, 2 May 2016, http://www.alhayat.com/m/story/15376923.
67. Abu Bakr al-Baghdadi, 'Hadha ma Wa'adahu 'llah wa-Rasuluhu', Mu'assasat al-Furqan, 3 November 2016, transcript available at http://www.jihadica.com/wp-content/uploads/2016/11/hadha.pdf.

9. PARRICIDE IN THE KINGDOM: GENEALOGY, NATIONALISM, AND THE ISLAMIC STATE CHALLENGE

1. David Gullette, *The Genealogical Construction of the Kyrgyz Republic: Kinship, State, and 'Tribalism'*, Folkestone: Global Oriental, 2010.
2. C. C. W. Taylor, 'Plato's Totalitarianism', in Richard Kraut (ed.), *Plato's Republic: Critical Essays*, Lanham, MD: Rowman & Littlefield, 1997.
3. John T. Scott and Vickie B. Sullivan, 'Patricide and the Plot of *The Prince*: Cesare Borgia and Machiavelli's Italy', *The American Political Science Review*, 88, 4 (1994).
4. Michael Cook, *Commanding Right and Forbidding Wrong in Islamic Thought*, Cambridge: Cambridge University Press, 2001.

5. For Saudi militants these injunctions are affirmed perhaps more intimately in a declaration by Muhammad ibn 'Abd al-Wahhab (drawn
from Qur'an 58:22): 'Those who assert the unicity of God … and
worship [him] … are not permitted to have friendly relations with
those who turn away from God and his messenger, even if these were
their fathers, sons, brothers, or kin group (*'ashira*).' Muhammad b.
'Abd al-Wahhab, 'Thalathu Masa'il', in *Mu'allafat al-Shaykh al-Imam
Muhammad b. 'Abd al-Wahhab*, vol. 1, Riyadh: Jami'at al-Imam
Muhammad b. Sa'ud al-Islamiyya, 1980, p. 375; in a variant on the
above injunction, Ibn 'Abd al-Wahhab elsewhere writes: 'He who has
pledged obedience to the Prophet and affirmed God's unicity is not
permitted to befriend one who attacked God and his Prophet, even
if [the latter] were his closest kin (*aqraba qarib*)': Muhammad b. 'Abd
al-Wahhab, *al-Usul al-Thalatha*, Amman: Dar 'Ammar, 1990, p. 8.

6. Thomas Friedman, 'Letter from Saudi Arabia', *The New York Times*,
25 November 2015. See also Ibn Salman's *Economist* interview: '[The
House of Saud] are a part of a national process; we are a part of the
local tribes of the country; we are part of the regions in the country;
we have been working together for the past three hundred years':
'Transcript: Interview with Muhammad bin Salman', *The Economist*,
6 January 2016.

7. Nadav Samin, *'Da'wa*, Dynasty, and Destiny in the Arab Gulf',
Comparative Studies in Society and History 58, 4 (2016).

8. Nadav Samin, *Of Sand or Soil: Genealogy and Tribal Belonging in Saudi
Arabia*, Princeton: Princeton University Press, 2015.

9. 'al-Dakhiliyya Tuhaddid Rawatib al-Manasib al-Qabaliyya', *al-Hayat*,
9 October 2015, goo.gl/B2Wycs, (accessed 14 September 2016).

10. 'Khitab Sayf al-Islam al-Qadhdhafi', YouTube, 2 February 2011,
https://www.youtube.com/watch?v=Pp6DFM9_NuU, (accessed 14
September 2016).

11. For a useful examination of the kingdom's tepid experiments with
such associations see Steffen Hertog, 'The New Corporatism in Saudi
Arabia: Limits of Formal Politics', in Abdulhadi Khalaf and Giacomo
Luciani (eds.), *Constitutional Reform and Political Participation in the Gulf*,
Dubai: Gulf Research Center, 2006.

12. Ruth Pike, *Linajudos and Conversos in Seville: Greed and Prejudice in
Sixteenth- and Seventeenth-Century Spain*, New York: Peter Lang, 2000.

13. Dale F. Eickelman, *Knowledge and Power in Morocco: The Education of a
Twentieth Century Notable*, Princeton: Princeton University Press, 1992,
p. 116.

14. 'Rashid Ibrahim al-Sufyan', Twitter, https://twitter.com/alsufaian
(accessed 14 September 2016).

15. 'abdullahfahad1417', Instagram, https://www.instagram.com/abdullah-fahad1417/?hl=en (accessed 14 September 2016).

16. 'Interview with 'Abdallah b. Muhammad al-Rashud', *Sawt al-Jihad* 3, November 2003, pp. 15–16; Osama Bin Laden, 'The Betrayal of Palestine', in Bruce Lawrence (ed.), *Messages to the World: The Statements of Osama Bin Laden*, London: Verso, 2005, pp. 3–14. An exception to this rhetorical deference is Bin Laden's interview with an Australian magazine in 1996, which Lawrence titles 'The Saudi Regime'.

17. '"Where is Khaled?" The English-subtitled interview', YouTube, 5 April 2011, https://www.youtube.com/watch?v=mxinAxWxXo8, (accessed 14 September 2016).

18. 'Interview with 'Abd al-'Aziz al-Muqrin', *Sawt al-Jihad* 1, September 2003, p. 22. The critique of state paternalism was also advanced by Juhayman al-'Utaybi in one of his pamphlets, *Risalat al-Imara wa-l-Bay'a*. There, he laments the fact that government positions are the 'sole source of sustenance' for religious scholars, who take them on the condition that they make no controversial claims and that they assert their moral authority against any challengers to the state. 'Utaybi's group grew to shun all government employment and condemned anyone who partook of it. See Juhayman al-'Utaybi, *Risalat al-Imara wa-l-Bay'a wa-l-Ta'a wa-Hukm Talbis al-Hukkam 'ala Talabat al-'Ilm wa-l-'Amma*, http://www.ilmway.com/site/maqdis/MS_20536.html (accessed 14 September 2016).

19. According to a well-known hadith, the Prophet Muhammad said to a supporter on the issue of tribal pride, 'Leave it alone, for it is a stinking matter (*muntina*).'

20. It is rumoured that al-Shatiri was later fired for unspecified transgressions by the Hay'a's director, 'Abd al-Latif Al al-Shaykh.

21. 'Sa'd al-Shatiri', Twitter, https://twitter.com/saaad10111 (accessed 14 September 2016).

22. Saad Abdullah Sowayan, 'Tonight My Gun is Loaded: Poetic Dueling in Arabia', *Oral Tradition*, 4, 1–2 (1989). In view of Sowayan's observations concerning the diminished gravity of *riddiyya* thematics in the oil age, we might observe here a return to consequence for that poetic form.

23. The Shutr, Sa'd al-Shatiri's kin group, are a sub-clan of the Mutayr Bedouin tribal confederation. While the Mutayr have a long history of opposition to Saudi domination, their leader during the Ikhwan revolt, Qad'an ibn Darwish, sided with Ibn Saud. See John S. Habib, *Ibn Saud's Warriors of Islam*, Leiden: Brill, 1979, p. 171.

24. Here the poet critiques the pursuit of tribal or national glory (*majd*).

25. *Ta's*, i.e. Bedouin-origin youth.

26. 'al-Radd 'ala 'Abid Al Sa'ud: Ya 'Asib al-Ra's, Waynak?', YouTube,

23 July 2014, https://www.youtube.com/watch?v=KcvNKE28IVw (accessed 14 September 2016).

27. 'Ya 'Asib al-Ra's' has been parodied multiple times. It has also been adapted by al-Nusra militants in a polemic against ISIS, by the Iraqi Shi'a militia movement al-Hashd al-Sha'bi after the 2016 reconquest of Fallujah, and by a Jordanian Ba'athist poet in commemoration of Saddam Hussein's 'assassination'. Significantly, the chant has been adopted by a Chadian ISIS bard in Benghazi, Libya and repurposed for ISIS's Libyan campaign.

28. The Special Forces are still referred to by the older poets as Nayif's soldiers or hawks (*suqur Nayif*), after their presumed boss, the late Saudi interior minister Nayif ibn 'Abd al-'Aziz. In perhaps classic patrimonial fashion, they are now known officially, or at least were until recently, as Suqur Muhammad ibn Nayif.

29. 'Jadid: Radd Qawi min Shabab Qabilat Harb 'ala Da'ish', YouTube, 24 July 2014, https://www.youtube.com/watch?v=bSvOP_ZAclI (accessed 14 September 2016).

30. 'Jadid: Radd Shabab al-Sa'udiyya Ha'il al-Shammari 2015 'ala Da'ish', YouTube, 26 July 2014, https://www.youtube.com/watch?v=voD6fqjn8XY (accessed 14 September 2016).

31. i.e., 'Anazi.

32. 'Radd 'Iyal Wayil 'ala Da'ish', YouTube, 27 July 2014, https://www.youtube.com/watch?v=N1HiqQE6Mao (accessed 14 September 2016).

33. 'Radd Juhayna ['] #Da'ish', YouTube, 30 July 2014, https://www.youtube.com/watch?v=ymqdZeJpU6g (accessed 14 September 2016).

34. Abu Mit'ib, i.e., the late King 'Abdullah ibn 'Abd al-'Aziz (d. 2014). His son Mit'ib led the Saudi Arabian National Guard (SANG).

35. 'Radd Bani Sulaym 'ala Da'ish: Ya 'Asib al-Ra's Waylak', YouTube, 27 July 2014, https://www.youtube.com/watch?v=GjOlEMx9WUI (accessed 14 September 2016).

36. 'Ya 'Asib al-Ra's Waynak', YouTube, 9 August 2014, https://www.youtube.com/watch?v=ZK8cN0iddVs (accessed 14 September 2016).

37. *Chalbin yuqawwad* is perhaps a reference to popular YouTube parody videos of dogs driving cars, as invoked by a young 'Utaybi poet, Abu Dhib al-'Atawi, who shares a surname with the famous vernacular (*nabati*) bard, Shlaywih al-'Atawi.

38. 'Ya 'Asib al-Ra's Waynak li-Abu Dhib al-'Atawi al-Rawqi', YouTube, 23 October 2014, https://www.youtube.com/watch?v=HBjYu9sDKtY (accessed 14 September 2016).

39. 'Qasida: Da'ish/Takfa', YouTube, 6 October 2015, https://www.youtube.com/watch?v=6hxacMBOEnI (accessed 14 September 2016).

40. Sunaytan addresses this point indirectly in his discussion of the varied connotations of the term Bedouin. Muhammad ibn Sunaytan, *al-*

Sa'udiyya: al-Siyasi wa-l-Qabila, Beirut: Arab Network for Research and Publishing, 2008, p. 26.

41. Kingdom of Saudi Arabia, 'The Basic Law of Governance', Ministry of Foreign Affairs, goo.gl/kGaQaa (accessed 14 September 2016).

42. Bernard Haykel et al., 'Introduction', in Bernard Haykel et al. (eds.), *Saudi Arabia in Transition: Insights on Social, Political, Economic and Religious Change*, Cambridge: Cambridge University Press, 2015, p. 41.

43. Toby C. Jones, 'The Dogma of Development: Technopolitics and Power in Saudi Arabia', in Haykel et al. (eds.), *Saudi Arabia in Transition*, p. 35.

44. Pascal Ménoret, *Joyriding in Riyadh: Oil, Urbanism, and Road Revolt*, Cambridge: Cambridge University Press, 2014, p. 116. Al-Rasheed considers the doctrine of Saudi exceptionalism in the context of the kingdom's gender politics, finding it to be more durable than do Jones and Menoret, yet no less ideological in origin and nature. Madawi Al-Rasheed, 'Caught Between Religion and State: Women in Saudi Arabia', in Haykel et al. (eds.), *Saudi Arabia in Transition*, pp. 305–6.

45. Jacob Collins, 'French Liberalism's "Indian Detour": Louis Dumont, the Individual, and Liberal Political Thought in Post-1968 France', *Modern Intellectual History* 12, 3 (2015).

46. Samin, *Of Sand or Soil*, chap. 2.

47. Scott and Sullivan, 'Patricide and the Plot of *The Prince*', p. 891.

48. This verse is absent from the 1 August 2014 version of the recitation, which was performed in front of several hundred Islamic State militants.

49. A shame, as opposed to a blessing.

10. SAUDI ARABIA AND THE COLD WAR

1. Toby Matthiesen is Senior Research Fellow in the International Relations of the Middle East at St Antony's College, University of Oxford. He is the author of *Sectarian Gulf: Bahrain, Saudi Arabia, and the Arab Spring That Wasn't* (2013) and *The Other Saudis: Shiism, Dissent and Sectarianism* (2015). toby.matthiesen@sant.ox.ac.uk. I would like to thank Helen Lackner, Avi Shlaim and the participants of the conference for their insightful comments on an earlier version of the paper.

2. Cited after Rachel Bronson, *Thicker than Oil: America's Uneasy Relationship with Saudi Arabia*, New York: Oxford University Press, 2006, p. 46.

3. Telegram From the Department of State to the Embassy in Saudi Arabia, Washington, 26 February 1966, National Archives and Records Administration, RG 59, Central Files 1964–66, POL 23–7 NEARE; https://history.state.gov/historicaldocuments/frus1964–68v21/d262.

4. William Simpson, *The Prince: The Secret Story of the World's Most Intriguing Royal, Prince Bandar bin Sultan*, New York: Regan Books, 2006, p. 112.

5. Odd Arne Westad, *The Global Cold War: Third World Interventions and the Making of Our Times*, Cambridge: Cambridge University Press, 2007.

6. Rachel Bronson is one of the few authors to emphasise this Cold War connection, stating that 'in many ways September 11 was the price we paid for winning the Cold War and the strategies we chose': Bronson, *Thicker than Oil*, pp. 3, 9. An edited volume that surveyed the field, for example, does not include a chapter on Saudi Arabia: see Yezid Sayigh and Avi Shlaim (eds.), *The Cold War and the Middle East*, 2nd edn, Oxford: Oxford University Press, 2003. Saudi Arabia is also hardly ever mentioned in Westad's otherwise remarkable account (Westad, *The Global Cold War*).

7. John Baldry, 'Soviet Relations with Saudi Arabia and the Yemen, 1917–1938', *Middle Eastern Studies* 20, 1 (1984), pp. 53–80; Fahd al-Qahtani, *Shuiu'iyyun fi al-Su'udiyya: Dirāsa fi al-'Alaqat al-Sufitiyya al-Su'udiyya*, n.p.: n.p., 1988.

8. Of the three kings, only Ibn Saud was to die while in office, and the revolution that overthrew Emperor Haile Selassie in 1974 was to lead to a major Saudi Cold War intervention in the Horn of Africa.

9. See, for example, Louise Fawcett, *Iran and the Cold War: The Azerbaijan Crisis of 1946*, Cambridge: Cambridge University Press, 1992.

10. David S. Painter, 'Oil, Resources, and the Cold War, 1945–1962', in Melvyn P. Leffler and Odd Arne Westad (eds.), *The Cambridge History of the Cold War*, vol. I: *Origins*, Cambridge: Cambridge University Press, 2012, pp. 486–507.

11. Robert Vitalis, *America's Kingdom: Mythmaking on the Saudi Oil Frontier*, 2nd edn, London: Verso, 2009.

12. I should like to thank Gregory Gause for reiterating this point. The USA and Britain, through their foreign intelligence services (in particular the CIA and MI6) and with the help of the American- and British-owned oil companies, devised a sophisticated 'oil denial' policy in the Persian Gulf region (including in Iraq, Iran, Saudi Arabia, and the smaller Gulf States). Under this policy, undercover agents were embedded within the oil companies, and trained to either destroy or plug oil wells in case of war. 'US, Britain Developed Plans to Disable or Destroy Middle Eastern Oil Facilities from Late 1940s to Early 1960s in Event of a Soviet Invasion', *National Security Archive*, 23 June 2016, http://nsarchive.gwu.edu/NSAEBB/NSAEBB552-US-and-Britain-planned-to-destroy-Middle-East-oil-facilities-in-case-of-Soviet-invasion-from-1940s-1960s.

13. Adam Hanieh, *Capitalism and Class in the Gulf Arab States*, New York: Palgrave Macmillan, 2011, chaps. 1 and 2.

14. David E. Spiro, *The Hidden Hand of American Hegemony: Petrodollar Recycling and International Markets*, Ithaca: Cornell University Press, 1999.

15. At Saudi Arabia's request, the holdings of all OPEC states were listed together so that the Saudi share would not directly be identifiable: 'The Untold Story behind Saudi Arabia's 41-Year US Debt Secret', Bloomberg, 31 May 2016, http://www.bloomberg.com/news/features/2016–05–30/the-untold-story-behind-saudi-arabia-s-41-year-u-s-debt-secret. See also 'Saudi Arabia's Secret Holdings of US Debt are Suddenly a Big Deal', Bloomberg, 22 January 2016, http://www.bloomberg.com/news/articles/2016–01–22/u-s-is-hiding-treasury-bond-data-that-s-suddenly-become-crucial. As of 2016, OPEC states were listed individually, and Saudi Arabia held around $100bn in US debt: 'Major Foreign Holders of Treasury Securities', Department of the Treasury/Federal Reserve Board, 18 January 2017, http://ticdata.treasury.gov/Publish/mfh.txt.

16. Toby Jones, 'Shifting Sands', *Foreign Affairs* (March/April 2006), https://www.foreignaffairs.com/reviews/review-essay/2006–03–01/shifting-sands.

17. Dianne Kirby (ed.), *Religion and the Cold War*, Basingstoke, Palgrave, 2003; Philip Emil Muehlenbeck (ed.), *Religion and the Cold War: A Global Perspective*, Nashville: Vanderbilt University Press, 2012.

18. Joyce Battle, *US Propaganda in the Middle East: The Early Cold War Version*, National Security Archive Electronic Briefing Book No. 78 (13 December 2002). The files that are cited in subsequent footnotes and that are available on the National Security Archive website are also discussed in this National Security Archive briefing.

19. United States, National Security Council, Executive Secretary Report to the United States, National Security Council, 'United States Objectives and Policies with Respect to the Arab States and Israel' [Annex to NSC 129], 7 April 1952, http://nsarchive.gwu.edu/NSAEBB/NSAEBB78/propaganda%20059.pdf.

20. United States Consulate General, Dhahran (Saudi Arabia), Letter from William A. Eddy to Dorothy Thompson, 7 June 1951. Source: National Archives, Record Group 59, Records of the Department of State, Lot Files, 57 D 298, http://nsarchive.gwu.edu/NSAEBB/NSAEBB78/propaganda%20026.pdf.

21. Cited after Bronson, *Thicker than Oil*, pp. 26f.

22. Bronson, *Thicker than Oil*, pp. 45f.

23. Department of State, Bureau of Near Eastern and South Asian Affairs, Office of Near Eastern Affairs, Memorandum from Frederick Awalt to Samuel K. C. Kopper, 'Conversation with Prince Saud', 10 March

1952. Source: National Archives, Record Group 59, Records of the Department of State, Lot File 57 D 298, http://nsarchive.gwu.edu/NSAEBB/NSAEBB78/propaganda%20055.pdf.

24. Bronson, *Thicker than Oil*, pp. 74–7.
25. Simon M. W. Collier, 'Countering Communist and Nasserite Propaganda: The Foreign Office Information Research Department in the Middle East and Africa, 1954–1963', Ph.D. thesis, University of Hertfordshire, 2013.
26. See, for example, Department of State, Cable from Dean Acheson to the United States Embassy, Egypt, 11 February 1952. Source: National Archives, Record Group 59, Records of the Department of State, Decimal Files, 1950–1954, http://nsarchive.gwu.edu/NSAEBB/NSAEBB78/propaganda%20053.pdf.
27. Deepa Kumar, 'The Right Kind of "Islam": News media representations of US-Saudi relations during the Cold War', *Journalism Studies*, (Published online: 05 Dec 2016).
28. There are a few exceptions, such as Reinhard Schulze, *Islamischer Internationalismus im 20. Jahrhundert: Untersuchungen zur Geschichte der Islamischen Weltliga*, Leiden: Brill, 1990 and Michael Farquhar, 'Saudi Petrodollars, Spiritual Capital, and the Islamic University of Medina: A Wahhabi Missionary Project in Transnational Perspective', *International Journal of Middle East Studies* 47, 4 (2015), pp. 701–21. Then there are a number of biographies praising Faysal such as Joseph Kéchichian, *Faysal: Saudi Arabia's King for All Seasons*, Gainesville: University Press of Florida, 2008. In an ironic twist, former Pravda correspondent and frequent visitor to the People's Democratic Republic of Yemen and the liberated areas of Dhofar, and historian of Saudi Arabia, Alexei Vassiliev, eventually also ended up writing a biography of Faysal: Alexei Vassiliev, *King Faisal of Saudi Arabia: Personality, Faith and Times*, London: Saqi Books, 2012.
29. Quoted after Bronson, *Thicker than Oil*, p. 181.
30. Malcolm Kerr, *The Arab Cold War: Gamal 'Abd al-Nasir and his Rivals, 1958–1970*, 3rd edn, Oxford: Oxford University Press, 1971.
31. Jesse Ferris, *Nasser's Gamble: How Intervention in Yemen Caused the Six-Day War and the Decline of Egyptian Power*, Princeton: Princeton University Press, 2013; Eugene Rogan and Tewfik Aclimandos, 'The Yemen war and Egypt's war preparedness in June 1967' in Wm. Roger Louis and Avi Shlaim (eds.), *The 1967 Arab-Israeli War: Origins and Consequences*, Cambridge: Cambridge University Press, 2012, pp. 149–164.
32. Ferris, *Nasser's Gamble*, pp. 114f.
33. Ferris, *Nasser's Gamble*, p. 108. For more on this period, in particular shifting US relations with Saudi Arabia and Arab nationalism, see

Nathan J. Citino, *From Arab Nationalism to OPEC: Eisenhower, King Saud, and the Making of US–Saudi Relations*, Bloomington: Indiana University Press, 2002; Salim Yaqub, *Containing Arab Nationalism: The Eisenhower Doctrine and the Middle East*, Chapel Hill: University of North Carolina Press, 2004.

34. Sarah Yizraeli, *The Remaking of Saudi Arabia: The Struggle between King Saud and Crown Prince Faysal, 1953–1962*, Tel Aviv: Moshe Dayan Center for Middle Eastern and African Studies, 1997.

35. Kamal Hasim, 'The ARAMCO (Letter from Saudi Arabia)', *World Marxist Review* 5 (May 1962), pp. 88f.

36. On 1 January 1964 the *'ulama'* reached a decision concerning the dispute between Saud and Faysal. But this did not resolve the conflict, and on 29 March 1964 the twelve leading *'ulama'* including the grand mufti issued a fatwa declaring that Saud should remain king in a nominal capacity, but that all affairs of internal and foreign politics should be handled by Faysal, the crown prince and prime minister. FO 371/174671/BS1015/14.

37. FO 371/174671/BS1015/41. For an analysis of this paradox, and of Saudi Arabia's complicated relationship with the NAM, see Gulshan Dhanani, 'Saudi Arabia and Non-Alignment', *International Studies* 20, 1–2 (1981), pp. 361–9.

38. Ferris, *Nasser's Gamble*, p. 261; Joseph Mann, 'King without a Kingdom: Deposed King Saud and His Intrigues', *Studia Orientalia Electronica* 1 (2013), pp. 26–40.

39. Stephanie Cronin, *Armies and State Building in the Modern Middle East: Politics, Nationalism and Military Reform*, London: I. B. Tauris, 2014, pp. 224–232; Toby Matthiesen, 'Migration, Minorities and Radical Networks: Labour Movements and Opposition Groups in Saudi Arabia, 1950–1975', *International Review of Social History* 59, 3 (Autumn 2014), pp. 473–504.

40. The first massive sale was agreed in December 1965: Bronson, *Thicker than Oil*, pp. 94–6.

41. Fred Halliday, *Revolution and Foreign Policy: The Case of South Yemen 1967–1987*, Cambridge: Cambridge University Press, 1990; Toby Matthiesen, 'Red Arabia: Anti-Colonialism, the Cold War, and the Long Sixties in the Gulf States', in: Chen Jian, Martin Klimke, Masha Kirasirova, Mary Nolan, Marilyn Young, Joanna Waley-Cohen, eds., *Routledge Handbook of the Global Sixties* (eds.), *Routledge Handbook of the Global Sixties* (London: Routledge, 2018, pp. 94–105). Abdel Razzaq Takriti, *Monsoon Revolution: Republicans, Sultans, and Empires in Oman 1965–1976*, Oxford: Oxford University Press, 2013.

42. See, for example, From American Embassy Jidda, to Secretary of State,

Washington, 'Faisal Visit: King's Preoccupation with Zionism–
Communism', 23 May 1971, RG 59, 1970–3, Political and Defense,
Box 2585, POL 7 SAUD; and William P. Rogers, 'Memorandum for
the President', 24 May 1971, RG 59, 1970–3, Political and Defense,
Box 2585, POL 7 SAUD, National Archives at College Park, Maryland.
They were also worried about cooperation between the left wing of
the Syrian Ba'ath Party and the PDRY on the Arabian Peninsula. See
Joseph Mann, 'The Syrian Neo-Ba'th Regime and the Kingdom of Saudi
Arabia, 1966–70', *Middle Eastern Studies* 42, 5 (2006), pp. 761–76.

43. Despite, or perhaps because, of the cooptation of a number of leftists, the Soviet Union and its allies encouraged the remaining Saudi
communists to constitute a formal communist party, the CPSA, which
received limited Soviet support until the collapse of the Soviet Union.
See Toby Matthiesen, 'Marxists in the Land of the Two Holy Places:
The Communist Party of Saudi Arabia, 1975–1991', *Journal of Cold
War Studies* (forthcoming).

44. Already during the March 1964 crisis, Omar Saqqaf and Kamal Adham
were sent to Beirut to prepare Arab opinion and to possibly arrange
a place of exile for King Saud. C. T. Crowe, Report of the Recent
Political Crisis, Jeddah, 2 April 1964, FO 371/174671/BS1015/18.
Kamal Adham was also in regular contact with the British embassy:
FO 371/174671/BS1015/29.

45. For more on Adham see David Holden and Richard Johns, *The House
of Saud*, London: Sidgwick & Jackson, 1981.

46. Holden and Johns, *The House of Saud*, p. 292f.; Owen L. Sirrs, *The
Egyptian Intelligence Service: A History of the Mukhabarat, 1910–2009*,
Abingdon: Routledge, 2010, p. 137; Joseph Kéchichian, 'The Man
behind the Scenes', *Gulf News*, 12 February 2010, http://gulfnews.
com/news/uae/general/the-man-behind-the-scenes-1.581564.

47. SOVIET MILITARY MISSION FOR NORTH YEMEN, 9 December
1974, 1974STATE269636, https://wikileaks.org/plusd/cables/1974
STATE269636_b.htm.

48. For more see Jonathan Beaty and S. C. Gwynne, *The Outlaw Bank: A
Wild Ride into the Secret Heart of BCCI*, New York: Random House,
1993.

49. Naif Bin Hethlain, *Saudi Arabia and the US since 1962: Allies in Conflict*,
London: Saqi, 2010, p. 190.

50. Nancy Mitchell, *Jimmy Carter in Africa: Race and the Cold War*, Washington
DC: Woodrow Wilson Center/Cold War International History Project,
2016.

51. Houchang Chehabi, 'South Africa and Iran in the Apartheid Era',
Journal of Southern African Studies 42, 4 (2016), pp. 687–709; Mohamed

Heikal, *The Return of the Ayatollah: The Iranian Revolution from Mossadeq to Khomeini*, London: André Deutsch, 1981, p. 112.

52. For the Cuban involvement in these conflicts see Piero Gleijeses, *Conflicting Missions: Havana, Washington, and Africa, 1959–1976*, Chapel Hill: University of North Carolina Press, 2002; Piero Gleijeses, *Visions of Freedom: Havana, Washington, Pretoria and the Struggle for Southern Africa, 1976–1991*, Chapel Hill: University of North Carolina Press, 2013.

53. MOROCCAN REQUEST FOR ASSISTANCE IN FINANCING ARMS PURCHASES, 14 May 1974, https://wikileaks.org/plusd/cables/1974STATE099959_b.html; MOROCCAN REQUEST FOR ASSISTANCE IN FINANCING ARMS, 19 May 1974, https://wikileaks.org/plusd/cables/1974JIDDA02742_b.html.

54. John Cooley, *Unholy Wars: Afghanistan, America and International Terrorism*, 3rd edn, London: Pluto Press, 2002, pp. 15–18.

55. Interview with Turki al-Faysal, cited in Robert Lacey, *Inside the Kingdom: Kings, Clerics, Modernists, Terrorists and the Struggle for Saudi Arabia*, London: Penguin, 2009, p. 66.

56. Heikal has given the earliest and so far most extensive account of the Safari Club, based on documents he was able to access in Iran after the revolution. Apart from Adham for Saudi Arabia, the agreement was signed by General Nassiri, head of SAVAK, for Iran, the director of intelligence for Egypt, Ahmed Duleimi, director of intelligence for Morocco, and Comte de Marenches for France. Cited after Heikal, *The Return of the Ayatollah*, pp. 113   f., 116.

57. Heikal, *The Return of the Ayatollah*, p. 114.

58. 'The Horn of Africa', Presidential Review Memorandum/NSC-21, 1 April 1977, http://nsarchive.gwu.edu/carterbrezhnev/docs_global_competition/Tab%202/19770401%20-%20The%20Horn%20of%20Africa,%20Presidential%20Review%20Memorandum.pdf; Donna R. Jackson, *Jimmy Carter and the Horn of Africa: Cold War Policy in Ethiopia and Somalia*, Jefferson: McFarland, 2007. For the Horn of Africa–Yemen–Saudi nexus see Holden and Johns, *The House of Saud*, pp. 467–78; and Jeffrey A. Lefebvre, 'Middle East Conflicts and Middle Level Power Intervention in the Horn of Africa', *Middle East Journal*, 50, 3 (Summer 1996), pp. 387–404.

59. Radoslav A. Yordanov, *The Soviet Union and the Horn of Africa during the Cold War: Between Ideology and Pragmatism*, Lanham, MD: Lexington, 2016.

60. Miriam M. Müller, *A Spectre is Haunting Arabia: How the Germans Brought their Communism to Yemen*, Bielefeld: Transcript Verlag, 2015, pp. 300f.

61. Zbigniew Brzezinski, *Power and Principle: Memoirs of the National Security Adviser, 1977–81*, New York: Farrar, Straus & Giroux, 1983, p. 181, cited in Bin Hethlain, *Saudi Arabia and the US since 1962*, p. 191.

62. Heikal, *The Return of the Ayatollah*, p. 114.
63. Sensing the momentum and the geostrategic importance of the Horn of Africa, parts of the European New Left supported the revolution, including Fred Halliday, a key advocate and scholar of leftist movements in the Persian Gulf and the Arabian Peninsula. See Fred Halliday and Maxine Molyneux, *The Ethiopian Revolution*, London: Verso, 1982.
64. Heikal, *The Return of the Ayatollah*, pp. 115f.; Saudi–US Relations Information Service (SUSRIS), 'Perspectives on Conflicts, Cooperation and Crises: A Conversation with Saudi Arabia's New Ambassador to the United States, Part 2', 2 March 2006, http://susris.com/articles/2006/interviews/060314-turki-interview-2.html.
65. David E. Long, *The United States and Saudi Arabia: Ambivalent Allies*, Boulder, CO: Westview Press, 1985, p. 123. For a detailed study of Saudi foreign policy towards and religious networks in Ethiopia see Haggai Erlich, *Saudi Arabia and Ethiopia: Islam, Christianity, and Politics Entwined* (Boulder, CO: Lynne Rienner, 2007).
66. See Bronson, *Thicker than Oil*, pp. 132–6.
67. Simpson, *The Prince*, pp. 124–6.
68. Bin Hethlain, *Saudi Arabia and the US since 1962*, pp. 191f.
69. The role of Morocco and Hassan II is particularly noteworthy. Heikal, *The Return of the Ayatollah*, p. 116.
70. See, for example, EGYPT—THE LIMITS OF SAUDI INFLUENCE AND ASAD, 15 August 1976, https://wikileaks.org/plusd/cables/1976CAIRO10937_b.html. Another US diplomatic cable claims that the Saudi–Egyptian relationship was primarily handled by Kamal Adham on the Saudi side and Ashraf Marwan on the Egyptian side. See SAUDI–EGYPTIAN CONNECTION, 1 September 1977, https://wikileaks.org/plusd/cables/1977CAIRO14610_c.html. Ashraf Marwan was later exposed as an Israeli spy, who passed information on the 1973 war plans to Israel, and who died in London in 2007 under mysterious circumstances: Uri Bar-Joseph, *The Angel: The Egyptian Spy who Saved Israel*, [[New York]]: HarperCollins, 2016.
71. Bronson, *Thicker than Oil*, pp. 177–81.
72. Bronson, *Thicker than Oil*, pp. 183–5; Bin Hethlain, *Saudi Arabia and the US since 1962*, pp. 193f. Simpson, *The Prince*, pp. 111–22.
73. Prince Bandar seems to have told his biographer that he personally handed over a suitcase with $10 million in cash to a priest at the Vatican Bank during a journey to Rome in 1983. He claims that this was money that had been overpaid by Saudi Arabia during the al-Yamamah deal with BAE systems and thus ended up being untraceable cash. This money was allegedly used to support the Christian Democrats' election campaign in order to keep the Italian Communist Party in

check. According to Bandar, this was an American plan that was decided upon by US president Ronald Reagan, British prime minister Margaret Thatcher, and Saudi crown prince Fahd. Saudi Arabia was asked to supply the money, so there was 'a deniability factor, because you would never see American fingerprints—or the British—on it.' According to Bandar, CIA director William Casey contacted him, and he obtained permission to go ahead from Fahd, and then carried out the mission: Simpson, *The Prince*, pp. 99–101, 148–50. David Ottaway, however, questions the account, arguing that it may not have been related to the general election of 1983 but the local elections of May 1985. He also states that US officials denied having had any knowledge of this: David Ottaway, *King's Messenger: Prince Bandar Bin Sultan and America's Tangled Relationship with Saudi Arabia*, New York: Walker & Company, 2008, pp. 62f.

74. Bronson, *Thicker than Oil*, pp. 135f.
75. Takriti, *Monsoon Revolution*.
76. Sirrs, *The Egyptian Intelligence Service*, pp. 140–2.
77. This is not the place to tell the story of the Saudi involvement in the Afghan jihad. For detailed accounts see, amongst others, Steve Coll, *Ghost Wars: The Secret History of the CIA, Afghanistan, and bin Laden, from the Soviet Invasion to September 10, 2001*, London: Penguin, 2005; Panagiotis Dimitrakis, *The Secret War in Afghanistan: The Soviet Union, China and Anglo-American Intelligence in the Afghan War*, London: I. B. Tauris, 2013; Thomas Hegghammer, *Jihad in Saudi Arabia: Violence and Pan-Islamism since 1979*, Cambridge: Cambridge University Press, 2010, pp. 24–30; and Bin Hethlain, *Saudi Arabia and the US since 1962*, pp. 123–49.
78. Saudi Arabia, however, maintained informal ties with Yugoslavia and Romania, and had good economic relations with the latter: *The Guardian*, 30 March 1985, Foreign Broadcast Information Service (FBIS).
79. Richard F. Staar (ed.), *1989 Yearbook on International Communist Affairs*, Stanford, CA: Hoover Institution, 1989, p. 499.
80. The sale was eventually revealed in the *Washington Post* in March 1988: Simpson, *The Prince*, pp. 152–67; Khaled bin Sultan and Patrick Seale, *Desert Warrior: A Personal View of the Gulf War by the Joint Forces Commander*, London: HarperCollins, 1995, pp. 137–152.
81. I thank Shuang Wen and Engseng Ho for drawing my attention to this point. See also Makio Yamada, 'Taiwan's Relations with Saudi Arabia: An Interview with Ibrahim Chao', 8 December, 2014, *Middle East Institute*, http://www.mei.edu/content/map/taiwan%E2%80%99s-relations-saudi-arabia-interview-ibrahim-chao. For background see

Naser M. al-Tamimi, *China–Saudi Arabia Relations, 1990–2012: Marriage of Convenience or Strategic Alliance?*, Abingdon: Routledge, 2014; Mohammed Turki Al-Sudairi, 'Sino-Saudi Relations: An Economic History', *GRC Papers*, August 2012.

82. 'Saudis Cultivate Ties with Kremlin', *The New York Times*, 5 December 1990.

83. Sonoko Sunayama, *Syria and Saudi Arabia: Collaboration and Conflicts in the Oil Era*, London: I. B. Tauris, 2007, p. 93.

84. Stéphane Lacroix, *Awakening Islam: The Politics of Religious Dissent in Contemporary Saudi Arabia*, Cambridge, MA: Harvard University Press, 2011; Madawi Al-Rasheed, *Contesting the Saudi State: Islamic Voices from a New Generation*, Cambridge: Cambridge University Press, 2007. For Saudi Arabia and the war see also Alan Munro, *An Arabian Affair: Politics and Diplomacy behind the Gulf War*, London: Brassey's, 1996; Khaled bin Sultan and Patrick Seale, *Desert Warrior: A Personal View of the Gulf War by the Joint Forces Commander*, London: HarperCollins, 1995.

85. For the primacy of Iran over Saudi Arabia in American Persian Gulf and broader Middle East Cold War strategy during the 1970s see Roham Alvandi, *Nixon, Kissinger, and the Shah: The United States and Iran in the Cold War*, Oxford: Oxford University Press, 2014.

11. KING SALMAN AND HIS SON: WINNING THE USA, LOSING THE REST

1. Simon Henderson, 'Young Saudi Leader's Landmark US Visit', Washington Institute, 13 June 2016, http://www.washingtoninstitute. org/policy-analysis/view/young-saudi-leaders-landmark-u.s.-visit (accessed 18 June 2017).

2. Julie Hirschfield Davis, 'Trump Meets Saudi Prince as US and Kingdom Seek Warmer Relations', *The New York Times*, 14 March 2017, https:// www.nytimes.com/2017/03/14/world/middleeast/mohammed-bin-salman-saudi-arabia-trump.html (accessed 18 June 2017).

3. Yara Bayoumy, 'Obama Administration Arms Sales Offers to Saudi Top $115 Billion', Reuters, 7 September 2016, http://www.reuters.com/ article/us-usa-saudi-security-idUSKCN11D2JQ (accessed 20 June 2017).

4. For the main points of Trump's speech see 'Donald Trump's Saudi Arabia Speech: Eight Key Points', *The Telegraph*, 21 May 2017, http://www. telegraph.co.uk/news/2017/05/21/donald-trumps-saudi-arabia-speech-eight-key-points/ (accessed 18 July 2017).

5. 'Donald Trump's Saudi Arabia Speech'.

6. 'Donald Trump's Saudi Arabia Speech'.

7. Jennifer Peck, 'Do Foreign Gifts Buy Corporate Political Action? Evidence from the Saudi Crude Discount Program', Job Market Paper, 2012, available at http://economics.mit.edu/files/8300 (accessed 25 September 2017).

8. Jeffrey Goldberg, 'The Obama Doctrine', *The Atlantic*, April 2016, https://www.theatlantic.com/magazine/archive/2016/04/the-obama-doctrine/471525/ (accessed 25 August 2017).

9. Seung Min Kim, 'Congress Hands Obama First Veto Override', *New York Times*, 9 September 2016, https://www.nytimes.com/2017/06/13/world/middleeast/trump-weapons-saudi-arabia.html?mcubz=0 (accessed 26 September 2017).

10. Matt Broomfield, 'UK Arms Sales to Saudi Arabia Worth 5.6 Billion under David Cameron', *The Independent*, 6 January 2016, http://www.independent.co.uk/news/uk/politics/uk-has-sold-56bn-of-military-hardware-to-saudi-arabia-under-david-cameron-research-reveals-a6797861.html (accessed 12 June 2017).

11. For an assessment of a 'Macron Doctrine' in the Arab world see Joseph Bahout, 'La difficile définition d'une "doctrine Macron" au Proche-Orient et au Maghreb', *OrientXXI*, 10 July 2017, http://orientxxi.info/magazine/la-difficile-definition-d-une-doctrine-macron-au-proche-orient-et-au-maghreb,1942 (accessed 19 July 2017).

12. Justin Huggler, 'Saudi Arabia Destabilising Arab World, German Intelligence Warns', *The Telegraph*, 2 December 2015, http://www.telegraph.co.uk/news/worldnews/middleeast/saudiarabia/12029546/Saudi-Arabia-destabilising-Arab-world-German-intelligence-warns.html (accessed 12 June 2017).

13. Lizzie Dearden, 'Saudi Arabia and Gulf States Support Islamic Extremism in Germany: Intelligence Report Finds', *The Independent*, 14 December 2016, http://www.independent.co.uk/news/world/europe/saudi-arabia-gulf-states-fund-islamic-extremism-germany-salafism-wahhabism-qatar-kuwait-islamists-a7473551.html (accessed 13 June 2017).

14. Saudi Embassy in Berlin, 'Saudi–German Economic Relations', available at http://www.saudibotschaft.de/en/information-for-german-business/ (accessed 29 August 2017).

15. Timothy Jones, 'Saudi Arabia "Wants No More German Weapons": Report', *DW News*, 30 April 2017, http://www.dw.com/en/saudi-arabia-wants-no-more-german-weapons-report/a-38647662 (accessed 29 August 2017).

16. 'Saudi Prince in Push for Iran Regime Change at Paris Opposition Conference', *Gulf News*, 9 July 2016, http://gulfnews.com/news/mena/iran/saudi-prince-in-push-for-iran-regime-change-at-paris-opposition-conference-1.1859664 (accessed 20 July 2017).

17. Kristian Coates Ulrichsen, 'Israel and the Arab Gulf States: Drivers and Directions of Change', Baker Institute for Public Policy, Rice University, September 2016, https://www.bakerinstitute.org/media/files/research_document/13eaaa71/CME-pub-GCCIsrael-090716.pdf (accessed 20 July 2017).

12. CHINA'S 'RISE' IN THE GULF: A SAUDI PERSPECTIVE

1. Wayne M. Morrison, 'China's Economic Rise: History, Trends, Challenges, and Implications for the United States', Congressional Research Service, https://www.fas.org/sgp/crs/row/RL33534.pdf (accessed 2 September 2016).
2. All figures were calculated by the author based on International Monetary Fund, 'World Economic Outlook Database, April 2017', https://goo.gl/Aq9yIn (accessed 21 April 2017).
3. See IMF, 'World Economic Outlook Database, April 2017'; IEA, 'Oil Market Report, 15 Mar. 2017', https://goo.gl/PdgOLL (accessed 21 April 2017); WTO, 'Trade Recovery Expected in 2017 and 2018, Amid Policy Uncertainty', https://goo.gl/dqGFsv (accessed 21 April 2017).
4. IMF, 'World Economic Outlook Database, April 2017'.
5. IEA, 'Oil Market Report, 15 March 2017'.
6. 'Full Text of Chinese President's Signed Article on Saudi Newspaper', Xinhua, https://goo.gl/OC78xJ (accessed 20 September 2016).
7. 'Full Text of Chinese President's Signed Article on Saudi Newspaper'.
8. 'The Trade Volume between China and Arab Countries Exceeds $ 200 billion in 2015', Xinhua, https://goo.gl/VNI1IQ (accessed 2 September 2016 (in Arabic)).
9. Centre for Economics and Business Research, 'CEBR's World Economic League Table', https://www.cebr.com/welt-2017/ (accessed 9 January 2017).
10. 'China, Saudi Arabia Ink Cooperation Deals', Xinhua, https://goo.gl/nuJ5az (accessed 24 September 2016).
11. 'China, Saudi Arabia Eye $65 billion in Deals as King Visits', Reuters, https://goo.gl/gcgKtY (accessed 21 April 2017).
12. See Saudi Aramco, 'Extending a Long History of Collaboration with China', https://goo.gl/4vG27G (accessed 18 September 2016); 'An Economic Forum in Beijing Discusses the Kingdom's Vision 2030 and the Initiative of One Belt One Road', Saudi News Agency, http://spa.gov.sa/1532924 (accessed 2 September 2016 (in Arabic)).
13. 'Feature: Chinese Technology Contributes to Saudi Arabia's Modernization', Xinhua, https://goo.gl/1oNulw (accessed 22 October 2016).

14. Saudi Ministry of Commerce and Investment, 'Huawei Obtain a Commercial License to Invest in Saudi Arabia', https://goo.gl/6223XS (accessed 21 October 2016).

15. American Enterprise Institute, 'China Global Investment Tracker', https://goo.gl/D6y3ak (accessed 11 January 2016).

16. 'An Economic Forum in Beijing'.

17. BMI Research, *China Going Global: Energy and Infrastructure Round-Up*, London: Business Monitor International, 2017, pp. 22, 25.

18. 'GCC Could Need $560bn of Deficit Finance by 2019', MEED, http://ow.ly/pC7y305fuoM (accessed 17 October 2016).

19. 'IDB Puts Islamic Finance on AIIB Drawing Board', Reuters, https://goo.gl/Yev3uH (accessed 27 October 2016).

20. 'StanChart Starts Direct Trading between Yuan, Saudi Riyal, UAE Dirham', Reuters, https://goo.gl/74hYyC (accessed 29 September 2016).

21. China's Ministry of Commerce, 'The 9th Round of China–GCC FTA Negotiation Concluded in Riyadh Saudi Arabia', https://goo.gl/xiP17R (accessed 9 January 2017).

22. Market Report Company, 'GCC and China to Ink FTA by Land 2016', https://goo.gl/0xKZTh (accessed 3 October 2016).

23. China's Ministry of Commerce, 'The 9th Round of China–GCC FTA Negotiation Concluded'.

24. US Energy Information Administration (EIA), 'Annual Energy Outlook 2016', https://www.eia.gov/forecasts/aeo/ (accessed 20 September 2016); IEA, 'Oil Market Report, 15 March 2017'.

25. 'Foreign Oil Dependence Up', *China Daily*, https://goo.gl/bDEIEv (accessed 23 April 2016).

26. 'IEA Warns of Capacity Squeeze Unless Investment "Rebounds Sharply"', *MEES*, https://goo.gl/4hh29z (accessed 21 April 2017).

27. 'IEA Warns of Capacity Squeeze Unless Investment "Rebounds Sharply"'.

28. 'IEA Warns of Capacity Squeeze Unless Investment "Rebounds Sharply"'.

29. BP, 'Energy Outlook 2035', https://goo.gl/VNJnKi (accessed 24 April 2017).

30. BP, 'Energy Outlook 2035'.

31. See Wang Yilin, 'Changes in China', China Oil & Gas, https://goo.gl/aBi1w4 (accessed 22 October 2016); Tian Chunrong, 'Oil Import and Export in China', China Oil & Gas, https://goo.gl/0Igjfe (accessed 22 October 2016); Wang Zhen, Zhang An, and Liu Mingming, 'China Crude Oil Imports and Oil Market-Oriented Reform', China Oil & Gas, https://goo.gl/7YokQo (accessed 22 October 2016); 'China's

Decline in Oil Production Echoes Globally', *Wall Street Journal*, https://goo.gl/rNf2AF (accessed 17 October 2016); 'A $24 Billion China Refinery Sees a Great Future in Plastics', Bloomberg, https://goo.gl/ZSp7xq (accessed 22 September 2016); and 'Low Oil Price Fuels Chinese Imports and Exports', *The Wall Street Journal*, https://goo.gl/vhzQQG (accessed 23 October 2016).

32. 'Chinese Crude Imports ('000 B/D)', *MEES*, https://goo.gl/Oh6lqe (accessed 29 October 2016).

33. 'IEA Warns of Ever-Growing Reliance on Middle Eastern Oil Supplies', *The Financial Times*, https://goo.gl/szEYQd (accessed 18 September 2016).

34. BP, 'Energy Outlook 2035'.

35. 'Saudi Arabia's Biggest Asian Oil Buyers Await Crown Prince Visit', Bloomberg, https://goo.gl/uLbehY (accessed 26 October 2016).

36. 'Saudi Arabia's Biggest Asian Oil Buyers Await Crown Prince Visit'.

37. See 'Saudi SABIC Says Chemicals Project in China to Cost $34 billion: TV', Reuters, https://goo.gl/j8RfJA (accessed 25 September 2016); 'Saudi Arabia's Biggest Asian Oil Buyers Await Crown Prince Visit'.

38. 'al-Benyan: $6 Billion SABIC's Investments in China', al-Arabiyya, https://goo.gl/0TJGPr (accessed 3 September 2016 (in Arabic)).

39. 'Saudi Vision 2030', http://vision2030.gov.sa/en (accessed 9 January 2017).

40. 'China Debt Load Reaches Record High as Risk to Economy Mounts', *The Financial Times*, https://goo.gl/bALqaJ (accessed 26 October 2016).

41. Economist Intelligence Unit, 'Country Report: China April 2017', http://country.eiu.com/china (accessed 24 April 2017); Economist Intelligence Unit, 'China: Hard Landing Looms', http://country.eiu.com/china (accessed 21 October 2016).

42. 'Arab Steel Industry Seeks Protection from Cheap Chinese Imports', *The National*, https://goo.gl/54baUQ (accessed 19 October 2016); 'Emal CEO Says Chinese oversupply is Threatening Aluminium Sector', MEED, http://ow.ly/bqxl305rL1q (accessed 23 October 2016).

43. See Gulf Petrochemicals & Chemicals Association, 'GCC Petchem Exports to China Continue to Rise, Despite Waning Demand', https://goo.gl/NaObUV (accessed 21 October 2016); John Richardson, Chris Qi, and John Baker, 'GCC Producers Should Watch China Closely', Gulf Petrochemicals & Chemicals Association, ICIS, https://goo.gl/ESUlnl (accessed 21 October 2016); Slavka Atanasova, 'Challenging Times Ahead for KSA', Oil & Gas, https://goo.gl/YPc4n9 (accessed 12 September 2016).

44. 'Chemicals Producers Must Adapt to Survive', MEED, https://goo.gl/U4XCN9 (accessed 21 October 2016).

45. BMI Research, 'Saudi Arabia Petrochemicals Report', https://goo.gl/kWJWY6 (accessed 29 October 2016).

46. BMI Research, *China's Petrochemicals Report Q4 2016*, London: Business Monitor International, 2016, p. 9.

47. BP, 'Energy Outlook 2035'.

48. 'Japan, Saudi Aramco Extend Okinawa Crude Storage Deal', Reuters, https://goo.gl/azbJbN (accessed 22 April 2017).

49. Naser M. al-Tamimi, *China–Saudi Arabia Relations, 1990–2012: Marriage of Convenience or Strategic Alliance?* London: Routledge, 2014, pp. 141–2.

50. World Bank, 'Doing Business 2017', http://www.doingbusiness.org/ (accessed 25 October 2016).

51. Sun Yi, 'China Must Adapt to Win Respect in Foreign Deals', *Global Times*, https://goo.gl/M4YCPO (accessed 14 October 2016).

52. 'Localisation is Triggering the Rise of GCC Oil Contractors', MEED, https://goo.gl/axrv6A (accessed 25 October 2016); 'MEED Top Oil and Gas Contractors', MEED, https://goo.gl/p9LnLi (accessed 25 October 2016).

53. 'China Must Adapt to Win Respect in Foreign Deals'.

54. 'Saudi Arabia Expands its Anti-Iran Strategy beyond the Middle East', Reuters, https://goo.gl/gC2zQB (accessed 13 September 2016).

55. Joel Wuthnow, 'Posing Problems without an Alliance: China–Iran Relations after the Nuclear Deal', Institute for National Strategic Studies, https://goo.gl/aRZl2Y (accessed 22 September 2016).

56. 'Xinhua Insight: China to Raise 2017 Defense Budget by Around 7 pct: Spokesperson', Xinhua, https://goo.gl/dutpDg (accessed 22 April 2017).

57. 'Trends in World Military Expenditure 2016', SIPRI Fact Sheet, https://goo.gl/qqymYl (accessed 24 April 2016).

58. 'Trends in World Military Expenditure 2016'.

59. 'R&D Funding Forecast 2016', *R&D Magazine*, https://goo.gl/ylhwtP (accessed 15 September 2016).

60. 'OECD Science, Technology and R&D Statistic: Main Science and Technology Indicators', https://goo.gl/yYk7QH (accessed 2 October 2016).

61. State Council of the People's Republic of China, 'Report of the Work of the Government (2016), delivered by the Premier of the State Council Li Keqiang', https://goo.gl/i4TU8O (accessed 13 September 2016).

62. 'R&D Funding Forecast 2016'.

63. 'China Poised to Top Global Corporate Patents', *Financial Times*, https://goo.gl/5Es1WK (accessed 22 April 2017).

64. 'China Poised to Top Global Corporate Patents'.
65. 'China Extends Run of Double-Digit Military Spending Increases', *Financial Times*, https://goo.gl/8AY153 (accessed 13 September 2016).
66. US Department of Defense, 'Military and Security Developments Involving the People's Republic of China 2016', Annual Report to Congress, https://goo.gl/hxTmNl (accessed 26 October 2016); BMI Research, *China Defence & Security Report 2016*, London: Business Monitor International, August 2016; Ronald O'Rourke, 'China Naval Modernization: Implications for US Navy Capabilities: Background and Issues for Congress', US Congressional Research Service 2016, https://www.fas.org/sgp/crs/row/RL33153.pdf (accessed 13 September 2016); US Department of Defense, 'Military and Security Developments Involving the People's Republic of China for 2016', https://goo.gl/crJYhv (accessed 15 September 2016); 'China's First Home-Made Aircraft Carrier Assembling', *People's Daily* Online, https://goo.gl/Kxikcy (accessed 29 October 2016); 'A Look at Progress on a Chinese Aircraft Carrier', Stratfor Analysis, https://goo.gl/msjKow (accessed 5 August 2016); 'China's Navy Makes Strides, Work Remains to Be Done', *Defence News*, https://goo.gl/Fr2691 (accessed 25 September 2016).
67. US–China Economic and Security Review Commission, 'China's Industrial and Military Robotics Development', https://goo.gl/PP5SYn (accessed 4 November 2016); Bradley Perrett, 'China's Plans for New, Long-Range Bomber', *Aviation Week*, https://goo.gl/f5YVXN (accessed 11 September 2016).
68. Jesse Karotkin, 'Trends in China's Naval Modernization', testimony before the US-China Economic and Security Review Commission, https://goo.gl/qHZrxP (accessed 10 September 2016).
69. 'China's Five Year Plan for Social and Economic Development (Full Text)', Xinhua, https://goo.gl/Ykpc9o (accessed 29 October 2016).
70. State Council of the People's Republic of China, 'Report of the Work of the Government (2015), delivered by the Premier of the State Council Li Keqiang', https://goo.gl/H6dIw9 (accessed 17 October 2016).
71. 'China's Military Spending: At the Double', *The Economist*, https://goo.gl/lfVsl1 (accessed 22 September 2016).
72. BMI Research, *China Defence & Security Report 2016*, p. 10.
73. O'Rourke, 'China Naval Modernization'; Centre for Strategic and International Studies (CSIS), 'Is China a Military Superpower?' https://goo.gl/JaPvFe (accessed 12 October 2016); Bill Gertz, 'China's Expanding its Military Power Projection Capabilities', *Asia Times*, https://goo.gl/fiJzYi (accessed 4 November 2016); Bruce Jones, David

Steven, and Emily O'Brien, 'Fueling a New Disorder? The New Geopolitical and Security Consequences of Energy', Brookings Institution, https://goo.gl/DbdmBz (accessed 16 September 2016).

74. 'China's Aircraft Carrier is Nothing to Fear', Bloomberg, https://goo.gl/gsbmtC (accessed 10 September 2016).

75. United Nations, 'UN Comtrade Database', http://comtrade.un.org/ (accessed 22 April 2017).

76. United Nations, 'UN Comtrade Database'.

77. 'China Crude Imports Hit Record Levels in 3Q16 as Middle East Volumes Soar ('000 B/D)', *MEES* 59, 43 (2016), p. 4.

78. IEA, 'Medium-Term Oil Market Report 2017', https://goo.gl/wu82Kw (accessed 22 April 2017); IEA, 'World Energy Outlook 2016', https://goo.gl/MwiUXk (accessed 22 April 2017).

79. Ministry of National Defence of the People's Republic of China, 'Full Text: China's Military Strategy', https://goo.gl/syHoQp (accessed 10 September 2016).

80. 'China Foreign Policy: Throwing out the Rule Book', *The Financial Times*, https://goo.gl/tlHmwZ (accessed 16 September 2016); 'China Builds First Overseas Military Outpost', *The Wall Street Journal*, https://goo.gl/A6AD6U (accessed 18 October 2016).

81. 'Supply Ships Critical to Chinese Maritime', Stratfor, https://goo.gl/sCG9lq (accessed 11 October 2016); 'China Advances Sea- and Land-Based Nuclear Deterrent Capabilities', IHS Jane's Defence Weekly, https://goo.gl/KKxqaY (accessed 7 October 2016).

82. 'Supply Ships Critical to Chinese Maritime'; 'China Advances Sea- and Land-Based Nuclear Deterrent Capabilities'.

83. 'Marines need to be beefed up to provide offshore support: expert', *Global Times*, https://goo.gl/szEYQd (accessed 23 April 2016).

84. Daniel Yergin, 'The Global Impact of US Shale', Project Syndicate, https://goo.gl/lvmVLG (accessed 10 October 2016).

85. White House, 'Remarks by President Obama in Address to the United Nations General Assembly', https://goo.gl/1DsHfg (accessed 26 September 2016); Tony Blair, 'Why the Middle East Matters: A Keynote Speech by Tony Blair', Office of Tony Blair, https://goo.gl/iSvy6c/ (accessed 27 September 2016); Anthony H. Cordesman, 'The Myth of US Energy Independence and the Realities of Burden Sharing', CSIS, https://goo.gl/9bVwSn (accessed 29 October 2016); Jeremy Shapiro and Richard Sokolsky, 'America's Core Middle East Interests are Already Secure', https://goo.gl/lYJJYu (accessed 18 September 2016).

86. EIA, 'International Energy Outlook 2017', https://goo.gl/giYdXN (accessed 9 January 2017).

87. Blair, 'Why the Middle East Matters'.

88. 'Saudis Have Few Options as they Push Tougher Foreign Policy', Reuters, https://goo.gl/VvOeQQ (accessed 15 September 2016).

89. Ministry of Foreign Affairs, People's Republic of China, 'Transcript of Foreign Minister Wang Yi's Interview with Belahodood of Al Jazeera', https://goo.gl/UlUYvF (accessed 2 October 2016).

90. Frederic Wehrey, 'A New US Approach to Gulf Security', Carnegie Endowment for International Peace, https://goo.gl/JsHPr3 (accessed 14 September 2016).

91. 'Saudi Scholarship Students in America Fall by 40,000', Arab News, https://goo.gl/yygNZa (accessed 23 September 2016).

92. 'al-Damak: The Deputy Crown Prince's Visit to China is a Milestone in the History of Relations between the Two Countries', al-Madina, https://goo.gl/cq0XS9 (accessed 3 September 2016 (in Arabic)); 'Program Helps Young Saudi's Study Abroad', China Daily, https://goo.gl/ULkK2o (accessed 24 October 2016).

93. Christopher M. Blanchard, 'Saudi Arabia: Background and US Relations', US Congressional Research Service, https://goo.gl/wiDC1E (accessed 23 September 2016); F. Gregory Gause III, 'The Future of US–Saudi Relations', Foreign Affairs 95, 4 (2016), p. 116.

94. Naser al-Tamimi, 'Analysis: China and Saudi Arabia: Reinvigorating Ties', Arab News, https://goo.gl/lEvAyI (accessed 22 April 2017).

95. 'Kingdom of Saudi Arabia to Launch Remote Sensing Satellite from China', Saudi Press Agency, http://spa.gov.sa/1448523 (accessed 22 October 2016); US–China Economic and Security Review Commission, 'China's Reported Ballistic Missile Sale to Saudi Arabia: Background and Potential Implications', https://goo.gl/nYnqU9 (accessed 26 September 2016); 'Saudi Arabia Buys High-Tech China Drones', Arab News, https://goo.gl/G5Vjyq (accessed 24 October 2016); 'UAE, Saudi Arabia Operating Chinese UAVs over Yemen', IHS Jane's Defence Weekly, https://goo.gl/3ITLVa (accessed 24 October 2016); 'China's BeiDou Navigation Satellite System Targets Global Service around 2020', Xinhua, https://goo.gl/WGtJ9x (accessed 31 October 2016); 'Beijing Missile Makers Cash in on Mideast and African Wars', The Financial Times, https://goo.gl/Kjqhir (accessed 28 October 2016).

96. 'Saudi Arabia to Build Chinese UAVs', IHS Jane's 360, https://goo.gl/wu1Qdm (accessed 21 April 2017).

97. Reza Akhlaghi, 'Candid Discussions: Kenneth Pollack on US Policy in the Middle East', Foreign Policy, https://goo.gl/YRwFgU (accessed 27 October 2016).

98. John J. Mearsheimer, 'Can China Rise Peacefully?' The National Interest, https://goo.gl/3VZLIx (accessed 19 October 2016).

SELECT BIBLIOGRAPHY

Books

1989 Yearbook on International Communist Affairs, Stanford, CA: Hoover Institution, 1989.

Aarts, Paul and Gerd Nonneman (eds.), *Saudi Arabia in the Balance: Political Economy, Society, Foreign Affairs*, London: Hurst & Co., 2005.

Aarts, Paul and Carolien Roelants, *Saudi Arabia: A Kingdom in Peril*, London: Hurst & Co., 2015.

al-'Abbud, 'Abd Allah ibn Salih ibn 'Abd Allah, *Juhud al-Mamlaka al-'Arabiyya al-Su'udiyya fi al-Da'wa ila Allah Ta'ala fi al-Kharij min Khilal al-Jami'a al-Islamiyya*, al-Madina al-Munawwara: al-Jami'a al-Islamiyya, 2004.

'Abduh, Muhammad, *al-A'mal al-Kamila*, Beirut: al-Mu'assasa al-'Arabiyya, 1980.

Abou El Fadl, Khaled, *The Great Theft: Wrestling Islam from the Extremists*, New York: Harper San Francisco, 2005.

Aburish, Said, *The Rise, Corruption and Coming Fall of the House of Saud*, London: Bloomsbury 1994.

Ahmad, Feroz, *The Turkish Experiment in Democracy 1950–1975*, London: C. Hurst & Co., 1977.

Ahmed, Shahab, *What is Islam? The Importance of Being Islamic*, Princeton: Princeton University Press, 2016.

al-'Ajmi, Muhammad bin Nasir, *al-Rasa'il al-Mutabadila*, Beirut: al-Basha'ir, 2001.

Alamer, Sultan et al., *Fi Tarikh al-Ouroba*, Beirut: Jusour, 2016.

al-Alusi, Mahmud Shukri, *Tarikh Najd*, Cairo: Madbouly, n.d.

Alvandi, Roham, *Nixon, Kissinger, and the Shah: The United States and Iran in the Cold War*, Oxford: Oxford University Press, 2014.

Asad, Talal, *The Idea of an Anthropology of Islam*, Occasional Papers Series, Washington, DC: Georgetown University, Center for Contemporary Arab Studies, 1986.

335

al-Athari, 'Abd Allah bin 'Abd al-Hamid, *al-Ghina' wa-l-Musiqa bayn al-Lahw wa-l-Wa'id*, Istanbul: Guraba, 2001.

———, *al-Iman: Haqiqatuhu, Khawarimuhu, Nawaqiduhu 'ind Ahl al-Sunna wa-l-Jama'a*, Riyadh: Madar al-Watan, 2003.

———, *al-Tawassul al-Mashru' wa-l-Mamnu': Anwa' wa Ahkam*, Istanbul: Guraba, 2013.

———, *al-Wajiz fi 'Aqidat al-Salaf al-Salih*, Riyadh: Wizarat al-Shu'un al-Islamiyya, 2002.

al-Athari, Abdullah, *Islamic Beliefs: A Brief Introduction to the 'Aqidah of Ahl as-Sunnah wal-Jama'ah*, Riyadh: International Islamic Publishing House, 2004.

Atia, Mona, *Building a House in Heaven: Pious Neoliberalism and Islamic Charity Egypt*, Minneapolis: University of Minnesota Press, 2013.

Ayoub, Mohammed and Hasan Kosebalaban (eds.), *Religion and Politics in Saudi Arabia: Wahhabism and the State*, Boulder: Lynne Rienner, 2009.

Barber, Benjamin R., *Jihad vs. McWorld*, London: Corgi, 2003.

Bayly, Christopher, *The Birth of the Modern World, 1780–1914: Global Connections and Comparisons*, Oxford: Blackwell, 2004.

Beaty, Jonathan and S. C. Gwynne, *The Outlaw Bank: A Wild Ride into the Secret Heart of BCCI*, New York: Random House, 1993.

Bin Hethlain, Naif, *Saudi Arabia and the US since 1962: Allies in Conflict*, London: Saqi, 2010.

Binder, Leonard, *Islamic Liberalism: A Critique of Development Ideologies*, Chicago: University of Chicago Press, 1988.

Black, P., *The Mystique of Modern Monarchy: With Special Reference to the British Commonwealth*, London: C. A. Watts & Co., 1954.

Bligh, A., *From Prince to King: Royal Succession to the House of Saud in the Twentieth Century*, New York: New York University Press, 1984.

Bonnefoy, Laurent, *Salafism in Yemen: Transnationalism and Religious Identity*, London: Hurst & Co., 2011.

Bronson, Rachel, *Thicker than Oil: America's Uneasy Relationship with Saudi Arabia*, New York: Oxford University Press, 2006.

Brown, Jonathan, *Hadith: Muhammad's Legacy in the Medieval and Modern World*, London: Oneworld, 2009.

Bunzel, Cole, *From Paper State to Caliphate: The Ideology of the Islamic State*, Washington, DC: Brookings Institution, 2015.

———, *The Kingdom and the Caliphate: Duel of the Islamic States*, Washington, DC: Carnegie Endowment for International Peace, 2016.

al-Buti, Said Ramadan, *al-Lamadhhabiyya Akhtar Bid'a Tuhaddid al-Shari'a al-Islamiyya*, 2nd edn, Damascus: n.p., 1970.

Chaudhry, Kiren Aziz, *The Price of Wealth: Economics and Institutions in the Middle East*, Ithaca: Cornell University Press, 1997.

Citino, Nathan J., *From Arab Nationalism to OPEC: Eisenhower, King Saud, and the Making of US–Saudi Relations*, Bloomington: Indiana University Press, 2002.

Coll, Steve, *Ghost Wars: The Secret History of the CIA, Afghanistan, and Bin Laden, from the Soviet Invasion to September 10, 2001*, London: Penguin, 2005.

Commins, David, *Islamic Reform: Politics and Social Change in Late Ottoman Syria*, New York: Oxford University Press, 1990.

————, *The Mission and the Kingdom: Wahhabi Power behind the Saudi Throne*, London: I. B. Tauris, 2006.

Cook, Michael, *Commanding Right and Forbidding Wrong in Islamic Thought*, Cambridge: Cambridge University Press, 2001.

Cooley, John, *Unholy Wars: Afghanistan, America and International Terrorism*, 3rd edn, London: Pluto Press, 2002.

Cronin, Stephanie, *Armies and State Building in the Modern Middle East: Politics, Nationalism and Military Reform*, London: I. B. Tauris, 2014.

Crystal, Jill, *Oil and Politics in the Gulf: Rulers and Merchants in Kuwait and Qatar*, Cambridge: Cambridge University Press, 1990.

Davidson, Christopher, *After the Sheikhs: The Coming Collapse of the Gulf Monarchies*, New York: Oxford University Press, 2013.

DeLong-Bas, Natana, *Wahhabi Islam: From Revival and Reform to Global Jihad*, London: I. B. Tauris, 2004.

Determann, Jorg Matthias, *Historiography in Saudi Arabia: Globalization and the State in the Middle East*, London: I. B. Tauris, 2014.

Dimitrakis, Panagiotis, *The Secret War in Afghanistan: The Soviet Union, China and Anglo-American Intelligence in the Afghan War*, London: I. B. Tauris, 2013.

Eickelman, Dale F. and James P. Piscatori (eds.), *Muslim Travellers: Pilgrimage, Migration, and the Religious Imagination*, London: Routledge, 1990.

el-Eseri, Abdullah b. Abdulhamid, *Ehl-i Sünnet ve'l-Cemaat'e Göre İman: Hakikati, Onu Zedeleyen ve Bozan Şeyler*, trans. Ahmed İyibildiren, Istanbul: Guraba, 2014.

————, *İslami Açıdan Müzik ve Teganni*, trans. Mustafa Öztürk, Istanbul: Guraba, 2013.

————, *Meşru ve Gayrımeşru Tevessül*, trans. Ahmet İyibildiren and Mustafa Öztürk, Istanbul: Guraba, 2013.

Farag, 'Abd al-Salam, *al-Jihad: al-Farida al-Gha'iba*, Amman: n.p., 1982.

Farquhar, Michael, *Circuits of Faith: Migration, Education, and the Wahhabi Mission*, Stanford: Stanford University Press, 2017.

Fawcett, Louise, *Iran and the Cold War: The Azerbaijan Crisis of 1946*, Cambridge: Cambridge University Press, 1992.

Ferris, Jesse, *Nasser's Gamble: How Intervention in Yemen Caused the Six-Day War and the Decline of Egyptian Power*, Princeton: Princeton University Press, 2013.

al-Ghazali, Muhammad, *al-Sunna al-Nabawiyya bayn Ahl al-Fiqh wa Ahl al-Ḥadith*, Cairo: Dar al-Shurouq, 1989.

Gullette, David, *The Genealogical Construction of the Kyrgyz Republic: Kinship, State, and 'Tribalism'*, Folkestone: Global Oriental, 2010.

Hamid, Shadi, *Islamic Exceptionalism: How the Struggle over Islam is Reshaping the World*, New York: St Martin's Press, 2016.

Halliday, Fred, *Arabia without Sultans*, New York: Penguin Books, 1975.

————, *Revolution and Foreign Policy: The Case of South Yemen 1967–1987*, Cambridge: Cambridge University Press, 1990.

Hanieh, Adam, *Capitalism and Class in the Gulf Arab States*, New York: Palgrave Macmillan, 2011.

Hasso, Frances, *Consuming Desires: Family Crisis and the State in the Middle East*, Stanford: Stanford University Press, 2011.

Haykel, Bernard, Thomas Hegghammer, and Stéphane Lacroix (eds.), *Saudi Arabia in Transition: Insights on Social, Political, Economic, and Religious Change*, Cambridge: Cambridge University Press, 2015.

Hegghammer, Thomas, *Jihad in Saudi Arabia: Violence and Pan-Islamism since 1979*, Cambridge: Cambridge University Press, 2010.

Heikal, Mohamed, *The Return of the Ayatollah: The Iranian Revolution from Mossadeq to Khomeini*, London: André Deutsch, 1981.

Herb, Michael, *All in the Family: Absolutism, Revolution and Democracy in the Middle East*, Albany: State University of New York Press, 1999.

Hertog, Steffen, *Princes, Brokers, and Bureaucrats: Oil and the State in Saudi Arabia*, Ithaca: Cornell University Press, 2010.

Hinnebusch, Raymond, *The International Politics of the Middle East*, 2nd edn, Manchester: Manchester University Press, 2015 [2003].

Holden, David, *The House of Saud*, London: Pan, 1982.

Holden, David and Richard Johns, *The House of Saud*, London: Sidgwick & Jackson, 1981.

House, Karen Elliott, *On Saudi Arabia: Its People, Past, Religion, Fault Lines, and Future*, New York: Alfred A. Knopf, 2012.

Ibn Qasim, 'Abd al-Rahman (ed.), *al-Durar al-Saniyya fi 'l-Ajwiba al-Najdiyya*, 8th edn, 16 vols., Riyadh: Warathat al-Shaykh 'Abd al-Rahman ibn Qasim, 2012.

Ibn Sunaytan, Muhammad, *al-Sa'udiyya: al-Siyasi wa-l-Qabila*, Beirut: Arab Network for Research and Publishing, 2008.

Jackson, Donna R., *Jimmy Carter and the Horn of Africa: Cold War Policy in Ethiopia and Somalia*, Jefferson: McFarland, 2007.

al-Jibrin, 'Abd al-Rahman ibn 'Abdullah, *U'jubat al-'Asr: Sirat Samahat al-Shaykh al-'Allama al-Imam 'Abdullah ibn 'Abd al-Rahman al-Jibrin*, Riyadh: Mu'assasat Ibn Jibrin al-Khayriyya, 2012.

Jones, Toby Craig, *Desert Kingdom: How Oil and Water Forged Saudi Arabia*, Cambridge, MA: Harvard University Press, 2010.

Kéchichian, Joseph, *Faysal: Saudi Arabia's King for All Seasons*, Gainesville: University Press of Florida, 2008.

Kéchichian, Joseph, *Legal and Political Reforms in Saudi Arabia*, New York: Routledge, 2013.

SELECT BIBLIOGRAPHY

————, *Succession in Saudi Arabia*, New York: Palgrave, 2001.

Kerr, Malcolm, *The Arab Cold War: Gamal 'Abd al-Nasir and his Rivals, 1958–1970*, 3rd edn, Oxford: Oxford University Press, 1971.

al-Kibsi, Gassan et al., *Saudi Arabia beyond Oil: The Investment and Productivity Transformation*, London and Dubai: McKinsey Global Institute, December 2015.

Kirby, Dianne (ed.), *Religion and the Cold War*, Basingstoke: Palgrave, 2003.

Kuran, Timur, *Private Truths, Public Lies: The Social Consequences of Preference Falsification*, Cambridge, MA: Harvard University Press, 1997.

La Boetie, E., *The Politics of Obedience: The Discourse of Voluntary Servitude*, Auburn, AL: Mises Institute, 1975.

Lacey, Robert, *Inside the Kingdom: Kings, Clerics, Modernists, Terrorist, and the Struggle for Saudi Arabia*, London: Penguin, 2010.

————, *The Kingdom*, London: Hutchinson, 1981.

Lacroix, Stéphane, *Awakening Islam: Religious Discourse in Contemporary Saudi Arabia*, trans. George Holoch, Cambridge, MA: Harvard University Press, 2011.

Lav, Daniel, *Radical Islam and the Revival of Medieval Theology*, Cambridge: Cambridge University Press, 2012.

Lefevere, André and Susan Bassnett (eds.), *Translation, History and Culture*, London: Pinter, 1990.

Le Renard, Amélie, *A Society of Young Women: Opportunities of Place, Power, and Reform in Saudi Arabia*, Stanford: Stanford University Press, 2014.

Long, David E., *The Kingdom of Saudi Arabia*, Gainesville: University of Florida Press, 1997.

————, *The United States and Saudi Arabia: Ambivalent Allies*, Boulder, CO: Westview Press, 1985.

Mabon, Simon, *Saudi Arabia and Iran: Power and Rivalry in the Middle East*, London: I. B. Tauris, 2016.

Mandaville, Peter. *Global Political Islam*, London: Routledge, 2007.

al-Maqdisi, Abu Muhammad, *al-Kawashif al-Jaliyya fi Kufr al-Dawla al-Sa'udiyya*, Amman: Minbar al-Tawhid wa-l-Jihad, 1989.

————, *Millat Ibrahim wa Da'wat al-Anbiya' wa-l-Mursalin* (c. 1984).

Massad, Joseph, *Islam in Liberalism*, Chicago: University of Chicago Press, 2015.

Matthiesen, Toby, *The Other Saudis: Shiism, Dissent, and Sectarianism*, Cambridge: Cambridge University Press, 2014.

————, *Sectarian Gulf: Saudi Arabia and the Arab Spring That Wasn't*, Stanford: Stanford University Press, 2013.

Meijer, Roel (ed.), *Global Salafism: Islam's New Religious Movement*, New York: Columbia University Press, 2009.

Ménoret, Pascal, *L'Énigme saoudienne: les Saoudiens et le monde 1744–2003*, Paris: La Découverte, 2003.

SELECT BIBLIOGRAPHY

————, *Joyriding in Riyadh: Oil, Urbanism, and Road Revolt*, Cambridge: Cambridge University Press, 2014.

Mitchell, Nancy, *Jimmy Carter in Africa: Race and the Cold War*, Washington DC: Woodrow Wilson Center / Cold War International History Project, 2016.

Mitchell, Richard, *The Society of the Muslim Brothers*, New York: Oxford University Press, 1993.

Mouline, Nabile, *The Clerics of Islam: Religious Authority and Political Power in Saudi Arabia*, trans. Ethan S. Rundell, New Haven: Yale University Press, 2014.

Muehlenbeck, Philip Emil (ed.), *Religion and the Cold War: A Global Perspective*, Nashville: Vanderbilt University Press, 2012.

Müller, Miriam M., *A Spectre is Haunting Arabia: How the Germans Brought their Communism to Yemen*, Bielefeld: Transcript Verlag, 2015.

Mumcu, Uğur, *Rabıta*, Ankara: Tekin Yayınevi, 1987.

al-Muslim, Muhammad Sa'id, *Sahil al-Dhahab al-Aswad: Dirasa Tarikhiyya Insaniyya li-Mintaqat al-Khalij al-'Arabi*, 2nd edn, Beirut: Manshurat Dar Maktabat al-Haya, 1962.

al-Obodi, Mohammed Nasir, *al-Mu'ajam al-Joghraphy li Bilad al-Qasim*, Riyadh: Thulothia Publishing House, 1978.

Ottaway, David, *King's Messenger: Prince Bandar Bin Sultan and America's Tangled Relationship with Saudi Arabia*, New York: Walker & Company, 2008.

Partrick, Neil (ed.), *Saudi Foreign Policy: Conflict and Cooperation*, London: I. B. Tauris, 2016.

Pétriat, Philippe, *Le Négoce des Lieux Saints: négociants hadramis de Djedda, 1850–1950*, Paris: Sorbonne, 2016.

al-Qahtani, Fahd, *Shiui 'Iyyun fi al-Su'udiyya: Dirasa fi al-'Alaqat al-Sufitiyya al-Su'udiyya*, n.p.: n.p., 1988.

Al-Rasheed, Madawi, *Contesting the Saudi State: Islamist Voices from a New Generation*, Cambridge: Cambridge University Press, 2007.

————, *A History of Saudi Arabia*, Cambridge: Cambridge University Press, 2010.

————, *A Most Masculine State: Gender, Politics and Religion in Saudi Arabia*, Cambridge: Cambridge University Press, 2013.

————, *Muted Modernists: The Struggle over Divine Politics in Saudi Arabia*, London: Hurst & Co. / Oxford University Press, 2015.

————, *Politics in an Arabian Oasis: The Rashidis of Saudi Arabia*, London: I. B. Tauris, 1991.

Al-Rasheed, Madawi (ed.), *Kingdom without Borders: Saudi Arabia's Political, Religious and Media Frontiers*, London: Hurst & Co., 2008.

al-Rebdi, Muhammad, *Buraydah: Nomowha al-Hadheri wa al-Aqatuha al-Iqlimiah*, Buraydah: n.p., 1986.

Rihani, A., *Ibn Saud of Arabia*, London: Constable & Co., 1928.

El-Rouayheb, Khaled, *Islamic Intellectual History in the Seventeenth Century:*

SELECT BIBLIOGRAPHY

Scholarly Currents in the Ottoman Empire and the Maghreb, Cambridge: Cambridge University Press, 2015.

Roy, Olivier, *The Failure of Political Islam*, London: I. B. Tauris, 1994 [1992].

———, *Globalized Islam: The Search for a New Ummah*, New York: Columbia University Press, 2004.

Rubin, Lawrence, *Islam in the Balance: Ideational Threats in Arab Politics*, Stanford: Stanford Security Studies, 2014.

Salime, Zakia, *Between Feminism and Islam: Human Rights and Sharia Law in Morocco*, Minneapolis: Regents of University of Minneapolis, 2011.

Samin, Nadav, *Of Sand or Soil: Genealogy and Tribal Belonging in Saudi Arabia*, Princeton: Princeton University Press, 2015.

Samore, Gary Samuel, *Royal Family Politics in Saudi Arabia (1953–1982)*, Ann Arbor: University Microfilms International, 1983.

Sayigh, Yezid and Avi Shlaim (eds.), *The Cold War and the Middle East*, 2nd edn, Oxford: Oxford University Press, 2003.

Schulze, Reinhard, *Islamischer Internationalismus im 20. Jahrhundert: Untersuchungen zur Geschichte der Islamischen Weltliga*, Leiden: Brill, 1990.

Scott, J., *Domination and the Arts of Resistance*, New Haven: Yale University Press, 1990.

———, *Weapons of the Weak: Everyday Forms of Peasant Resistance*, New Haven: Yale University Press, 1985.

al-Shamsi, Mansoor, *Islam and Political Reform in Saudi Arabia: The Quest for Political Change and Reform*, London: Routledge, 2011.

al-Shihabi, A., *The Saudi Kingdom: Between the Jihadi Hammer and the Iranian Anvil*, Princeton: Markus Wiener Publishers, 2016.

Simpson, William, *The Prince: The Secret Story of the World's Most Intriguing Royal, Prince Bandar bin Sultan*, New York: Regan Books, 2006.

Sirrs, Owen L., *The Egyptian Intelligence Service: A History of the Mukhabarat, 1910–2009*, Abingdon: Routledge, 2010.

Spiro, David E., *The Hidden Hand of American Hegemony: Petrodollar Recycling and International Markets*, Ithaca: Cornell University Press, 1999.

Sunayama, Sonoko, *Syria and Saudi Arabia: Collaboration and Conflicts in the Oil Era*, London: I. B. Tauris, 2007.

Takriti, Abdel Razzaq, *Monsoon Revolution: Republicans, Sultans, and Empires in Oman 1965–1976*, Oxford: Oxford University Press, 2013.

Tamam, Husam, *Tasalluf al-Ikhwan: Ta'akul al-Utruha al-Ikhwaniyya wa Su'ud al-Salafiyya fi Jama'at al-Ikhwan al-Muslimin*, Alexandria: Bibliotheca Alexandrina/Future Studies Unit, 2010.

al-Tamimi, Naser M., *China–Saudi Arabia Relations, 1990–2012: Marriage of Convenience or Strategic Alliance?*, Abingdon: Routledge, 2014.

al-Torki, Soraya, *Women in Saudi Arabia: Ideology and Behavior among the Elite*, New York: Columbia University Press, 1986.

SELECT BIBLIOGRAPHY

al-Torki, Soraya and Camillia Fawzi El-Solh, *Arab Women in the Field: Studying your Own Society*, Syracuse: Syracuse University Press, 1988.

Valentine, Simon Ross, *Force and Fanaticism: Wahhabism in Saudi Arabia and Beyond*, Oxford: Oxford University Press, 2015.

Vassiliev, Alexei, *The History of Saudi Arabia*, London: Saqi Books, 1997.

―――, *King Faisal of Saudi Arabia: Personality, Faith and Times*, London: Saqi Books, 2012.

Vitalis, Robert, *America's Kingdom: Mythmaking on the Saudi Oil Frontier*, Stanford: Stanford University Press, 2007.

Wagemakers, Joas, *A Quietist Jihadi: The Ideology and Influence of Abu Muhammad al-Maqdisi*, Cambridge: Cambridge University Press, 2012.

Weismann, Itzchak, *Taste of Modernity: Sufism Salafiya, and Arabism in Late Ottoman Damascus*, Leiden: Brill, 2001.

Westad, Odd Arne, *The Global Cold War: Third World Interventions and the Making of Our Times*, Cambridge: Cambridge University Press, 2007.

Yamani, Mai, *The Cradle of Islam: The Hijaz and the Quest for an Arabian Identity*, London: I. B. Tauris, 2004.

Yaqub, Salim, *Containing Arab Nationalism: The Eisenhower Doctrine and the Middle East*, Chapel Hill: University of North Carolina Press, 2004.

al-Yassini, Ayman, *al-Din wa-al-Dawla fi al-Mamlaka al-'Arabiyya al-Su'udiyya*, London: Saqi, 1990; trans. as *Religion and State in the Kingdom of Saudi Arabia*, Boulder, CO: Westview Press, 1985.

Yizraeli, Sarah, *The Remaking of Saudi Arabia: The Struggle between King Saud and Crown Prince Faysal, 1953–1962*, Dayan Center Papers 121, Tel Aviv: Moshe Dayan Center for Middle Eastern and African Studies, 1997.

―――, *Politics and Society in Saudi Arabia: The Crucial Years of Development, 1960–1982*, London: Hurst & Co., 2012.

Yolcu, Abdullah, *Kur'an ve Sünnet'in Işığında İslam'ın Şartları*, Istanbul: Guraba, 2010.

―――, *Selef-i Salihin Akidesi: Ehl-i Sünnet ve'l-Cemaat*, Istanbul: Guraba, 2014.

Yordanov, Radoslav A., *The Soviet Union and the Horn of Africa during the Cold War: Between Ideology and Pragmatism*, Lanham, MD: Lexington, 2016.

Chapters in edited volumes

Adraoui, Mohamed-Ali, 'Salafism in France: Ideology, Practices and Contradictions', in Roel Meijer (ed.), *Global Salafism: Islam's New Religious Movement*, New York: Columbia University Press, 2009, pp. 364–83.

Bonnefoy, Laurent, 'How Transnational is Salafism in Yemen?' in Roel Meijer (ed.), *Global Salafism: Islam's New Religious Movement*, London: Hurst & Co., 2009, pp. 321–41.

Bonnefoy, Laurent, 'Salafism in Yemen: A "Saudisation"?' in Roel Meijer (ed.),

Global Salafism: Islam's New Religious Movement, New York: Columbia University Press, 2009, pp. 323–40.

Brown, Nathan J., 'Constitutional Revolutions and the Public Sphere', in Marc Lynch (ed.), *The Arab Uprisings Explained: New Contentious Politics in the Middle East*, New York: Columbia University Press, 2014, pp. 67–83.

Cook, Michael, 'The Expansion of the First Saudi State: The Case of Washm', in C. Bosworth, C. Issawi, and A. Udovitch (eds.), *The Islamic World from Classical to Modern Times: Essays in Honor of Bernard Lewis*, Princeton: Darwin Press, 1988, pp. 661–99.

Al Fahad, Abdulaziz, 'Rootless Trees: Genealogical Politics in Saudi Arabia', in Bernard Haykel, Thomas Hegghammer, and Stéphane Lacroix (eds.), *Saudi Arabia in Transition: Insights on Social, Political Economic and Religious Change*, Cambridge: Cambridge University Press, 2015, pp. 263–91.

Gause, F. Gregory, III, 'Official Wahhabism and the Sanctioning of Saudi–US Relations', in Mohammed Ayoob and Hasan Kosebalaban (eds.), *Religion and Politics in Saudi Arabia: Wahhabism and the State*, Boulder, CO: Lynne Rienner Publishers, 2009, pp. 135–40.

Hammond, Andrew, 'Rereading Jihadi Texts: Between Subalternity and Policy Discourse', in Noha Mellor and Khalil Rinnawi (eds.), *Political Islam and Global Media: The Boundaries of Religious Identity*, Abingdon: Routledge, 2016, pp. 67–85.

Hasan, Nourhaidi, 'Ambivalent Doctrines and Conflicts in the Salafi Movement', in Roel Meijer (ed.), *Global Salafism: Islam's New Religious Movement*, New York: Columbia University Press, 2009, pp. 169–88.

Haykel, Bernard et al., 'Introduction', in Bernard Haykel et al. (eds.), *Saudi Arabia in Transition: Insights on Social, Political, Economic and Religious Change*, Cambridge: Cambridge University Press, 2015, pp. 1–12.

Haykel, Bernard, 'On the Nature of Salafi Thought and Action', in Roel Meijer (ed.), *Global Salafism: Islam's New Religious Movement*, New York: Columbia University Press, 2009, pp. 33–57.

Hertog, Steffen, 'The New Corporatism in Saudi Arabia: Limits of Formal Politics', in Abdulhadi Khalaf and Giacomo Luciani (eds.), *Constitutional Reform and Political Participation in the Gulf*, Dubai: Gulf Research Center, 2006, pp. 239–73.

———, 'Saudi Arabia's Political Demobilization in Regional Comparison: Monarchical Tortoise and Republican Hares', in Laura Guazzone and Daniela Pioppi (eds.), *The Arab State and Neo-Liberal Globalization: The Restructuring of State Power in the Middle East*, Reading: Ithaca Press, 2009, pp. 73–95.

Hroub, Khaled, 'Salafi Formations in Palestine', in Roel Meijer (ed.), *Global Salafism: Islam's New Religious Movement*, New York: Columbia University Press, 2009, pp. 222–44.

Jones, Toby C., 'The Dogma of Development: Technopolitics and Power in

Saudi Arabia', in Bernard Haykel et al. (eds.), *Saudi Arabia in Transition: Insights on Social, Political, Economic and Religious Change*, Cambridge: Cambridge University Press, 2015, pp. 31–47.

Lacroix, Stéphane, 'Between Revolution and Apoliticism: Nasir al-Din al-Albani and his Impact on the Shaping of Contemporary Salafism', in Roel Meijer (ed.), *Global Salafism: Islam's New Religious Movement*, New York: Columbia University Press, 2009, pp. 59–82.

Luciani, Giacomo, 'From Private Sector to National Bourgeoisie: Saudi Arabian Business', in Paul Aarts and Gerd Nonneman (eds.), *Saudi Arabia in the Balance: Political Economy, Society, Foreign Affairs*, New York: New York University Press, 2006, pp. 144–81.

Makdisi, George, 'Law and Traditionalism in the Institutions of Learning of Medieval Islam', in Gustave Grunebaum (ed.), *Theology and Law in Islam*, Wiesbaden: Harrassowitz, 1971, pp. 75–88.

Meijer, Roel, 'Introduction', in Roel Meijer (ed.), *Global Salafism: Islam's New Religious Movement*, New York: Columbia University Press, 2009, pp. 1–32.

Melchert, Christopher, 'Muhammad Nasir al-Din al-Albani and Traditional Hadith Criticism', in Elisabeth Kendall and Ahmad Khan (eds.), *Reclaiming Islamic Tradition: Modern Interpretations of the Classical Heritage*, Edinburgh: Edinburgh University Press, 2016, pp. 33–51.

Painter, David S., 'Oil, Resources, and the Cold War, 1945–1962', in Melvyn P. Leffler and Odd Arne Westad (eds.), *The Cambridge History of the Cold War*, vol. 1: *Origins*, Cambridge: Cambridge University Press, 2012, pp. 486–507.

Pall, Zoltan, 'Salafi Dynamics in Kuwait: Politics, Fragmentation and Change', in Francesco Cavatorta and Fabio Merone (eds.), *Salafism after the Arab Awakening: Contending with People's Power*, London: Hurst & Co, 2017, pp. 169–86.

Piscatori, James, 'Islamic Values and National Interest: The Foreign Policy of Saudi Arabia', in Adeed Dawisha (ed.), *Islam in Foreign Policy*, Cambridge: Cambridge University Press, 1983, pp. 33–53.

Al-Rasheed, Madawi, 'Caught Between Religion and State: Women in Saudi Arabia', in Bernard Haykel et al. (eds.), *Saudi Arabia in Transition: Insights on Social, Political, Economic and Religious Change*, Cambridge: Cambridge University Press, 2015, pp. 292–313.

———, 'Circles of Power: Royals and Society in Saudi Arabia', in P. Aarts and G. Nonneman (eds.), *Saudi Arabia in the Balance: Political Economy, Society, Foreign Affairs*, London: Hurst & Co., 2005, pp. 185–213.

———, 'The Local and the Global in Saudi Salafi–Jihadi Discourse', in Roel Meijer (ed.), *Global Salafism: Islam's New Religious Movement*, London: Hurst & Co., 2009, pp. 301–20.

———, 'Saudi Internal Dilemmas and Regional Responses to the Arab

Spring', in Fawaz Gerges (ed.), *The New Middle East: Protest and Revolution in the Arab World*, Cambridge: Cambridge University Press, 2014, pp. 353–79.

—————, 'Sectarianism as Counter-Revolution: Saudi Responses to the Arab Uprisings', in Nader Hashemi and Danny Postel (eds.), *Sectarianization: Mapping the New Politics of the Middle East*, London: Hurst & Co., 2017, pp. 143–58.

Redissi, Hamadi, 'The Refutation of Wahhabism in Arabic Sources, 1745–1932', in Madawi Al-Rasheed (ed.), *Kingdom Without Borders: Saudi Political, Religious and Media Frontiers*, London: Hurst & Co., 2008, pp. 157–81.

El-Rouayheb, Khaled, 'From Ibn Hajar al-Haytami (d. 1566) to Khayr al-Din al-Alusi (d. 1899): Changing Views of Ibn Taymiyya among non-Hanbali Sunni Scholars', in Yossef Rapoport and Shahab Ahmed (eds.), *Ibn Taymiyya and his Times*, Karachi: Oxford University Press, 2010, pp. 269–318.

Sindi, Abdullah M., 'King Faisal and Pan-Islamism', in Willard A. Beling (ed.), *King Faisal and the Modernisation of Saudi Arabia*, London: Croom Helm, 1980, pp. 184–201.

Steinberg, Guido, 'The Wahhabi Ulama and the Saudi State: 1745 to the Present', in Paul Aarts and Gerd Nonneman (eds.), *Saudi Arabia in the Balance: Political Economy, Society, Foreign Affairs*, New York: New York University Press, 2005, pp. 11–34.

—————, 'The Wahhabiyya and Shi'ism, from 1744/45 to 2008', in Ofra Bengio and Meir Litvak (eds.), *The Sunna and Shi'a in History: Division and Ecumenism in the Muslim Middle East*, New York: Palgrave, 2011, pp. 163–82.

Utvik, Bjørn Olav, 'The Ikhwanization of the Salafis: Piety in the Politics of Egypt and Kuwait', *Middle East Critique* 23, 1 (2 January 2014), pp. 5–27.

van Ess, Josef, 'The Logical Structure of Islamic Theology', in Gustave Grunebaum (ed.), *Logic in Classical Islamic Culture*, Wiesbaden: Harrassowitz, 1970, pp. 21–50.

Voll, John Obert, 'Islam as a Community of Discourse and a World System', in Akbar S. Ahmed and Tamara Sonn (eds.), *The Sage Handbook of Islamic Studies*, London: Sage, 2010, pp. 3–16.

Zürcher, Eric, 'The Importance of Being Secular: Islam in the Service of the National and Pre-National State', in Celia Kerslake, Kerem Öktem, and Philip Robins (eds.), *Turkey's Engagement with Modernity: Conflict and Change in the Twentieth Century*, London: Routledge Curzon, 2005, pp. 55–68.

Journal articles

Aba Namay, R., 'Constitutional Reforms: A Systematisation of Saudi Politics', *Journal of South Asian and Middle Eastern Studies* 16, 3 (1993), pp. 43–88.

Abner, Elihugh, 'The Collapse of Saudi Arabia and the Cataclysmic Power

Shift in the Middle East', *Journal of International Affairs* 69, 2 (2016), pp. 169–73.

Ahmad, Feroz, 'Islamic Reassertion in Turkey', *Third World Quarterly* 10, 2 (1988), pp. 750–69.

Aidi, Hisham, 'Let us be Moors: Islam, Race and "Connected Histories",' *Middle East Report* 229 (1 December 2003), pp. 42–53.

Baldry, John, 'Soviet Relations with Saudi Arabia and the Yemen, 1917–1938', *Middle Eastern Studies* 20, 1 (1984), pp. 53–80.

Bellin, E. 'Reconsidering the Robustness of Authoritarianism in the Middle East: Lessons from the Arab Uprisings', *Comparative Politics* 44, 2 (2012), pp. 127–49.

Chehabi, Houchang, 'South Africa and Iran in the Apartheid Era', *Journal of Southern African Studies* 42, 4 (2016), pp. 687–709.

Christmann, Andreas, 'Islamic Scholar and Religious Leader: A Portrait of Shaykh Muhammad Sa'id Ramadan al-Buti', *Islam and Christian–Muslim Relations* 9, 2 (1998), pp. 149–69.

Coast, D., and J. Fox, 'Rumour and Politics', *History Compass* 13, 5 (2015), pp. 222–34.

Dhanani, Gulshan, 'Saudi Arabia and Non-Alignment', *International Studies* 20, 1–2 (1981), pp. 361–9.

Dresch, P., 'The Significance of the Course Events Take in Segmentary Systems', *American Ethnologist* 13, 2 (1986), pp. 309–24.

al-Fahad, A., 'Ornamental Constitutionalism: The Saudi Basic Law of Governance', *Yale Journal of International Law* 30 (2005), pp. 375–96.

Farquhar, Michael, 'Saudi Petrodollars, Spiritual Capital, and the Islamic University of Medina: A Wahhabi Missionary Project in Transnational Perspective', *International Journal of Middle East Studies* 47, 4 (2015), pp. 701–21.

Foley, Sean, 'When Collision Emerges as Unexpected Harmony: Saudi Responses to the Arab Spring', *Contemporary Review of the Middle East* 1, 1 (2014), pp. 53–74.

al-Fuqayhi, 'Ali ibn Muhammad ibn Nasir, 'Wahdat al-Umma Hiya Tariq al-Khalas', *Majallat al-Jami'a al-Islamiyya bi-l-Madina al-Munawwara* 58 (Rabi' al-Akhir-Jumada al-Akhira 1403 H.).

Gause, F. Gregory III, 'The Future of US–Saudi Relations', *Foreign Affairs* 95, 4 (2016), pp. 114–26.

Griffel, Frank, 'What Do we Mean by "Salafi"? Connecting Muhammad 'Abduh with Egypt's Nur Party in Islam's Contemporary Intellectual History', *Die Welt des Islams* 55 (2015), pp. 186–220.

Hasim, Kamal, 'The ARAMCO (Letter from Saudi Arabia)', *World Marxist Review* 5 (May 1962), pp. 88f.

Hegghammer, Thomas, 'The Rise of Muslim Foreign Fighters: Islam and the

Globalization of Jihad', *International Security* 35, 3 (Winter 2010), pp. 53–91.

Hertog, Steffen, 'Rentier Militaries in the Gulf: The Price of Coup-Proofing', *International Journal of Middle East Studies*, 43, 3 (August 2011), pp. 400–2.

Ibrahim, Ahmed Fekry, 'Rethinking the Taqlid–Ijtihad Dichotomy: A Conceptual-Historical Approach', *Journal of the American Oriental Society* 136, 2 (April–June 2016), pp. 285–303.

'Interview with 'Abd al-'Aziz al-Muqrin', *Sawt al-Jihad* 1, September 2003, p. 22.

'Interview with 'Abdallah b. Muhammad al-Rashud', *Sawt al-Jihad* 3, November 2003, pp. 15–16.

Jones, C., 'Seeing Like an Autocrat: Liberal Social Engineering in an Illiberal State', *Perspectives on Politics* 1, 13 (2015), pp. 24–41.

Jones, Toby, 'Shifting Sands: The Future of US–Saudi Relations', *Foreign Affairs* 85, 2 (March/April 2006), pp. 164–70.

Kersten, Carool, 'Critical Islam: Muslims and their Religion in a Post-Islamist World', *Singapore Middle East Papers* 10, 1 (2015), pp. 107–124.

Khan, Bilal, Muhammad Khurram Khan, and Khaled S. Alghathbar, 'Biometrics and Identity Management for Homeland Security Applications in Saudi Arabia', *African Journal of Business Management* 4, 15 (2010), pp. 296–306.

Kuran, Timur, 'Now out of Never: The Element of Surprise in the East European Revolution of 1989', *World Politics* 44, 1 (1991), pp. 7–48.

Lauzière, Henri, 'The Construction of Salafiyya: Reconsidering Salafism from the Perspective of Conceptual History', *International Journal of Middle East Studies* 42 (2010), pp. 369–89.

Lefebvre, Jeffrey A., 'Middle East Conflicts and Middle Level Power Intervention in the Horn of Africa', *Middle East Journal*, 50, 3 (Summer 1996), pp. 387–404.

Le Renard, Amelie, '"Only for Women": Women, the State, and Reform in Saudi Arabia', *Middle East Journal* 62, 4 (2008), pp. 610–29.

Maisel, Sebastian, 'The New Rise of Tribalism in Saudi Arabia', *Nomadic Peoples*, 18, 2 (2014), pp. 100–22.

Mandaville, Peter, 'Transnational Muslim Solidarities and Everyday Life', *Nations and Nationalism* 17, 1 (1 January 2011), pp. 7–24.

Mann, Joseph, 'King without a Kingdom: Deposed King Saud and his Intrigues', *Studia Orientalia Electronica* 1 (2013), pp. 26–40.

Mann, Joseph, 'The Syrian Neo-Ba'th Regime and the Kingdom of Saudi Arabia, 1966–70', *Middle Eastern Studies* 42, 5 (2006), pp. 761–6.

Matthiesen, Toby, 'Marxists in the Land of the Two Holy Places: The

Communist Party of Saudi Arabia, 1975–1991', *Journal of Cold War Studies* (forthcoming).

————, 'Migration, Minorities and Radical Networks: Labour Movements and Opposition Groups in Saudi Arabia 1950–1975', *International Review of Social History*, 59, 3 (2014), pp. 473–504.

————, 'Shi'i Historians in a Wahhabi State: Identity Entrepreneurs and the Politics of Local Historiography in Saudi Arabia', *International Journal of Middle East Studies* 47, 1 (2015), pp. 25–45.

Menaldo, Victor, 'The Middle East and North Africa's Resilient Monarchs', *Journal of Politics*, 74, 3 (July 2012), pp. 707–22.

Mitchell, Timothy, 'McJihad: Islam in the US Global Order', *Social Text* 20, 4 (2002), pp. 1–18.

Mouline, N., 'Power and Generational Transition in Saudi Arabia', *Critique Internationale* 46 (2010), pp. 125–46.

Al-Otaibi, Saud, 'The Resilience of Monarchy in the Middle East: A Case Study of Saudi Arabia', *Journal of King Saud University*, 10 (1998), pp. 69–80.

Ramadan, Muhi al-Din, 'Wa-Lam Yazil A'da' al-Umma Yamkuruna', *Majallat al-Jami'a al-Islamiyya bi-l-Madina al-Munawwara* 10, 2 (September 1977).

Al-Rasheed, Madawi, 'Saudi Regime Resilience after the 2011 Arab Uprisings', *Contemporary Arab Affairs* 9, 1 (2016), pp. 13–26.

————, 'The Shi'a of Saudi Arabia: A Minority in Search of Cultural Authenticity,' *British Journal of Middle Eastern Studies*, 25, 1 (1998), pp. 121–38.

Rifai, Ola, 'Online Mobilization for Civil and Political Rights in Saudi Arabia', *Asian Politics and Policy* 6, 3 (2014), pp. 500–4.

Samin, Nadav, '*Da'wa*, Dynasty, and Destiny in the Arab Gulf', *Comparative Studies in Society and History* 58, 4 (2016), pp. 935–54.

Scott, D., 'The Saudi Paradox', *Foreign Affairs* 83, 1 (2004), pp. 35–51.

Scott, James C., John Tehranian, and Jeremy Mathias, 'The Production of Legal Identities Proper to States: The Case of the Permanent Family Surname', *Comparative Studies in Society and History* 44, 1 (2002), pp. 4–44.

Sirry, Mun'im, 'Jamal al-Din al-Qasimi and the Salafi Approach to Sufism', *Die Welt des Islams* 51, 1 (2011), pp. 75–108.

Sowayan, Saad Abdullah, 'Tonight my Gun is Loaded: Poetic Dueling in Arabia', *Oral Tradition* 4, 1–2 (1989), pp. 151–73.

Utas, Mats, 'Victimcy, Girlfriending, Soldiering: Tactic Agency in a Young Woman's Social Navigation of the Liberian War Zone', *Anthropological Quarterly* 78, 2 (2005), pp. 403–30.

Wagemakers, Joas, 'Protecting Jihad: The Sharia Council of the Minbar al-Tawhid wa-l-Jihad', *Middle East Policy* 18, 2 (2011), pp. 148–62.

SELECT BIBLIOGRAPHY

Wiktorowicz, Quintan, 'Anatomy of the Salafi Movement', *Studies in Conflict and Terrorism* 29, 3 (2006), pp. 207–39.

Yom, S. and F. Gregory Gause, III, 'Resilient Royals: How Arab Monarchies Hang On', *Journal of Democracy* 23, 4 (2012), pp. 74–88.

Zubaida, Sami, 'The Fragments Imagine the Nation: The Case of Iraq', *International Journal of Middle East Studies* 34, 2 (2002), pp. 205–15.

INDEX

INDEX

INDEX

INDEX

cal reform 128; repression of 9, 225; and sectarianism 11, 12; and Syria 11–12; women 118, 128, 290n12, 290n17
Islamophobia 131
Isma'ilis 27, 161
Israel 18: and Egypt 230; and the Safari Club 230; and Saudi Arabia 19, 248–9; Six-Day War 223; and USA 233, 237–7

Jabhat al-Taharrur al-Watani: see National Liberation Front
Jabhat al-Nusra 207
al-Jama'a al-Salafiyya al-Muhtasiba (Salafi Hisba Group, Salafi Group for Promoting Virtue and Preventing Vice) 152
Jamaat-i Islami 155
al-Jami, Muhammad Aman 178
Japan 259, 261
al-Jasir, Hamad 107, 109, 201
al-Jaza'iri, Jabir Abu Bakr 170
al-Jazeera 19, 128, 244, 248, 265
Jenkins, John 242
jihad: financing of 227; first Saudi state and 185; and Salafiyya 159; against Saudi regime 184; and Wahhabiyya 5, 15, 184, 189
Jihadi Salafism 150, 183, 184, 190–3
jihadism: and anti-communism 25, 239; and foreign hostages 189; and parricide 24, 197–206, 210; and poetry 24, 189, 206–10; Salafi jihadism 15, 41, 42; and state paternalism 204–6; and Wahhabiyya 4–5, 15, 24, 184, 189, 191–2, 193
Jones, Toby 211, 288n13
Jordan: monarchy 48; Saudi sup-

port for 230, 267; Saudi outreach to 3, 17
Jordan, Robert 265
al-Jubair, Adil 247
judiciary: dominated by religious forces 92; promise of independence for 78; state funded 79
al-Juhani, Khalid 202, 205
Juhayman group 153
Justice Against Sponsors of Terrorism Act (JASTA) 20, 42, 241, 266
Justice and Development Party (AKP) 157, 158

Karotkin, Jesse 261
Kevseri, Mehmed Zahid 152
Khalaf, Roula 62
Khalid ibn 'Abd al-'Aziz, King 53, 54, 226
Khalid ibn Bandar 88
Khalid ibn Faysal, Prince 120
al-Khatib, Muhibb al-Din 151
Khattab 204
King Fahd Complex for Printing the Holy Qur'an 155
kinship nationalism 201–2, 203, 204, 206, 208–9, 210–11
Kulliyyat al-Shari'a 187
Kuran, Timur 101–3, 114
Kuwait: expulsion of Iraq 37, 232, 233

Lajnat al-Difa' 'an al-Huquq al-Shar'iyya: see Committee for the Defence of Legitimate Rights
Lauzière, Henri 162
Lebanon 10: Iranian intervention in 12, 243–4, 246, 260; Saudi intervention in 267
Lefevere, André 161

358

INDEX

Thatcher, Margaret 325n73
al-Thunayan, Iffat bint Ahmad 226
Truman, Harry S.: administration
221
Trump, Donald 1, 20, 25–6, 235,
236, 237–42, 249, 266: adminis-
tration 42, 240
Tunisia: and Arab uprisings 17; fall
of monarchy 33
Turkey: intervention in Syria 157;
Islamism in 157; Islamization
of 157; Kurdish nationalism
157; and Qatar crisis 248;
Saudi Arabia and 18, 19, 147,
157, 248; Salafi texts 158–62;
Salafiyya in 23, 157–62; Sufism
in 159, 161; USA and 237–8
Turki ibn 'Abd al-'Aziz, Prince 53,
60, 69
Turki ibn 'Abdullah (r. 1824–34)
(Saudi emirate) 51
Turki ibn Bandar 61
Turki ibn Faysal, Prince 120, 226,
230, 246
Turkish–Islamic Synthesis (*Türk
İslam Sentezi*) 157
al-Tuwaijri, Khalid 61
Twitter 3, 61, 125, 128, 134, 136,
158, 204, 207: Twittersphere
128; **see also** Mujtahid ibn
Harith ibn Hamam

Uganda 230
'ulama' 23, 64, 150, 152, 153, 155,
156, 162, 224, 315n18, 321n36
umma 166, 168, 169, 170, 171,
172, 173–4, 181
Umm Ruqayba festival 202
UK: British protectorates 33; and
the Cold War 222, 229, 233,
325n73; Middle East policy 224;
and Muslim Brotherhood 242–3;
and oil 220; and Saudi Arabia

219, 242–3; weapons sales to
Saudi Arabia 242, 243; and
Yemen 225
United Arab Emirates (UAE) 33,
41, 236, 242, 248
USA: CIA 225, 231; and China
267; and the Cold War 217, 221,
222–3, 227, 229, 23, 325n73;
economy 251, 254, 261; and
financing of jihad 227; and Gulf
region 264–5, 267; and Iran 10,
41, 42, 237, 238–9; and Iraq
18, 189, 247; military presence
in Saudi Arabia 187, 220, 233;
and oil 218; and Saudi Arabia 1,
7, 18, 19–20, 21, 22, 25–6, 31,
37, 38, 41–2, 211, 217, 218,
219–20, 221–2, 225, 235, 236,
237–42, 247, 252, 266, 267,
268; and Syria 42, 238; weapons
sales to Morocco 227; weapons
sales to Saudi Arabia 20, 41, 225,
238, 241, 266; and Yemen 41,
266
'Utayba festival 202
al-'Utaybi, Juhayman 66, 152, 155,
315n18
al-'Uthaymin, Muhammad 158,
183

Venezuela 258
Vision 2030 8, 16, 38, 39–40, 43,
50, 63, 87, 90, 92, 93, 134–5,
141, 241, 293n50, 294n56
Voice of the Arabs 77
Voll, John 179

Wahba, Mustafa Hafiz 224
Wahhabis 3: critical of Saudi state
187–8; emirate of Riyadh 51,
185; and first Saudi emirate 50,
185; and jihad 185, 189–90; and